ARCHITECTURAL
DETAILING
IN CONTRACT INTERIORS

ARCHITECTURAL DETAILING
IN CONTRACT INTERIORS

WENDY W. STAEBLER

Whitney Library of Design
an imprint of Watson-Guptill Publications/New York

*With heartfelt thanks for
their contributions to*
Elaine Bell and Jonathan Staebler

Also to
**Florence Agnew
Dayna Elliott
Elizabeth Harper
Margaret Holly
Robin Robertson
Sue Wiggins Strite**

Sandra Brown
Betsy Laurino
Robin Rosenthal
Christine Swenson
Andrew Schrader
Donald Widdoes

At the Whitney Library of Design
Julia Moore
Cornelia Guest
Areta Buk
Ellen Greene

Special thanks to
Herman Miller, Inc.

Illustration opposite Table of Contents: Axonometric
view of canopy *in situ*, Alabama Power Company headquarters,
Birmingham, Alabama. Architecture/Interior Design: Geddes
Brecher Qualls Cunningham; Gresham, Smith and Partners.
From detail on pages 54 and 55.

Text copyright © 1988 by Wendy W. Staebler

First published 1988 in New York by the Whitney Library of Design
an imprint of Watson-Guptill Publications
a division of Billboard Publications, Inc.
1515 Broadway, New York, N.Y. 10036

Library of Congress Cataloging-in-Publication Data

Staebler, Wendy W.
  Architectural detailing in contract interiors.

  Includes index.
  1. Architecture—United States—Details.
2. Architectural drawing—United States—Detailing.
3. Interior architecture—United States. I. Title.
NA2840.S73 1988   720′ 92′2   88-271
ISBN 0-8230-0242-X

Manufactured in Japan

First Printing, 1988

2 3 4 5 6 7 8 9 / 93 92

To Beverly Russell, Julia Moore, and Paula Rice Jackson

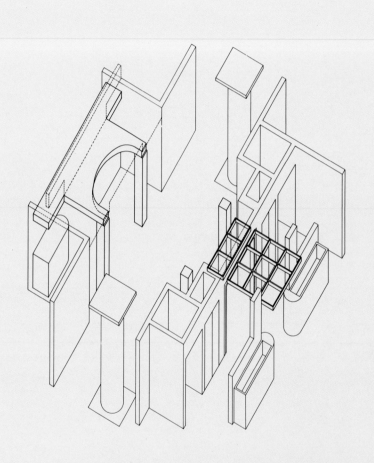

CONTENTS

FOREWORD

FOR ANYONE ON the fast-track visiting-lecturer circuit, the time spent shuttling by car from the airport to the college campus and then back to the airport is often the most productive and valuable segment of the lecturer's visit. I use the time to exhaustively question the person captured behind the driver's seat, usually my host. I learn about the politics and economics of the community I have dropped into, the trends in building and design, the student mood. And I also inquire about the reaction by local readers to the magazine I edit.

Of course, I always emphasize that I am not seeking pats on the back, but rather, genuine and frank criticism. I like to learn from opposing viewpoints, particularly those from outside of the major coastal metropolitan centers. This way, I reason, improvements can be made which will benefit everyone.

Really constructive criticism can lead to giant leaps forward, and such was the case in the summer of 1984, when I was being driven to the airport following a lecture at Oklahoma State University. At the wheel was Professor Ron Raetzman, who had invited me to speak at the School of Architecture. Ron told me that the only drawings of interior detailing that he could show his students were in *Architectural Graphic Standards*, a well-known reference work—but these drawings were totally inadequate in terms of preparing students for work in the real world *today* and were hopelessly out-of-date. For instance, the standard height of a restaurant bar, he said, was calculated on the height of a long-obsolete 1940s refrigerator.

He reasoned that in the archives of innumerable interior design firms lay quantities of finish detail drawings, probably gathering dust, that were created for specific projects and never used again. What a treasury of information! Couldn't it be mined—and put to use in published form? He persuaded me that *Interiors* magazine had an obligation to pursue this idea.

Any doubts I had about designers sharing this wealth of information gratis was immediately put to rest by Raetzman himself. Designers, he said, were schooled in the principle of show-and-tell. They were educated to share. And, indeed, he quickly proved this to be the case by initiating a mailing that brought forth positive response. From that point on, a new editorial service feature, to be called "Design Files," was in the works.

When I asked Wendy Staebler, then *Interiors* Special Features Editor, to start soliciting drawings from design firms for this feature, she met with willing cooperation. Giant tubes of blueprints started rolling into the office. Then the fun started—or rather the trouble. The real effort in getting these finish details into publishable format went into editing and selecting the final drawings—distilling them down to the minimal few that would explain enough of the project so that any designer could use them.

What followed, naturally, from the monthly magazine feature was this comprehensive volume of finish detailing that makes available many more details in a format that enables and invites study and comparison. I suspect the book will not only become a text in schools, but a valuable resource in design offices as well. It is a product of generosity that will be shared for decades to come. It is particularly gratifying to see an idea born in a brief automobile journey in the Oklahoma prairie come such a long way. I must salute Ron Raetzman as the generator and Wendy Staebler as the executor and thank them for the opportunity to be mediator.

Beverly Russell, Editor-in-Chief, *Interiors*

PREFACE

WHEN MIES VAN DER ROHE remarked to a colleague that "God is in the details," he was summing up what every architect and interior designer learns by experience, if not by education: A building, of whatever size, is merely an anonymous shell until it has been defined, refined, and made personal by the designer's detailing imprimatur.

There are two kinds of detailing. Functional details address functional concerns: how planes intersect or abut; how appendant structures, both interior and exterior, are supported; how labyrinthine ductwork and plumbing and electrical lines are integrated with a building's framework. Architects and interior designers, working with engineers and other consultants, consider functional detailing from the first day of design development. It is an unfortunate truth that because these details are hidden by the framework of the building structure, owners and end-users rarely appreciate the finesse with which they are often rendered.

Finish detailing, on the other hand, is completely visible. Its quality affects the end-user's conscious or unconscious appreciation and ultimate opinion of a building to a degree that may sometimes be disproportionate. All schools of architecture up to and including the Beaux Arts understood this principle and raised the level of finish detailing in their buildings to what was, in many cases, an art form in itself.

The Internationalist, Moderne, and Modernist eras in architecture changed the rules of finish detailing, which underwent, paradoxically, a gradual yet seemingly abrupt streamlining process. By the early 1960s, leading American firms like Skidmore, Owings & Merrill had reduced ornamental detailing to a Minimalist discipline. But inspired practitioners of Minimalism opened up an unforeseen Pandora's box in their reductionist efforts, giving tacit permission for less talented or less ideologically motivated builders to impose graceless speculative structures whose stringent budgetary limitations precluded any but the most cursory attention to finish detailing.

Postmodernism, associated with advocates Michael Graves and born-again Modernist Philip Johnson, heralded a reevaluation of the design and detailing process. Although Postmodernism was short-lived in its most stylistic extremes, enthusiastic popular response to the movement stimulated a permanent shift of focus toward thoughtful, fully developed and integrated finish detailing that takes to heart the satisfaction of human scale.

Architectural Detailing in Contract Interiors is a compilation and celebration of the renaissance in finish detailing that has typified the design work completed by mainstream American architecture and interior design firms within the last five years, work which witnesses the evolution from Postmodernism to a more current attitude dubbed, for lack of more precise description, Neoclassical Modernism or Neoconstructionist Modernism.

The details in this volume, although disparate in geographic genesis, level of sophistication, and degree of complexity, share a unifying and encouraging quality of balance. It is balance that finds the confident middle ground between detailing that is too literal in its historical references and that which is defiantly avant garde. This balance confines expression of ego to a comfortable range between that which is monumental and that which is apologetically self-effacing. It is weighted between detailing that is overwrought in its ornamentation and that which is too spare. And finally, it is a balance between sensibilities that are somber and those that are frankly flamboyant.

A superb showcase of finish detailing undertaken without undue budgetary constraint is the private dining room of Shell Central Offices at The Hague, Netherlands. Charles Pfister Associates of San Francisco visually enriched the room by articulating the walls in handcrafted Anigre paneling inlaid with brushed brass.

Pfister's design team located a Dutch craftsman who painstakingly installed the paneling and brass strips piece by piece, working from the center of one wall. Only after the work was completed did the craftsman confess that one mistake would have required tearing out all the finished walls.

Pfister's attention to detailing quality was reinforced by the precisely gauged application of gold leaf to cove soffit fascias and by the specification of real plaster to the tautly controlled tray ceiling.

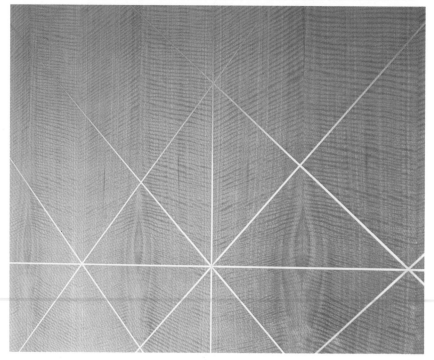

The *trompe l'oeil* embossing of the elevator doors found on floors two through twenty-four of Chicago's Merchandise Mart exemplify creative detailing rendered on a tight budget.

Larson Associates of Chicago, Illinois, developed the detail to duplicate the pattern of the building's original ground floor elevator doors at nominal expense. The design team abstracted the primary design pattern from the original doors and applied it to the upper floor doors in a vertically worked silkscreen process.

Each of the details in *Architectural Detailing in Contract Interiors* was selected for its successful resolution of a particular design problem, without regard to the cost involved in achieving the client's goals. Some details are splendid by-products of projects without any budgetary constraints, such as the wood and brass wall for the Shell Central Offices in The Hague, Netherlands, by Charles Pfister Associates. Others have ingeniously gotten the most effect for the least outlay; the *trompe l'oeil* elevator door by Larson Associates for the Merchandise Mart in Chicago is one of those. The book is intended as a visual form in which to examine, compare, and evaluate the variety of ways in which different designers have attacked and solved similar generic problems.

Those of us who produced *Architectural Detailing in Contract Interiors* were led to some surprising discoveries about the current practice of architecture and interior design in America. On the positive side, we verified that there are many more practitioners with real detailing prowess than is generally acknowledged, and that they are not all working in coastal or urban locations. We discovered scores of geographically dispersed, bright, thoughtful, and talented professionals who are enriching our built environment in every region of the United States and around the world.

Conversely, we also discovered two surprising shortcomings in current finish detailing practice, both of which seem to be the consequence of incomplete professional training. One is that a number of architectural and interior design firms—large and small, distinguished and unknown—turn out detail drawings with technical deficiencies. Although the drawings solicited for publication in this book were to blend presentation and working-drawing characteristics—and as such differ from the drawings used for client or builder review—much of the work *initially* submitted was characterized by weaknesses that detract from any drawing: bad line-weight control, poor lettering, and inadequate dimensioning or notation. We might all do well to study the example of Michael Graves, whose drawings are paradigms of the art and science of visualization.

Poor-quality drafting from professionals is merely puzzling. An apparent lack of fundamental technical knowledge, or construction know-how, is a more serious concern. Despite increasingly rigorous technical requirements in our architecture and interior design curriculums, and despite the proliferation of continuing education programs for practicing professionals, technical knowledge about detailing construction continues to be passed on to the often-maligned general contractor, millworker, or mason. If we are to come of age as an industry, we must be willing to abandon the posture that "the architect and designer design; the builder builds." If we take an oath acknowledging that we are "responsible for the public health, safety, and welfare," we ought to be taking the trouble to insure that the public well-being is, in fact, protected. Furthermore, if we have shown the sensitivity required to design something of lasting beauty (as the details in this book clearly demonstrate), we should be able to communicate to each other, to our clients, and to the general public how that beauty is to be realized in three-dimensional form.

Criticism may seem inappropriate in view of the enormous debt we owe to every one of the people who cooperated in this project. We hope these observations will not be construed as anything other than what they are intended to be—information with constructive implications. We are grateful beyond words to all the architects, interior designers, and design firm staff members who graciously donated their work, as well as a great deal of their personal time, to the implementation of this project. These thanks extend to those whose work, for reasons of space limitations, could not be included in this volume. Their generous participation in what has become a collaborative achievement in the best design tradition is deeply appreciated.

This exquisite detail drawing by Ron Berlin of the office of Michael Graves, Architect, clearly communicates high standards of professionalism. The detail—an elevator cab for The Humana Building, Louisville, Kentucky—is found on pages 116 and 117.

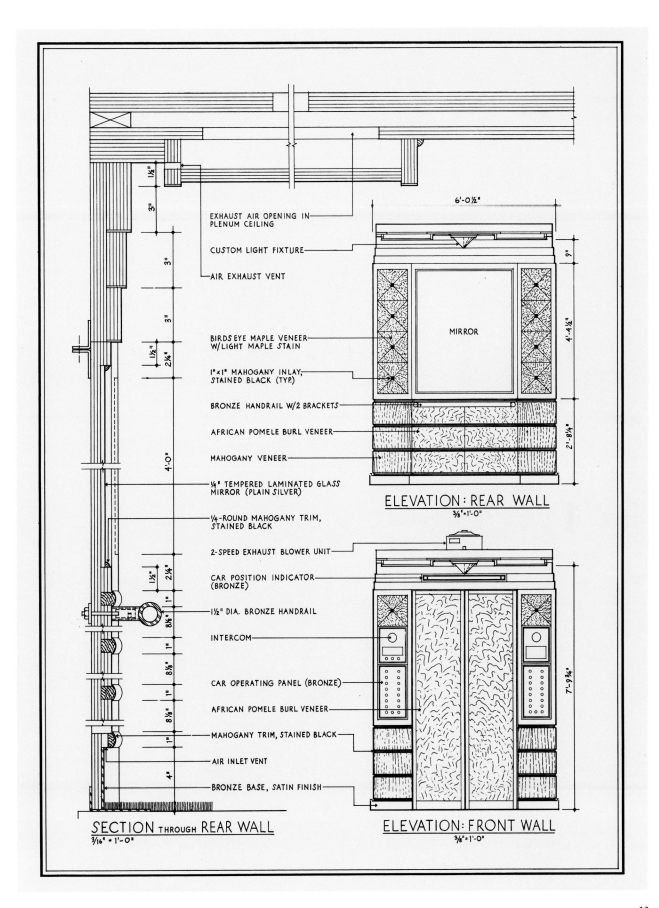

EXHAUST AIR OPENING IN PLENUM CEILING

CUSTOM LIGHT FIXTURE

AIR EXHAUST VENT

BIRDS EYE MAPLE VENEER W/LIGHT MAPLE STAIN

1"×1" MAHOGANY INLAY, STAINED BLACK (TYP.)

BRONZE HANDRAIL W/2 BRACKETS

AFRICAN POMELE BURL VENEER

MAHOGANY VENEER

¼" TEMPERED LAMINATED GLASS MIRROR (PLAIN SILVER)

¼-ROUND MAHOGANY TRIM, STAINED BLACK

2-SPEED EXHAUST BLOWER UNIT

CAR POSITION INDICATOR (BRONZE)

1½" DIA. BRONZE HANDRAIL

INTERCOM

CAR OPERATING PANEL (BRONZE)

AFRICAN POMELE BURL VENEER

MAHOGANY TRIM, STAINED BLACK

AIR INLET VENT

BRONZE BASE, SATIN FINISH

MIRROR

6'-0½"

9"

4'-4½"

2'-8¼"

ELEVATION: REAR WALL
3/8"=1'-0"

7'-9¾"

SECTION THROUGH **REAR WALL**
3/16" = 1'-0"

ELEVATION: FRONT WALL
3/8"=1'-0"

ARCHWAY

THE ROSEWOOD CORPORATION
Dallas, Texas

Architecture/Interior Design
3D/International, Inc., Dallas
Millwork
The Wigand Corporation
Photography
© Chas McGrath

THE RECEPTION ROOM of The Rosewood Corporation in Dallas, Texas, requires a quick double take to differentiate it from the entry halls found in elegant turn-of-the-century residences. Such an impression was exactly what the client requested. The Dallas design office of 3D/International, Inc., was asked to furnish Rosewood with an elegant corporate office that would be romantic in concept and timeless in design. According to the project architect, 3D/I responded to this "once-in-a-lifetime" opportunity with exquisite detailing that justified the expenditure of every dollar.

Of principal importance among the reception-room details is a series of four archways (*elevation 2*; *section 4*). The wooden archways were shop constructed and finished on site by the Wigand Corporation of Colorado Springs, Colorado. Emeric Wigand, a German millwork craftsman, worked hand in hand with the architect to select the finest woods and establish the custom moldings.

Unlike the millwork installed in most traditionally styled offices, the archways at The Rosewood Corpora-tion are constructed of solid, rather than veneered, hardwoods. 3D/I spec-ified the use of American cherry wood with a seventeen-step finishing process for the reception areas. Each piece was hand selected before being stained, waxed, finished, aged, and distressed. The twenty Wigand crafts-people lived on the job site twenty-four hours a day for two and a half months while completing the finish-ing process.

3D/I imposed the exacting stan-dards of Wigand's craftsmanship on tangential details rendered in other materials. A radius light cove super-imposed above the reception-room paneling was constructed of lath and plaster, as were the suspended ceil-ings in adjacent offices (*section 3*).

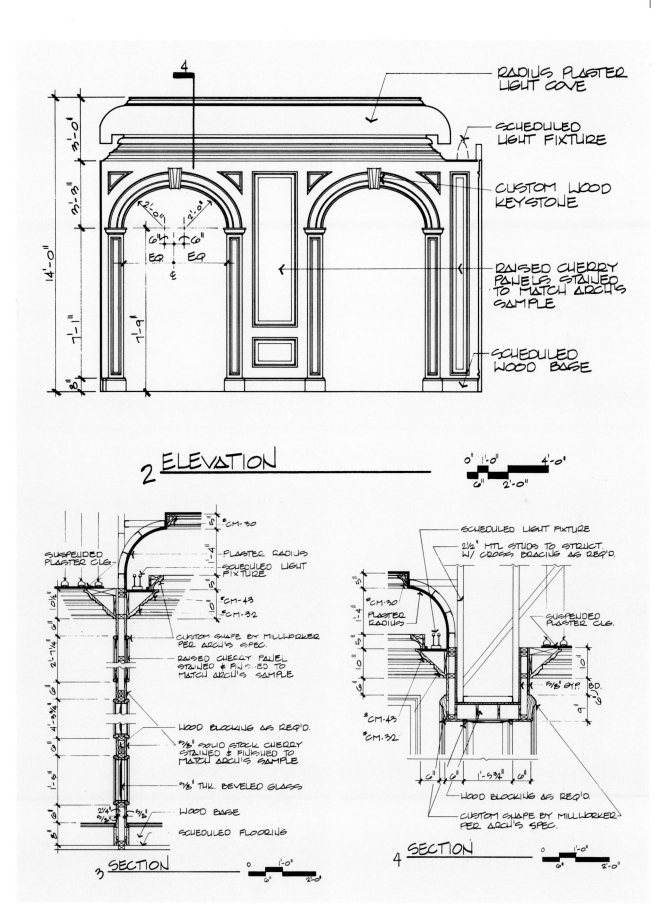

RADIUS PLASTER LIGHT COVE

SCHEDULED LIGHT FIXTURE

CUSTOM WOOD KEYSTONE

RAISED CHERRY PANELS STAINED TO MATCH ARCH'S SAMPLE

SCHEDULED WOOD BASE

2 ELEVATION

0" 1'-0" 4'-0"
6" 2'-0"

SUSPENDED PLASTER CLG.

#CM-30
PLASTER RADIUS
SCHEDULED LIGHT FIXTURE
#CM-43
#CM-32

CUSTOM SHAPE BY MILLWORKER PER ARCH'S SPEC.

RAISED CHERRY PANEL STAINED & FINISHED TO MATCH ARCH'S SAMPLE

WOOD BLOCKING AS REQ'D.

5/8" SOLID STOCK CHERRY STAINED & FINISHED TO MATCH ARCH'S SAMPLE

5/8" THK. BEVELED GLASS

WOOD BASE

SCHEDULED FLOORING

3 SECTION

0" 1'-0"
6" 2'-0"

SCHEDULED LIGHT FIXTURE

2½" MTL STUDS TO STRUCT. W/ CROSS BRACING AS REQ'D.

#CM-30
PLASTER RADIUS

SUSPENDED PLASTER CLG.

5/8" GYP. BD.

#CM-43
#CM-32

6" 6" 1'-5¾" 6"

WOOD BLOCKING AS REQ'D.

CUSTOM SHAPE BY MILLWORKER PER ARCH'S SPEC.

4 SECTION

0" 1'-0"
6" 2'-0"

ARCHWAY

EPSON COMPUTER SHOWROOM
Haverford, Pennsylvania

Interior Design
Hearst & Company Architecture, Inc.
Design Team
Nan Hearst, Michael Garavaglia,
Vicki Simon, Jim Fagler,
Laura Nettleton, Teri Behm Clawson
Fabrication
Alex L. Pronzato, Inc.
Photography
© Matt Wargo

"VITALITY" AND "HUMOR" are not words that readily come to mind when product showrooms are being discussed or reviewed, particularly when the product being displayed is a machine. But the Epson Computer showroom, designed by Hearst & Company Architecture, Inc., of San Francisco, merits these terms of descriptive praise and more.

Epson asked the design team to develop prototypical detailing components that might later be adapted to variously dimensioned showroom spaces nationwide. To convey the businesslike attitude of the Japanese parent company, Epson asked that the design package be "solid, but not dull." To encourage American end-user enthusiasm for the product, Epson requested detailing "which conveys a sense of playfulness and energy."

Hearst & Company interpreted the Epson wish list by developing a set of detailing components, which, in their building-block format, symbolically echo the modularity of Epson's computers and visually convey a sense of Zen-like simplicity, enlivened by a child's palette of bold color.

The detail components are flexible groupings of stripped-down architectural elements—columns, spheres, lintels, and sliding screens—that may be arranged and rearranged according to on-site conditions. For Epson's Philadelphia showroom, located in 60,000 square feet of raw industrial space, the design team had enough room to install the full array of components in a variety of configurations for diverse purposes.

The entrance to the Philadelphia showroom is announced by a 12'-6"-high archway, constructed of columns spaced 5'-5" apart. The columns support two 9-inch-diameter spheres and a pierced triangular lintel (*portal elevation*). Behind the archway a wall of sliding screens opens to the showroom proper and the training room and offices beyond.

Additional budget constraints encountered after the construction phase of the project had begun forced the design team to make finish-material substitutions. Project director Nan Hearst warns: "Budget cuts which occur well into the project are, unfortunately, not all that uncommon. New designers should be aware of that possibility and be ready to adapt their solutions accordingly." For Epson, the Hearst design team quickly substituted faux finishes on plywood and low-grade wood stock for the finely grained woods and stone they had originally envisioned (*column plan; wall section*). Having achieved visual parity with the original design concept, the Hearst team allocated its "extra" money to recessing light fixtures into the tops of the columns for additional theatricality (*free-standing column section*).

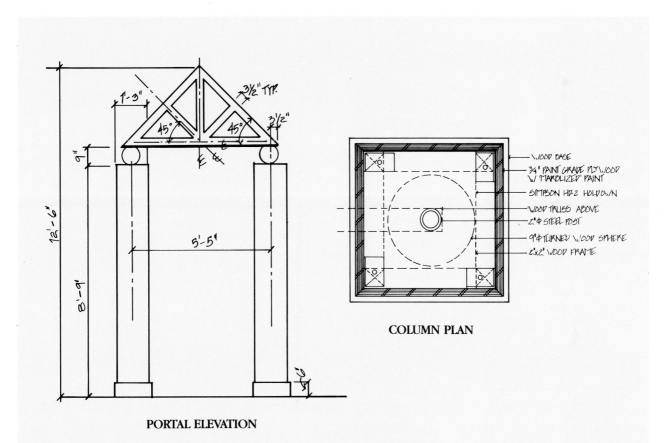

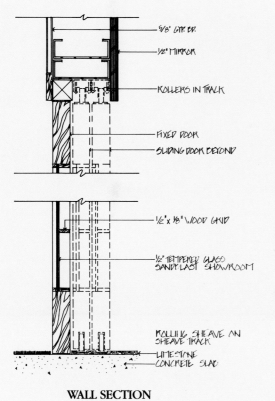

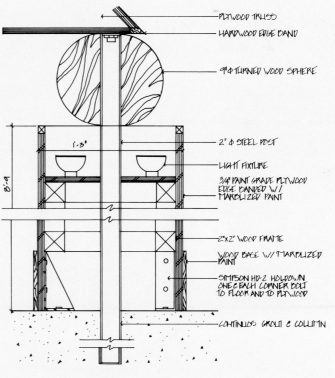

PORTAL ELEVATION

COLUMN PLAN

WALL SECTION

FREE-STANDING COLUMN SECTION

ARCHWAY

EYES NIGHTCLUB
Kansas City, Missouri

Interior Design
Kelly and Lehn
Design Team
Thomas Lehn, Kathleen Kelly,
Kay Boehr, Rick Prater,
Brian Griffiths
Consulting Architect
J. Christopher Gale & Co.
Faux Finishes
Human Nature Designs
Neon
Sign Graphics, Inc.
Neon Fabrication
Kansas City Neon
Photography
© E. G. Schempf

NEOCONSTRUCTIONIST detailing is a phenomenon that until recently was rarely seen in America's heartland. The work of the fledgling Kansas City, Missouri, firm Kelly and Lehn, however, proves that geography has nothing to do with pizazz. The firm's design for Eyes, a nightclub in downtown Kansas City owned by Victor Fontana, epitomizes nothing less than the chic insouciance of SoHo in downtown Manhattan.

According to Kathleen Kelly, "the name of the nightclub—Eyes—refers to ones senses of visual and psychic perception. Altering those perceptions was our number one conceptual design priority."

Customers entering the 7,000-square-foot nightclub are immediately transported from the nineteenth-century brick warehouse environment advertised by the exterior of the building to an intentionally disorienting world of cavernous black space—defined by theatrically lighted stainless steel, concrete, wire mesh, and neon. The jarring, but immediately intriguing, "expectation-versus-reality" entryway experience is a stimulating one. Thomas Lehn asserts that "it takes about two seconds for the customer to adjust his or her expectations of the space from the known to the unknown. The immediate response is then anticipation. Everyone wants to know what's next."

Kelly and Lehn devised a number of transitional details to steer customers through the space from one activity-intensive area to the next. One such detail is a rampway promenade—framed by a Neoconstructionist archway/portal—to the upper lounge. The archway is constructed of plywood piers painted in faux stone, from which angled galvanized metal wings, or "capitals," protrude in a vertical forced perspective. A "lintel"—which suggests the surge of a laser beam—is actually a fire-engine red neon tube suspended between the narrow extremities of the capitals. The edges of the capitals and the adjacent wire-mesh partition walls are defined against the black ceiling by the glow of neon tube extensions that show through circular perforations in the galvanized metal wings and in the metal partition wall cap (*ramp section and elevation*).

An inverted version of the archway reverses the orientation of the forced perspective (*ramp section*). Neon tubing runs at floor level from the broad base of one wing to the other. The wing forms are constructed of banded steel framing covered in wire mesh, within which faux-painted plywood "water panels" are recessed for depth-perception distortion (*ramp section and elevation*).

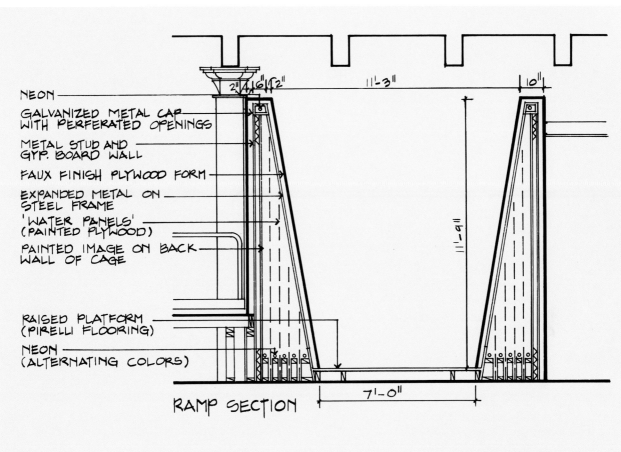

NEON

GALVANIZED METAL CAP
WITH PERFORATED OPENINGS

METAL STUD AND
GYP. BOARD WALL

FAUX FINISH PLYWOOD FORM

EXPANDED METAL ON
STEEL FRAME

'WATER PANELS'
(PAINTED PLYWOOD)

PAINTED IMAGE ON BACK
WALL OF CAGE

RAISED PLATFORM
(PIRELLI FLOORING)

NEON
(ALTERNATING COLORS)

2" 16" 2"   11'-3"   10"

11'-9"

7'-0"

RAMP SECTION

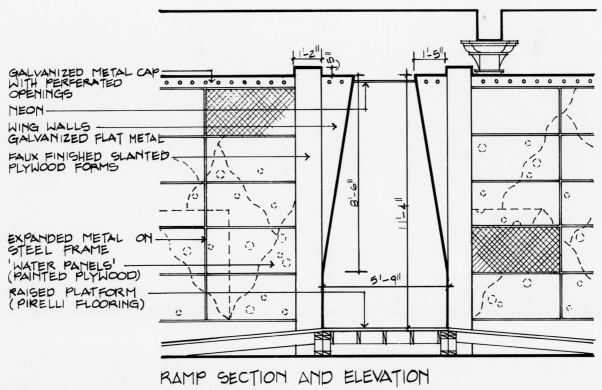

GALVANIZED METAL CAP
WITH PERFORATED
OPENINGS

NEON

WING WALLS
GALVANIZED FLAT METAL

FAUX FINISHED SLANTED
PLYWOOD FORMS

EXPANDED METAL ON
STEEL FRAME

'WATER PANELS'
(PAINTED PLYWOOD)

RAISED PLATFORM
(PIRELLI FLOORING)

1'-2" 5"   1'-5"

8'-6"

11'-4"

5'-9"

RAMP SECTION AND ELEVATION

BANK CHECKWRITING COUNTER

FIRST REPUBLIC BANK
Houston, Texas

Interior Design
Gensler and Associates/Architects,
Houston
Design Team
Antony Harbour, Bill Livingston,
Gregory Burke (drawings)
Fabrication
Brochsteins
Photography
© Chas McGrath

IN DETAILING First Republic Bank of
Houston, Texas, where large expanses
of granite cover almost every visible
surface in the public areas, Gensler
and Associates/Architects of Houston
adopted a "more-is-more" attitude.
The carefully planned and finely
crafted planar simplicity of the granite
surfaces creates an understated counterpoint to the complex, monumen-
talist architecture of Johnson/Burgee
Architects.

On the main banking floor, the
Gensler design team selected circular
granite slabs for the countertops of
strategically placed checkwriting
counters (*plan*). A ring of tubular
brass poles rising from the hub of
each granite work surface supports
five glass-shaded light fixtures (*elevation*). The translucent fixtures illuminate electronic fittings for consumer
banking. The fittings are embedded in
a polished brass centerpiece, which,
in turn, has been recessed into the
granite slab (*detail*).

The weight of the granite countertop and its pedestal base configuration called for structural reinforcement and stabilizing at both the floor
and writing-height levels. Brass tubing
bisects a brass anchor plate located
above grade. The 5-inch brass tubes
intersect below grade with a ⅜-inch-
thick steel plate bolted to the cement-
slab subfloor. At the countertop level,
a ⅜-inch-thick steel shelf provides
support for the granite top
(*elevation*).

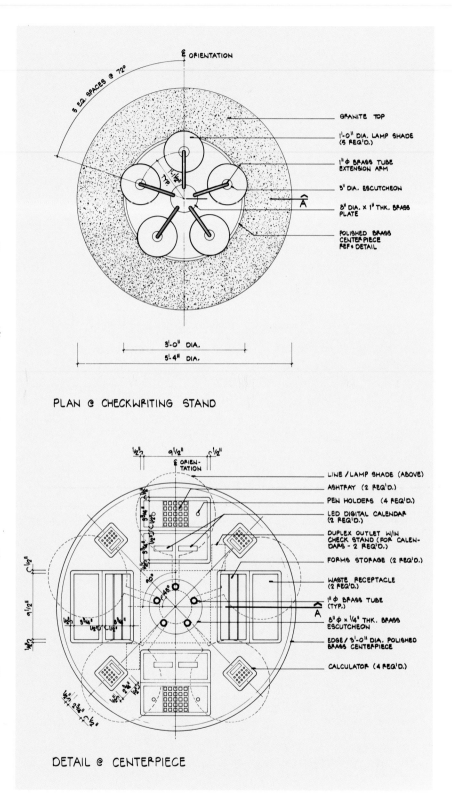

PLAN @ CHECKWRITING STAND

DETAIL @ CENTERPIECE

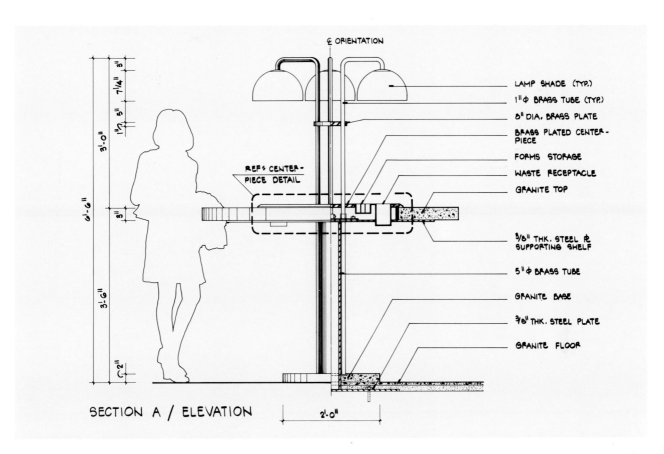

¢ ORIENTATION

LAMP SHADE (TYP.)
1"∅ BRASS TUBE (TYP.)
8" DIA. BRASS PLATE
BRASS PLATED CENTER-PIECE
FORMS STORAGE
WASTE RECEPTACLE
GRANITE TOP

3/8" THK. STEEL ℄ SUPPORTING SHELF

5"∅ BRASS TUBE

GRANITE BASE

3/8" THK. STEEL PLATE

GRANITE FLOOR

REF: CENTER-PIECE DETAIL

SECTION A / ELEVATION

2'-0"

BANK CHECKWRITING COUNTER

THE BANK OF BALTIMORE
Baltimore, Maryland

Interior Design
RTKL Associates Inc.

Design Team
Les Bates, Michael Gotwald,
Kim Johnston, Ria Zake

Fabrication
N. L. Lighting

Lighting Consultant
Theo Kondos

Photography
© Victoria Lefcourt

RTKL ASSOCIATES INC. of Baltimore/ Washington, D.C., and The Bank of Baltimore approached the renovation of the bank's downtown headquarters with a determination to project a "new, up-to-date image." A more challenging proviso for RTKL in developing that image was to "maintain a posture of respect for the building's Classical architecture," which is based on the Erechtheum on the Acropolis in Athens.

The first step for RTKL in the renovation process was archaeological. The original fifty-foot ceilings and stately windows of the main banking room were obscured by a floor constructed in the 1950s, which bisected the room horizontally. To the design team's dismay, the demolition process revealed that most of the original detailing had been removed during that "modernization." However, the lower half of the windows were re-exposed and served as a basis for the classic detailing and motifs used in the design of the railings, checkwriting counter, and teller counter.

A less courageous design firm might have used the dearth of original detailing as a reason to change course to a more modern interior. Instead, RTKL proceeded resolutely by designing a traditional turn-of-the-century mezzanine-over-banking-floor configuration, which includes an intelligently edited array of modern details replete with understated Neoclassical allusions.

A new coffered ceiling detail is reinforced by the architectural strength of the most prominent detail designed by RTKL for the space—a handsome, Neoclassically styled checkwriting counter constructed of three finely balanced tones of polished marble, statuary finish bronze, and etched glass. The counter is highlighted by an elegant bronze torchiere (*elevation*). Each of the counter's finish materials (*section*) echoes a form or finish visible elsewhere on the floor. The paneled marble counter fascia rises from the marble floor, the etched-glass dividing panels reiterate the pattern of the original windows, and the bronze panel frames and torchiere restate the finish vocabulary of the tellers' windows.

The checkwriting counter exemplifies multifunctional detailing at its best. In addition to storing ubiquitous banking paraphernalia (such as pens, calendars, and form bins), the counter separates and controls the traffic flow of the checkwriting, queuing, and management waiting areas. It also houses the return air duct enclosures for the entire floor and provides a pedestal for the dramatic torchiere, which highlights the new coffered ceiling.

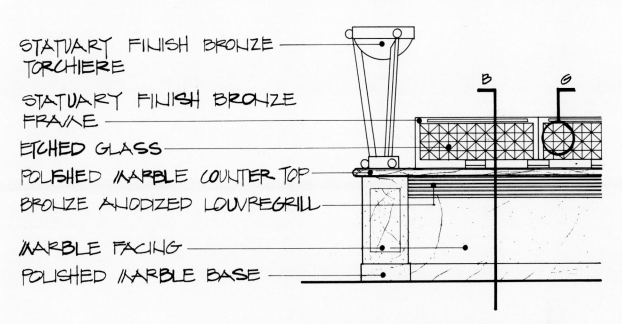

STATUARY FINISH BRONZE TORCHIERE

STATUARY FINISH BRONZE FRAME

ETCHED GLASS

POLISHED MARBLE COUNTER TOP

BRONZE ANODIZED LOUVREGRILL

MARBLE FACING

POLISHED MARBLE BASE

B   G

A.   ELEVATION - CHECKWRITING COUNTER

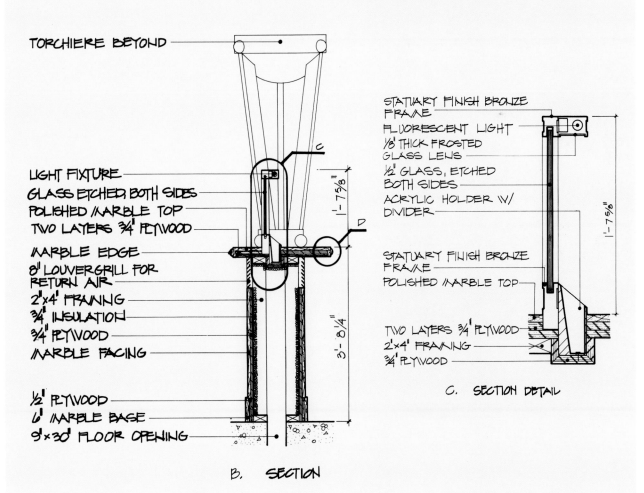

TORCHIERE BEYOND

LIGHT FIXTURE
GLASS ETCHED BOTH SIDES
POLISHED MARBLE TOP
TWO LAYERS 3/4" PLYWOOD

MARBLE EDGE
8" LOUVERGRILL FOR RETURN AIR
2"x4" FRAMING
3/4" INSULATION
3/4" PLYWOOD
MARBLE FACING

1/2" PLYWOOD
6" MARBLE BASE
9"x30" FLOOR OPENING

C

D

1'-7 5/8"

3'-8 1/4"

B.   SECTION

STATUARY FINISH BRONZE FRAME
FLUORESCENT LIGHT
1/8" THICK FROSTED GLASS LENS
1/2" GLASS, ETCHED BOTH SIDES
ACRYLIC HOLDER W/ DIVIDER

STATUARY FINISH BRONZE FRAME
POLISHED MARBLE TOP

TWO LAYERS 3/4" PLYWOOD
2"x4" FRAMING
3/4" PLYWOOD

1'-7 5/8"

C.   SECTION DETAIL

BANK TELLER STATION

FIRST REPUBLIC BANK
Houston, Texas

Interior Design
Gensler and Associates/Architects,
Houston
Design Team
Antony Harbour, Bill Livingston,
Gregory Burke (drawings)
Fabrication
Intrepid
Photography
© Chas McGrath

AT FIRST REPUBLIC BANK in Houston, Texas, Gensler and Associates/Architects of Houston was charged with developing a "grandiloquent but not grandiose" interior detailing package for the banking hall designed, architecturally, by John Burgee Architects with Philip Johnson. As a footnote to

their request, First Republic Bank asked Gensler to provide detailing that would "reinforce the Dutch burgher aspect of the space, rather than evoking a church or chapel-like atmosphere."

The program called for a number of teller stations to be located immediately in front of one of the long, leather-paneled interior walls of the vast banking floor. In developing dimensions for the nineteen-person teller station, the design team's task was to find an appropriate balance in scale between the limitations of human ergonomic standards and the height of the hall's ceiling.

The solution was to substitute "solid" materials for massive form. The public face of each 4'-11" by 4'-4" module is covered in solid blocks of

alternating white and red granite (*elevation @ teller's line*). Although each individual unit is relatively small, the abutment of nineteen units side by side adds dimensional impact when the line is perceived as a whole.

Each teller station unit is topped by a 1'-6"-high screen, complete with a swinging gate window. The screens are constructed of escutcheon-statuary brushed bronze, a material that recalls turn-of-the-century teller cages (*elevation detail; sections A–C*).

Because economy was an issue in the development of the teller stations, the private, or inside, face of each station reveals plastic laminate. Countertops and pigeonholes enclose CRTs and surmount a steel safe at each station (*elevation @ teller's station*).

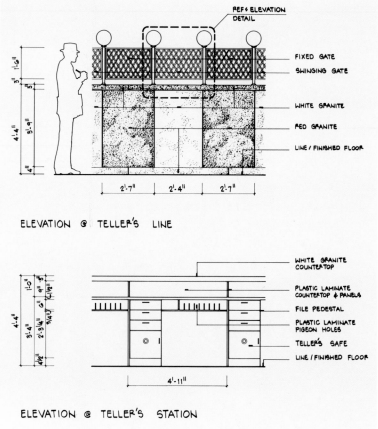

ELEVATION @ TELLER'S LINE

ELEVATION @ TELLER'S STATION

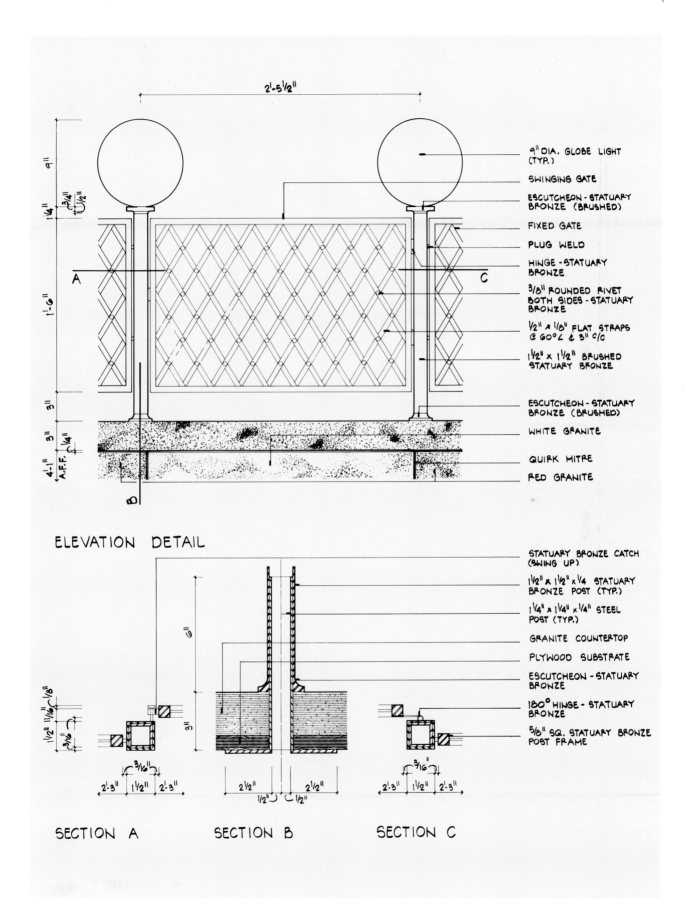

2'-5½"

9" DIA. GLOBE LIGHT (TYP.)

SWINGING GATE

ESCUTCHEON - STATUARY BRONZE (BRUSHED)

FIXED GATE

PLUG WELD

HINGE - STATUARY BRONZE

3/8" ROUNDED RIVET BOTH SIDES - STATUARY BRONZE

½" x 1/8" FLAT STRAPS @ 60°∠ & 3" C/C

1½" x 1½" BRUSHED STATUARY BRONZE

ESCUTCHEON - STATUARY BRONZE (BRUSHED)

WHITE GRANITE

QUIRK MITRE

RED GRANITE

9"

¾"

½"

¼"

A

1'-6"

C

3"

3"

¼"

4'-1"

A.F.F.

B

ELEVATION DETAIL

STATUARY BRONZE CATCH (SWING UP)

1½" x 1½" x ¼ STATUARY BRONZE POST (TYP.)

1¼" x 1¼" x ¼" STEEL POST (TYP.)

GRANITE COUNTERTOP

PLYWOOD SUBSTRATE

ESCUTCHEON - STATUARY BRONZE

180° HINGE - STATUARY BRONZE

5/8" SQ. STATUARY BRONZE POST FRAME

9"

3"

½" 11/16" 1/8"

3/16"

3/16"

2'-3" 1½" 2'-3"

2½" 2½"

½" ½"

3/16"

2'-3" 1½" 2'-3"

SECTION A   SECTION B   SECTION C

25

BANK TELLER STATION

THE BANK OF BALTIMORE
Baltimore, Maryland

Interior Design
RTKL Associates Inc.
Design Team
Les Bates, Michael Gotwald,
Kim Johnston, Ria Zake
Marble
Architectural Marble Importers
Millwork
Columbia Woodworking
Lighting Consultant
Theo Kondos
Photography
© Victoria Lefcourt

TELLER STATION locations at the newly renovated Bank of Baltimore are demarcated by updated Neoclassical window frames, which add elemental strength in elevation to an established Neoclassical ambience. RTKL Associates Inc. of Baltimore/Washington, D.C., developed the detail in response to the client's request for "an up-to-the-minute, nonstodgy image which respects the bank's heritage and the building's Classical architecture."

RTKL positioned the 3'-3½"-high teller station counter along the longitudinal rear wall of the main banking room in a circulation-conscious alcove created by a newly installed mezzanine balcony. As a consequence, Bank of Baltimore tellers gain the benefit of the more soothing incandescent lighting that is recessed into coffered panels beneath the mezzanine flooring. (Most bank tellers work with harsh fluorescent lighting.)

The windows of the teller stations are constructed of statuary finish, square-edged bronze tubes. A domed indicator light is front mounted on the pediment of each window frame (*section—indicator light*). When a station is free, the light is activated by a sensor strip recessed into the marble fascia of the counter. The light is deactivated when the sensor's range of sensitivity is blocked by the presence of a customer (*elevation; section at teller window*).

The pedimented windows are laterally braced by modular openwork bronze frames, which reiterate the patterning of the room's original windows, as well as the pattern of the mezzanine railing (*elevation*). Glass directional signage panels, which are back painted and enclosed in similarly scaled bronze frames, are installed above the openwork bronze braces at a central counter location.

RTKL showed particular finesse in its selection of finish materials for the teller stations. The bronze, glass, and marble enrich the space without overwhelming it. The design team accented the long span of the gray/white counter subtly, specifying a contrasting dark gray marble for the baseboard alone and a siena marble for the bullnosed counter ledge and window block. The restrained color composition of the expansive unit helps to deemphasize its mass, a maneuver aided by the more complex coloration of a tricolor marble floor.

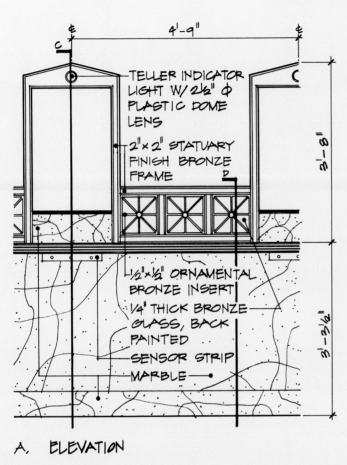

4'-9"

TELLER INDICATOR LIGHT W/ 2½" φ PLASTIC DOME LENS

2" x 2" STATUARY FINISH BRONZE FRAME

3'-8"

½" x ½" ORNAMENTAL BRONZE INSERT

¼" THICK BRONZE GLASS, BACK PAINTED

SENSOR STRIP

MARBLE

3'-3½"

A. ELEVATION

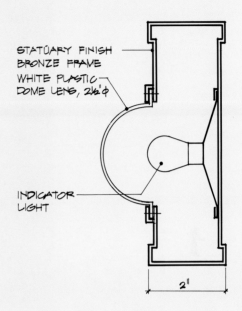

STATUARY FINISH BRONZE FRAME

WHITE PLASTIC DOME LENS, 2½" φ

INDICATOR LIGHT

2"

E. SECTION - INDICATOR LIGHT

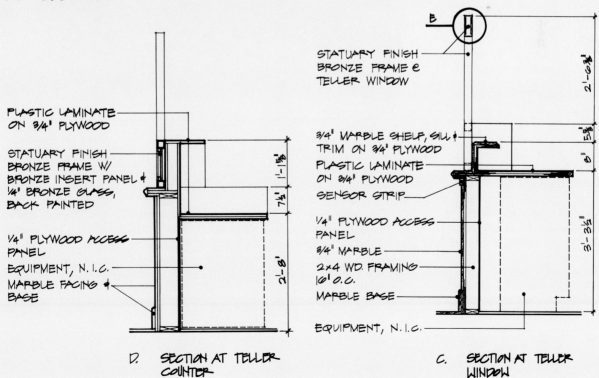

PLASTIC LAMINATE ON ¾" PLYWOOD

STATUARY FINISH BRONZE FRAME W/ BRONZE INSERT PANEL & ¼" BRONZE GLASS, BACK PAINTED

¼" PLYWOOD ACCESS PANEL

EQUIPMENT, N.I.C.

MARBLE FACING & BASE

1'-1⅝"

7½"

2'-8"

D. SECTION AT TELLER COUNTER

STATUARY FINISH BRONZE FRAME @ TELLER WINDOW

¾" MARBLE SHELF, SILL & TRIM ON ¾" PLYWOOD

PLASTIC LAMINATE ON ¾" PLYWOOD

SENSOR STRIP

¼" PLYWOOD ACCESS PANEL

¾" MARBLE

2x4 WD. FRAMING 16" O.C.

MARBLE BASE

EQUIPMENT, N.I.C.

2'-6¾"

5⅛"

8"

3'-3⅜"

C. SECTION AT TELLER WINDOW

BANQUETTE

CAFFE ROMA INTERNATIONAL
New York City

Interior Design
Haverson-Rockwell Architects
Design Team
David S. Rockwell, Jay M. Haverson
Mural Painting
Decorative Painting Specialists
(William van Ess, Pamela Lassiter)
Mural Lighting Control
Litelab
Woodworking
Baltic Woodworking
Photography
© Mark Ross Photography, Inc.

BY PAINTING A 45-foot-long brick wall in subtle gradations of color and detailing a backlit banquette to draw attention to a wall as the focal point of Caffe Roma International, in Manhattan, Haverson-Rockwell Architects of New York City solved a number of design problems and in the process paid homage to the pointillist art of Georges Seurat.

The brick wall, discovered during initial demolition, was not only an unattractive color but was also marred by settling cracks and fissures. Although the client requested an atmosphere filled with "character, texture, and warmth," David S. Rockwell characterizes the wall as having "a little too much character." Furthermore, the bare wall "was the wrong character for the Mediterranean courtyard mood we were trying to create."

The decision to treat the wall as a mural altered the normal progression of the design's development—an anomaly that allowed the design team to reconfigure the banquette to include the now-essential light box. The 3'-6"-high ergonomically scaled banquette, which rests on a recessed plywood base, was drawn into the dining area by an additional 1'-4" to accommodate the new light trough (*elevation*). A backbrace partition, or stepping wall, constructed of birch plywood separates the banquette from the trough (*section*). Capping the dividing partition with half-round molding and installing inset lattice panels resulted in a credible garden wall (*elevation*).

The light box—concealed by the stepping wall—houses an incandescent flood lamp superimposed by a four-color striplight. In consequence, the painted wall may appear—according to mood—blue, lavender, pink, or green. Heat build-up, resulting from the concentration of lighting fixtures within an enclosed space, might have been a cause of owner anxiety. However, because the fixtures were installed as free-standing devices braced by lateral metal studs within the light box, air circulates freely. Excess heat is diffused by the intake of colder air through intermittently placed grilles in the recessed banquette base (*elevation*).

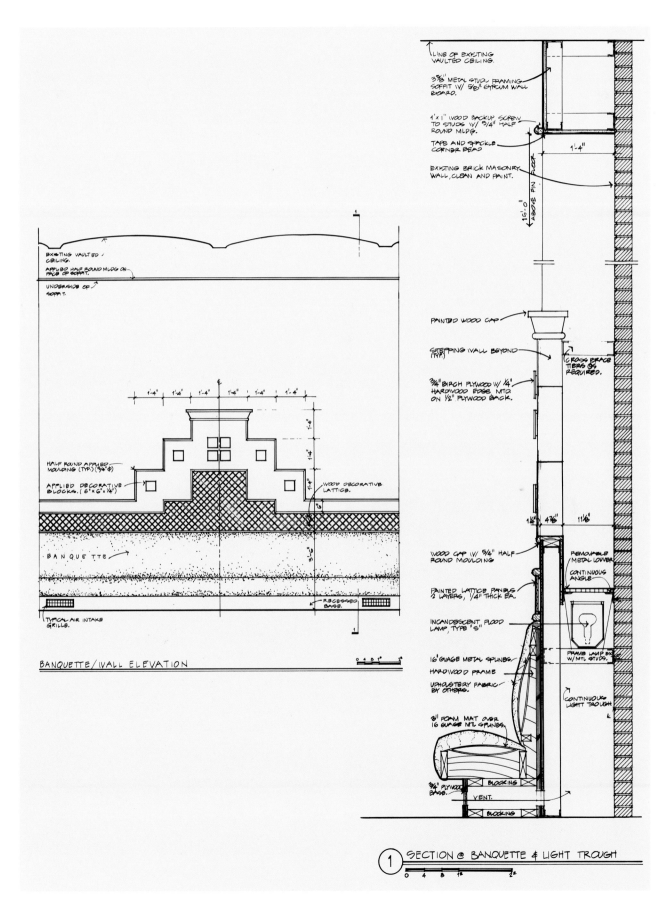

BANQUETTE/WALL ELEVATION

1. SECTION @ BANQUETTE & LIGHT TROUGH

BANQUETTE

GOLDEN TULIP BARBIZON HOTEL
New York City

Interior Design
Judith Stockman & Associates
Design Team
Judith Stockman, Steve Smith
Banquette Fabrication
Beaver Furniture
***Trompe l'oeil* Painting**
Richard Haas
Photography
© Langdon Clay

DURING THE BARBIZON'S much-chronicled era as a residential hotel for women, the mezzanine level of the hotel was used as a "pointedly public" lounge— or the only space in which guests might entertain male visitors. The passage of time, new management, and the design skills of Judith Stockman & Associates have changed that perspective. Today, the mezzanine level of the hotel, now called the Golden Tulip Barbizon Hotel, houses a public restaurant that is "pointedly private" in its solicitous regard for its customers' personal space. As a consequence, The Barbizon restaurant has become one of the most popular spots on Manhattan's Upper East Side for drinking or dining.

The design team worked closely with graphic designer Milton Glaser to revamp and upgrade the space, which now, in accordance with the owner's mandate, "seats 125 people, meets code requirements, and gives customers a refreshing sense of spatial privacy." However, meeting the client's list of quantity, as well as quality, priorities was no simple task. Although the total square footage allocated for use by the restaurant might be deemed generous by most urban standards, the narrow, peninsular configuration around three sides of an atrium proved problematic.

In response, the Stockman design team devised a number of space-saving strategies, the most important of which was a three-sectioned banquette, which follows the linear configuration of the atrium railing. Because Stockman believes that "detailing should be, wherever possible, multifunctional," the banquette at the hotel does much more than provide space-saving seating. The banquette is back mounted on hollow framing that simultaneously conceals much of the restaurant's indirect lighting.

Within the hollow backframe, two angle-mounted fluorescent strips bounce warm-temperature light toward the ceiling and highlight the railing from a lobby perspective. The railing definition is made possible by translucent panels, which face the atrium-side elevation of the unit's framework (*section*). Light-fixture maintenance and bulb replacement are made possible by removable banquette seat cushions.

Stockman and Steve Smith expanded the space visually with other devices: a barrel-vaulted skylight, recessed wall niches, and the *trompe l'oeil* mural painted on the atrium ceiling.

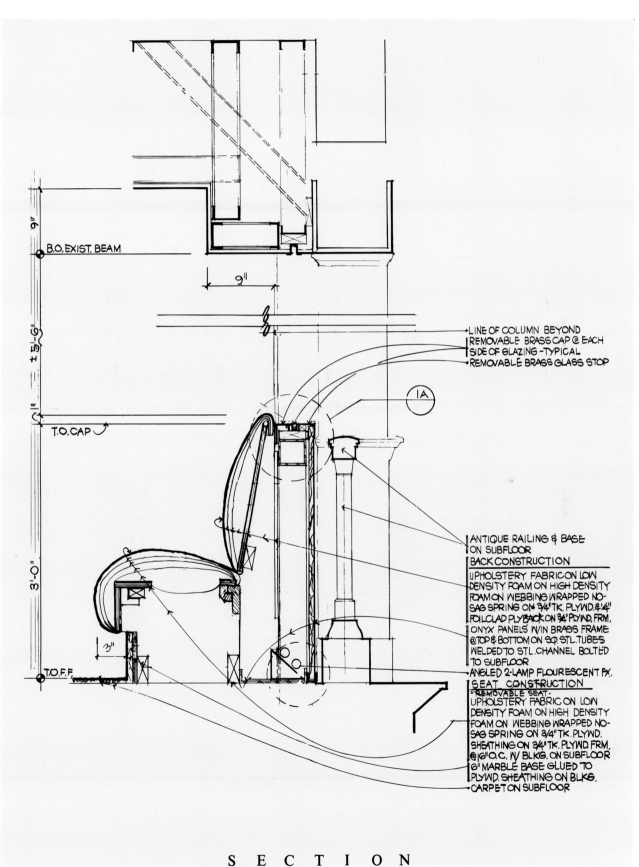

9"

B.O. EXIST. BEAM

9"

±5'-6"

6"

T.O. CAP

3'-0"

3"

T.O.F.F.

LINE OF COLUMN BEYOND
REMOVABLE BRASS CAP @ EACH
SIDE OF GLAZING -TYPICAL
REMOVABLE BRASS GLASS STOP

1A

ANTIQUE RAILING & BASE
ON SUBFLOOR
BACK CONSTRUCTION
UPHOLSTERY FABRIC ON LOW
DENSITY FOAM ON HIGH DENSITY
FOAM ON WEBBING WRAPPED NO-
SAG SPRING ON 3/4" TK. PLYWD. & 1/4"
FOIL CLAD PLY BACK ON 3/4" PLYWD. FRM,
ONYX PANELS W/IN BRASS FRAME
@ TOP & BOTTOM ON SQ. STL. TUBES
WELDED TO STL. CHANNEL BOLTED
TO SUBFLOOR
ANGLED 2-LAMP FLOURESCENT FX.
SEAT CONSTRUCTION
REMOVABLE SEAT-
UPHOLSTERY FABRIC ON LOW
DENSITY FOAM ON HIGH DENSITY
FOAM ON WEBBING WRAPPED NO-
SAG SPRING ON 3/4" TK. PLYWD.
SHEATHING ON 3/4" TK. PLYWD. FRM,
@ 16" O.C. W/ BLKG. ON SUBFLOOR
6" MARBLE BASE GLUED TO
PLYWD. SHEATHING ON BLKG.
CARPET ON SUBFLOOR

S E C T I O N

BAR

CAROLINE'S
New York City

Architecture/Interior Design
Dorf Associates
Design Team
Martin Dorf, Hugh Boyd,
Robert McGrath, Jonathan Hutchings,
Susan Cummings, Lorraine Knapp
(renderings)
Terrazzo Work
Port Morris
Terrazzo Panel Framework
Osborne Woodworking
Metalwork
Birk Iron Works
Lighting Consultant
Domingo Gonzales Design
Photography
© Durston Saylor

"SHANTYTOWN CHIC" might best describe the atmosphere at Caroline's, a restaurant/comedy club located within the old Fulton Street Fish Market district in lower Manhattan. By reinterpreting the architectural vocabulary of a formerly down-and-out neighborhood—broken glass, corroding copper, and rusting metal—Dorf Associates has written an encouraging story of neighborhood rejuvenation, while answering the owner's request for "detailing which makes *objets d'art* from everyday objects."

Working within a 10,000-square-foot "long and narrow industrial shell," the Dorf design team installed a dramatic backlit iridescent 60'-0" bar on each of two floors. The bars not only reiterate the fish-market ambience but also increase the linear division between a 200-seat comedy club and a 90-seat restaurant. Although the configuration and lateral orientation of the bars break the space into a series of smaller, more intimate areas, their repetition ties the floors together as a compositional whole.

The bar fabrication was a matter of innovative technique as well as an example of the inventive use of materials. For the curved portion of the translucent structure, ½-inch-thick Plexiglas panels were bent around arced wooden templates; the flat portions were assembled in 3'-0" modules. The panels were then abraded to provide an adhesion-receptive surface for a ⅜-inch-deep poured-in mixture of "great glittery goo"—an asphalt-colored epoxy terrazzo embedded with shards of blue and green glass.

When hardened, the panels were ground and polished and then secured to the galvanized steel frame by concealed fasteners. The flicker of interior fluorescent fixtures adds a watery shimmer to the fascia of the bar, which is protected from actual water seepage by the light-enhancing reflectors on which they are mounted (*section*). Fluorescent-tube replacement is effected through intermittently placed hinged panels (*detail*).

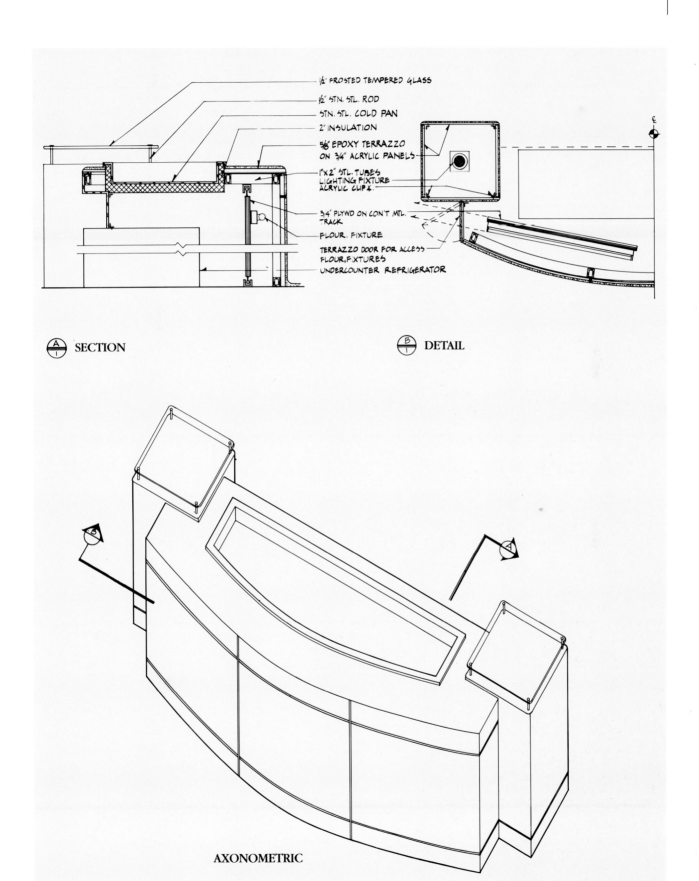

½" FROSTED TEMPERED GLASS
½" STN. STL. ROD
STN. STL. COLD PAN
2" INSULATION
⅝" EPOXY TERRAZZO
ON ¾" ACRYLIC PANELS
1"x2" STL. TUBES
LIGHTING FIXTURE
ACRYLIC CLIP ⅘.
¾" PLYWD ON CON'T MTL.
TRACK
FLOUR. FIXTURE
TERRAZZO DOOR FOR ACCESS
FLOUR. FIXTURES
UNDERCOUNTER REFRIGERATOR

Ⓐ SECTION

Ⓑ DETAIL

AXONOMETRIC

BAR

EYES NIGHTCLUB
Kansas City, Missouri

Interior Design
Kelly and Lehn
Design Team
Thomas Lehn, Kathleen Kelly,
Kay Boehr, Rick Prater, Brian Griffiths
Consulting Architect
J. Christopher Gale & Co.
Fabrication
Arabian Construction Company
(formerly Black Oak
Construction Company)
Neon
Sign Graphics, Inc.
Neon Fabrication
Kansas City Neon
Photography
© E. G. Schempf

AFICIONADOS OF the Emerald City in *The Wizard of Oz* will experience a nostalgic sense of déjà vu at Eyes Nightclub in Kansas City, Missouri. There, a larger-than-life stage-set atmosphere detailed in Neoconstructionist materials powerfully suggests that magical things may happen.

Illusionist art began at Eyes Night- club with the application of a second- ary interior skin constructed of pink and blue neon-backlighted Kalwall. For owner Victor Fontana, project designers Kathleen Kelly and Thomas Lehn, principals of an up-and-coming Kansas City design firm, came up with this clever detailing solution in re- sponse to the owner's desire for an "enclosed and surreal" environment. The interior the designers had to work with—a 7,000-square-foot land- marked brick warehouse, overbur- dened with oddly shaped windows. Kelly and Lehn used the backlighted Kalwall for detailing continuity in areas throughout the space, imposing it with particular effect as a dramatic backdrop to a large semicircular bar.

This 25'-wide by 14'-11"-deep bar at Eyes Nightclub is constructed of flex- ible, corrugated galvanized metal sheathing which easily conforms to the bar's semicircular- to semiellip- tical-shaped plywood subframe (*plan*). Small gold plastic buttons snap into place over regularly spaced metal screwheads, which were driven through the corrugated metal fascia into the plywood frame from the outside to add subtle punctuation to the ribbing pattern (*section*). Although the bar's sturdy countertop is prag- matically rendered in plastic laminate over a double 1⅛-inch plywood-on- masonite subframe, the correspond- ing double edging detail of fluted stainless steel recalls the opulence of an Art Deco diner (*detail*).

Of particular note is the elegantly controlled use of accent lighting. The nosecone-shaped backbar with its stepped glass shelves is faced in clear fiberglass awning sheeting. The back- bar is illuminated from within by green neon tubes that accentuate its similarity to the bar's fascia. They also differentiate the bar's corrugation from that of the bar fascia.

Brilliant blue neon glows in con- trast from behind a narrow steel-mesh band, which runs horizontally at counter height the length of the Kalwall backdrop wall, and from neon halos that surround framing metal column culverts.

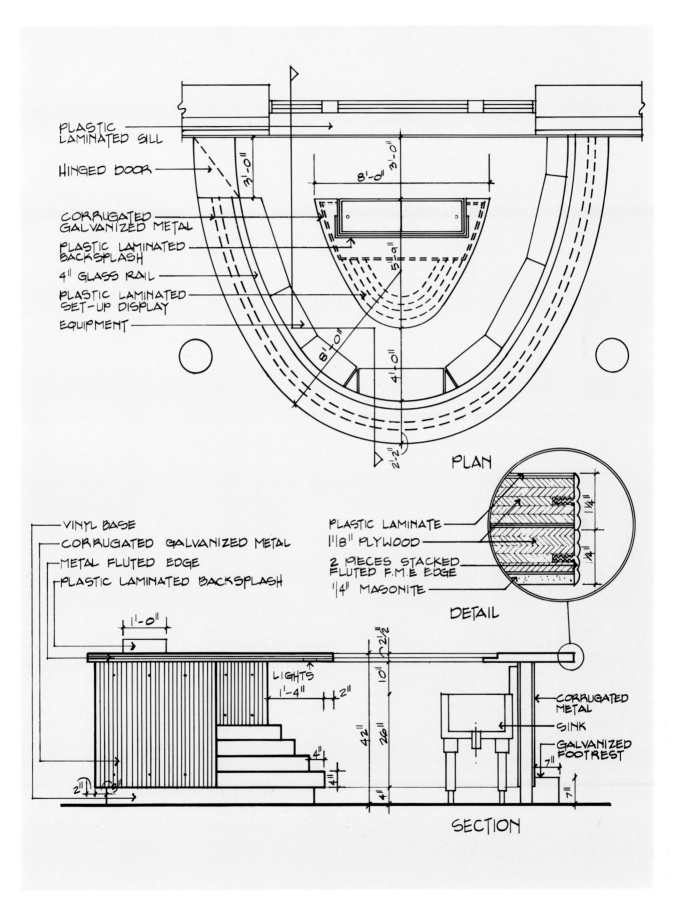

PLASTIC LAMINATED SILL

HINGED DOOR

CORRUGATED GALVANIZED METAL

PLASTIC LAMINATED BACKSPLASH

4" GLASS RAIL

PLASTIC LAMINATED SET-UP DISPLAY

EQUIPMENT

8'-0"

3'-0"

3'-0"

5'-9"

8'-0"

4'-0"

2'-2"

PLAN

VINYL BASE

CORRUGATED GALVANIZED METAL

METAL FLUTED EDGE

PLASTIC LAMINATED BACKSPLASH

PLASTIC LAMINATE

1 1⁄8" PLYWOOD

2 PIECES STACKED FLUTED F.M.E EDGE

1⁄4" MASONITE

1⁄4"

1⁄4"

DETAIL

1'-0"

2 1⁄2"

LIGHTS

1'-4"   2"

10"

42"

26"

4"

4"

4"

2"

0"

CORRUGATED METAL

SINK

GALVANIZED FOOTREST

7"

7"

SECTION

BAR

B. SMITH'S RESTAURANT
New York City

Architecture/Interior Design
Anderson/Schwartz
Design Team
Ross Anderson, G. Wesley Goforth,
Frederic Schwartz, Malcolm Kaye,
Amy Lann
Fabrication
Aileron Design, Inc.
(Kathryn Biddinger, R. Carroll Todd)
Photography
© Elliott Kaufman

MANY MANHATTAN RESTAURATEURS attempt to shield their patrons from the clamor of the street scene outside by wrapping their spaces in either upholstered walls or sound-absorbent carpeting. Having thus established acoustic control, they then seat their unluckier customers at tables as close as possible to the entrance.

A different approach was taken at the stylish theater-district establishment B. Smith's Restaurant, where Anderson/Schwartz of New York City imposed a laterally oriented bar as a buffer zone between the street and a spacious dining room. The bar area "invites the outside in," while the contrasting motif of the dining room "pushes the inside out."

B. Smith's Restaurant, owned by New York City's modeling doyenne Barbara Smith, is located on a busy Eighth Avenue corner. The location inspired the design team's choice of "street vocabulary" finishing materials. These were abstracted from the view through the windows and further tie together the interior bar and the exterior world. The palette—reminiscent of the colors in a super realist painting by Richard Estes—is correspondingly industrial: clear glass shelves, white walls, reflective stainless steel bar cladding, and an opaque gray concrete slab floor.

The bar itself is constructed of 16-gauge stainless steel screwed to a ½-inch plywood subframe. The steel panels are joined with stainless steel fasteners, and the panel joints have been welded seamlessly smooth. The pattern on the sloped fascia of the bar was produced by swirling a grinder over the surfaces after the panels were in place (*section*).

Both the bar and the welded carbon steel footrail are bolted to the base concrete slab, which is held in place by a metal pan floor. The design team mixed the concrete with bits of metal and glass to create an "exterior" sidewalk in the bar's interior.

The illusion of bringing the outside in is reinforced by the backbar "window" (*front elevation*) and the adjacent archway/stairs that allow bar patrons to look into the dining room in much the same way that people outside on the street look into the bar. The dining room's palette of earth-toned residential materials—ochre-painted walls, taupe carpeting, hardwood chairs, and lightly stained wood floors—contrasts elegantly with the cool tones of the bar. Further definition of the dining space as an interior room is provided by a staircase wall mural rendered in saturated colors.

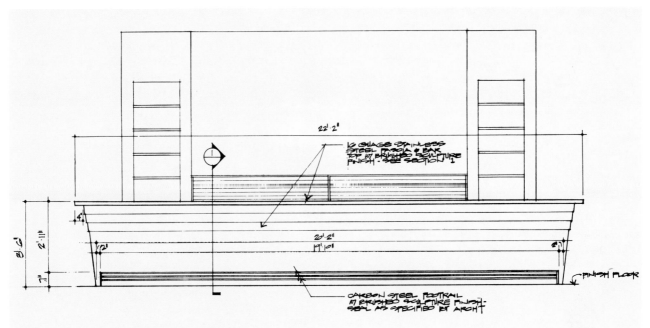

16 GUAGE STAINLESS
STEEL FASCIA & BAR
TOP W/ BRUSHED SCULPTURE
FINISH - SEE SECTION 1

22'-2"

22'-2"
19'-10"

CARBON STEEL FOOTRAIL
W/ BRUSHED SCULPTURE FINISH-
SEAL AS SPECIFIED BY ARCH'T

FINISH FLOOR

FRONT ELEVATION @ BAR
SCALE 1/2"=1'-0"

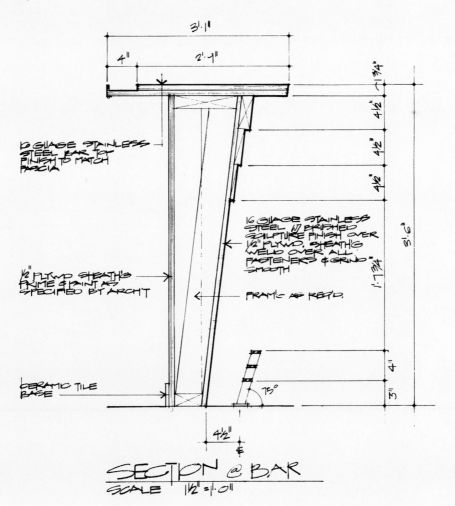

16 GUAGE STAINLESS
STEEL BAR TOP
FINISH TO MATCH
FASCIA

1/2" PLYWD SHEATH'G
PRIME & PAINT AS
SPECIFIED BY ARCH'T

CERAMIC TILE
BASE

3'-1"

4"   2'-7"

1 3/4"

4 1/2"

4 1/2"

4 1/2"

16 GUAGE STAINLESS
STEEL W/ BRUSHED
SCULPTURE FINISH OVER
1/2" PLYWD. SHEATH'G
WELD OVER ALL
FASTENERS & GRIND
SMOOTH

FRAM'G AS REQ'D.

3'-6"

1'-1 3/4"

4"

3"

75°

4 1/2"

SECTION @ BAR
SCALE 1 1/2"=1'-0"

BOARDROOM TABLE

SHELL CENTRAL OFFICES HEADQUARTERS
The Hague, Netherlands

Architecture/Interior Design
Charles Pfister Associates

Design Team
Charles Pfister, Pamela Babey,
Joseph Matzo, Miguel Solé,
Deborah Lewis, James Tung,
James Leal

Fabrication
Lems & V.d. ven B.V.

Photography
© Jaime Ardiles-Arce

FOR THE SHELL CENTRAL OFFICES elegant headquarters, located in The Hague, Netherlands, Charles Pfister Associates of San Francisco designed a boardroom table, which, according to Pfister, "does just about everything but launch rocket ships." His remark aptly describes the remarkably sophisticated technical capabilities built into the 13.4-meter-long table, a modular unit constructed of reinforced steel, Mapa burl veneer, polished bronze, and Rosso Turco granite.

Because the table must accommodate as many as thirty-six conferees, audio and visual clarity across the table's vast surface were primary requirements of the design team. To obtain maximum clarity, they decided to sink a battery of dual-control sound, teleconferencing, video, and recording systems at each station around the table. The challenge was how to do so unobtrusively.

The design team worked with the Wilkie Organization, a European audio-visual consultant to adapt high-quality professional componentry to corporate, trouble-free use. Each station was fitted on two sides with speakers enclosed in perforated brass covers. At the twist of a recessed dial located on the table's apron, the speakers can be modulated for voice honing, amplification, or muting. There are two black grommets at each station. One anchors a discreetly scaled pencil-rod light pole, which identifies which person is speaking; the other anchors a pencil-rod microphone (*section–conference table; plan @ speakers*). Both components are detachable. A set of auxiliary microphones are concealed in the granite berm, which nominally serves the more pedestrian function of providing a stain-proof surface for water pitchers and coffee carafes (*plan @ granite berm*). The light fixture and microphone work in tandem. Additional portable controls, which individually monitor a sixteen-screen video wall, may be plugged in at each station. This enables conferees to make presentations while seated, with supplementary narrative material comfortably at hand.

Pfister's design team provided a mute adjustment at the chairman's station, enhancing it so that he or she may elect to cut off any—or all—of the other thirty-five speakers.

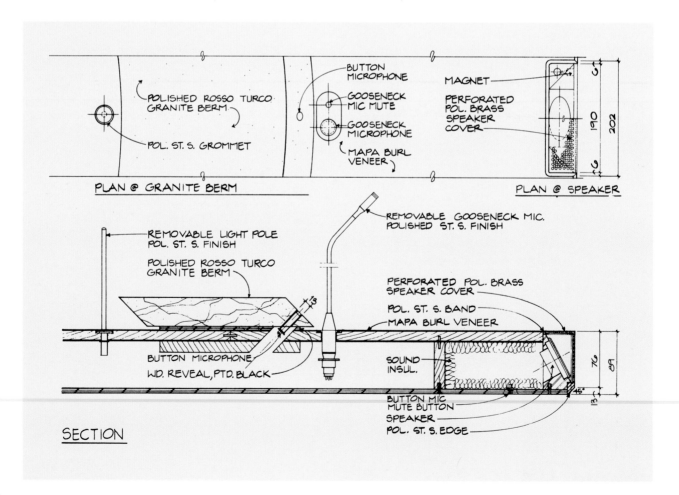

BOARDROOM TABLE

LOCAL NO. 1115, AFL-CIO HEADQUARTERS
Westbury, New York

Westbury, Interior Design
Sidney Philip Gilbert & Associates
Design Team
Sidney Gilbert, William Whistler,
Daniel Goldschmiedt
Millwork
Samuel Kapzis
Photography
© Norman McGrath

LOCAL NO. 1115 of the AFL-CIO commissioned Sidney Philip Gilbert & Associates of New York City to design their headquarters in Westbury, New York. The building was to fulfill a number of functions: office space for the union's management, medical and legal clinics for the members, and facilities for meetings and recreation.

As a reflection of their confidence in SPGA, the union leadership allowed the firm to make all of the design decisions. Their only request

was that the design of the 1,000-square-foot boardroom help to put the union on an equal psychological footing with management representatives during the negotiations that would be conducted there. The budget constraints were minimal. In response, the design team produced an award-winning boardroom interior that is sensitive to its mandate and entirely original.

The designers concluded that the boardroom table should be detailed simply so that it would not conflict with the room's strong architectural statement. The table's form evolved from functional considerations. As a meeting place for potentially difficult negotiations, the table needed a clear division of space. A tripartite division was required for negotiations at which arbitrators would be present along with representatives of labor and management. For other negotiations only a two-part division was necessary. The result was the arc-and-straight-line design (*plans*), which has

a clear head-of-table position opposite the opening in the straight side (where arbitrators in negotiations or leaders in internal meetings are seated) and two well-defined straight sides. The opening into the center area permits stenographers and recorders to be seated within easy hearing of all parties.

Not all of the uses of the table are so serious. When membership get-togethers are held here and in adjoining rooms, buffets are spread on the tabletop.

The construction is as simple and sturdy as the table is elegant. All surfaces are oak veneer (*plans*), and all nosing is solid oak. There is no interior bracing (*vertical section*). The strength of the glued joints and the natural rigidity of the table shape obviated the need for it, permitting the table to rest on standard commercial levelers, which are not affixed to the floor.

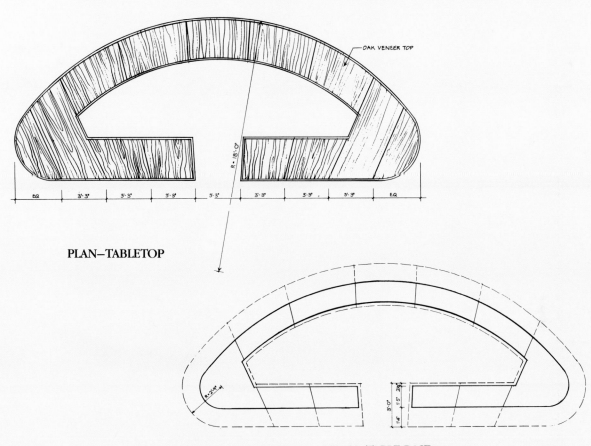

OAK VENEER TOP

R = 18'-0"

EQ | 3'-3" | 3'-3" | 3'-3" | 3'-3" | 3'-3" | 3'-3" | 3'-3" | EQ

PLAN—TABLETOP

R = 2'-4"

3'-0" | 1'-5" | 2½"
¼"

PLAN—TABLE BASE

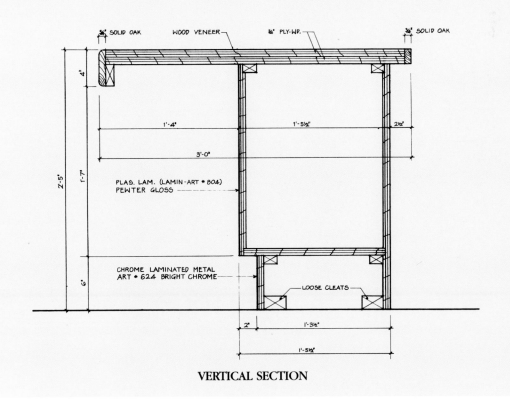

¾" SOLID OAK   WOOD VENEER   ¾" PLY-WD.   ¾" SOLID OAK

4"

1'-4"   1'-5½"   2½"

3'-0"

2'-5"   1'-7"

PLAS. LAM. (LAMIN-ART # 804)
PEWTER GLOSS

6"

CHROME LAMINATED METAL
ART # 624 BRIGHT CHROME

LOOSE CLEATS

2"   1'-3½"

1'-5½"

VERTICAL SECTION

BOARDROOM TABLE

ALABAMA POWER COMPANY
Birmingham, Alabama

Architecture/Interior Design
Geddes Brecher Qualls Cunningham;
Gresham, Smith and Partners
Design Team
James Snyder, Kim Haskell,
Lisa Hansel
Millwork
Walter P. Sauer & Sons
Audio-Visual Consultant
Ancha Electronics
Photography
© Durston Saylor

THE CURVATURE OF the boat-shaped boardroom table at the Alabama Power Company is so sleek and the electronic componentry contained within it so sophisticated that one

might expect it to represent the United States in the next America's Cup. Instead, the table has found a permanent berth in the boardroom of the Alabama Power Company, where it represents the acumen of company officials in commissioning the furniture detail design from Geddes Brecher Qualls Cunningham of Philadelphia (working with Gresham, Smith and Partners of Birmingham, Alabama, on the overall project).

The client suggested the table's elliptical configuration and required a 26-person seating capacity. All other design decisions were deferred to the GBQC team. Although constraints from the client were few, there were three other controlling factors that demanded either circumvention or

accommodation. First, regardless of its construction venue, the table was to be transported to the eighteenth floor on a standard-sized freight elevator. Second, electronic specifications dictated setting concealed microphones 16 to 18 inches from the edge of the table at a 60-degree angle; and third, speakers were to be mounted at a 45-degree angle to the surface of the table.

Faced with these "unlimited" parameters, the design team, led by James Snyder, took a punchlist approach in resolving specific problems. As a starting point, the circumference of the table was determined by mathematical equation—the dimensions of the room minus a 12-foot distance from the table's edge to the projection

screen, and 6 feet from the widest point of the ellipse points to the side walls. A fine-tuning adjustment to give each station 2'-8″ of elbow room and the decision to avoid stations at either end of the table for clear paths of vision to the projection screen determined the final dimensions: a clean, streamlined 37'-8.5″ in length by a 9'-4″ width at the broadest section of the elliptical curve—with the whole broken into sections for ease of transportation (*framing plan/pedestal plan*).

To conceal the necessary wiring for electrical features, the table was designed with a hollow base. Controls for the management of audio-visual equipment, including the projection screen, room lighting, window treat-ment, and conference calls, are contained at chair level in two drawers, one at one end and the other in the middle of the table; at floor level, the controls are located in the center base (accessible by a removable panel); and, at standing height, the controls are on the adjoining podium surface. Refinements to the electronic componentry included installation of amplified and modulated microphone paths and bilaterally positioned zoned speakers that maintain a constant conversational zone.

Aesthetic considerations were addressed last but are certainly not least in their positive impact on the overall design. Mahogany veneers in slats of 16 inches were applied to the particleboard subframes and surfaces, as well as to the elevated tabletop and the 45-degree angled apron. The design team used the veneer patterns to allude to traditional designs without literally reproducing them. The central starburst on the tabletop is flanked by butt-matched grains matched center to center to form echoing elliptical shapes. The writing surfaces were wrapped in leather, and both wood and leather surfaces were trimmed in bullnosed mahogany molding (*plan*). At the edge of the table, the bullnose was dropped 1/16 inch to further enhance the stylistic allusion to traditional forms. The table legs were constructed of solid mahogany, and the base panels are mahogany veneer.

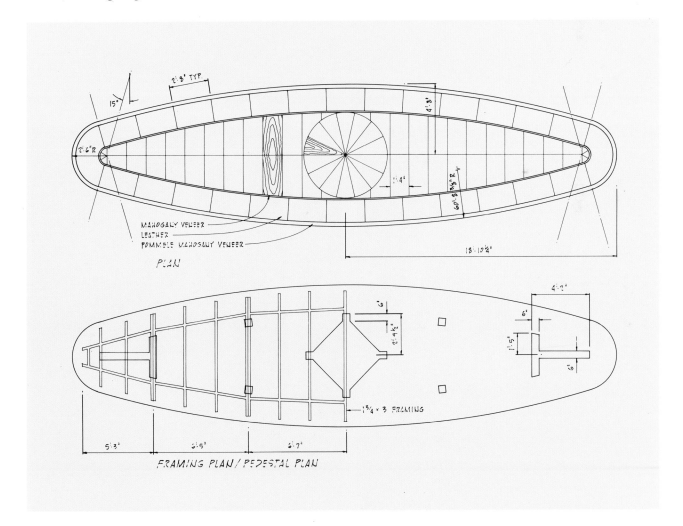

PLAN

FRAMING PLAN / PEDESTAL PLAN

BOOKCASE

SOUTH STREET SEAPORT MUSEUM BOOK AND CHART STORE
New York City

Architecture/Interior Design
Beyer Blinder Belle
Design Team
John H. Beyer, Robert Bayley,
John H. Stubbs
Staircase Fabrication
Sal Cagno
Bookcase Fabrication
Harkins and Maeger
Photography
© Paul Warchol (left); © Roy Wright (right)

AMIDST THE HONKY-TONK atmosphere of any successful urban waterfront re-development project, one or two spaces of surprising quality and interest often appear. So it is at the South Street Seaport in Manhattan, where a nautical map/bookstore, designed by Beyer Blinder Belle of New York City, sets a tone of permanence and dignity.

The bookstore occupies the ground floor of a modest but pure Greek Revival structure, dating from about 1836. To the design team members, the building's architecture reflected the rough-and-ready spirit of the original seaport. Therefore, they resolved to adapt the building to its new use by honoring the original materials—without the limitations of reproducing the style of any specific period.

The design team had already gutted the interiors and renovated the exteriors of the entire surrounding block. It began the bookstore project with a shell of its own making, as well as a three-month deadline, a bare-bones budget, and an 18-inch differential in floor elevation between the alley and street entrances.

To resolve the disparity in floor heights, the design team produced a 36'-long by 8'-3"-high wall of book-cases, which, at the juncture of a new four-riser staircase, metamorphose into cabinets on the lower level. The bookcases are built-out 3 inches from the wall to hide existing wiring and plumbing and are detailed with adjustable, pin-and-hole shelving.

On the opposite side of the double staircase (the two halves of which are separated by the base of a purely decorative nineteenth-century iron column), the design team imposed a 10'-0" sloped display cabinet at a 90-degree angle aligning flush with the staircase. The cabinet accommodates photograph bins, adjustable display racks, drawer storage on the lower-floor level, cabinet storage on the upper-floor level, and cabinet storage that spans the stairwall (*section*).

The millwork throughout the store was constructed of dark-stained sugar pine over plywood. The joints are either mitered and glued or screwed. The baseboards, which serve as closure strips, are nailed to the cabinet frames. The hardware is brass, and the hinges are surface mounted. The stairs and floor are constructed of 5-inch white oak slats that were stained and joined tongue in groove. The stock-part brass stair railing was custom fitted.

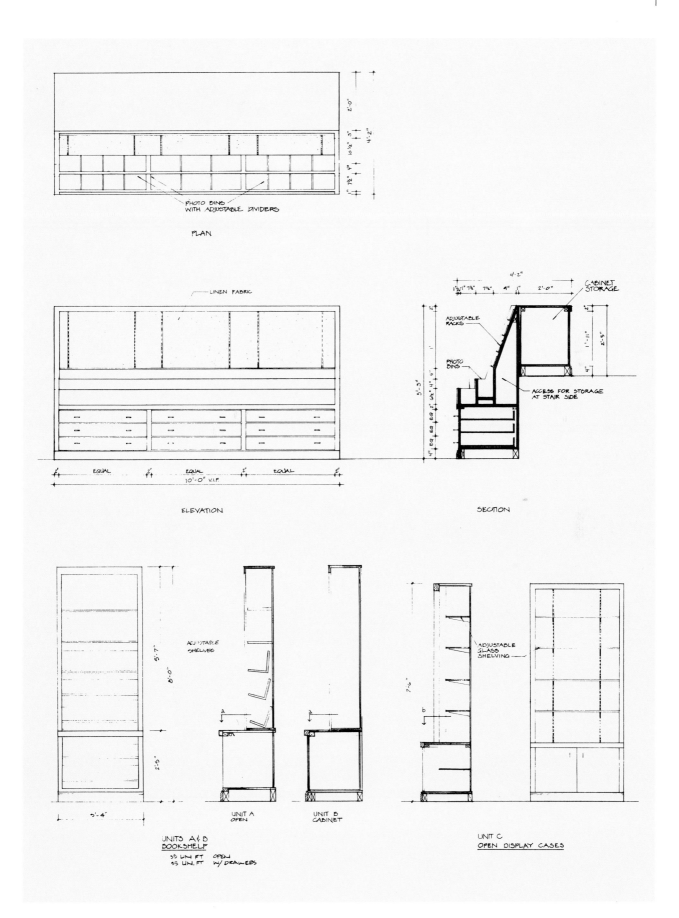

PHOTO BINS
WITH ADJUSTABLE DIVIDERS

PLAN

2'-0"
3"
10½"
4"
7½"
1"
4'-2"

LINEN FABRIC

ELEVATION

EQUAL   EQUAL   EQUAL
10'-0" V.I.F.

4'-2"
1" 2½"1" 7½"   7½"   4" 1"   2'-0"

CABINET
STORAGE

ADJUSTABLE
RACKS

PHOTO
BINS

ACCESS FOR STORAGE
AT STAIR SIDE

2"
2"
1'-11"
2'-5"
4"

5'-5"
4" EQ EQ 2½"4½"4" 4"

SECTION

ADJUSTABLE
SHELVES

5'-7"
6'-0"

2'-5"

5'-4"

a

UNIT A
OPEN

a

UNIT B
CABINET

UNITS A & B
BOOKSHELF
  33 LIN. FT   OPEN
  33 LIN. FT   W/ DRAWERS

ADJUSTABLE
GLASS
SHELVING

7'-6"

b

UNIT C
OPEN DISPLAY CASES

BOOKSTACKS

MAYER, BROWN & PLATT
Chicago, Illinois

Architecture/Interior Design
John Burgee Architects
(John Burgee, Partner;
Philip Johnson, Design Consultant)
Design Team
John Burgee, Philip Johnson,
Alan Ritchie, Ralf Torke,
Joseph Katanik
Lighting Consultant
Claude R. Engle
Color Consultant
Donald Kaufman Color
Metalwork
Steven T. Baird Architect & Associates
Photography
© Jon Miller, Hedrich-Blessing

JOHN BURGEE'S FORMER partner and current design consultant, Philip Johnson, once worked with Ludwig Mies van der Rohe, author of the famous dictum "less is more." This Miesian statement has had several implications, among them that good design should be made to appear simple no matter what complexities the actual construction might involve. In his magisterial library design for the Chicago law firm of Mayer, Brown & Platt, Burgee and Johnson have turned that dictum around in the service of post-Postmodern eclecticism. An example of this inversion is that the construction of the law firm's stately library hall and its bookstacks on two levels is considerably simpler than the elaborate architectural elements employed would suggest.

The client asked only that the library be "the central feature" of the offices Burgee and Johnson were commissioned to design at 190 South LaSalle Street in Chicago. (The building is also a Burgee and Johnson design.) The firm's budget was not extravagant, which made the use of ordinary materials desirable. Otherwise, Burgee and Johnson were given a free hand in the design.

The building's exterior incorporates historical motifs, but these did not determine the library's design. Although generally fifteenth-century Italianate in impression, the library, according to Burgee, "does not quote any specific source."

The two-story, vaulted-ceiling library concept was suggested by the firm's occupation of the top floors of the gabled building. The stepped-in vertical progression of the built-out walls was dictated by the slope of the exterior roof (*section detail 2*).

The simplicity of the plan is apparent in the construction, which consists of three elements: the bookcases themselves, which are standard steel units; the walls and ceiling of gypsum board; and the columns, arches, railings, chandeliers, stairs, brackets, and ceiling straps, which are the chief ornamental elements. All of the elements are cast aluminum, painted in variegated colors (*partial elevation*). Even the end caps of the lower-level stacks are painted sheet metal. Cast-aluminum grilles cover the vents. The grating of the mezzanine floor is steel.

The construction of the cast-aluminum portion of the library demonstrates the advantages first recognized in the cast-iron works of the nineteenth century. The main structural and ornamental elements of the library were cast as discrete pieces (*partial elevation*). It was then a simple process to join them together with stainless-steel bolts. In essence, the structure was put together in the manner of a large erector set.

The walls and vaulted ceiling were more difficult to construct, although less complex in componentry. The ceiling is suspended by wire from channels spanning the vault. The wires are anchored to furring channels, which, in turn, support steel angles to which the gypsum board is affixed. The aluminum straps are screwed to the gypsum board.

Ambient lighting is provided by five chandeliers. With the exception of the lighting installed in the ceilings over the aluminum spiral staircases at each end of the mezzanine, no incandescent lighting has been recessed into the ceiling (another measure of the design's essential simplicity). Other lighting originates as concealed fluorescent tubes in the soffit above the mezzanine stacks and in the ceiling of the lower-level stack areas (*section @ mezzanine floor*). Reading lamps are placed on each of the tables along the central row. Natural illumination emanates from the four sets of triple windows—one set at each end of the library axis and one centered in each side wall. Each set of windows includes a circular window within a vault—replaying the theme of the dominant arches.

Burgee and Johnson employed a somber paint palette in dressing up the metal and gypsum-board elements. Their ochre, cream, black, and gray-green choices parallel the serious colors preferred by publishers of lawbooks. In the library space, however, these colors are enlivened by the luminosity of the ceiling, by the end walls, and by the vigor of the carpet. As a result, the overall effect of the color scheme is serious but not dark.

Burgee and Johnson's open yet unified plan for the Mayer, Brown & Platt library dramatically answers the firm's request for a central focal point for their office. In addition, the library is actually easy to use. Unlike in many traditional library layouts, in Burgee and Johnson's there are no narrow corridors to hide the crucial reference texts and no dark recesses to endure while reading. By providing the drama and interest inherent in the vaulted space, the spiral steps, and the mezzanine catwalk, Burgee and Johnson's design helps to alleviate the tedium of research. Mayer, Brown & Platt and its employees have been well served.

BOOKSTACKS

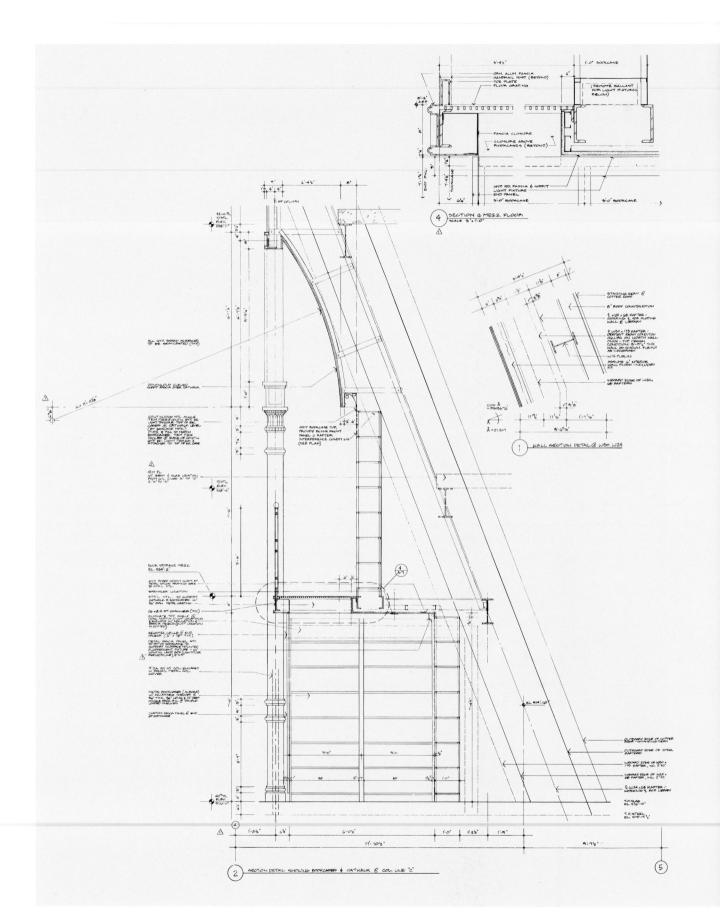

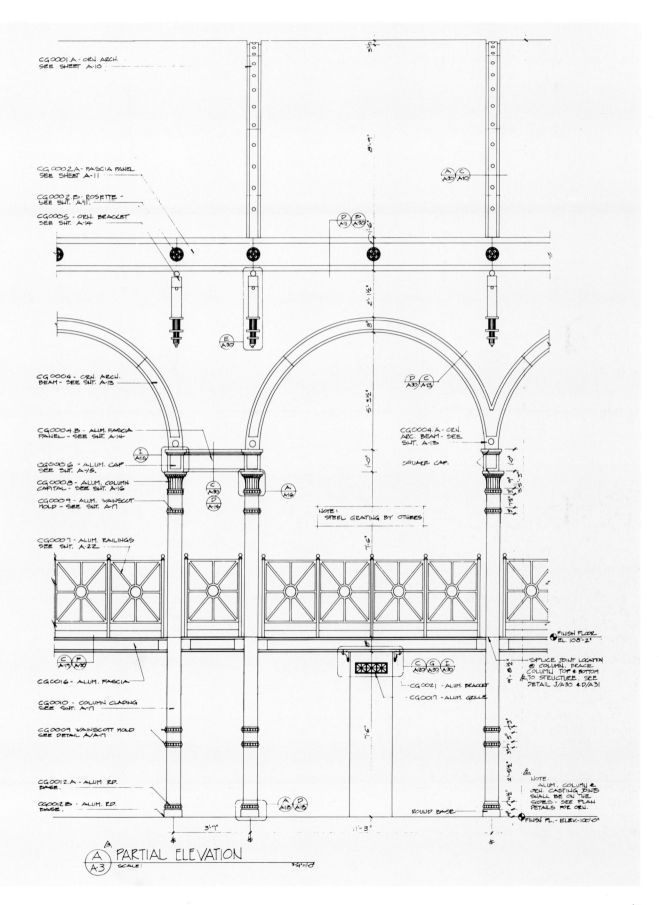

CG0001.A - ORN. ARCH.
SEE SHEET A-10

CG0002.A - FASCIA PANEL
SEE SHEET A-11

CG0002.B - ROSETTE -
SEE SHT. A-11

CG0005 - ORN. BRACKET
SEE SHT. A-14

CG0004 - ORN. ARCH.
BEAM - SEE SHT. A-13

CG0004.B - ALUM. FASCIA
PANEL - SEE SHT. A-14

CG0006 - ALUM. CAP.
SEE SHT. A-15.

CG0008 - ALUM. COLUMN
CAPITAL - SEE SHT. A-16

CG0009 - ALUM. WAINSCOT
MOLD - SEE SHT. A-17

CG0007 - ALUM. RAILINGS
SEE SHT. A-22

CG0016 - ALUM. FASCIA

CG0010 - COLUMN CLADING
SEE SHT. A-17

CG0009 WAINSCOT MOLD
SEE DETAIL A/A-17

CG0012.A - ALUM. RD.
BASE

CG0012.B - ALUM. RD.
BASE

CG0004.A - ORN.
ARC. BEAM - SEE
SHT. A-13

SQUARE CAP.

NOTE:
STEEL GRATING BY OTHERS

CG0021 - ALUM. BRACKET

CG0017 - ALUM. GRILLE

FINISH FLOOR
EL. 108'-2"

SPLICE JOINT LOCATION
@ COLUMN. BRACE
COLUMN TOP & BOTTOM
& TO STRUCTURE. SEE
DETAIL J/A30 & D/A31

NOTE:
ALUM. COLUMN &
ORN. CASTING JOINTS
SHALL BE ON THE
SIDES - SEE PLAN
DETAILS FOR ORN.

ROUND BASE

FINISH FL. - ELEV.-100'0"

3'-7"   11'-3"

A PARTIAL ELEVATION
A3   SCALE: 3/4"=1'-0"

BREAKFRONT

HEADQUARTERS, A FINANCIAL SERVICES CORPORATION
New York City

Architecture/Interior Design
Kohn Pedersen Fox Conway
Design Team
Patricia Conway, Randolph Gerner,
Miguel Valcarcel, Ruxandra Panaitescu,
Richard Kronick, Teri Figliuzzi
Fabrication
Walter P. Sauer & Sons Inc.
Photography
© Paul Warchol

A MAJOR FINANCIAL services institution wanted to demonstrate its respect for tradition in its landmark corporate headquarters in Manhattan. Corporate executives communicated this wish to Kohn Pedersen Fox Conway of New York City as a desire for a "colonial" interior environment.

The design team analyzed the stylistic characteristics of colonial design and concluded that a literal interpretation of the style would result in a less sophisticated interior than was appropriate for the executive suite. Nor did the raw interior space present a physical bias toward a faithfully reproduced "colonial" interior. The lofty, top-floor vaulted space created by architect Edward Larrabee Barnes would have been squandered by the usual colonial design. Research suggested that Georgian architecture, as interpreted by Thomas Jefferson, was a better stylistic alternative.

A massive mahogany breakfront stands against the wall opposite the imposing boardroom window. In functional terms, the breakfront is nothing more than a complex projection booth. But its stupendous scale belies such pedestrian usage, and its proportions show some of the slight tendency toward Mannerism apparent in the architectural elements of the room itself. The cabinet encloses VCRs, film projectors, slide and television projectors (two of each so that any medium can be shown in split screen), and a processor for computer-graphics generation, as well as a complete audio reproduction capability. The 48-inch double-window opening is backed by a curtain that is automatically drawn for screenings.

Projection occurs through the water-clear glass, to a theater-sized screen that is lowered in front of the window.

The breakfront's Georgian pediment is supported by 70-inch, solid mahogany columns with hand-carved Corinthian capitals. Each base is trimmed with a polished brass scotia, matched by a narrower brass astragal beneath the capital (*elevation*).

The 26-foot-diameter boardroom table seats thirty-two and gives preference to no one. The visible inner face of the table is simply a rectangle replicated thirty-two times, with each replication divided from those in adjacent positions by fluted columns of quasi-Ionic character.

The table is constructed entirely of wood, except for the screws in some interior pieces, the electrical lines, the brass rosettes above each column, and the leather inserts on each desktop. Crotch-grain mahogany, in split medallions, was specified for the interior rectangles of the inner face of the table; straight-grain Honduras mahogany veneers the columns that separate the rectangles from one another and from the cornice "supported" by the columns. Hand-rubbed, semi-closed-pore mahogany covers the tabletop. Surrounding each mahogany rectangle in the inner face are strips of sandalwood.

The electronic componentry within each station of the table includes a microphone concealed in the brass lamp and two desktop edge-concealed speakers. The electronic effect is muted; each speaker's voice is merely enhanced.

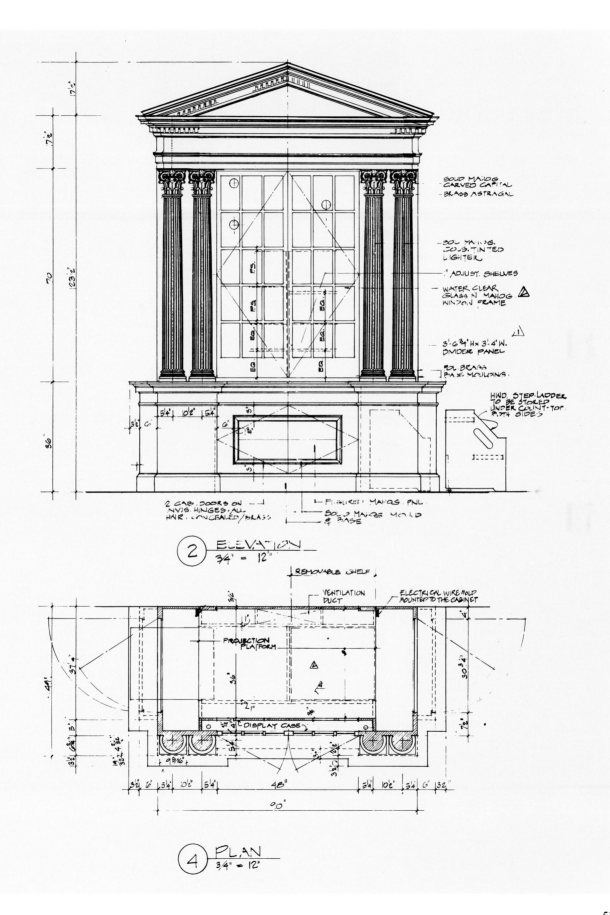

SOLID MAHOG.
CARVED CAPITAL
BRASS ASTRAGAL

SOL. MAHOG.
DOORS-TINTED
LIGHTER

"ADJUST. SHELVES

WATER CLEAR
GLASS N MAHOG
WINDOW FRAME

3'-6¾" H x 3'-4" W.
DIVIDER PANEL

SOL. BRASS
BASE MOULDING.

HWD. STEP-LADDER
TO BE STORED
UNDER COUNT-TOP
& TH4 SIDES

2 GAB. DOORS ON
INVIS. HINGES. ALL
HWR. CONCEALED/BRASS

FIGURED MAHOG. PNL.
SOLID MAHOG MOLD
& BASE

② ELEVATION
¾" = 12"

REMOVABLE SHELF

VENTILATION
DUCT

ELECTRICAL WIRE MOLD
MOUNTED TO THE CABINET

PROJECTION
PLATFORM

DISPLAY CASE

④ PLAN
¾" = 12"

BRIDGE

DEUTSCHE BANK
TAUNUSANLAGE
Frankfurt, West Germany

Architecture/Interior Design
Charles Pfister Associates;
Robinson Mills + Williams;
ABB Architekten
Design Team
Joseph Matzo, Sara Galbraith,
James Leal (Charles Pfister Associates);
Andrew Belschner, James Budzinsky
(Robinson Mills + Williams)
Sculpture
Richard Lippold
Photography
© Jaime Ardiles-Arce

"BRIDGING THE GAP" was the operative concern of Charles Pfister Associates of San Francisco for their interior design of the Deutsche Bank headquarters in Frankfurt, West Germany. Pfister's mandate—from the client and collaborating architects, ABB Architekten of Frankfurt, West Germany, and Robinson Mills + Williams of San Francisco—was to achieve an impression of "stately dignity" by unifying complex and eccentric spatial geometry. The bank's interior was composed of two hexagonal towers, a four-story entrance atrium, and a four-story ancillary building set asymmetrically to the site.

Respecting the economic wisdom of Euclidean geometry—the shortest distance between two points being a straight line—Pfister's team imposed two bridge spans over the reception atrium. The bridges were designed to provide direct access from the elevator banks in one tower to those in the other. The first bridge is set at 45 degrees to a reflecting pool on the ground floor. The second bridge is set at 90 degrees to the first; thereby also crossing the pool at 45 degrees. The configuration was adopted for structural reasons. An added visual benefit in elevation is the compositional framing of both a Richard Lippold bronze sculpture suspended from the ceiling and a red-granite relief sculpture of the bank's logo, located at the end axis of the reflecting pool.

The design team treated the fascias of the two bridges differently to add drama and an element of surprise to otherwise straightforward problem-solving devices. Both spans are constructed of poured-in-place concrete. The upper span uses the same plate-glass-and-chrome guardrail as the mezzanine—set at 30 inches from the floor, according to German code, rather than the 42 inches required by American code (*section B*). Lower bridge spans are finished in flush panels of granite, which reiterate finish materials of the logo wall and pool lining. The other, a diagonal bridge, is soffited in an inverted stairstep of crenellated bar-stock stainless steel. The crenellated configuration was adapted to avoid the "oil-can" buckling that often occurs in the application of large sheets of steel. The sheets were folded and welded into place to avoid potential flaws in seaming (*section A*).

Charles Pfister's insistence on craftsmanlike workmanship in his corporate projects applies to both small and large details. The sparkle of stainless steel was used to demarcate the juncture of columns to floor and columns to ceilings. Bands of ½-inch-thick bar-stock stainless steel encircle the columns and branch out in tangential strips to cover HVAC ducts in reflective ribbons. Rather than inserting utilitarian air-slot segments, the team designed custom air slots, which were carved from the solid stainless steel bar stock.

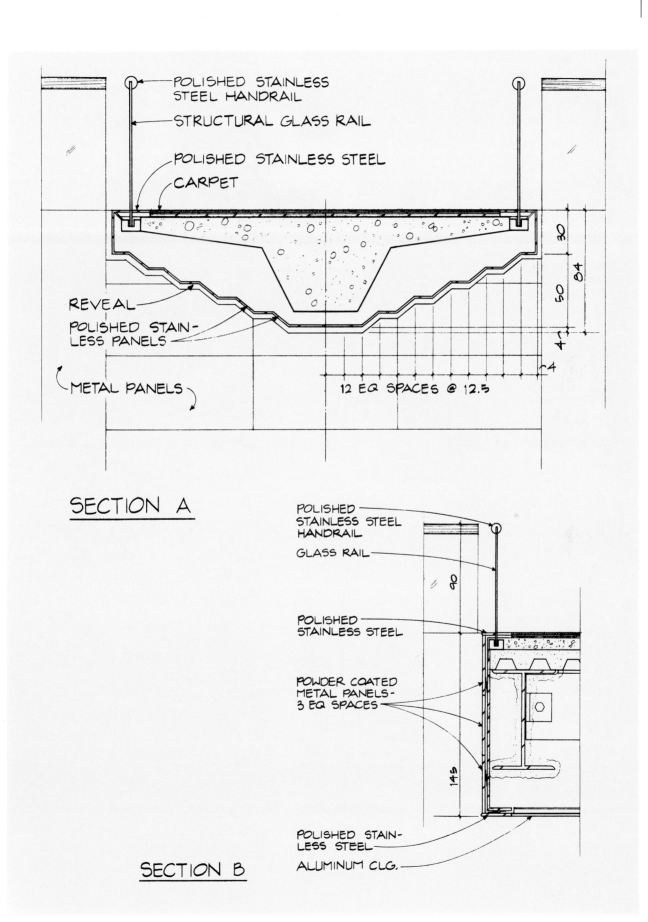

POLISHED STAINLESS
STEEL HANDRAIL

STRUCTURAL GLASS RAIL

POLISHED STAINLESS STEEL

CARPET

30

84

50

41

4

REVEAL

POLISHED STAIN-
LESS PANELS

METAL PANELS

12 EQ SPACES @ 12.5

SECTION A

POLISHED
STAINLESS STEEL
HANDRAIL

GLASS RAIL

90

POLISHED
STAINLESS STEEL

POWDER COATED
METAL PANELS-
3 EQ SPACES

145

POLISHED STAIN-
LESS STEEL

ALUMINUM CLG.

SECTION B

53

CANOPY

ALABAMA POWER COMPANY
Birmingham, Alabama

Architecture/Interior Design
Geddes Brecher Qualls Cunningham;
Gresham, Smith and Partners
Design Team
James Snyder, Charles Alexander,
Elaine Ciufo, James Rowe
Fabrication
Akira Wood; Melco Wood Fixtures
Photography
© Durston Saylor (above);
© Paul Warchol (below)

WHO'S WHO ON THE executive floor of
the Alabama Power Company's headquarters in Birmingham, Alabama, is
never in question. By virtue of good
detailing, who's where is made
equally clear. Such demarcation was
made possible by the collaborative
design efforts of Geddes Brecher
Qualls Cunningham of Philadelphia
and Gresham, Smith and Partners of
Birmingham, who worked together to
produce two differently detailed but
aligned transitional canopies. One
canopy signals the passage to and
from the business dining room; the
other announces the entrance to the
president's suite.

To stress the significant difference
in hierarchical importance between
the two canopies, the design team
developed a different form for each.
The lattice-work dining room canopy
is as light and airy as the eighteenth-
floor room it occupies. The semi-
elliptical canopy outside of the president's suite is as solid and serious as
the office it demarcates.

Certain characteristic construction
features, however, tie both canopies
together: Both are fabricated of mahogany veneer over particleboard
frames and are partially supported by
square columns. Each is designed as a
positive/negative spatial composition
and refers to the bullnose mahogany
planters below (*axonometric*).

As a final unifying factor, the canopies were similarly lighted. Cove-
concealed lamps above the president's
canopy bounce indirect light off the
ceiling, and uplights hidden within
the dining room's entrance partition
wall reflect off the plaster above the
slatted-wood ceiling (*reflected ceiling
plan.*)

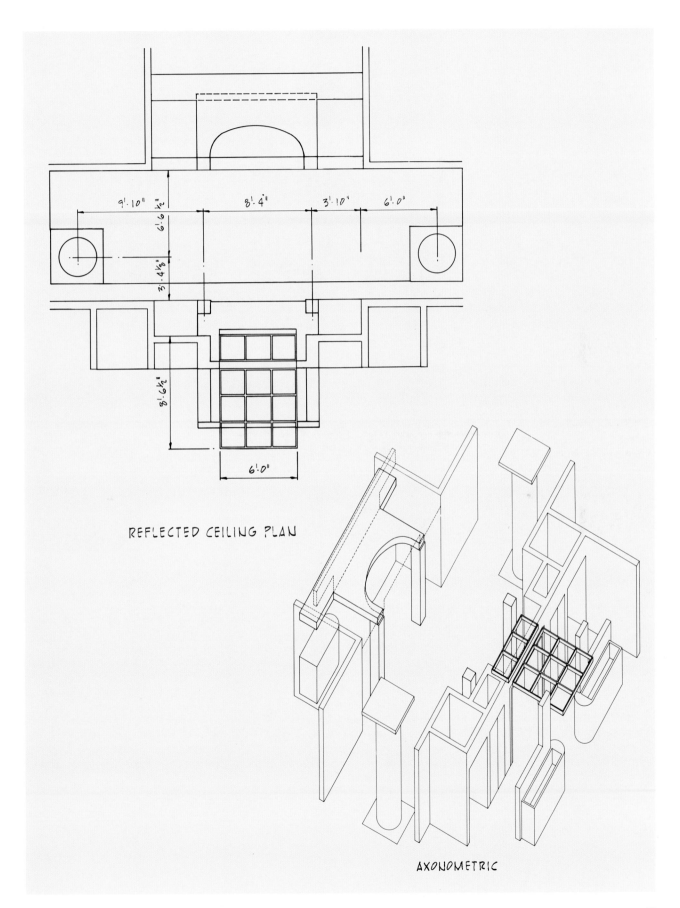

REFLECTED CEILING PLAN

9'-10"   4½"   8'-4"   3'-10"   6'-0"

6'-9"

3'-4⅝"

3'-6⅝"

6'-0"

AXONOMETRIC

CANOPY

DIANE VON FURSTENBERG BOUTIQUE
New York City

Architecture/Interior Design
Michael Graves, Architect
Design Team
Michael Graves, Theodore Brown,
Thomas Rowe, Robert Marino,
Steven Sivak, Patrick Burke,
Ron Berlin (drawings)
Lighting Consultant
Douglas Baker
Fabrication
Pavarini Construction
Photography
© Peter Aaron, ESTO

MICHAEL GRAVES envisioned the Diane Von Furstenberg Boutique in Manhattan's Sherry Netherland Hotel as a cabinet or wardrobe—a concept entirely in keeping with the store's deep, narrow spaces and its product line of high-fashion clothing and accessories.

With that abstract concept in mind, the task for the design team was to work within the narrow confines of the 16-foot-wide space—as well as within the restrictions of the New York Landmarks Preservation Commission, which has jurisdiction over any alterations to the Fifth Avenue building—to devise a space plan and detailing package that would allow the "cabinet" to be perceived as "open" rather than "closed."

The solution was to create, within the front room of the gutted two-story space, a mezzanine—or "shelf"—on the south and east walls. The mezzanine was located on the second-story level. The open vertical volume is further defined on the north wall by a newly installed staircase (*mezzanine plan; section looking north*).

The mezzanine and stair having formed the interior of the cabinet, the secondary problem was to develop a storefront facade on the west—or Central Park–facing wall—which would enhance the open-door illusion. The Graves team designed a predominantly glass-front facade that is, at the same time, sympathetic to the building's original architecture.

As the space plan defines the cabinet's outline, finely scaled and crafted detailing defines and refines its stylistic venue. The crown of the Neoclassical composition is a curved canopy, or cornice detail, which surmounts the two-story central space. The canopy is constructed of wood lattice strips that were painted with an oxidized turquoise finish. The finish was achieved by applying a dry-brush technique over a base coat.

The canopy is framed by a bird's-eye maple veneer soffit, which is, in turn, supported by paired, lathe-turned wood columns (*cornice soffit*). The columns have been ebonized (soaked through with color) "to allow the grain to retain its vitality" and to prevent wear and tear from becoming apparent. The columns are braced by a brushed-steel handrail, which is punctuated by brass fasteners (*elevation/section*).

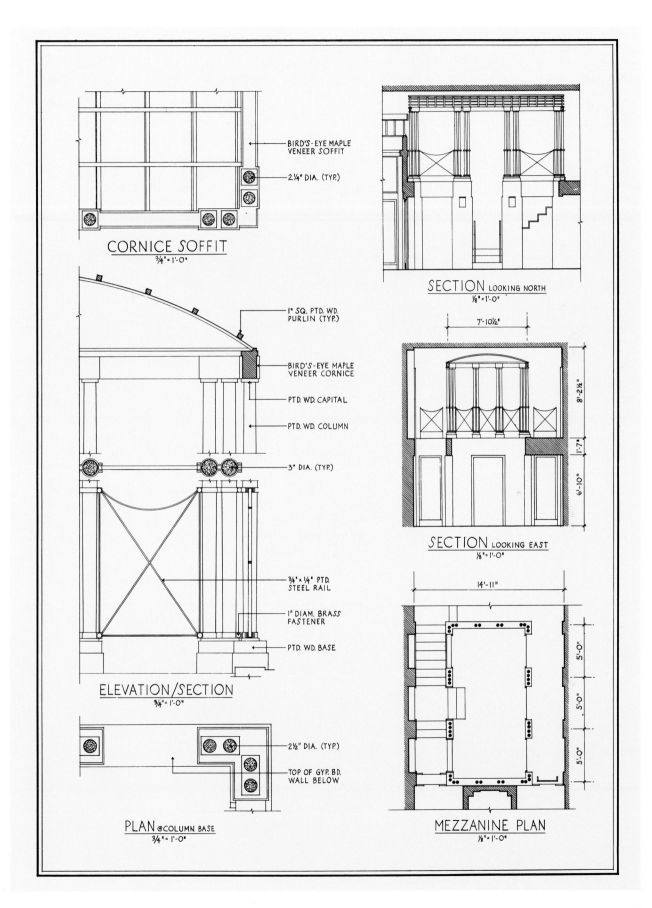

CORNICE SOFFIT
3/4"=1'-0"

BIRD'S-EYE MAPLE
VENEER SOFFIT

2¼" DIA. (TYP.)

SECTION LOOKING NORTH
⅛"=1'-0"

7'-10½"

8'-2½"

1'-7"

6'-10"

SECTION LOOKING EAST
⅛"=1'-0"

1" SQ. PTD. WD.
PURLIN (TYP.)

BIRD'S-EYE MAPLE
VENEER CORNICE

PTD. WD. CAPITAL

PTD. WD. COLUMN

3" DIA. (TYP.)

¾" × ¼" PTD.
STEEL RAIL

1" DIAM. BRASS
FASTENER

PTD. WD. BASE

ELEVATION/SECTION
3/4"=1'-0"

2½" DIA. (TYP.)

TOP OF GYP. BD.
WALL BELOW

14'-11"

5'-0"

5'-0"

5'-0"

PLAN @COLUMN BASE
3/4"=1'-0"

MEZZANINE PLAN
⅛"=1'-0"

CANOPY

THOS. MOSER, CABINETMAKERS & WEATHEREND ESTATE FURNITURE
Princeton Forrestal Village
Princeton, New Jersey

Architecture/Interior Design
Snyder · Snyder
Design Team
Susan Nigra Snyder, James P. Snyder, Nora Wren Kerr
Millwork
Phoenix Construction Company; Frank DeMarco, Alex Kwiatkowski, Julius Fekete
Photography
© Durston Saylor

THE PRINCETON-BASED Thos. Moser, Cabinetmakers & Weatherend Estate Furniture is the first out-of-state retail outlet for these two highly respected New England furniture companies. Both companies previously sold their handcrafted products exclusively from their Maine factories, through their own mail-order catalogs, or through print ads placed in upscale magazines.

Toombs Development Company of New Canaan, Connecticut, regard the store, located in their Princeton Forrestal Village shopping complex, as a "prototype capable of being adapted to various sites throughout the country." Toombs commissioned Architects Snyder · Snyder, a husband-and-wife architectural team from Philadelphia, to design the complex's pivotal space. According to Toombs executive Norbert Young, Snyder · Snyder was chosen because "we saw, in their work, a sensibility of quality and restraint similar to that of the Thos. Moser and Weatherend furniture products."

Snyder · Snyder was given 1,710 square feet of raw construction space within which to work, a $73,800 (or $43 per-square-foot) budget, and a stultifying five-week design-development and construction deadline. The budget and time constraints—as well as the architects' appreciation of the products' inherent beauty—dictated a decidedly spare solution.

According to Susan Nigra Snyder, "a pure museum approach was too formal for the store's suburban location" (just off a parking-lot rampway). Instead, the design team developed a detailing package that emphasizes the juxtaposition of informal indoor/outdoor space. The concept evolved naturally from both the exterior approach to the store and from the intended end-usage of the products—Weatherend's furniture is intended for outdoor use, while Moser's is strictly for use in interiors.

Snyder · Snyder utilized two specific details to subtly communicate their "indoor/outdoor" theme. The more important of the two, a circular gridded canopy, is hung just inside the store's front door (*axonametric*). The 17'-0"-diameter, 1'-0"-deep canopy is hung concentrically over a circular pine-plank platform. The canopy

evokes the shadows, sounds, and smells of a traditional small-town front porch.

The canopy, which is suspended by steel rods threaded through the wood and connected to the steel roof structure above, was constructed on-site on the floor and was then hoisted into place by hydraulic jacks. The canopy grid is built of 1½-inch Douglas fir, framed by a laminated plastic apron.

The products are displayed both as *objets d'art* on stepped platforms near the window and in display rooms against the rear wall of the store. The display rooms are demarcated by a floor-to-ceiling partition built of clapboard siding and "window" frames, and by canvas curtains. Both devices work with the sea blue/green walls to suggest the geographic coastal origins of the products. The photograph and signage panels mounted on the interior partitions describe each company's history and manufacturing process.

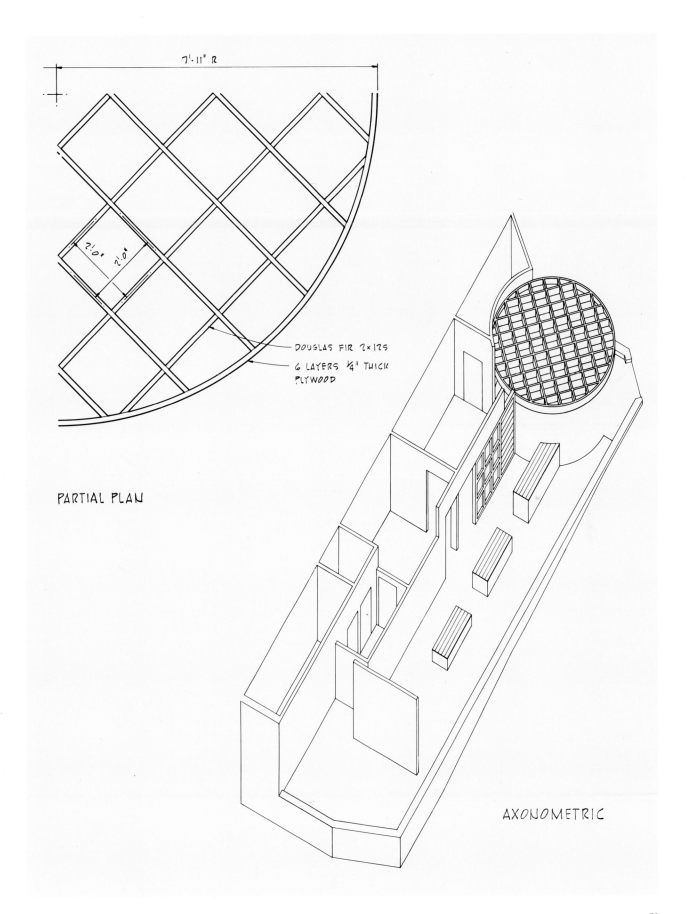

7'-11" R

7'-0"   7'-0"

DOUGLAS FIR 2×12s

6 LAYERS ¼" THICK
PLYWOOD

PARTIAL PLAN

AXONOMETRIC

CARREL

CARRINGTON, COLEMAN, SLOMAN & BLUMENTHAL
Dallas, Texas

Interior Design
ISD Incorporated, Houston
Design Team
Jim Hanlin, Barbara Burkhardt,
Nancy Lindsay
Fabrication
Robert Shaw Manufacturing
Photography
© Chas McGrath

A DARK, MUSTY WARREN of library stacks and inadequately proportioned research carrels overflowing with piles of file folders was definitely not the image Carrington, Coleman, Sloman & Blumenthal, a progressive Dallas law firm, had in mind for their new library. The law firm, which owns an impressive modern art collection, asked ISD Incorporated of Houston to develop a "light-filled, modern interior," which would, nonetheless, "reference the traditional decor associated with the profession."

Because the firm was converting its collection of legal reference material from books to microfiche and computer, there was no pressure to cover the walls with traditional bookcase shelving; the fortuitous timing of the conversion allowed ISD to design low bookshelves and carrel partitions. These open the space to a periphery window wall through a circulation corridor colonnade.

The research carrels and bookshelves are slab constructions with knock-down fasteners. Both are finished in flat-cut and bird's-eye maple veneers over high-density particleboard, or panelcore, base frames. A bird's-eye perspective of the carrel units (*axonometric*) reveals mirror-image imposition of storage shelves and work surfaces within the island carrels, which were hard wired on site for concealed task lights (*section*).

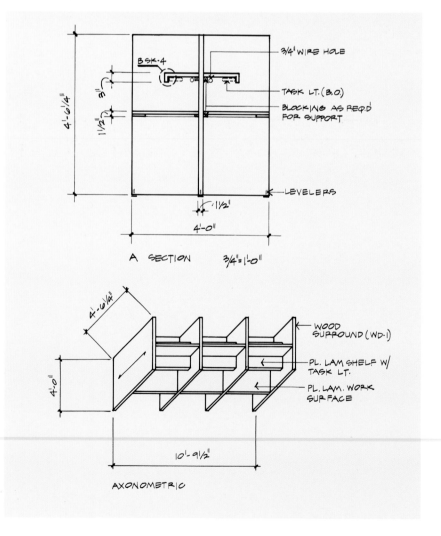

CARREL

PILLSBURY, MADISON & SUTRO
San Francisco, California

Interior Design
Robinson Mills + Williams
Design Team
Matthew Mills, Robert Hayes,
Steven Tierney, Carolyn Chow
Fabrication
Traditional Woodwork
Marquetry Specialist
Darker Marqueterie
Photography
© Paul Peck of RMW

THE 25,000-SQUARE-FOOT satellite office of Pillsbury, Madison & Sutro, one of the West Coast's largest law firms, boasts its own self-contained library. Robinson Mills + Williams of San Francisco developed a number of its custom details.

The decision to use carrels in the new satellite library was dictated by the interplay between shelf-space requirements and structural limitations on load placement. RMW combined stack space with the library tables originally contemplated as reading locations. The result was the carrel depicted—a table surrounded on three sides by bookcases. These low stacks relieve some of the load that would otherwise be borne by the alternating high stacks.

The unusual 13-foot length (11 feet of table surface) matches the length of the alternating high bookcases (*back elevation*). The 1'-⅜"-deep shelves are standard for law-book storage. The shelves themselves are premanufactured, standard steel units, which were incorporated at the client's request.

The shelving was designed to accommodate built-in lighting. Space was built-in for conduits through the millwork, and the vertical panels above the tabletop can be removed to provide room for lighting fixtures (*section*).

Working with a comfortable budget, RMW was able to extend throughout the library the paneling and other design motifs established for the rest of the office. The finish wood used on the carrels—and on the bookcases and paneling generally—is light maple veneer. A marquetry specialist inlaid the veneer with thin, parallel strips of East African mahogany.

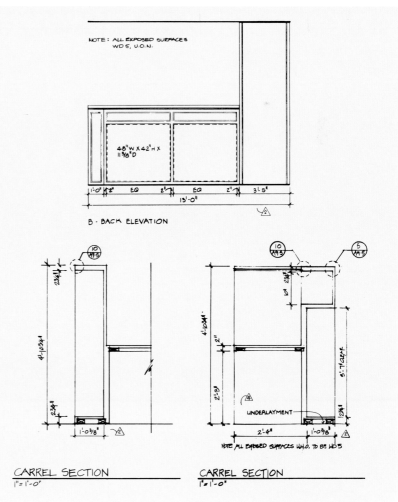

NOTE: ALL EXPOSED SURFACES WD 5, U.O.N.

48" W X 42" H X 11⅜" D

13'-0"

B · BACK ELEVATION

CARREL SECTION
1" = 1'-0"

CARREL SECTION
1" = 1'-0"

NOTE: ALL EXPOSED SURFACES W.O. TO BE WD 5

UNDERLAYMENT

CEILING

SHELL CENTRAL OFFICES HEADQUARTERS
The Hague, Netherlands

Architecture/Interior Design
Charles Pfister Associates
Design Team
Charles Pfister, Pamela Babey,
Joseph Matzo, Miguel Solé,
Deborah Lewis, James Tung,
James Leal
Fabrication
Lems & v.d. Ven B.V.
Photography
© Jaime Ardiles-Arce

THE HEADQUARTERS of Shell Central Offices, one of the three largest industrial corporations in the world, are located in The Hague. As a logical consequence of its location within the geographically removed and ineffably reserved Dutch capital, in its design mandate the company included the descriptive terms "subtlety and restraint"—as well as the cautionary proviso, "quality without pretension."

San Francisco's Charles Pfister Associates realized those intentions in detailing that enhances the sophisticated space planning the firm had already accomplished throughout the four-story management-block sector of the complex (see page 38). The Pfister firm, which has a reputation for detailing "writ large," turned out equally fine detailing for this project—written large, medium, and small.

The coffered ceiling of a modestly dimensioned (26'-0" × 15'-0") bar located adjacent to a vestibule and an executive dining room illustrates Pfister's deft hand at more delicate detailing. The design team assessed the ceiling as "the only plane within the space with inherent detailing potential" and then selected a coffered treatment as "the ceiling type which would best carry through to the dining room, while recalling the layering effect typical of traditional Dutch architecture."

Pfister's layers began with the wire suspension of a particleboard ceiling (framed in a standard T-channel system) from anchor bolts in the structural slab. Sisal matting, like that applied to the walls for acoustic control, was glued to the exposed side of the particleboard. The actual coffering was implemented in three additional layers: first, by the application of gridded brass angles screwed into the particleboard; second, by the concentric application of a lacquered-wood-glued-to-bleached-teak grid (a recurrent theme throughout the building); and third, by the imposition of a finish frame grid, coated in opulent gold leaf (*partial reflected ceiling plan*).

A Pfister trademark is the discreet integration of ventilation systems into ceiling detail. In the bar area, that integration was accomplished by the insertion of end-to-end rows of sheet metal conduits and air supply and return boots into slotted channel reveals between frames (*supply air slot @ dining room ceiling*). The head covers for the building's sprinkler outlets are also inserted at the interstices of coffers. Incandescent downlighting fixtures without baffles or lenses accentuate the depth of the ceiling's projection.

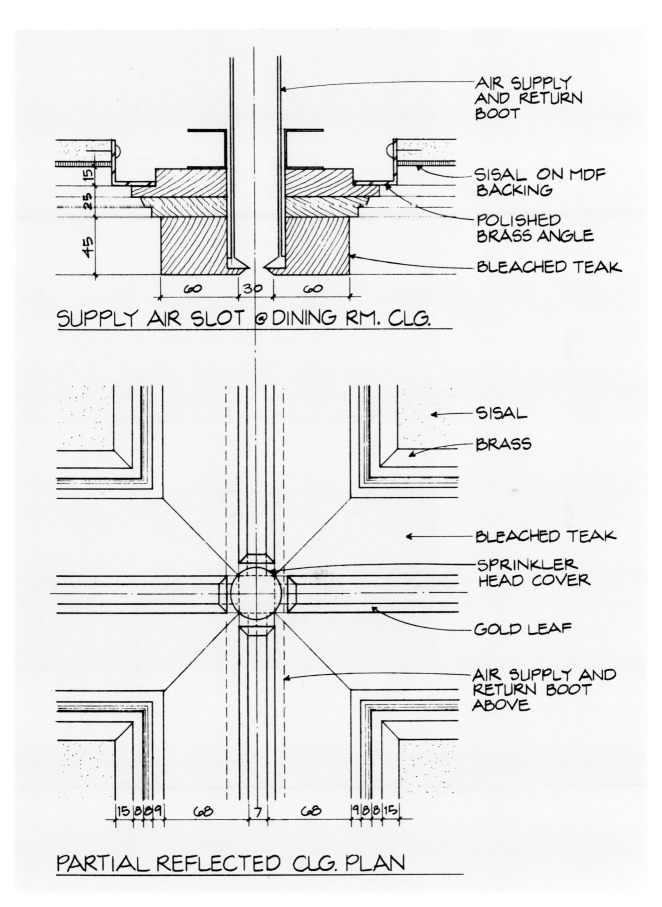

AIR SUPPLY
AND RETURN
BOOT

SISAL ON MDF
BACKING

POLISHED
BRASS ANGLE

BLEACHED TEAK

15 25 45

60 30 60

SUPPLY AIR SLOT @ DINING RM. CLG.

SISAL

BRASS

BLEACHED TEAK

SPRINKLER
HEAD COVER

GOLD LEAF

AIR SUPPLY AND
RETURN BOOT
ABOVE

15 8 8 9 68 7 68 9 8 8 15

PARTIAL REFLECTED CLG. PLAN

CEILING

DUBAI HYATT HOTEL
Dubai, United Arab Emirates

Architecture/Interior Design
3D/International, Inc., Houston
Fabrication
General Drapery
Photography
© Ed Stewart

IN DUBAI, one of the United Arab Emirates on the Persian Gulf, the Hyatt hotel chain decreed a subtle pleasure-dome—an "Arabian-nights" club for drinking, dancing, and dinner conversation.

Hyatt built an entire hotel complex based on plans developed by 3D/International, Inc., of Houston, Texas. 3D/I was also commissioned by Hyatt to design the hotel's interiors, including the in-house nightclub. In describing its wishes for the nightclub interior, Hyatt instructed 3D/I to create an environment with a flavor "not too gaudy, not too disco." Because most patrons of the club would be American or Saudi businessmen, Hyatt asked that the ambience be "similar to, but more romantic than their accustomed gathering places back home."

3D/I laid out a conventional footprint for the club's approximately 5,000 square feet, providing table and seating room for 150, a dance floor, and a small stage for revues. 3D/I then treated the walls and privacy partitions unconventionally, wrapping them in a dark blue fabric meant to recall the sea.

To suggest the clear, sparkling sky of the desert night on the club's ceiling, 3D/I again had recourse to fabric. This time it was used in a more frankly romantic manner—three cascading swags of gossamer Sol-R-Veil (a panne cloth of polyester) were loosely stretched and draped over the width of the club. Each swag was laterally stitched together from the manufacturer's 17-inch widths.

Steel grommets are sewn, at 30-centimeter intervals, into each horizontal swag hem. The hems are fastened over eyehooks welded to the steel-tube-and-pipe support system

(*wall support; intermediate support*). The support system includes a slot-and-screw slide mechanism to adjust tension in the swags.

The technical specifications of the fabric are: 14.4 average maximum spec optical density; fabric count: 60 by 30; weight: 13.36 ounces per linear yard. The result, in layman's terms, is a "silvery" fabric finish, caused by a

weave that is wide enough to allow semitranslucence. The glittering, gossamer effect is accentuated by the placement of a rectangular grid of incandescent track lights above the fabric. The tracks themselves are screwed to a unistrut frame, which, in turn, is attached to the structural ceiling by threaded rods (*ceiling support*).

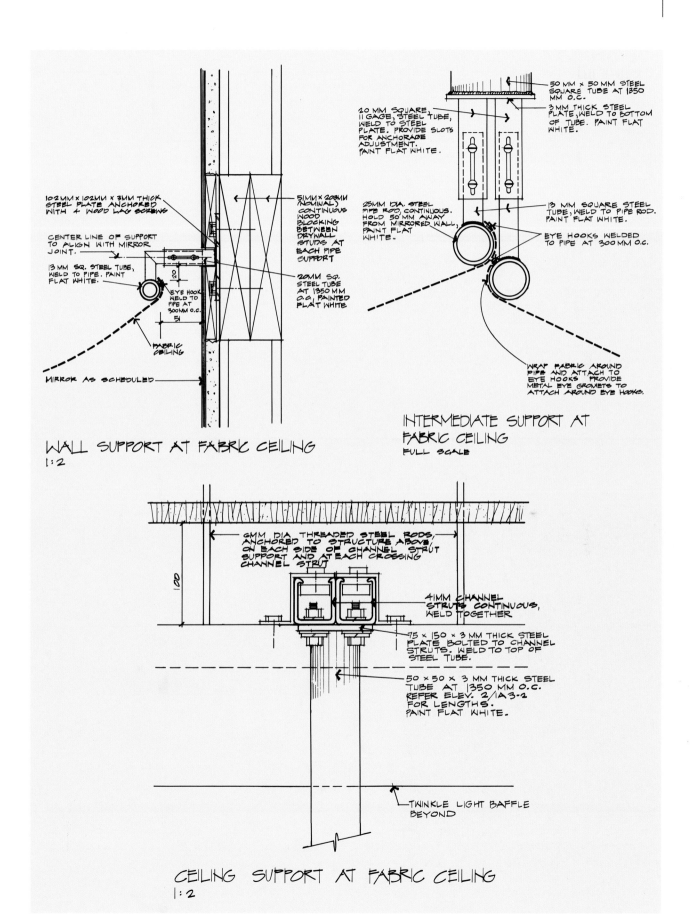

102MM x 102MM x 3MM THICK
STEEL PLATE ANCHORED
WITH 4 WOOD LAG SCREWS

CENTER LINE OF SUPPORT
TO ALIGN WITH MIRROR
JOINT.

13 MM SQ. STEEL TUBE,
WELD TO PIPE. PAINT
FLAT WHITE.

EYE HOOK
WELD TO
PIPE AT
300MM O.C.

FABRIC
CEILING

MIRROR AS SCHEDULED

51MM x 203MM
(NOMINAL)
CONTINUOUS
WOOD
BLOCKING
BETWEEN
DRYWALL
STUDS AT
EACH PIPE
SUPPORT

20MM SQ.
STEEL TUBE
AT 1350 MM
O.C. PAINTED
FLAT WHITE

WALL SUPPORT AT FABRIC CEILING
1:2

20 MM SQUARE,
11 GAGE, STEEL TUBE,
WELD TO STEEL
PLATE. PROVIDE SLOTS
FOR ANCHORAGE
ADJUSTMENT.
PAINT FLAT WHITE.

25MM DIA. STEEL
PIPE ROD, CONTINUOUS.
HOLD 50 MM AWAY
FROM MIRRORED WALL.
PAINT FLAT
WHITE.

50 MM x 50 MM STEEL
SQUARE TUBE AT 1350
MM O.C.

3 MM THICK STEEL
PLATE, WELD TO BOTTOM
OF TUBE. PAINT FLAT
WHITE.

13 MM SQUARE STEEL
TUBE, WELD TO PIPE ROD.
PAINT FLAT WHITE.

EYE HOOKS WELDED
TO PIPE AT 300 MM O.C.

WRAP FABRIC AROUND
PIPE AND ATTACH TO
EYE HOOKS. PROVIDE
METAL EYE GROMETS TO
ATTACH AROUND EYE HOOKS.

INTERMEDIATE SUPPORT AT
FABRIC CEILING
FULL SCALE

6MM DIA. THREADED STEEL RODS,
ANCHORED TO STRUCTURE ABOVE
ON EACH SIDE OF CHANNEL STRUT
SUPPORT AND AT EACH CROSSING
CHANNEL STRUT

41MM CHANNEL
STRUTS CONTINUOUS,
WELD TOGETHER

75 x 150 x 3 MM THICK STEEL
PLATE BOLTED TO CHANNEL
STRUTS. WELD TO TOP OF
STEEL TUBE.

50 x 50 x 3 MM THICK STEEL
TUBE AT 1350 MM O.C.
REFER ELEV. 2/1A3-2
FOR LENGTHS.
PAINT FLAT WHITE.

TWINKLE LIGHT BAFFLE
BEYOND

CEILING SUPPORT AT FABRIC CEILING
1:2

CEILING

**U.S. POST OFFICE
STATE OF ILLINOIS CENTER**
Chicago, Illinois

Interior Design
Loebl Schlossman & Hackl
Design Team
David A. Marks, Hans D. Lagoni,
Steve Schmidt
Photography
© Barry Rustin

THE BOLD DESIGN of the State of Illinois Center in Chicago inspired the U.S. Postal Service to request a "lively, interesting, and dramatic" interior for its branch to be located within the building. Chicago's Loebl Schlossman & Hackl took up the challenge by creating an interior in which the "fast, hard materials engender a sense of kinetic activity in people as they move through the space."

The Postal Service leased an L-shaped area of 2,870 square feet, located just off the lower level of the building's colossal circular atrium. Working within the constraints of the post office's budget and its "American-products-only" rule, the designers fitted a number of subtly detailed curves into the two-story space. The curvilinear counters of the postal station proper (on the floor above the lockbox area shown in the photograph) and the barrel-vaulted ceiling (which joins the intersecting corridors of the lockbox zone on the lower level) intentionally reflect the strong shapes of the atrium and the building's exterior facade.

The shallow vaulted rib-and-slat ceiling is constructed with standard ceiling-system components generally used for flat ceilings. To create the barrel-vault configuration, the ribs were bent in the field to the proper shape; they were then wire suspended from the structural ceiling—approximately 4½ feet from the structure to the top of the rib curve. The aluminum slats were clipped with standard fasteners to the ribs, which define the curve of the ceiling. The system's stability was assured by anchoring the perimeter of the ceiling to the metal studs, which define the outer limits of the space occupied by the post office. The design team specified a factory-painted silver finish for the longitudinal aluminum slats.

As part of the detailing package for the project, Loebl Schlossman & Hackl designed free-standing, private post-office boxes, which are flush fitted in elevation with the suspended vault ceiling (*elevation*). Each "wall" slat runs the entire length of its corridor—from the gypsum-board wall section at the entrance end to the groin. The groin is not ribbed; slat simply abuts slat (*reflected ceiling plan*).

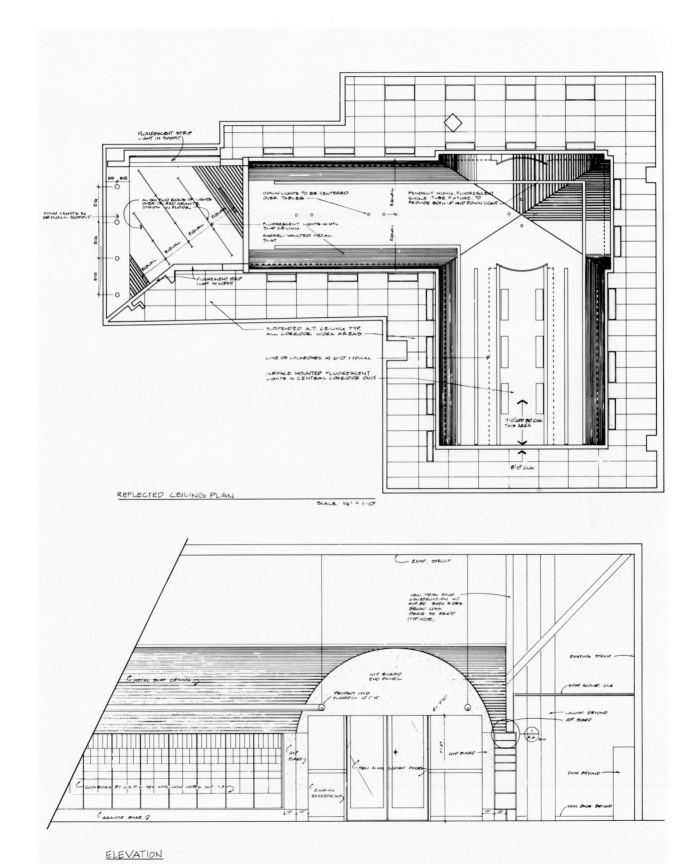

FLOURESCENT STRIP
LIGHT IN SOFFIT

DOWN LIGHTS IN
DRYWALL SOFFIT

ALIGN TWO ROWS OF LIGHTS
OVER CARVED GRANITE
STRIPS IN FLOOR.

EQ EQ

EQUAL EQUAL EQUAL

EQUAL

FLOURESCENT STRIP
LIGHT IN SOFFIT

DOWN LIGHTS TO BE CENTERED
OVER TABLES

FLUORESCENT LIGHTS IN MTL
SLAT CEILING

BARREL VAULTED METAL
SLAT

PENDANT HUNG, FLUORESCENT
SINGLE TUBE FIXTURE, TO
PROVIDE BOTH UP AND DOWN LIGHT.

1'-0"

EQUAL

SUSPENDED A.T. CEILING TYP.
ALL CORRIDOR WORK AREAS

LINE OF LOCKBOXES AT 6'-0" TYPICAL

SURFACE MOUNTED FLUORESCENT
LIGHTS IN CENTRAL CORRIDOR ONLY

7'-0" GYP. BD. CLG.
THIS AREA

8'-0" CLG.

REFLECTED CEILING PLAN

SCALE 1/4" = 1'-0"

EXIST. STRUCT

NEW METAL STUD
CONSTRUCTION W/
GYP. BD. BOTH SIDES
BELOW CLG.
BRACE AS REQ'D
(TYP. NOTE)

METAL SLAT CEILING

GYP. BOARD
END PANEL

PENDANT MTD
FLUORESC. 4 FT FT

R = 7'-0"

GYP.
BOARD

7'-2"

1 A
G

EXISTING STRUCT

SUSP. ACOUST. CLG.

COLUMN BEYOND
GYP. BOARD

LOCKBOXES BY U.S.P.S. SEE APPLICABLE NOTES SHT. A3

NEW ALUM. GLAZED DOORS

EXISTING
STOREFRONT

GYP. BOARD

GRANITE BASE

DOOR BEYOND

VINYL BASE BEYOND

ELEVATION

67

CLOCK TOWER

CAROLINE'S
New York City

Architecture/Interior Design
Dorf Associates
Design Team
Martin Dorf, Hugh Boyd,
Lorraine Knapp (renderings)
Fabrication
Birk Iron Works (railings);
Metal Forms, Inc. (stainless clock)
Photography
© Durston Saylor

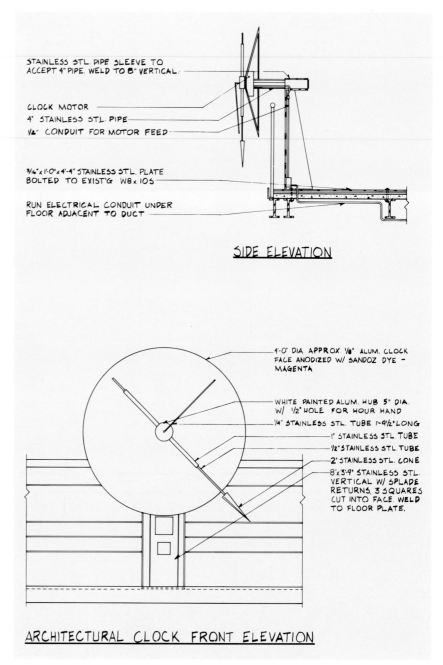

STAINLESS STL. PIPE SLEEVE TO
ACCEPT 4" PIPE. WELD TO 8" VERTICAL.

CLOCK MOTOR
4" STAINLESS STL. PIPE
½" CONDUIT FOR MOTOR FEED

3/16"x 1'-0"x 4'-4" STAINLESS STL. PLATE
BOLTED TO EXIST'G W8 x 105

RUN ELECTRICAL CONDUIT UNDER
FLOOR ADJACENT TO DUCT

SIDE ELEVATION

4'-0" DIA. APPROX. ⅛" ALUM. CLOCK
FACE ANODIZED W/ SANDOZ DYE –
MAGENTA

WHITE PAINTED ALUM. HUB 5" DIA.
W/ ½" HOLE FOR HOUR HAND
¼" STAINLESS STL. TUBE 1-9½" LONG
1" STAINLESS STL. TUBE
½" STAINLESS STL. TUBE
2' STAINLESS STL. CONE
8"x 3'-9" STAINLESS STL.
VERTICAL W/ SPLADE
RETURNS, 3 SQUARES
CUT INTO FACE. WELD
TO FLOOR PLATE.

ARCHITECTURAL CLOCK FRONT ELEVATION

DESIGNERS OFTEN GO for a show-stopping focal point when detailing their projects. As a variation on that theme, Dorf Associates of New York City designed a "show-starting" clock tower for Caroline's, a restaurant-cum-comedy club in lower Manhattan.

The clock accomplishes several functions within the converted warehouse. In addition to establishing a focal point that draws attention to the height of the space by night and the skylight by day, the clock ceremoniously announces two comedy shows nightly. Like a mobile, the kinetic movement of the clock's hand adds metronomic animation to the space.

Like the other details designed by Dorf for Caroline's (see pages 32 and 155), the clock tower celebrates "the refinement of rubble." The clock's fabrication in anodized aluminum symbolizes the phoenixlike potential of the fragmented cans that litter the neighborhood. The 4'-0"-diameter clock face was shaped as a cone. It was then brushed with magenta sandoz dye to diminish glare and to suggest a streak of lightning. The cone configuration is reiterated by the clock hand, which is constructed of a 2-foot stainless steel cone (the arrow) that pierces the 5-inch-diameter painted aluminum hub with a telescoping ½- and 1-inch stainless steel shaft. The hand is counterweighted by "feathers," which are abstracted in the form of a stainless steel cylinder (*front elevation*).

The clock tower itself is fabricated of satin-brushed stainless steel. The tower is bolted at a right angle to a stainless steel plate, which is, in turn, bolted through the 8-inch by 10-inch wood-plank finish floor to an I-beam-reinforced concrete slab. The electrical conduit that controls the motorized clock runs under the slab floor to an adjacent duct (*side elevation*). Three diminishing square cutouts run the length of the tower as a decorative device that effectively lessens the perception of the tower's dimensions.

COLUMN

CAFFE ROMA INTERNATIONAL
New York City

Architecture/Interior Design
Haverson-Rockwell Architects
Design Team
David S. Rockwell, Jay M. Haverson
Fabrication
Tiger Construction Corporation
Photography
© Mark Ross Photography, Inc.

LOFTS USED TO BE TREATED as if they were museum or gallery spaces. The formula for renovation was correspondingly rigid—spaces were stripped down to bare walls, bare floors, and exposed structural columns. The walls and columns were painted white; the floors were refinished and stained, or, as a variation on a theme, were sometimes covered in industrial carpeting in shades ranging from warm to dark gray.

Caffe Roma International in Manhattan, completed in 1986, is an example of the dramatic change of approach in loft design. Lofts are still valued for their spaciousness (Caffe Roma International has 5,500 square feet) and they are still valued for their high ceilings (Caffe Roma International's are 17 feet high). But vivid color has replaced white as the wall finish of choice, and selectively applied texture and ornamentation are de rigueur.

The implementer of Caffe Roma International's transformation from a standard-issue loft to an airy Mediterranean courtyard was Haverson-Rockwell Architects, a New York City–based architectural team with an award-winning record in restaurant design. To build an essentially low-key background environment, Haverson-Rockwell divided the space into more intimate dining areas with the judicious imposition of perforated partitions. The saturated peach walls were wrapped with lattice garden panels for continuity, and subtle pockets of visual interest were created with reflective mirror panels enhanced by concealed theatrical lighting.

Haverson-Rockwell allowed the handsome concrete-encased steel structural columns to command center-stage attention. The columns were given a Zolatone finish, and new bases and moldings were punched out with brilliant white paint. To further emphasize their importance to the space as a primary architectural element, the column capital that would have been hidden by partitioning was exposed in a shadowbox format and starkly lit by powerful 300-watt uplights against a contrasting backdrop of cerulean blue (*section*).

The designers expanded on the column-as-treasured-artifact theme by affixing Italianate paintings of a man and woman on the rest-room doors located on either side of the column shaft.

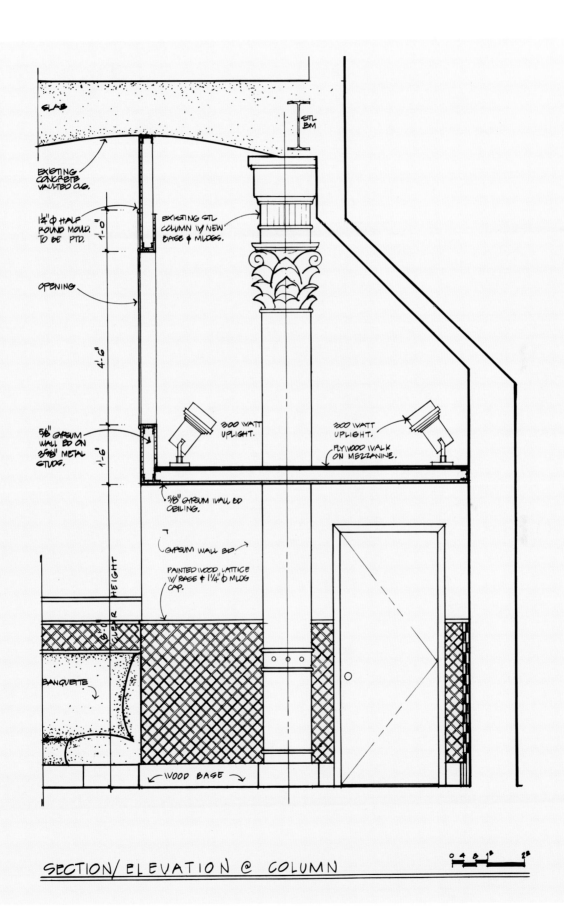

SLAB

EXISTING
CONCRETE
VAULTED CLG.

1¼" Ø HALF
ROUND MOULD.
TO BE PTD.

1'-0"

OPENING

EXISTING STL.
COLUMN W/ NEW
BASE & MLDGS.

STL.
BM.

4'-6"

5/8" GYPSUM
WALL BD. ON
3⅝" METAL
STUDS.

1'-6"

300 WATT
UPLIGHT.

300 WATT
UPLIGHT.

PLYWOOD WALK
ON MEZZANINE.

5/8" GYPSUM WALL BD
CEILING.

CLEAR HEIGHT

8'-0"

GYPSUM WALL BD.

PAINTED WOOD LATTICE
W/ BASE & 1¼" Ø MLDG
CAP.

BANQUETTE

WOOD BASE

SECTION / ELEVATION @ COLUMN

0 4 8 1'   2'

71

Column Enclosure

THIRD NATIONAL BANK
Nashville, Tennessee

Architecture/Interior Design
Kohn Pedersen Fox Associates PC
Fabrication
Wasco/E.C.A. Marble Granite
Photography
© Jock Pottle

NEW YORK CITY–BASED Kohn Pedersen Fox Associates PC is known for designing carefully proportioned and sensitively detailed new buildings that assimilate easily into their architectural environs. As a result, when the Murphree Company commissioned KPF to design the Third National Bank building in Nashville, Tennessee, it asked only that the interior and exterior of the building be "simple and elegant."

KPF chose to develop a detailing package based on the simplicity and elegance of the stylistic elements found in an Egyptian-revival church located directly across the street from the job site. Nowhere is that intention more evident than in the 3,200-square-foot lobby, where an Egyptian sensibility is manifest in the massive scale of three structural column enclosures.

The marble-clad column enclosures are constructed of 8'-0" square bases. The bases are articulated to trapezoidal panels that slant upward and inward to papyruslike, proto-Doric capitals. The coffered ceiling of the lobby was originally planned to "sit" on top of the capitals. However, KPF accommodated a later client request for a 30'-0" ceiling height by extending the column an additional 10 feet. The column enclosure was not rescaled because the unclad extension—veneered in thin-coat plaster—was judged as "also appropriate to the proportionality of Egyptian papyrus columns."

The enclosures, which are of serpeggiante marble that matches the floor material, actually cover two different shapes of concrete structural columns. The two outer columns are five sided, while the center column is square (*elevation*). The marble panels are hung from hooks welded to a steel unistrut system built around the structural columns. The panels are butt joined at the outer edges, and the inner edges of the corner notches are mitered. An epoxy thermal-gluing process was used to bond the edges.

The column colonnade, in conjunction with wall pilasters and ceiling joists, divides the lobby into eight subspaces (*reflected ceiling plan*). Each space is defined by its own chandelier (see page 152).

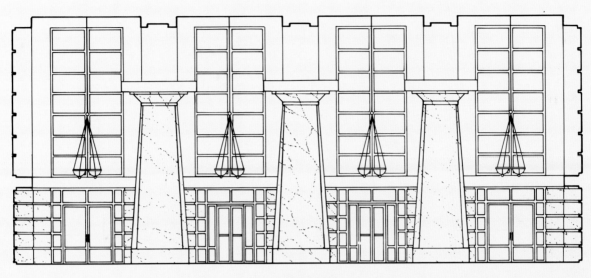

ELEVATION

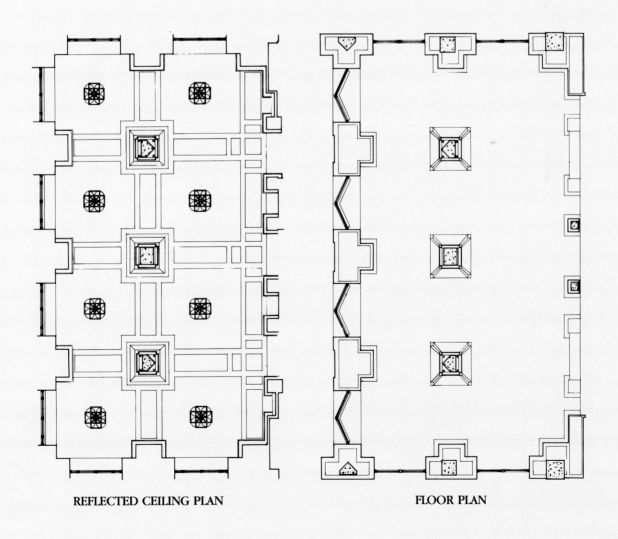

REFLECTED CEILING PLAN   FLOOR PLAN

COLUMN ENCLOSURE

EYES NIGHTCLUB
Kansas City, Missouri

Interior Design
Kelly and Lehn

Design Team
Thomas Lehn, Kathleen Kelly,
Kay Boehr, Rick Prater,
Brian Griffiths

Consulting Architect
J. Christopher Gale & Co.

Neon
Sign Graphics, Inc.

Neon Fabrication
Kansas City Neon

Dance Floor Lighting and Sound System
Blackstone Audio Visual, Inc.

Photography
© E. G. Schempf

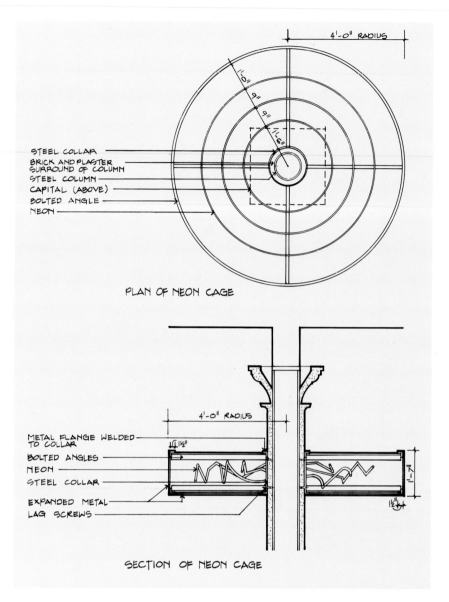

PLAN OF NEON CAGE

STEEL COLLAR
BRICK AND PLASTER SURROUND OF COLUMN
STEEL COLUMN
CAPITAL (ABOVE)
BOLTED ANGLE
NEON

4'-0" RADIUS

METAL FLANGE WELDED TO COLLAR
BOLTED ANGLES
NEON
STEEL COLLAR
EXPANDED METAL
LAG SCREWS

4'-0" RADIUS

SECTION OF NEON CAGE

KINETIC MOVEMENT OCCURS on more than one level at Eyes Nightclub in Kansas City, Missouri. As part of a quintessentially Neoconstructionist environment, Kelly and Lehn has designed a neon cage that both surrounds and is "invisibly" attached to a classic nineteenth-century composite steel column. Placed below the capital, this cage is a detailing filip that adds an aura of excitement to an otherwise straightforward architectural element.

Kelly and Lehn added the neon cage detail to the column as a pragmatic, problem-solving lighting solution as well as to enhance visual excitement. The design team realized early on that a 14'-0" ceiling was uncomfortably low, psychologically at least, for an open, 7,000-square-foot space. Painting the ceiling black was a first step in trying to make the ceiling invisible. But as a design sleight-of-hand maneuver, it was not enough to fool the eye completely. The column-mounted neon cage evolved as a secondary attack on the problem to arrest the eye of the beholder and to serve as a visual stop, or canopy, above which there is nothing but the capital itself to attract attention.

The three-ring neon cage also serves as a pivotal directional device, lighting the preferred routes to peripheral rest rooms as well as to the dance floor. Neon rings operate independently and may be adjusted for color and intensity by a control panel monitored by the nightclub's disc jockey.

The 4'-0" radius expanded-metal cage containing the three circular neon tubes (*plan*) is held in place by a tripartite support structure—horizontally parallel bolted angles welded to metal flanges, which in turn are screwed through horizontally parallel steel collars into the steel column itself (*section*).

COMPUTER WORKSTATION

HEADQUARTERS, A FINANCIAL SERVICES CORPORATION
New York City

Interior Design
Kohn Pedersen Fox Conway
Design Team
Patricia Conway, Randolph Gerner,
Judy Swanson, Miguel Valcarcel,
Ruxandra Panaitescu, Teri Figliuzzi,
Anne Manning
Fabrication
Specifications Built Corp.
Photography
© Paul Warchol

NEW YORK CITY'S Kohn Pedersen Fox Conway had definite ideas about how to plan and detail the eleven stories of general office space lying beneath the spectacular executive floors that are part of the headquarters of a major financial services corporation in New York City (see page 50). The design team wanted the lower floors to reflect—in spirit if not in literal detail—the Jeffersonian Georgian styling aesthetic of the executive suite. Their second concern was to design the workstation so that the privacy of the user would be respected—even within an open floor plan. And third, they wanted to build flexibility into the open plan.

KPFC accomplished all of these goals by designing a beautifully articulated custom workstation system, which is particularly useful for enclosing now-ubiquitous computer equipment. (The design is currently undergoing review for a United States patent.) Although the design team worked with raw space in their development of the system, specific dimensions of the workstations were determined in part by the atypical 4'-8" building module. In detailing the system, the feel of the Georgian design upstairs was re-created by the use of painted wood panels and moldings, with a suggestion of Georgian cornices.

Privacy was given its due by building up the exterior partitions of the custom stations with 2'-8"-high window panels. Many standard open workstations incorporate walls of this height, but most do so at the price of blocking out light transmission. Here

the panes are of sandblasted glass, which preserves the sense of privacy while admitting ambient light. Each pane also includes a 1-inch clear border so that visual cues of activity outside the station may be readily perceived (*elevation at workwall*).

For flexibility, KPFC designed components (*exploded view*) that can be assembled into three basic workstations, each of which answers a specific corporate need. The F station is a secretarial workplace; the E station accommodates junior professionals; the D station is planned for those more senior, or for those who need the larger table that the station incorporates. E and F stations are physically complementary and are intended to adjoin. Either station can be transformed into a D station by shifting the only two movable elements—the workwall and the storage wall (*exploded view*). All of the elements are free-standing and rest on levelers, which are not affixed to the floor.

The walls of the workstation system

were specifically designed to accommodate current and future electrical loads. The panels contain continuous-wire management cavities and slots (*section @ machine station*), to which easy access is permitted by top-hinged acoustical panels above the work surface.

The storage walls contain ambient Octron lighting fixtures in the molding/light trays (*section @ machine station*). These fixtures double as task lighting by virtue of removable diffusing lenses in the overhead panel.

The workstation panels are fabricated of particleboard painted with a urethane-based paint specially created for this project. The slightly pebbly surface is durable and can be rubbed and even washed with no ill effect (a particularly important consideration since the color is white). The panels are hung flush on an all-steel frame with Z-clips. Panels pop off for repair and reconfiguration. All work surfaces are stained in cherry veneer with solid cherry nosing.

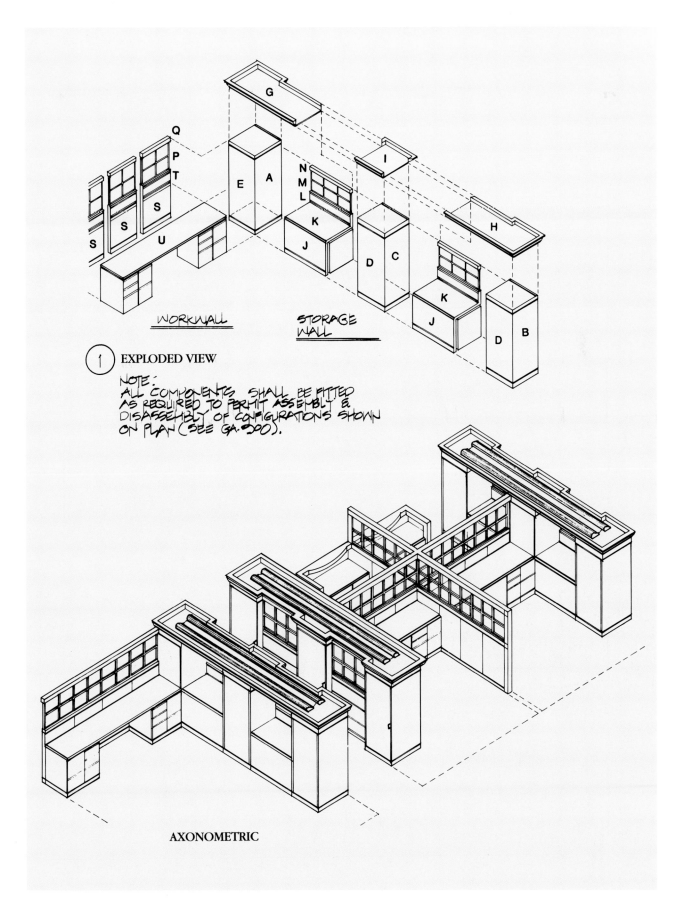

Q

P

T

S S U

WORKWALL

G

E A

N M L

K

J

STORAGE WALL

I

D C

H

K

J

D B

1 EXPLODED VIEW

NOTE:
ALL COMPONENTS SHALL BE FITTED
AS REQUIRED TO PERMIT ASSEMBLY &
DISASSEMBLY OF CONFIGURATIONS SHOWN
ON PLAN (SEE GA·300).

AXONOMETRIC

COMPUTER WORKSTATION

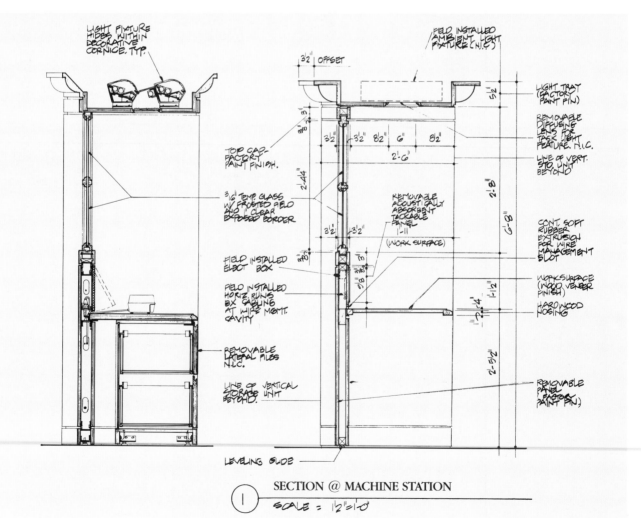

LIGHT FIXTURE HIDES WITHIN DECORATIVE CORNICE. TYP.

FIELD INSTALLED AMBIENT LIGHT FIXTURE (N.I.C.)

3'2" OFFSET

LIGHT TRAY (FACTORY PAINT FIN.)

REMOVABLE DIFFUSING LENS FOR TASK LIGHT FEATURE. N.I.C.

LINE OF VERT. STO. UNIT BEYOND

TOP CAP - FACTORY PAINT FINISH.

3/16" TEMP GLASS W/ FROSTED FIELD AND CLEAR EXPOSED BORDER

REMOVABLE ACOUSTICALLY ABSORBENT TACKABLE PANEL (WORK SURFACE)

CONT. SOFT RUBBER EXTRUSION FOR WIRE MANAGEMENT SLOT

FIELD INSTALLED ELECT. BOX

FIELD INSTALLED HORIZ. RUNS EX CABLING AT WIRE MGMT. CAVITY

WORKSURFACE (WOOD VENEER FINISH)

HARDWOOD NOSING

REMOVABLE LATERAL FILES N.I.C.

LINE OF VERTICAL STORAGE UNIT BEYOND.

REMOVABLE PANEL (FACTORY PAINT FIN.)

LEVELING GUIDE

① SECTION @ MACHINE STATION

SCALE = 1 1/2" = 1'-0"

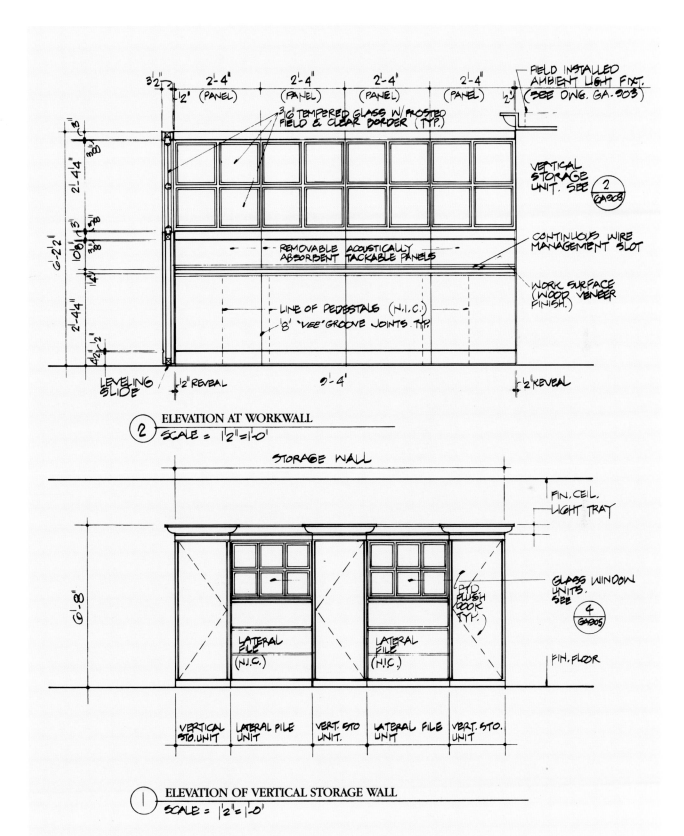

FIELD INSTALLED
AMBIENT LIGHT FIXT.
(SEE DWG. GA-903)

3½" | 2'-4" (PANEL) | 2'-4" (PANEL) | 2'-4" (PANEL) | 2'-4" (PANEL) | ½"

1½" (PANEL)

3/6" TEMPERED GLASS W/ FROSTED
FIELD & CLEAR BORDER (TYP.)

VERTICAL
STORAGE
UNIT. SEE ②/GA903

CONTINUOUS WIRE
MANAGEMENT SLOT

REMOVABLE ACOUSTICALLY
ABSORBENT TACKABLE PANELS

WORK SURFACE
(WOOD VENEER
FINISH.)

LINE OF PEDESTALS (N.I.C.)
8" "VEE" GROOVE JOINTS TYP.

6'-2½"

2'-4¼"

2'-4¼"

LEVELING
SLIDE
½" REVEAL
0'-4"
½" REVEAL

② ELEVATION AT WORKWALL
SCALE = 1½"=1'-0"

STORAGE WALL

FIN. CEIL.
LIGHT TRAY

6'-8"

LATERAL
FILE
(N.I.C.)

LATERAL
FILE
(N.I.C.)

(PTD
FLUSH
DOOR
TYP.)

GLASS WINDOW
UNITS. SEE
④/GA905

FIN. FLOOR

VERTICAL
STO. UNIT | LATERAL FILE
UNIT | VERT. STO.
UNIT. | LATERAL FILE
UNIT | VERT. STO.
UNIT

① ELEVATION OF VERTICAL STORAGE WALL
SCALE = 1½"=1'-0"

Computer Workstation

FOOTE, CONE & BELDING
San Francisco, California

Architecture/Interior Design
Whisler-Patri
Design Team
Joel Hendler, Rod Glasgow,
Paul Travis, David Tann (renderings)
Fabrication
Design Workshops
Lighting Consultant
Architectural Lighting
(David Malman)
Photography
© Bill Hedrich, Hedrich-Blessing

OFFICE WORKSTATIONS are designed to house standard office equipment. In the past ten years, computers have become as common as desktop type-writers in the work place. The result has been a decade-long era of experimentation and modification in workstation design. In 1984 Whisler-Patri of San Francisco broke with standard dimensioning with a computer workstation designed for the San Francisco offices of Foote, Cone & Belding. Whisler-Patri's design not only restores the logical visual orientation of the end-user but also conceals the computer monitor in an offset cylinder of particularly pleasing scale and form.

The tripartite station—consisting of a file/storage wall, a return and writing desk, and a computer-enclosure cylinder—is built as a free-standing unit intended for flexible configuration. At the offices of Foote, Cone & Belding, the unit was installed as a one-person station that faces the flow of corridor traffic outside of an executive office. The workstation functions equally well in flat-side-by-flat-side pairs; as mirror-image, back-to-back pairs in the center of a room; or as a set of four.

The Whisler-Patri workstation, which was designed as an "intentionally residential" piece of furniture, offers an alternative to the more commonly used steel-pole-and-panel-cloth systems. To accentuate the importance of personal comfort within the work environment, the design team specified luxurious leathers, ash veneers, and a chrome kickplate as finish materials for the module (*ax-*

AXONOMETRIC VIEW OF RECEPTION DESK

ASH TOP
ASH CABINETS
ASH TOP/TRIM
LEATHER COVERING

RECEPTION DESK ELEVATION

ASH SHELF/TOP
ASH CABINETS
LEATHER COVERING
CHROME BASE

onometric). However, more utilitarian materials may be substituted.

Whisler-Patri designated three primary work areas within the workstation detailed for the company's secondary receptionist (whose primary function is to monitor a computer-operated message center): the 11'-6" by 4'-4" by 2'-2" rear storage wall accommodates an articulated keyboard, a PBX board, message slots

and cabinets for telephone directories, and the computer printer; the 2'-0" by 3'-1" by 5'-6" curved desk and modesty panel houses a pencil drawer on one arm and a regular writing surface plus an articulated keyboard on the other; and the 4'-4" by 3'-0"-diameter cylinder houses the computer monitor mounted on a perforated shelf above a ventilating fan (*elevation*).

CONFERENCE TABLE

THE CHICAGO DOCK & CANAL TRUST
Chicago, Illinois

Interior Design
Lohan Associates (Mike Heider)
Fabrication
Imperial Woodworking Company
Photography
© Nick Merrick, Hedrich-Blessing

ALTHOUGH IT IS GENERALLY TRUE that "a sum is greater than its parts," the conference/model display table designed by Lohan Associates of Chicago for the marketing center of The Chicago Dock & Canal Trust demonstrates the converse—occasionally the "parts" are as great as their sum.

The conference table has a four-panel demountable work surface that is superimposed over hydraulic electric lifts concealed within its pedestal. The table's design ingeniously answers a perplexing problem commonly encountered by architects, developers, and management companies: how to provide ready-access storage for cumbersome architectural models in a space that must otherwise be used for regular "elbow-room" conferencing. Lohan Associates developed the prototype table with a generous—but not lavish—budget.

The modularity of the table is not confined to the removable tabletop "leaves." The base sections, side and end base encloser panels, lift access doors, interior base liner, and marble support plates were intentionally planned to accommodate off-site sectional construction, standard freight-elevator transit, and on-site installation (*isometric*). The lift mechanism has no hard wires. Instead, the mechanism is monitored from a hand-held, 8-inch remote control, which also controls the room's ambient and task lighting, window drapery, and wall-recessed display panels.

Finish materials for the table were selected to add color and textural "splash" to the unit. Cafe Rosita marble inserts and solid cherry trim (*plan 1*) were specified to "complete rather than compete with" the visual strength of an architectural model.

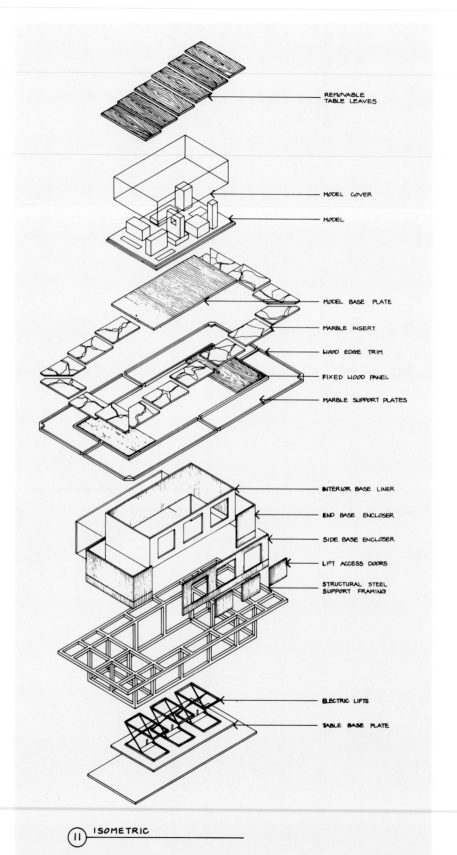

REMOVABLE TABLE LEAVES

MODEL COVER

MODEL

MODEL BASE PLATE

MARBLE INSERT

WOOD EDGE TRIM

FIXED WOOD PANEL

MARBLE SUPPORT PLATES

INTERIOR BASE LINER

END BASE ENCLOSER

SIDE BASE ENCLOSER

LIFT ACCESS DOORS

STRUCTURAL STEEL SUPPORT FRAMING

ELECTRIC LIFTS

TABLE BASE PLATE

11 ISOMETRIC

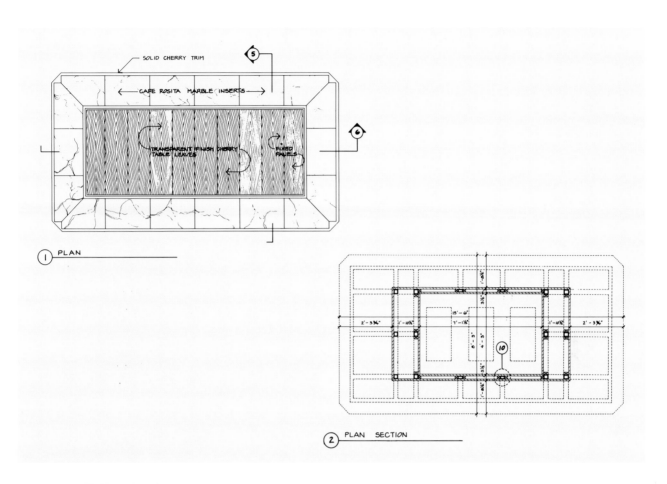

SOLID CHERRY TRIM

CAPE ROSITA MARBLE INSERTS

TRANSLUCENT FINISH CHERRY TABLE LEAVES

FIXED PANELS

① PLAN

② PLAN SECTION

15' - 6"

2' - 3¾" 1' - 10½" 7' - 1½" 1' - 10½" 2' - 3¾"

DIRECTORY

CROCKER NATIONAL BANK
San Francisco, California

Architecture/Interior Design
Gensler and Associates/Architects,
San Francisco
Design Team
John Bricker, Barbara Leistico
Fabrication
Thomas-Swan Sign Company
Photography
© David Wakely

AS A PROVISO IN GRANTING permission for the construction of Crocker National Bank's proposed corporate headquarters and commercial center, San Francisco's city planners required that the bank renovate its landmarked, but somewhat shopworn, existing building. Crocker's renovation mandate to Gensler and Associates/Architects of San Francisco was, therefore, "to preserve as much and innovate as little as possible."

The existing signage, however, was a hodgepodge of dissimilar styles bearing little relationship to the building or to any particular historical period. Gensler gained client approval for a completely new and comprehensive signage program.

For the development of a standardized directory, the design team began with the intention of incorporating historical motifs from the building. The arched outline of the directory mirrors the principal wall molding, although it is clearly an up-to-date design signature in tune with the bank's new center to which the directory's map refers.

The directory is constructed simply. A single piece of ½-inch clear, tempered, waterwhite glass is edged and laterally supported in a ⅝-inch channel opening and bolted with concealed fasteners in a satin-finish bronze frame. The weight of the glass is borne by two brass L-braces secured to the frame with flathead screws, and a strip of adhesive foam tape cushions the glass panel. The directory's frame is constructed of three welded, rectangular, 1-inch by 3-inch sections of hollow bronze. The frame's legs are set through the finish floor into steel footplates bolted to the concrete slab flooring and concealed by ornamental brass plates (*front and side elevations*).

The typography is silkscreened onto the front of the glass, and the background blue (which is the blue color of the corporate logo) is surface sprayed on the back. The diagrams are also silkscreened on the back for flexibility and may be changed without disturbing any of the lettering on the front surface. The bank is now a Wells Fargo Bank.

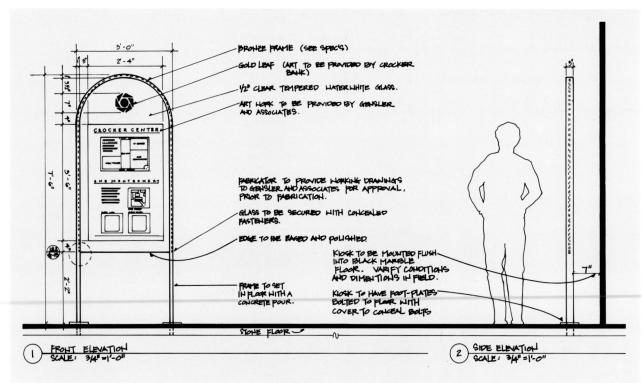

① FRONT ELEVATION
SCALE: 3/4" = 1'-0"

② SIDE ELEVATION
SCALE: 3/4" = 1'-0"

DIRECTORY

1001 PENNSYLVANIA AVENUE
Washington, D.C.

Architecture/Interior Design
Hartman-Cox Architects
Design Team
George Hartman, Graham Davidson
Fabrication
Belsinger Sign Company
Photography
© Durston Saylor

THE NEWLY CONSTRUCTED office tower at 1001 Pennsylvania Avenue in Washington, D.C., is located just down the street from the White House. Like its neighbor's, the building's prestigious address stimulates considerable competition for occupancy. 1001 was designed by Hartman-Cox Architects, also of Washington, D.C.

Proud holders of leases in 1001 announce their presence on a suitably grand alphabetical lobby directory detailed in hand-wrought bronze, glass, and green marble. At a cost of $10,000 per unit, Hartman-Cox detailed a "picture-frame" directory, which is recessed into a marble surround and

bolted into a concrete masonry wall. A further recess into the base construction wall houses a 15-watt lamp for backlighting the decorative "union jack" screen (*section*). The screen mirrors, in miniature, the patterned railing that surrounds the lobby on the mezzanine level (page 177). Access to the magnetized nameplate board (*detail of nameplate board*) is achieved through ¼-inch laminated glass-and-bronze frame doors, which open on bronze pivot hinges (*plan of frames @ hinge*). A fire annunciator panel is inserted in the lower portion of the directory unit, discreetly answering fire safety–code requirements for the concourse.

The craftsmanship involved in the design and construction of the unit far exceeds the client's original request for a directory that "blends with the traditional style of the architecture but is easy to read and readily changed." Of particular note are the beautifully molded bronze frames, which vary incrementally in width and forward projection (*frame and wire construction detail*).

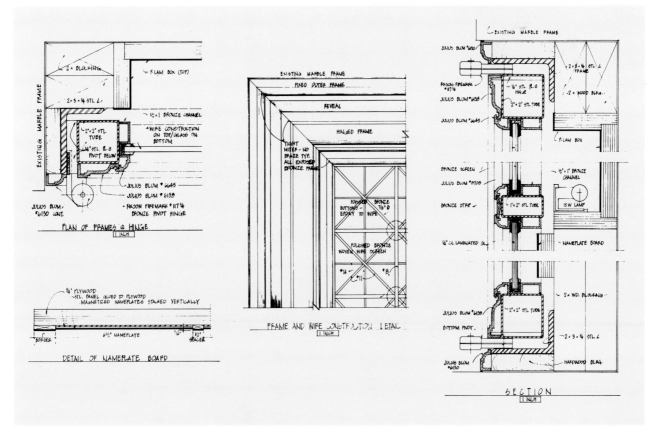

DIRECTORY

168 NORTH CLINTON STREET
Chicago, Illinois

Architecture/Interior Design
Pappageorge Haymes Ltd.
Design Team
George Pappageorge,
David A. Haymes, Keith Lasko
Fabrication
Vector
Photography
© Abby Sadin

IN INCREASING NUMBERS, warehouses and other structures originally designed for light industrial purposes are being retrofitted for condominium sales or for office-building tenancy. Adaptive reuse project designers capitalize on whatever architectural strengths the buildings possessed originally and then "integrate the up-to-date." Architects Pappageorge Haymes Ltd. of Chicago took on just such a project for Thrush & Company—the rehabilitation of a six-story 1890s building at 168 North Clinton Street in Chicago.

The client wanted a "clean and sophisticated" focal point for the redesigned lobby, which would contrast stylistically with the exposed brick walls and heavy fir joists of the original construction. Pappageorge Haymes delivered a slim, "space-age" directory whose whimsical dome adds an element of sculptural detailing to the 340-square-foot space.

The cylindrical directory is located on an axis running from the center of the entrance's double door frame to the panel between the two elevator doors and is immediately visible from the inside or outside of the building.

The directory was fabricated in two primary pieces: a free-standing 8'-6"-high cylindrical column constructed of rolled-and-welded stainless steel sheeting and a stainless steel domed "canopy" (*east-west section*). The column is bolted through the terrazzo-over-wood floor to a ¼-inch steel plate on the basement ceiling. A smoked glass door inside a continuous vertical reveal on the side of the column protects a strip of film on which the tenants' names are shown in reverse. The directory list is backlit with vertical fluorescent tube lighting. The glass door is hinged to permit removal of the film for name changes (*directory sections*). The canopy is suspended from the exposed wood construction of the lobby's ceiling by steel rods that were welded to the canopy and screwed into ceiling-mounted receptors (*east-west section*).

Together, the cylinder and dome provide the principal source of lobby illumination. The top of the column hides a standard can incandescent uplight fixture, without baffle or lens. The light is directed against the lower surface of the canopy, where by reflection it is diffused over the entire lobby area.

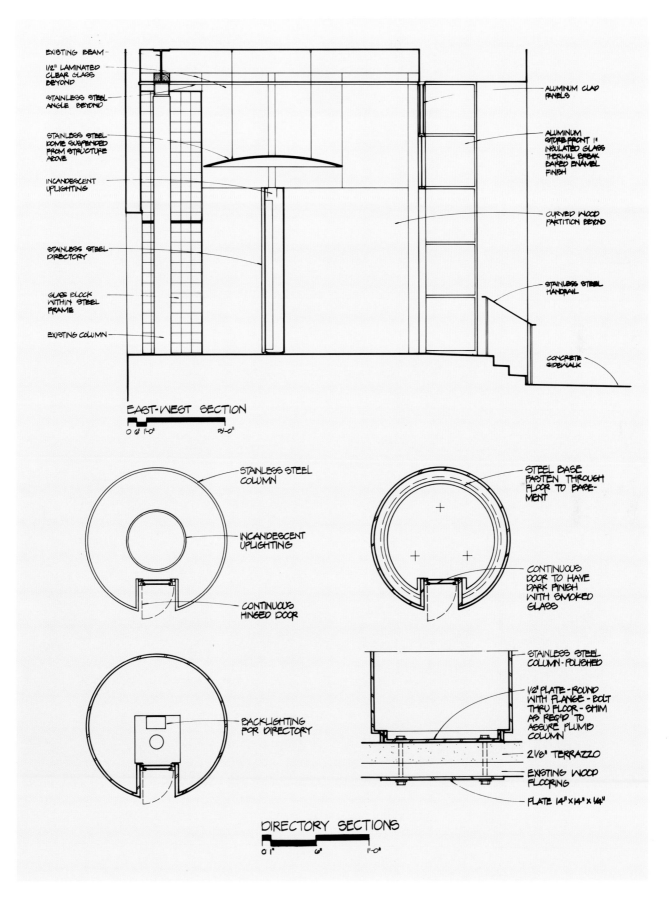

EXISTING BEAM

1/2" LAMINATED
CLEAR GLASS
BEYOND

STAINLESS STEEL
ANGLE BEYOND

STAINLESS STEEL
DOME SUSPENDED
FROM STRUCTURE
ABOVE

INCANDESCENT
UPLIGHTING

STAINLESS STEEL
DIRECTORY

GLASS BLOCK
WITHIN STEEL
FRAME

EXISTING COLUMN

ALUMINUM CLAD
PANELS

ALUMINUM
STOREFRONT 1"
INSULATED GLASS
THERMAL BREAK
BAKED ENAMEL
FINISH

CURVED WOOD
PARTITION BEYOND

STAINLESS STEEL
HANDRAIL

CONCRETE
SIDEWALK

EAST-WEST SECTION

0 6' 1'-0"   3'-0"

STAINLESS STEEL
COLUMN

INCANDESCENT
UPLIGHTING

CONTINUOUS
HINGED DOOR

STEEL BASE
FASTEN THROUGH
FLOOR TO BASE-
MENT

CONTINUOUS
DOOR TO HAVE
DARK FINISH
WITH SMOKED
GLASS

BACKLIGHTING
FOR DIRECTORY

STAINLESS STEEL
COLUMN - POLISHED

1/2" PLATE - ROUND
WITH FLANGE - BOLT
THRU FLOOR - SHIM
AS REQ'D TO
ASSURE PLUMB
COLUMN

2 1/8" TERRAZZO

EXISTING WOOD
FLOORING

PLATE 14" X 14" X 1/4"

DIRECTORY SECTIONS

0 1"   6"   1'-0"

DISPLAY CABINETS

MUSEUM OF ART AND ARCHAEOLOGY, MICHAEL G. CARLOS HALL

Emory University, Atlanta, Georgia

Architecture/Interior Design
Michael Graves, Architect

Design Team
Michael Graves, Theodore Brown, Patrick Burke, Karen Wheeler Nichols, Anita Rosskam, Thomas Rowe, Susan Butcher, Leslie Mason, Michael Kuhling, David Rockwood, Rico Cedro, Randall King

Millwork
Craftsman Products

Photography
© Steven Brooke

IN MUSEUM DESIGN there are two schools of thought. One supports the notion that the artifact in question should be displayed in an environment that is as neutral as possible. The other school affirms the belief that the environment's decorative detailing should enrich the artifact itself.

Emory University in Atlanta,

Georgia, commissioned Graves to renovate the 2,200-square-foot interior of the Michael C. Carlos Hall. The building, a three-story marble-clad structure designed by Henry Hornbostel in 1916, currently houses the departments of art history and anthropology and the Museum of Art and Archaeology.

For the museum portion of the building, Graves and his design team developed a prototypical vitrine (or display case) that is varied in size, as well as in vertical or horizontal orientation, for specific exhibition purposes.

In developing the cabinet configurations, the design team respected the client's mandate that "each unit must provide plenty of light, without heat build-up." These pragmatic considerations dictated the inclusion of concealed air filters, temperature controls, and a clear glass panel in the top of each cabinet (*plan*).

Fifty-three cabinets were shop-built in Toronto, Canada, trucked to Atlanta, and installed on site. Due to the

efficiency of the craftspeople, the cost per cabinet unit was lower than for standard museum fixtures.

Graves scaled the unit in a classical two-to-one ratio elevation proportion, in which each 2'-2⅝" base unit is surmounted by a 4'-10¾" upper cabinet (*elevation*). The base cabinets are constructed of stained bird's-eye maple veneer (a Graves signature) over plywood panel frames. Both sills and feet are rendered in solid ebonized beech. The 7/16-inch clear laminated glass panels in the upper cabinets are held in place by painted aluminum frames, anchored, in turn, by bird's-eye maple–veneered wooden corner posts inlaid with ebony (*section; detail*). The cabinets are intentionally "furniturelike." According to job captain Patrick Burke, the cabinets are "as fine as Biedermeier, as bold as Egyptian, and, most importantly, consistent with the character of the building."

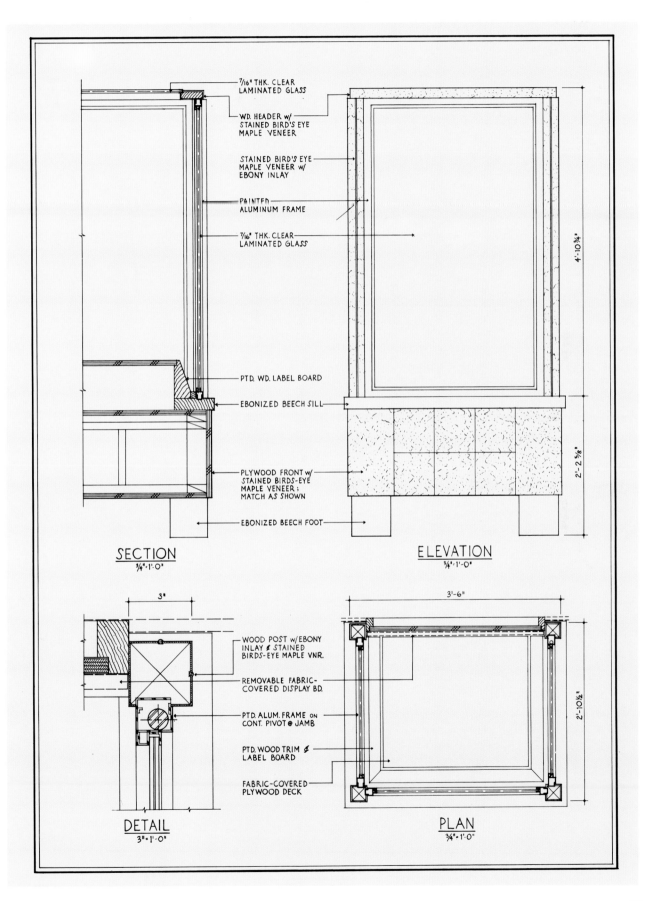

7/16" THK. CLEAR
LAMINATED GLASS

WD. HEADER w/
STAINED BIRD'S EYE
MAPLE VENEER

STAINED BIRD'S EYE
MAPLE VENEER w/
EBONY INLAY

PAINTED
ALUMINUM FRAME

7/16" THK. CLEAR
LAMINATED GLASS

PTD. WD. LABEL BOARD

EBONIZED BEECH SILL

PLYWOOD FRONT w/
STAINED BIRDS-EYE
MAPLE VENEER ;
MATCH AS SHOWN

EBONIZED BEECH FOOT

SECTION
3/4"=1'-0"

ELEVATION
3/4"=1'-0"

4'-10 3/4"

2'-2 5/8"

3"

WOOD POST w/EBONY
INLAY & STAINED
BIRDS-EYE MAPLE VNR.

REMOVABLE FABRIC-
COVERED DISPLAY BD.

PTD. ALUM. FRAME on
CONT. PIVOT @ JAMB

PTD. WOOD TRIM &
LABEL BOARD

FABRIC-COVERED
PLYWOOD DECK

DETAIL
3"=1'-0"

PLAN
3/4"=1'-0"

3'-6"

2'-10 1/2"

DISPLAY CABINETS

COLLINS & AIKMAN SHOWROOM
Atlanta, Georgia

Interior Design
Eva Maddox Associates, Inc.
(Patrick Grzybek)
Fabrication
The Sawmill
Photography
Nick Merrick, Hedrich-Blessing

COLLINS & AIKMAN, a major carpet manufacturer, commissioned Eva Maddox Associates, Inc., of Chicago to design their Atlanta Merchandise Mart showroom as a "progressive marketing tool" that would emphasize not only the company's traditional image within the industry but also its boldly colored new product line.

The design team responded to the client's wish by adopting a Viennese Secessionist approach, in which a unified design concept is integrated at all levels. At the Collins & Aikman showroom, the product itself becomes part of the design.

For the anchoring architectural element, detail designer Patrick Grzybek conceived eight display cabinets. Each cabinet is designed as an island, so that displays may be mounted on each side. The shelves and drawers of the cabinets are flush fitted as built-in, floor-to-ceiling units. The result is a completely "integrated" effect, achieved by constructing the base and crown of each unit in gypsum board to match the walls and ceiling of the showroom. A ½-inch metal reveal, painted black, separates a maple baseboard from the gypsum board. The cabinet unit is supported by internal wooden studs that are affixed to the floor with expanding fasteners (*vertical section @ slant shelves*).

Each lacquered particleboard shelf is supported by ¼-inch wooden pegs, clip mortised to the shelf at 3-inch intervals (*vertical section @ slant shelves*). The shelf height may be adjusted by moving pins from one bored hole to another in the veneered side-support panels. One-quarter-inch painted wood fascia strips are glued to each shelf edge (*vertical section @ slant shelves*).

The woodwork on one side of each cabinet is lacquer-painted hardwood. On the reverse side and on the walls of the interior niche above the drawers, the woodwork is solid maple trim over maple veneer (*vertical section @ drawer unit*). Maple was chosen as an "honest" wood, symbolically representing traditional values.

The drawers are fabricated of ¾-inch particleboard veneered with exterior maple and interior oak. Stylized pulls were specified to harmonize with the showroom's overall motifs.

The neutral background provided by the showroom cabinetry allows the carpet-sample colors to make a forceful self-marketing statement. In addition, bright carpet samples were inset into the showroom floor. To enable customers to judge carpet colors full size, the samples were also inset in the vertically framed 5'-10" by 2'-6" panels within each display unit (*elevation @ display unit*). The sloped shelf arrangement, with one sample per shelf, allows the complete color spectrum of the product line to be seen simultaneously, eliminating the need for outdated carpet showroom "waterfall" fixtures.

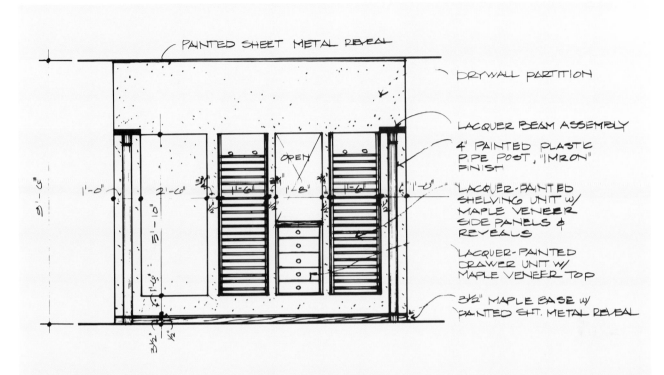

PAINTED SHEET METAL REVEAL

DRYWALL PARTITION

LACQUER BEAM ASSEMBLY

4" PAINTED PLASTIC PIPE POST, "IMRON" FINISH

LACQUER-PAINTED SHELVING UNIT W/ MAPLE VENEER SIDE PANELS & REVEALS

LACQUER-PAINTED DRAWER UNIT W/ MAPLE VENEER TOP

3½" MAPLE BASE W/ PAINTED SHT. METAL REVEAL

OPEN

ELEVATION @ DISPLAY UNIT

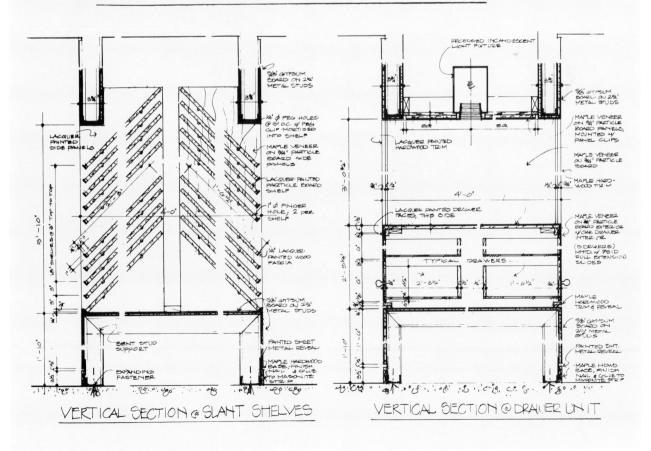

LACQUER PAINTED SIDE PANELS

5/8" GYPSUM BOARD ON 2½" METAL STUDS

¼" Ø PEG HOLES @ 2" O.C. W/ PEG CLIP MORTISED INTO SHELF

MAPLE VENEER ON ¾" PARTICLE BOARD SIDE PANELS

LACQUER-PAINTED PARTICLE BOARD SHELF

1" Ø FINGER HOLE; 2 PER SHELF

¼" LACQUER-PAINTED WOOD FASCIA

5/8" GYPSUM BOARD ON 2½" METAL STUDS

BENT STUD SUPPORT

EXPANDING FASTENER

PAINTED SHEET METAL REVEAL

MAPLE HARDWOOD BASE; FINISH, NAIL & GLUE TO MASONITE STRIP

VERTICAL SECTION @ SLANT SHELVES

RECESSED INCANDESCENT LIGHT FIXTURE

5/8" GYPSUM BOARD ON 2½" METAL STUDS

MAPLE VENEER ON ¾" PARTICLE BOARD PANELS, MOUNTED W/ PANEL CLIPS

MAPLE VENEER ON ¾" PARTICLE BOARD

MAPLE HARDWOOD TRIM

LACQUER PAINTED HARDWOOD TRIM

LACQUER PAINTED DRAWER FACES, THIS SIDE

MAPLE VENEER ON ¾" PARTICLE BOARD EXTERIOR W/ OAK DRAWER INTERIOR (5 DRAWERS) MNTD W/ 75LB FULL EXTENSION SLIDES

TYPICAL DRAWERS

MAPLE HARDWOOD TRIM & REVEAL

5/8" GYPSUM BOARD ON 2½" METAL STUDS

PAINTED SHT. METAL REVEAL

MAPLE HWD. BASE, FINISH NAIL & GLUE TO MASONITE STRIP

VERTICAL SECTION @ DRAWER UNIT

91

DISPLAY ISLAND

MALLARDS
Chicago, Illinois

Architecture/Interior Design
Eva Maddox Associates, Inc.
(Patrick Grzybek)
Fabrication
Northwestern Millworks
Photography
© Barbara Karant

MALLARDS, A VENERABLE retail clothing emporium in Chicago, asked Eva Maddox Associates, Inc., to create a "functional, flexible, and stylish" display unit that would enhance the store's value-priced merchandise—without overpowering a modestly scaled budget. Because Mallards is located in a high-ceilinged, loftlike space, a secondary function for the display units was to define more intimate shopping areas within the store's 6,800 square feet of space.

By creating free-standing, factory-built display islands, Maddox designer Patrick Grzybek answered Mallards' mandate for layout flexibility and economy. By limiting the dimensions of the islands in elevation and mounting them on casters, Grzybek also maintained the integrity of the existing high ceilings and old hardwood floors.

As delineated in their final form, the display islands are simply constructed. A quarter-moon-shaped backdrop panel is cantilevered vertically from a hardwood skid-styled base platform, which has been mounted on casters for mobility (*elevation*). The quarter-moon backdrop panel was adopted to provide back-to-back display fixture adaptability. It also adds graphic display "punch."

Grzybek designed an alternative version of the island module to increase display flexibility. In the expanded unit, the straight side of the quarter-moon shape was used to brace two partial partitions, which, between them, support a rod for clothes on hangers. The curved edge of the back panel supports a cubbyholed shelving unit for folded clothes.

In compliance with the client's request, these modestly priced display units were factory built using toned materials in single colors. The subframe is constructed of ¾-inch plywood, to which plastic laminate has been applied to the quarter-moon panel (*vertical section*). The platform on which the unit rests is constructed of rough-sawn pine covered with a clear finish over its 6'-0" length (*plan*).

92

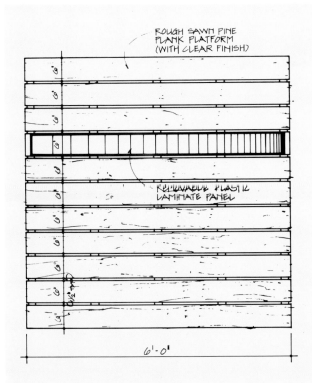

ROUGH SAWN PINE
PLANK PLATFORM
(WITH CLEAR FINISH)

REMOVABLE PLASTIC
LAMINATE PANEL

6'-0"

PLAN @ DISPLAY UNIT

PLASTIC
LAMINATE ON
3/4" PARTICLE
BOARD REMOVABLE
PANEL.

5'-0" RADIUS

3/4" PLYWOOD
SUB FRAME.

ROUGH SAWN
PINE PLANK
PLATFORM.

6'-0"

ELEVATION @ DISPLAY UNIT

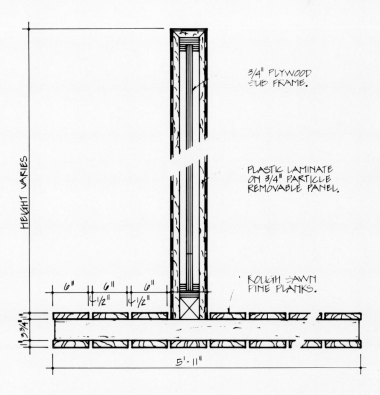

3/4" PLYWOOD
SUB FRAME.

PLASTIC LAMINATE
ON 3/4" PARTICLE
REMOVABLE PANEL.

ROUGH SAWN
PINE PLANKS.

HEIGHT VARIES

6"   6"   6"

5'-11"

VERTICAL SECTION @ DISPLAY UNIT

DISPLAY NICHE

CARRINGTON, COLEMAN, SLOMAN & BLUMENTHAL
Dallas, Texas

Interior Design
ISD Incorporated, Houston
Design Team
Jim Hanlin, Nancy Lindsay,
Barbara Burkhardt
Fabrication
Robert Shaw Manufacturing
Photography
© Chas McGrath

THE DALLAS, TEXAS, law firm Carrington, Coleman, Sloman & Blumenthal, commissioned ISD Incorporated of Houston to design its first office in an "assertive, progressive" image, softened by "references to traditional symbols." The Modernist detailing ISD produced in response avoids stylistic clichés. Instead, the detailing evokes a more subtle recollection of traditional solidity and conservatism by virtue of its fine craftsmanship.

As part of the detailing program, ISD designed a conference-room display niche that intentionally positions a wired and VCR-ready storage credenza in a recess away from the circulation pattern. ISD chose not to install cabinets above the credenza so that artwork from the firm's impressive collection might be more advantageously displayed.

The 3'-0"-high scribed credenza is veneered, both inside and out, with flat-grain maple that was washed, as were the floors, with a white pigment to achieve an "untreated" finish. ISD wrapped the wall panels behind the credenza in Velcro-fastened Shan silk (*front elevation*).

The 6'-0" by 2'-4" polished granite slab countertop is separated from the wall by a polished aluminum angle (*section*). Each flush overlay door is hung from full overlay spring-loaded concealed hinges. A finger reveal provides access to the hardware-free doors and pencil drawers. The

drawer's front panel is dovetailed to its sides with applied front (*section*). Two MR16, low-voltage pinspot lamps are recessed into the dry-wall soffit.

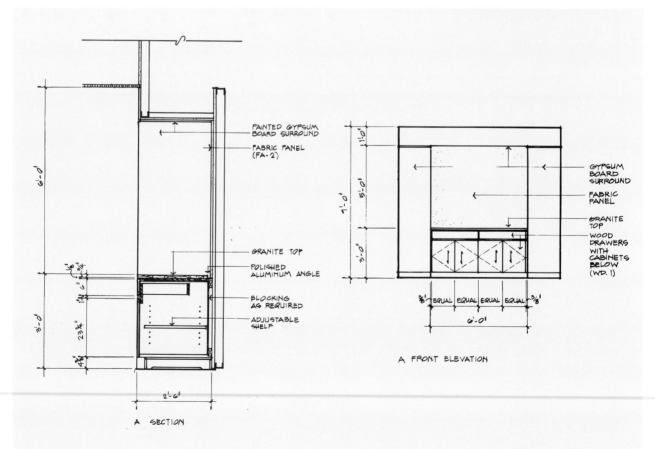

PAINTED GYPSUM BOARD SURROUND

FABRIC PANEL (FA-2)

GRANITE TOP

POLISHED ALUMINUM ANGLE

BLOCKING AS REQUIRED

ADJUSTABLE SHELF

A SECTION

GYPSUM BOARD SURROUND

FABRIC PANEL

GRANITE TOP

WOOD DRAWERS WITH CABINETS BELOW (WD. 1)

A FRONT ELEVATION

DISPLAY NICHE

NEW YORK CITY DEPARTMENT OF INVESTIGATION OFFICES
New York City

Architecture/Interior Design
Perkins & Will
Design Team
Aaron B. Schwartz, John J. Fallon,
Robert L. Luntz, Orlando Marin
Fabrication
Panner Woodworking
Photography
© James R. Morse

THE NEW YORK CITY Department of Investigation (DOI) is a somber outfit in a serious business. In consequence, Perkins & Will of New York City received a "no-frills" mandate and a taxpayer-conscious budget of $40.25 per square foot for the 86,960-square-foot office design project.

Despite the budgetary constraints, DOI did not want to convey either a drab or a dour image. Instead, they asked Perkins & Will to produce an interior that would project a "high-quality, highly professional" ambience. Perkins & Will countered by finding solutions that relied heavily on efficiently standardizing design components of good, but not lavish, materials.

The design team's skill at providing quality design using basic materials is particularly evident in a 300-square-foot conference room where the primary detail—a display niche/storage wall—employs several office standard features: wood doors (fabricated of red-oak veneer panel over solid wood blocking), a wood countertop, bronze hardware, recessed lighting, reveals, and routing to provide texture (*elevation*). All of the niche's joints are glued and screwed, and the hinges are concealed (*detail sections*).

The display niche is lit by a recessed incandescent fixture concealed by the gypsum-board soffit. Perkins & Will gave the niche an intentionally anonymous character for display flexibility. Thus far, DOI has chosen to fill the niche with exotic varieties of flowers. One door flanking the niche conceals office-supply storage; the other leads to a pantry, which is also accessed from the outside corridor.

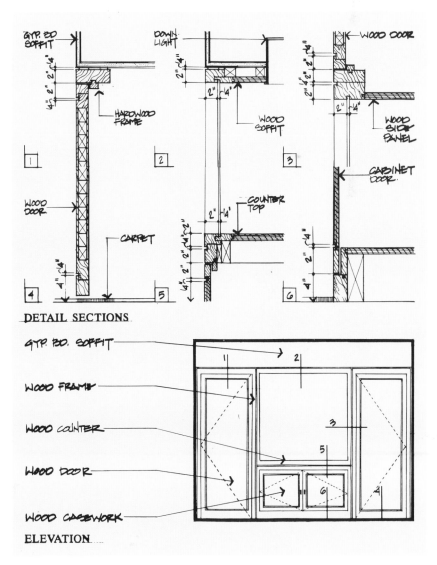

DETAIL SECTIONS

ELEVATION

DISPLAY PANELS

THE CHICAGO DOCK & CANAL TRUST
Chicago, Illinois

Interior Design
Lohan Associates (Mike Heider)
Fabrication
Claridge Products and Equipment
Photography
© Nick Merrick, Hedrich-Blessing

MOTORIZED, MOVABLE display panels that
are recessed into an unobtrusive
niche are an integral part of a con-
jurer's "now-you-see-it-now-you-don't"
detailing package Lohan Associates of
Chicago designed for the Chicago
Dock & Canal Trust marketing center.

Lohan project designer Mike
Heider designed the panels to work
in conjunction with a conference/
model display table (page 82) located
in a dual-purpose room used either
for business-suit conferencing or for
shirt-sleeved review of architectural
models, drawings, and renderings.

The design of the display-panel
system was adapted and modified
from a mechanism originally conceived for university and conference
center blackboards. The display-unit
opening, furred in from the existing
wall, contains two 4'-0" by 16'-0"
panels that slide up and down from a
motor assembly housing concealed
behind the upper reaches of the
fabric-wrapped partition wall (*detail
4*). A matching fabric wraps the cork
core of the movable panels. The
panels are counterweighted to accommodate display materials ranging from
light paper to heavy mounted and
framed photographs and renderings.

Movement of the panels is
monitored from a hand-held remote
control. In its boardroom guise both
panels are raised above the line of
vision, revealing a fabric-wrapped
back panel that matches the surrounding wall treatment. In the fully
lowered position the panels are
braced by two trough beds, which
have been carved into a cherry countertop shelf. Two finely routed grooves
in front of the troughs provide bracing for stand-up display (*detail 4*).

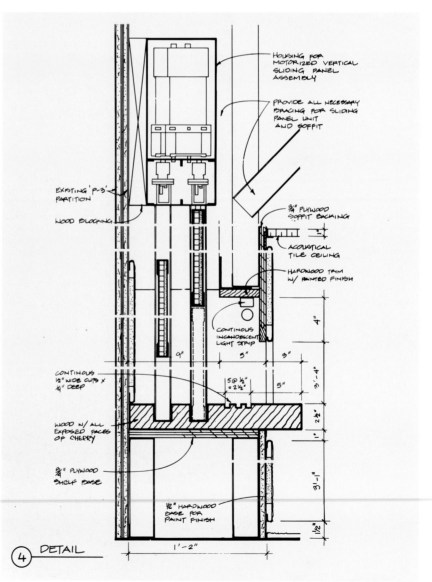

DISPLAY PEDESTAL

I. MAGNIN
Santa Clara, California

Pedestal Design
Cole Martinez Curtis and Associates
Design Team
Dennis Takeda, Paul Lechleiter,
Diane Minn, Miki Yoo, Joseph Magnetti,
Matthew Marten (drawing)
Fabrication
University Casework Systems, Inc.
Photography
© Toshi Yoshimi

LIKE ANY OTHER PRODUCT of small proportion, women's shoes tend to lose consumer impact when displayed in large quantities. The executives of I. Magnin's Santa Clara, California, store asked Cole Martinez Curtis and Associates of Marina del Rey to design a shoe-display fixture that would both "attract attention to and isolate" their higher-end product lines.

After assessing the wide but shallow space allocated to the ground-floor shoe department, the design team determined that a relatively tall, free-standing fixture with "theater-in-the-round" approachability would stop or

at least slow traffic—particularly if the display fixture were placed up front at the traffic-corridor margin of the department. To focus the consumer's attention on the displayed shoes, the design team developed a stepped display system composed of transparent shelves (*axonometric*). Against the solid background of the display pedestal's opaque core, an array of shoes is highlighted on both sides and at each end of the pedestal.

In dimensioning the pedestal, the designers used as their norm a vertical 5'-0" standing line of vision and an accessible 3'-0" counter height. In order to showcase a variety of shoes with differing heel heights, the shelves were placed at 1'-0" intervals in elevation (*section*). Terminal ends of the pedestal were given radial curves to increase the number of shoes displayed as well as to insure the public's safety.

To integrate the high-visibility fixture with display units in the adjacent cosmetic and accessories departments, finish materials for the display pedestal were selected to echo the

materials used in those adjacent departments. The pedestal core is faced in bird's-eye maple veneer over particleboard and is trimmed in black semi-gloss enamel. The edges of the ½-inch clear glass shelves are cut and polished.

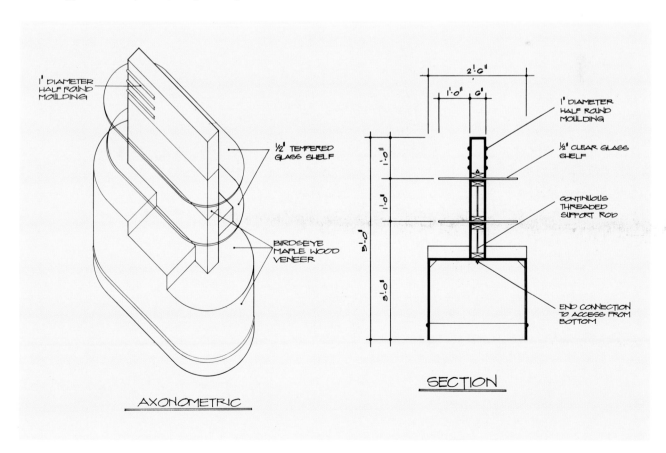

AXONOMETRIC

SECTION

1' DIAMETER HALF ROUND MOULDING

½" TEMPERED GLASS SHELF

BIRDSEYE MAPLE WOOD VENEER

2'-6"

1'-0" 6"

1'-0"

1'-0"

3'-0"

3'-0"

1' DIAMETER HALF ROUND MOULDING

½" CLEAR GLASS SHELF

CONTINUOUS THREADED SUPPORT ROD

END CONNECTION TO ACCESS FROM BOTTOM

DISPLAY SHELVES

MDC WALLCOVERINGS SHOWROOM
Chicago, Illinois

Architecture/Interior Design
Eva Maddox Associates, Inc.
(Patrick Grzybek)
Fabrication
Triangle Grand Construction
Photography
© Orlando Cabanban

IN RESPONSE TO AN MDC Wallcoverings management request that all six thousand samples of their varied product line be visible in the company's Chicago Merchandise Mart showroom, Eva Maddox Associates, Inc., of Chicago designed an innovative pullout sample display shelf/wall storage system, which has become the showroom's primary design element as well.

With only 2,500 square feet in which to accommodate sample display, a conference room, a storage room, and a lounge area, space at the MDC showroom was at a premium. "Comfortable compression" of display volume was the essential feature of the Maddox solution. The samples are packed tightly together with just enough margin for them to be pulled out easily for inspection. Thoughtful color groupings enhance the visual impact of the closely spaced display shelves by allowing each bolt to blend in tonal gradation with its neighbor. The result is a wave of color across the space.

The design team actually detailed two different sample-display shelf systems: one is a vertically oriented display for vinyl wallcoverings; the other is for horizontally stored upholstery fabric and wallcoverings.

The shelving is constructed of ¾-inch high-density particleboard for the back, top, ends, and base assembly (*display unit isometric*) and ¼-inch masonite for the shelves and dividers (*vertical section*). All of the surfaces are painted with black lacquer. Twenty-one 12-inch-deep shelves, with 3-inch vertical or horizontal spacing, rise above a 1'-0" base. The vertical or horizontal supports are spaced at 1-foot intervals over the 20-foot length of each case. Any exposed joints are mitered and glued. The shelves are interlocked to vertical or horizontal supports with glued dado joints; internal joinery is square shouldered. The cabinet is essentially free standing at a distance ranging from 2'-4" to 4'-4" from the showroom's wall (*plan detail*). Although the cabinet is not affixed to the floor, its rear-mounted two-by-four wood-stud support wall is braced against the gypsum board with two-by-four studs screwed to the frame.

The design team devised a custom-fabric bolt mechanism to facilitate sample inspection. Each bolt, or spindle device, consists of a 1¼-inch particleboard panel around which the sample is wound, sandwiched between end flange side panels of 1'-1" by 2½" high-gloss black Plexiglas. The side panels act as skids on which the bolts can easily be slid in and out.

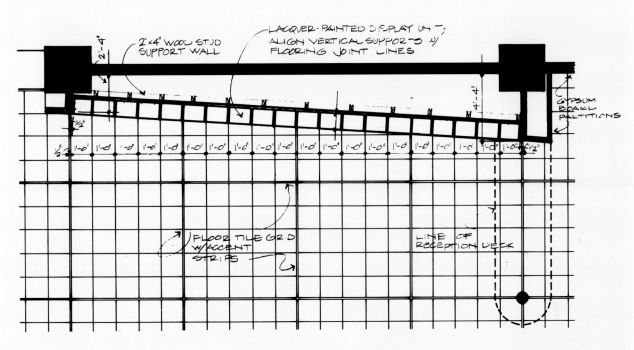

PLAN DETAIL @ FABRIC DISPLAY UNIT

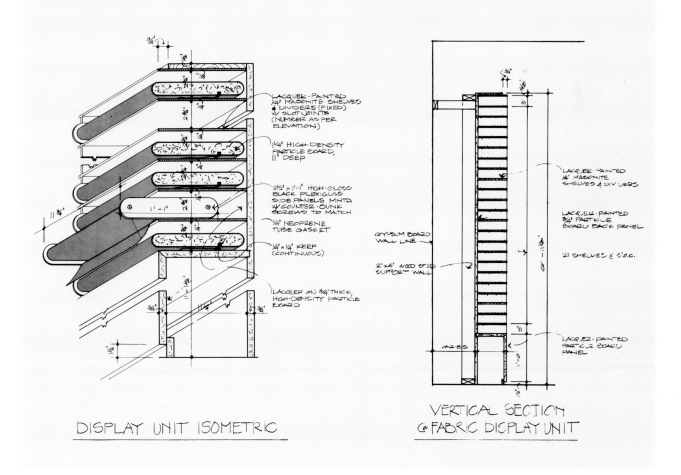

DISPLAY UNIT ISOMETRIC

VERTICAL SECTION
@ FABRIC DISPLAY UNIT

DISPLAY SHELVES

GALLERY NILSSON
New York City

Architecture/Interior Design
Judith Stockman & Associates
Design Team
Judith Stockman, Peter Valentini
Fabrication
Marx Glassworks
Lighting Consultant
Harry Gitlin
Photography
© Durston Saylor

SOME DESIGN PROJECTS rely on detailing for enhancement. In others, details *are* the project. At the Gallery Nilsson in Manhattan's SoHo district, Judith Stockman & Associates of New York City devised a decidedly dramatic character for the minimalist space by leaving out everything *but* the Swedish art-glass product itself and the counter and shelves on which it is displayed.

Prospective customers are lured from the street into the heart of the narrow gallery by the sinuous curve of the serpentine counter. Stockman developed the eye-catching device as part of an overall scheme to treat the entire gallery as a window display—in answer to the owner's request for "exterior visibility." Visual attraction to the space from outside is enhanced further by ceiling-mounted, suspended-rod halogen fixtures, which are concentrically aligned with the curved counters below.

Although counter space at the Gallery Nilsson is generously allocated, the Stockman design team supplemented those display surfaces with cantilevered light-box display shelving units along both peripheral walls. The shelves are an important design element, adding an angular expression of the stark black-and-white color palette as a geometric counterpoint to the curvilinear forms.

The shelves were designed in a stair-step configuration to provide maximum, unshadowed exposure for the glass objects on the shelves' lower levels. The shelves were wall mounted at counter height to provide ease in product handling. Like the counters, the shelves are delineated by black vertical planes, while the horizontal display surfaces are white. Unlike the counters' surfaces, which are covered in plastic laminate, the shelving surface is constructed of sandblasted clear glass. The glass was selected to diffuse the series of pink and blue fluorescent tubes that extend laterally beneath each unit. The specific lighting sequence of alternating color temperatures is designed to enhance the sculptural definition of the one-of-a-kind glass objects, while not interfering with their genuine pigments.

The ¼-inch-thick translucent glass shelf panels rest on continuous black-felt spacer strips, which are mounted on ¾-inch plywood box frames. The exterior surfaces of the frames are finished in plastic laminate, while the interior surfaces are painted white (*section*). The light-box shelves are attached to the wall framing with wood braces at 4'-2" on center, as well as to a continuous ledger and knee wall. One-quarter inch black glass panels are glued to the perimeters of the completed units.

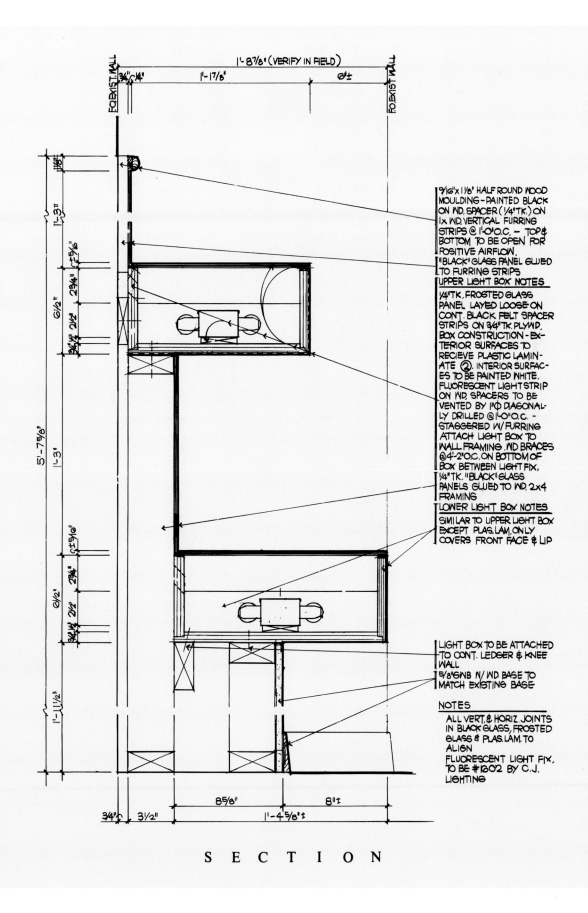

9/16"x 1⅛" HALF ROUND WOOD
MOULDING - PAINTED BLACK
ON WD. SPACER (¼"TK.) ON
1x WD. VERTICAL FURRING
STRIPS @ 1'-0"O.C. — TOP &
BOTTOM TO BE OPEN FOR
POSITIVE AIRFLOW.
"BLACK" GLASS PANEL GLUED
TO FURRING STRIPS
UPPER LIGHT BOX NOTES

¼"TK. FROSTED GLASS
PANEL LAYED LOOSE ON
CONT. BLACK FELT SPACER
STRIPS ON ¾"TK. PLYWD.
BOX CONSTRUCTION - EX-
TERIOR SURFACES TO
RECIEVE PLASTIC LAMIN-
ATE ②. INTERIOR SURFAC-
ES TO BE PAINTED WHITE.
FLUORESCENT LIGHT STRIP
ON WD. SPACERS TO BE
VENTED BY 1"∅ DIAGONAL-
LY DRILLED @ 1'-0"O.C. —
STAGGERED W/ FURRING
ATTACH LIGHT BOX TO
WALL FRAMING. WD BRACES
@ 4'-2"O.C. ON BOTTOM OF
BOX BETWEEN LIGHT FIX.
¼"TK. "BLACK" GLASS
PANELS GLUED TO WD. 2x4
FRAMING
LOWER LIGHT BOX NOTES

SIMILAR TO UPPER LIGHT BOX
EXCEPT PLAS. LAM. ONLY
COVERS FRONT FACE & LIP

LIGHT BOX TO BE ATTACHED
TO CONT. LEDGER & KNEE
WALL
⅝"GWB W/ WD. BASE TO
MATCH EXISTING BASE

NOTES

ALL VERT. & HORIZ. JOINTS
IN BLACK GLASS, FROSTED
GLASS & PLAS. LAM. TO
ALIGN
FLUORESCENT LIGHT FIX.
TO BE #1202 BY C.J.
LIGHTING

SECTION

DISPLAY WINDOW

BLOOMINGDALE'S
Boca Raton, Florida

Interior Design
Walker Group/CNI
Design Team
Martin Jerry, Waldo Sarjeant,
Errol Spence, Kevin Rice
Fabrication
Modern Woodcraft
Photography
© John Wadsworth

BY GENERAL CONSENSUS, Bloomingdale's, headquartered at 59th Street and Lexington Avenue in New York City, is—as its promotional slogan boasts—"like no other store in the world."

What brings hordes of consumers to Bloomingdale's year after year is due in part to the design acumen of Walker Group/CNI, a New York City–based design firm with a history of retail success. Walker Group/CNI supplements its skills in space planning with two other areas of expertise relevant to the retail industry: display/exhibition planning and graphic design.

Each of these skills was called upon when the design team developed the fashion-of-the-month display windows for the Bloomingdale's stores in Florida. Martin Jerry, vice president and director of design for Walker, designed the large display windows as a signature detail—one that would "unify focal-point display in the stores' 60'-0"-high, 3,800-square-foot atriums."

The windows are constructed (as exhibition cases often are) as clear glass boxes. The edges are joined glass to glass with clear vinyl adhesive.

What makes the windows unique is their size—which, in glass area alone, is 12'-0" square—and their suspension 17 feet above the atrium floor—a fact that does not show in the photograph. The windows are cantilevered out from the second-floor framing. The cantilevered effect is heightened by the soffit architecture that appears to suspend the glass display windows from the ceiling.

The display window floors are covered in carpeting, which abuts to the carpeting of the regular sales floor. Display lighting is provided in the soffit by a floor-mounted spotlight positioned unobtrusively in one forward corner. Access to the windows for changing displays is made possible by passing through the space next to the floating low wall, which stands free of the display windows. The display signage is applied vinyl-adhesive stencils, which may be replaced as the displays are changed.

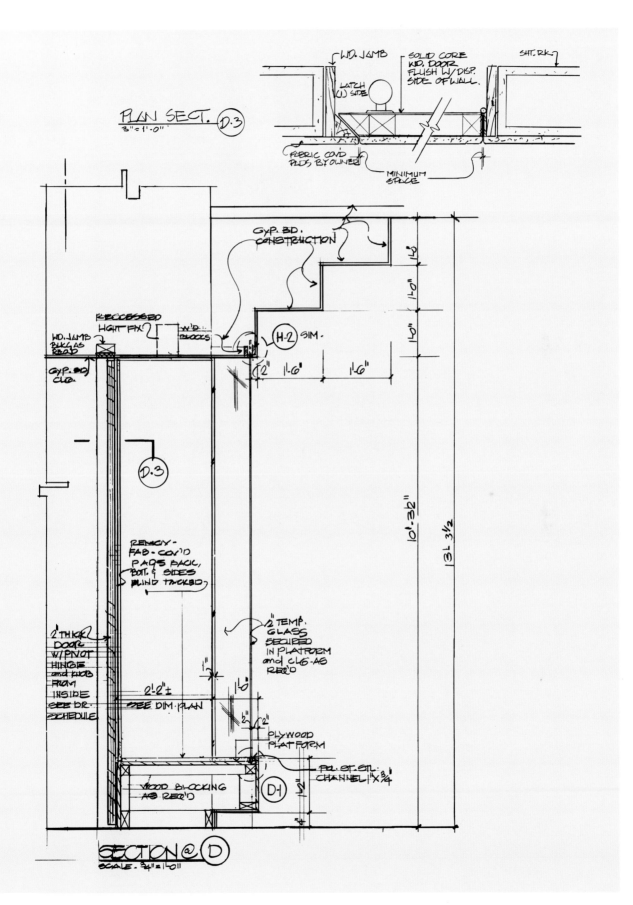

PLAN SECT. D.3
3" = 1'-0"

WD. JAMB
SOLID CORE
WD. DOOR
FLUSH W/ DISP.
SIDE OF WALL.
SHT. RK.
LATCH
(L) SIDE
FABRIC COV'D
PADS BY OWNER
MINIMUM
SPACE

GYP. BD.
CONSTRUCTION

1'-6"
1'-0"
1'-6"

RECESSED
LIGHT FIX.
W'D.
BLOCKS
H-2 SIM.

WD. JAMB
BLKG AS
REQ'D

GYP. BD.
CLG.

2" 1'-6" 1'-6"

D.3

10'-3½"
13'-3½"

READY-
FAB. COV'D
PADS BACK,
BOTT. & SIDES
BLIND TACKED

½" TEMP.
GLASS
SECURED
IN PLATFORM
and CLG. AS
REQ'D

2" THICK
DOOR
W/ PIVOT
HINGE
and KNOB
FROM
INSIDE
SEE DR.
SCHEDULE

1"
1½"

2'-2" ±
SEE DIM. PLAN

2" 2"

PLYWOOD
PLATFORM

WOOD BLOCKING
AS REQ'D

D-1

FOL. ST. STL.
CHANNEL 1" X ¾"

SECTION @ D
SCALE: ¾" = 1'-0"

DOORS

SHELL CENTRAL OFFICES HEADQUARTERS
The Hague, Netherlands

Architecture/Interior Design
Charles Pfister Associates

Design Team
Charles Pfister, Joseph Matzo,
Pamela Babey, Deborah Lewis,
Miguel Solé, James Tung,
James Leal

Fabrication
Clemens Schlatt

Photography
Peter Aaron, ESTO

IF THERE ARE SKILLED craftsmen still at work around the world, San Francisco's Charles Pfister Associates knows who they are, where to find them, and what they do best. Pfister's clients derive a double advantage from the firm's sleuthing skill—for what Pfister does best is the detailing only such craftsmen can render.

Pfister was asked to develop a number of details at Shell Central Offices headquarters in The Hague, Netherlands (see pages 38 and 62). Among them was a "light-transmitting screening device," which would separate the entrance to the executive offices from the public corridor and the dining and conference room spaces. After submitting several options for client review, the design team finally recommended partition walls and doors constructed of meticulously designed sandblasted and beveled etched glass (*sandblasted & beveled pattern*).

The design team worked with German glasscutters to develop a four-step glass treatment process. First the raw glass panel is sandblasted. The cutting pattern is then drawn on a computer, which then prints the design on transfer film with a peel-off back. After the pattern has been affixed to the sandblasted glass panels, a grinding wheel cuts the panel at three different depth levels. At the same time, two additional wheels cut as a jig. (During this phase of the process, three different degrees of abrasion are used before the polishing process is begun.) In the last step, the entire piece is carefully washed and cleaned to remove any silica dust that might dim the freshly worked surface. The tedious process results in what Charles Pfister calls "the largest Waterford glass in the world."

To accentuate the glitter of the V-groove cut glass, the design team devised an innovative door pull and push plate of brushed and polished steel and polished brass (*pull/push plate*). On the doors' opposite side, a stainless steel counter pull of simple design was installed.

The doors are set within frames that reflect the polished metals of the door pull and push plate. Panels of matching laminated glass are mounted on either side of the door frames (*jamb*). Like the doors, the panels have been sandblasted and V-grooved.

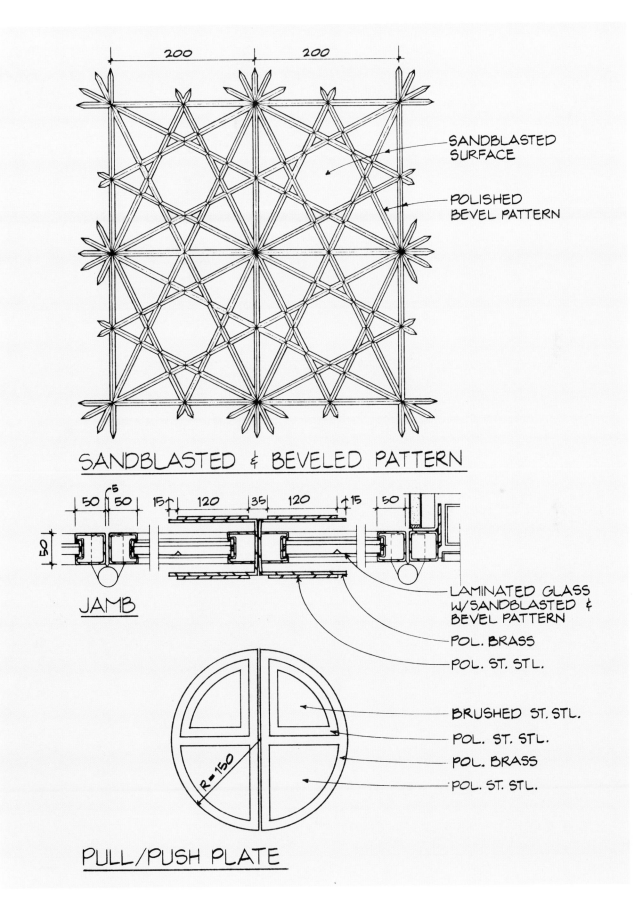

200 | 200

SANDBLASTED
SURFACE

POLISHED
BEVEL PATTERN

SANDBLASTED & BEVELED PATTERN

50 | 50 | 5 | 15 | 120 | 35 | 120 | 15 | 50

50

JAMB

LAMINATED GLASS
W/SANDBLASTED &
BEVEL PATTERN
POL. BRASS
POL. ST. STL.

R-150

BRUSHED ST. STL.
POL. ST. STL.
POL. BRASS
POL. ST. STL.

PULL/PUSH PLATE

Door/Door Surround

THE ROSEWOOD CORPORATION
Dallas, Texas

Architecture/Interior Design
3D/International, Inc.
Millwork
The Wigand Corporation
Photography
© Chas McGrath

GRANDIOSE, NECESSARILY expensive, and potentially tacky gestures of every kind are perceived by outsiders to be ubiquitous components of Texas design. The headquarters of The Rosewood Corporation in Dallas, designed by the Dallas office of 3D/International, Inc., defies such regional stereotyping. 3D/I's design makes an architectural detailing statement that

is—although suitably grand and certainly costly—first and foremost dignified, tasteful, and timeless.

Not one inch of the detail was mass produced. Everything from the millwork to the hardware and trim was custom built to 3D/I's specifications (*elevation*). All of the glass was hand beveled, and every molding was hand carved (*details*). The knotholes and cracks were enhanced as part of a painstaking seventeen-step finishing process.

The client allowed the design team a free hand in determining the detailing, stipulating only that the "final product should match the craftsmanship standards of turn-of-the-century residences."

The Rosewood Corporation re-

ceived value for its investment (see also page 14). The quality of both the detailing and millwork is superb. This is epitomized by the 26'-6" by 14'-6" door/door surround constructed of 2½-inch American cherry, ⅝-inch beveled glass doors, side panels, and transom (*elevation*; *section*), which separate the reception area from the primary conference room. The glass-paned door/door surround was designed to showcase the massively scaled but delicately traced fanlight window in the conference room. According to the 3D/I project architect, "we thought it would be a loss if Rosewood visitors were unable to note the dramatic view from the boardroom."

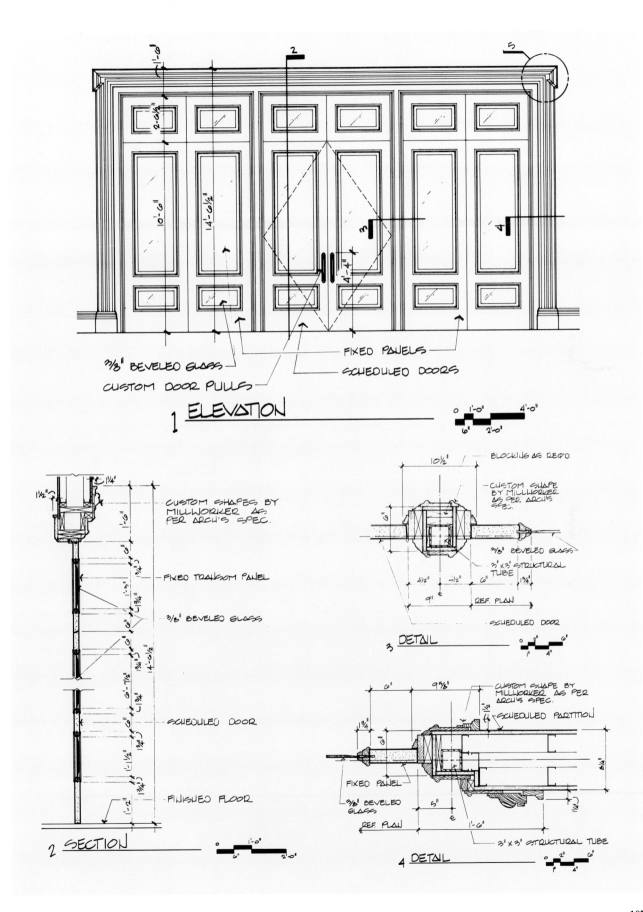

3/8" BEVELED GLASS

CUSTOM DOOR PULLS

FIXED PANELS

SCHEDULED DOORS

1 ELEVATION

0 1'-0"   4'-0"
  6"   2'-0"

CUSTOM SHAPES BY MILLWORKER AS PER ARCH'S SPEC.

FIXED TRANSOM PANEL

3/8" BEVELED GLASS

SCHEDULED DOOR

FINISHED FLOOR

2 SECTION

0   1'-0"
  6"   2'-0"

BLOCKING AS REQ'D

CUSTOM SHAPE BY MILLWORKER AS PER ARCH'S SPEC.

3/8" BEVELED GLASS

3"x3" STRUCTURAL TUBE

REF. PLAN

SCHEDULED DOOR

3 DETAIL

0   2"   6"
  1"   4"

CUSTOM SHAPE BY MILLWORKER AS PER ARCH'S SPEC.

SCHEDULED PARTITION

FIXED PANEL

3/8" BEVELED GLASS

REF PLAN

3"x3" STRUCTURAL TUBE

4 DETAIL

0   2"   6"
  1"   4"

DOOR/DOOR SURROUND

WEST SHELL REALTORS
Cincinnati, Ohio

Interior Design
Space Design International Inc.

Design Team
James T. Fitzgerald, Charles L. Nickel,
Randi Bayer, Pamela McDonel,
Judith K. Dilts

Woodwork
Art Woodworking, Inc. (Ronald Simmons)
Charles L. Nickel, Space Design International's senior project designer, worked
with junior architect Randi Bayer and
principal-in-charge James T. Fitzgerald
to develop the door details. Ronald
Simmons of Art Woodworking, Inc., of
Cincinnati supervised detail fabrication
and installation.

Photography
© Patrick Brown

ENTREPRENEURIAL CLIENTS are often more
assertive in making design statements
about their success than are corporate-ladder executives. Space Design
International Inc. of Cincinnati, Ohio,
had just such an unabashed client in
George Ballou II. The SDI design
team was instructed to "pull out all
the stops" in their finish detailing, so
that the headquarters of West Shell
Realtors, Ballou's newly purchased
real-estate company, would reflect the
client's high profile in the local economic scene.

SDI responded to Ballou's request
for a traditional office environment
within a modern building by rendering a number of contemporary details
in a traditional manner. The most
striking is a curved-wall concourse of
significantly scaled, floor-to-ceiling
double doors, which demarcate the
transition from the reception area to a
series of private executive offices and
a boardroom.

The sweeping curved wall has a
49'-6" radius to the facing wall. The
concave arc was imposed for two
reasons: to graphically identify the
location of upper-echelon management offices and to symbolically suggest the Ohio River, which flows past
the building thirty stories below in a
concentric curve.

The crinkle-glass-paned doors from
the reception area (*elevation A*), the

solid-panel office and boardroom
doors, and the door surrounds are all
constructed of matched-grain Honduran mahogany (*door section B-B*).
Because the 9' 0" doors are fitted
floor to ceiling, the surrounds' fluted
pilasters end in sloped-crown capitals
that break the curve and permit the
doors to be recessed a full 18 inches.
A 3-inch solid mahogany turned cylinder smoothly accommodates the
juncture of the pilaster's vertical elevation to the sloped plane of the capital
(*elevation A*).

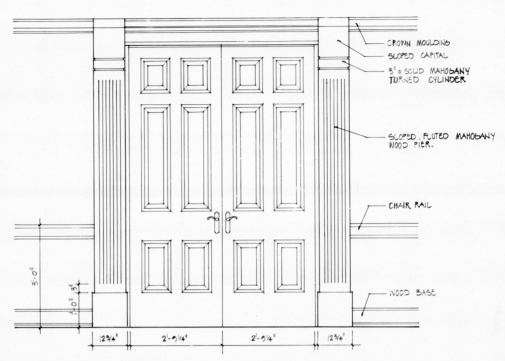

CROWN MOULDING
SLOPED CAPITAL
3" ø SOLID MAHOGANY TURNED CYLINDER

SLOPED, FLUTED MAHOGANY WOOD PIER.

CHAIR RAIL

WOOD BASE

3'-0"
1'-0" 3"

12 3/4" 2'-9 1/4" 2'-9 1/4" 12 3/4"

ENTRY DOOR ELEVATION 'A'

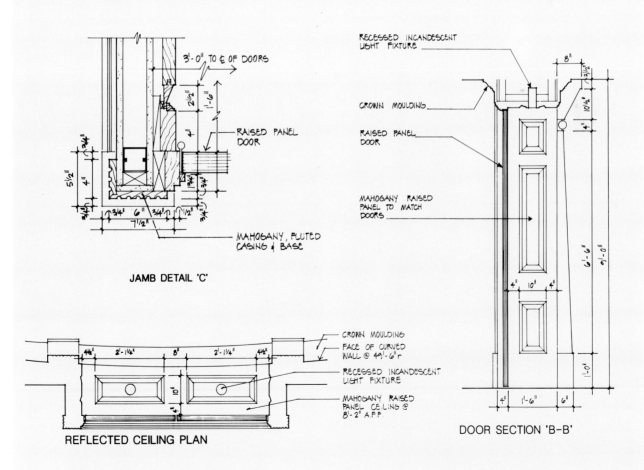

3'-0" TO ℄ OF DOORS
2 1/2"
1'-6"
1"
RAISED PANEL DOOR

3/4"
5 1/2" 4"
3/4" 3/4"
3/4" 6" 3/4" 1/2"
7 1/2"

MAHOGANY, FLUTED CASING & BASE

JAMB DETAIL 'C'

RECESSED INCANDESCENT LIGHT FIXTURE
8"
2 3/4"
10 1/2"

CROWN MOULDING

RAISED PANEL DOOR

4"

MAHOGANY RAISED PANEL TO MATCH DOORS

4" 10" 4"
6'-6"
9'-0"
1'-0"
4" 1'-6" 6"

DOOR SECTION 'B-B'

CROWN MOULDING
FACE OF CURVED WALL @ 49'-6" r
RECESSED INCANDESCENT LIGHT FIXTURE
MAHOGANY RAISED PANEL CEILING @ 8'-2" A.F.F.

4 1/2" 2'-1 1/4" 8" 2'-1 1/4" 4 1/2"
10"
4"

REFLECTED CEILING PLAN

109

DOOR SURROUNDS

ALABAMA POWER COMPANY
Birmingham, Alabama

Architecture/Interior Design
Geddes Brecher Qualls Cunningham;
Gresham, Smith and Partners
Design Team
James Snyder, Mark Williams,
James Thorington, Lynn Bush
Fabrication
Melco Wood Fixtures
Photography
© Durston Saylor

WHEN A CORPORATE headquarters project has been detailed well, one of the qualities that emerges is a sense of continuity from one area of the building to another. At the Alabama Power Company in Birmingham, Alabama, Geddes Brecher Qualls Cunningham in collaboration with Gresham, Smith and Partners has achieved subtle, but nonetheless spectacular, visual continuity by repeating detail forms throughout the building and by substituting within those forms a variety of finish materials that are appropriate to differing levels of formality and hierarchical importance.

James Snyder, director of interior design for GBQC, showed particular sensitivity to both architectural uniformity and employee morale in detailing the door surrounds, which occur at every cut-through corridor along each floor's mechanical core. By imposing a standard door surround grid that consists of three elements—the wainscot, casing, and lintel—Snyder was able to specify three finish-material standards. These help to graphically identify both floor operation and level of seniority.

For the public spaces on the lower floors (where some degree of impersonality is desired), the wainscot, casing, and lintels are rendered in polished, honed, and thermal-finished granite panels. A bisecting signage valance of polished stainless steel provides additional textural contrast (see page 206). On twelve operation floors, where informality is encouraged, the wainscot fields are rendered in 4-inch by 4-inch ceramic tile, while the casing is constructed of granite slab. To form a unifying background for disparate materials, the grout was tinted to a color value two shades

lighter than the tile. The lintels on the operation floors are finished in flat-grain mahogany (*architrave elevation A; details 1–5*). The mahogany lintels on the operation floors presage the finishes for the executive offices located on the seventeenth and eighteenth floors, where "formality with warmth" was required. There, the entire composition of wainscot, casing, and lintel is rendered in polished mahogany (*architrave elevation B; details A–E*).

The construction of the door surrounds was thoughtfully planned to facilitate simple imposition on site. The stone and wood lintels and prefinished standing and running trim were shop-cut and fabricated. Stonework was placed on plaster spots and held in place with steel anchors. Tile components were shipped to the site and mounted in ⅛-inch, thin-set mortar beds on Portland cement plasterboard panels. The mahogany lintels and trim were scribed to the walls and flooring. Small variations in lateral casing imposition were planned for field adjustment and were concealed by variations in the trim.

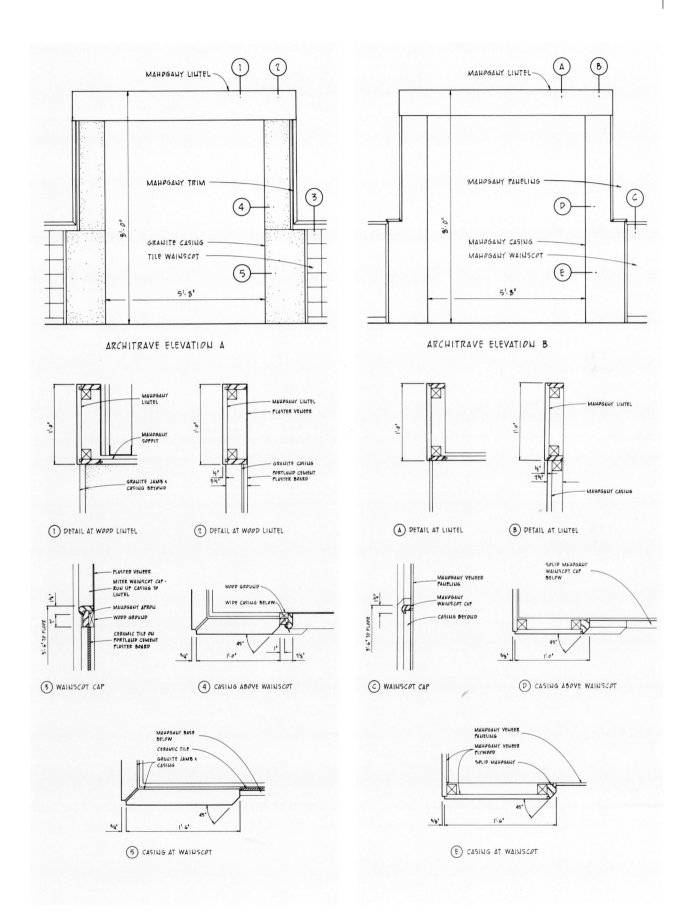

MAHOGANY LINTEL ①②

MAHOGANY TRIM ④

GRANITE CASING

TILE WAINSCOT ⑤ ③

8'-0"

5'-8"

ARCHITRAVE ELEVATION A

MAHOGANY LINTEL Ⓐ Ⓑ

MAHOGANY PANELING Ⓓ Ⓒ

MAHOGANY CASING

MAHOGANY WAINSCOT Ⓔ

8'-0"

5'-8"

ARCHITRAVE ELEVATION B

MAHOGANY LINTEL

MAHOGANY SOFFIT

GRANITE JAMB & CASING BEYOND

1'-0"

① DETAIL AT WOOD LINTEL

MAHOGANY LINTEL

PLASTER VENEER

GRANITE CASING

PORTLAND CEMENT PLASTER BOARD

1'-0"

½"
¾"

② DETAIL AT WOOD LINTEL

MAHOGANY LINTEL

1'-0"

Ⓐ DETAIL AT LINTEL

MAHOGANY LINTEL

MAHOGANY CASING

1'-0"

¼"
2½"

Ⓑ DETAIL AT LINTEL

PLASTER VENEER

MITER WAINSCOT CAP - RUN UP CASING TO LINTEL

MAHOGANY APRON

WOOD GROUND

CERAMIC TILE ON PORTLAND CEMENT PLASTER BOARD

1¼"
3'-6" TO FLOOR

③ WAINSCOT CAP

WOOD GROUND

WIDE CASING BELOW

45°
¾" 1'-0" 1" 2½"

④ CASING ABOVE WAINSCOT

MAHOGANY VENEER PANELING

MAHOGANY WAINSCOT CAP

CASING BEYOND

1¼"
3'-6" TO FLOOR

Ⓒ WAINSCOT CAP

SOLID MAHOGANY WAINSCOT CAP BELOW

45°
⅜" 1'-0"

Ⓓ CASING ABOVE WAINSCOT

MAHOGANY BASE BELOW

CERAMIC TILE

GRANITE JAMB & CASING

45°
¾" 1'-6"

⑤ CASING AT WAINSCOT

MAHOGANY VENEER PANELING

MAHOGANY VENEER PLYWOOD

SOLID MAHOGANY

45°
⅜" 1'-6"

Ⓔ CASING AT WAINSCOT

ELEVATOR CAB

1001 PENNSYLVANIA AVENUE
Washington, D.C.

Architecture/Interior Design
Hartman-Cox Architects
Design Team
George Hartman, Graham Davidson
Elevator Fabrication
Hauenstein and Burmeister
Photography
© Durston Saylor

IT IS NOT EASY TO SUGGEST permanence, stability, and affluence in a 7-foot by 6-foot enclosure. To do so is a particular achievement when the enclosure in question is an elevator, a structure which repeatedly rises and falls on what we may subliminally fear to be potentially questionable cables. Therefore, it is to Hartman-Cox Architects' credit that office residents of 1001 Pennsylvania Avenue in Washington,

D.C., take for granted that sense of security.

Hartman-Cox Architects derived its elevator design by interpreting the client's directive in literal terms. Cadillac-Fairview Urban Development Corporation asked for "elevators which echo the architectural themes of the building." In response, Hartman-Cox combined the elemental architectural forms of the lobby—there rendered in marble—with the mahogany paneling specified as finish materials in most tenant spaces. The design team maintained the relative scale of the elements to one another, thereby imposing balanced but smaller mahogany corner-set pilasters (*plan @ corner column*) and entablatures within the elevator cab.

There are twenty-four elevators, each entered through mirror-finish bronze doors, framed by beveled and

mitered slabs of verdegris marble. On either side of the doors inside the cab are mirror-finish bronze control panels (*front wall cab elevation*). Mahogany-veneer panels on the side and rear walls are symmetrically balanced and hung with metal clips so that any one panel may be individually removed if damaged by vandals (*rear and side wall cab elevations*).

Hartman-Cox obviated ubiquitous elevator glare by installing forty 25-watt incandescent lamps 4 inches on center around the periphery of the cab ceiling. Indirect lighting bounces off the mahogany-paneled ceiling from a lucifer strip mounted at a 10-degree angle (*wall/cornice profile*). The lighting intensity is controlled by a low-voltage dimmer mounted on the roof of the cab, as well as by a suspended and paneled coved ceiling (*suspended ceiling detail*).

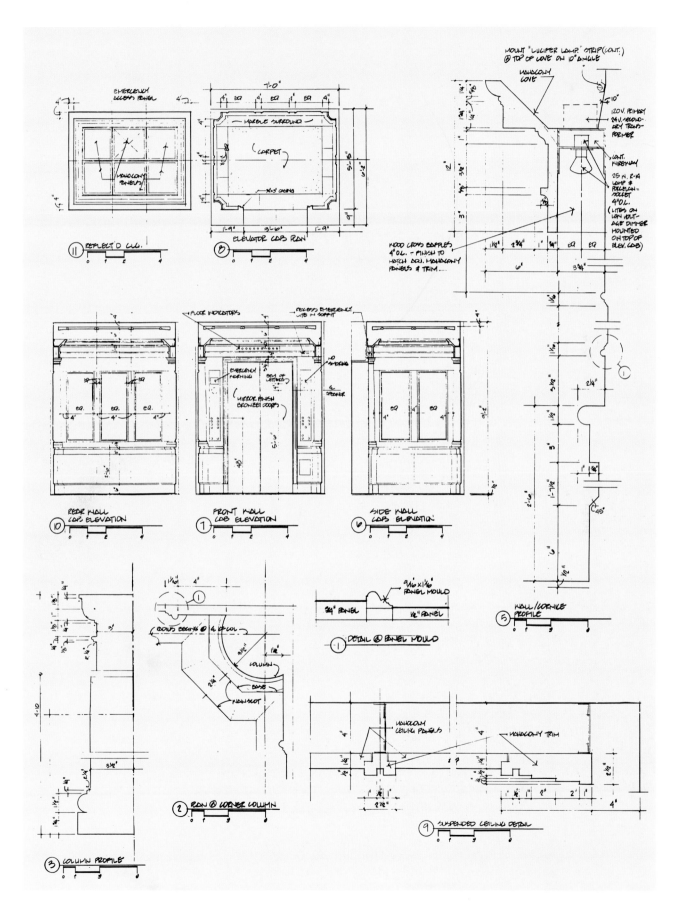

ELEVATOR CAB

ALABAMA POWER COMPANY
Birmingham, Alabama

Architecture/Interior Design
Geddes Brecher Qualls Cunningham;
Gresham, Smith and Partners
Design Team
James Snyder, Elaine Ciufo
Fabrication
Westinghouse Elevator Company
Photography
© Paul Warchol

AN ELECTRONIC VOICE announces destination points to occupants of the elevator cabs at the Alabama Power Company's corporate headquarters in Birmingham, Alabama. Should one tarry, the same voice politely requests that the doors be allowed to close. Such technological sophistication is impressive but is not nearly as impressive as the design sophistication exhibited by Geddes Brecher Qualls Cunningham of Philadelphia, who detailed the elevator cabs with as much concern for aesthetics as for high-tech componentry.

GBQC inferred its mandate from a client remark that "because the elevator is the one space in the building that every employee sees everyday, it should be good looking." Other client preferences included "a durable, maintainable floor, and an 'unsittable' railing."

Because the design of the elevator cab was part of the massive renovation and new construction project GBQC undertook in collaboration with Gresham, Smith and Partners of Birmingham, Alabama, GBQC's James Snyder worked closely with Alabama Power Company's Ken Penuel and Floyd Harrell and with the Westinghouse Elevator Company to determine the load capacity and number of elevators required. Sixteen elevators were finished at a unit cost of $20,000, exclusive of flooring. The price was negotiated before the cab detailing began; therefore, an additional design constraint was to specify finishes that would fall within predetermined budget figures.

Stylistically, Snyder designed the cab as a "thematic transition" from the granite finishes of the lobby to the granite and mahogany finishes of the higher floors. The design team rendered the transition symbolically, designing a patterned granite floor for the cab and specifying mahogany paneling for the walls and ceiling. Because the cabs would be subject to crash tests only after the finishing work was installed, the design team scaled down each element to increase its impact tolerance. Granite tile, laid in a diamond pattern, was further reinforced by a thickset wire-meshed mortar bed. Half-heart wood-paneling sections, matched from the center, were hung from the steel shell on knockdown wood fasteners.

Snyder designed an elegant "two-story" handrail that belies its functional genesis. A stainless steel barrier-free rail, mounted to code, is surmounted by a polished-wood finish rail with a rectangular face and a back that is curved for hand comfort (*handrail details*). Reveals between each wall panel were carefully sized ¼ inch so that the handrail brackets might be recessed and bolted to the steel wall without gouging or marring the wood. As a detail within a detail, reveal surfaces were covered with mylar strips for further finishing.

Snyder used the dropped ceiling to reflect the floor pattern, substituting, in tonal value, positive for negative; in material, he substituted mahogany and pecan for gray and rose granite (*axonometric*). Incandescent cove lighting was adjusted in the field (*section at light cove*), and, as a lighting embellishment, a dimmer panel was installed behind the swing return. A generous steel cove base facilitates maintenance (*base detail*).

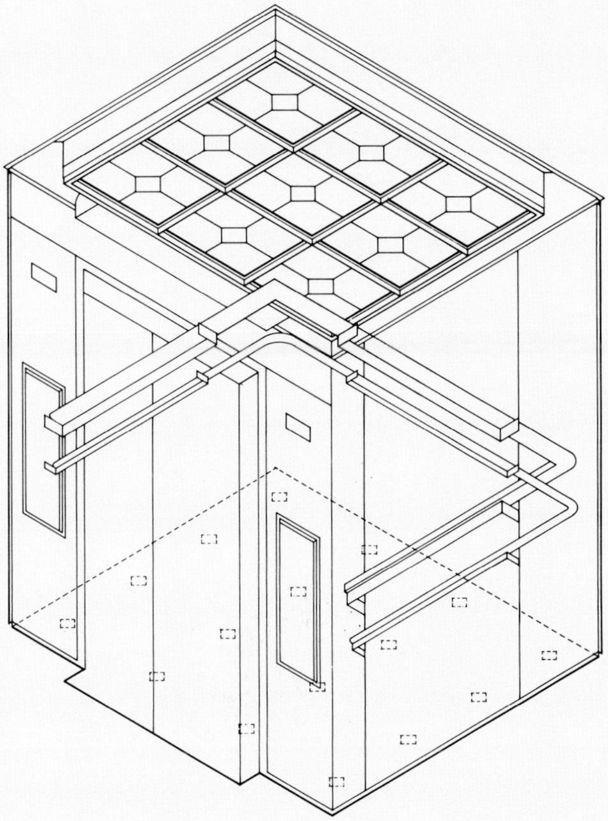

AXONOMETRIC

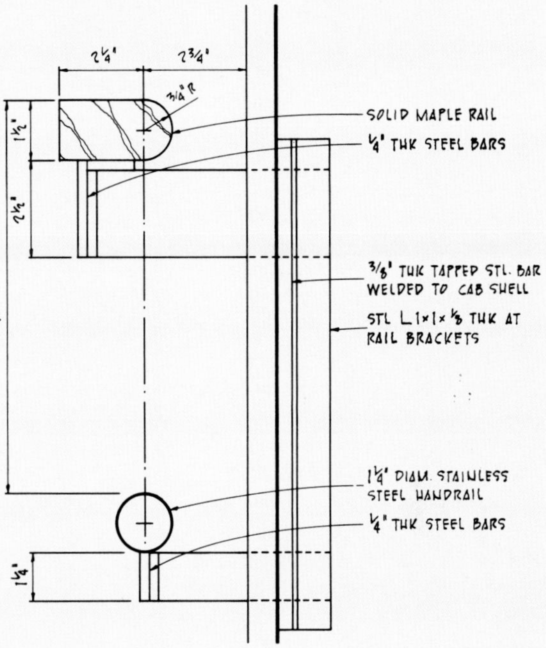

HANDRAIL DETAILS

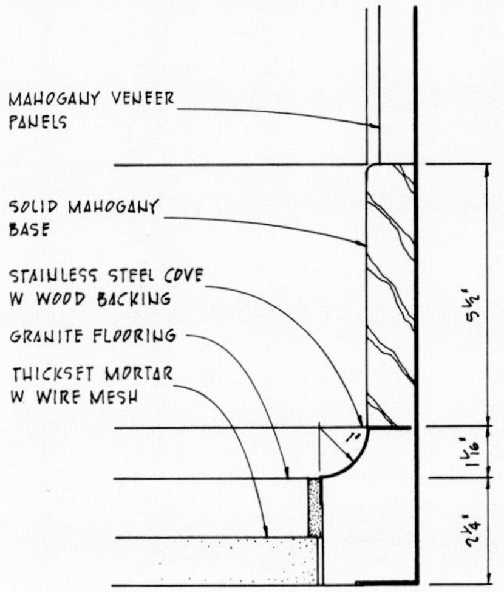

2¼"   2¾"

¾" R

1½"

2½"

10"

SOLID MAPLE RAIL

¼" THK STEEL BARS

⅜" THK TAPPED STL. BAR WELDED TO CAB SHELL

STL L 1×1×⅛ THK AT RAIL BRACKETS

1¼" DIAM. STAINLESS STEEL HANDRAIL

¼" THK STEEL BARS

1¼"

MAHOGANY VENEER PANELS

SOLID MAHOGANY BASE

STAINLESS STEEL COVE W WOOD BACKING

GRANITE FLOORING

THICKSET MORTAR W WIRE MESH

5½"

1"

1½"

2¼"

BASE DETAIL

VENT SLOTS IN CANOPY W DUST COVER

WIRING ACCESS HOLES

VENT HOLES

LIGHTS & LENSES AT WALLS & RETURNS ONLY

5½"

3⅜"

5½"

MAHOGANY CEILING GRID W. PECAN INLAID MAHOGANY VENEER PANELS

STAINLESS STEEL SOFFIT AT DOORS ONLY

MAHOGANY VENEER WALL PANELS

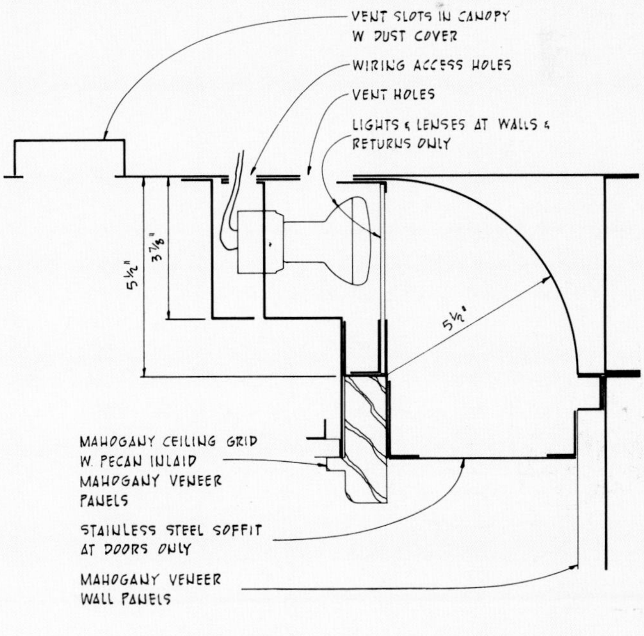

SECTION AT LIGHT COVE

ELEVATOR CAB

THE HUMANA BUILDING
Louisville, Kentucky

Architecture/Interior Design
Michael Graves, Architect, and Graves/
Warnecke, a joint venture of
Michael Graves, Architect, and
John Carl Warnecke & Associates

Design Team
Michael Graves, Terence W. Smith,
Juliet Richardson-Smith,
Peter Hague Neilson, David R. Teeters,
Lee Hamptian, William Collins,
Susan Butcher, Ron Berlin (drafting)

Elevator Consultant
John A. Van Deusen & Associates

Fabrication
Armor Elevator Co.

Photography
© Paschall/Taylor

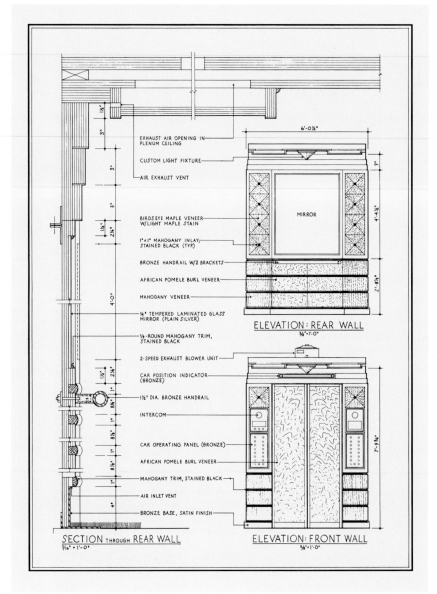

ELEVATION: REAR WALL
³⁄₈"·1'-0"

SECTION THROUGH REAR WALL
³⁄₁₆" · 1'-0"

ELEVATION: FRONT WALL
³⁄₈"·1'-0"

THE PARTICULAR TALENT of the office of Michael Graves is to design original buildings that also convey an intellectual awareness of historical form. Another hallmark of Graves's work is to integrate well-crafted details that reiterate the project's overall architectural forms.

The elevator cabs at The Humana Building in Louisville, Kentucky, represent elegant renditions of both characteristics. In fulfilling Humana's overall project request for "a sense of solidity and endurance," Graves transformed the cab shells from standard, code-certified steel chassis into "executive anterooms" by designing and installing exotically patterned grained wood panels of light and dark finish.

The cab walls were paneled in three primary wood veneers: lightly stained bird's-eye maple, African pomele burl, and mahogany (*elevation: rear wall*). Each wall and ceiling panel was constructed of rabbeted and glued veneer segments. The segments were then glued to plywood backing panels and trimmed in ebonized mahogany. The reverse side of each plywood panel was also veneered to prevent warping. The assembled panels were hung with blind fasteners from the steel chassis structure. So that the entire interior could be simply dismantled, the corner panels were not glued or connected. As a result, all the panels may be removed from their mounting hooks.

The back wall of the cab displays a

4'-1½"-high silvered mirror of tempered, laminated glass. The mirror was glued and clipped to the plywood backing and framed in mahogany. A 1½-inch-diameter bronze handrail, supported by welded bronze tubes that have been bolted to the wall through the plywood backing, is mounted underneath the mirror (*section through rear wall*). The operating panels, faced with bronze plates screwed to steel underframes, flank the pomele burl doors (*elevation: front wall*).

Illumination of the cab is provided by a bronze-fitted, sandblasted glass ceiling fixture, which is one of a type

designed by Graves for use throughout the building. The fixture is set into a ceiling panel raised 3 inches above the ceiling plane. The raised framing of the panel conceals exhaust vents. Air is drawn up by an electric blower concealed above the light fixture (*elevation: front wall*). The air inlet vent is hidden behind covering trim near the base of the rear wall (*section through rear wall*).

An escape hatch is concealed in the side wall, which most nearly adjoins another elevator. The hatch's covering panel is European hinged and is accessed by a fire-department skeleton key latch.

Elevator Surround

**ONE POST OFFICE SQUARE
ONE EXETER PLAZA**
Boston, Massachusetts

Interior Design
Jung/Brannen Associates, Inc.
Design Team
Robert Brannen, Robert Hsiung,
John Willand (One Exeter Plaza)
Fabrication
Moliterno Stone Sales, Inc.;
Euromarble
Photography
© Nick Wheeler

IN 1978 THE BEACON COMPANIES commissioned Jung/Brannen Associates, Inc., to design the interior of their upscale new speculative office building at One Post Office Square in Boston, Massachusetts. The client and the design firm agreed that as a finish material marble would best express the image of "luxury and high quality" The Beacon Companies wanted the building's public spaces to project. However, the high cost of marble

posed a problem. To achieve parity between the cost of marble and the developer's budget, Jung/Brannen invented a new marble construction technique.

The veneering process Jung/Brannen developed substantially reduces the cost of using patterned marble in interiors. The collaborative fabricator of the marble panels is a firm from Carrara, Italy, which quarries the marble, cuts it into shaped, laminate-thin strips, and then veneers the marble laminate onto travertine panels measuring approximately 3½ feet by 5 feet. Moliterno, a Providence, Rhode Island, stone installer, constructs the panels on site upon arrival in the United States.

Jung/Brannen demonstrated its mastery of the new technique by employing it in the design of an elevator surround in another building in Boston owned by Boylston Partners, One Exeter Plaza. In that project, four marbles were used: Breccia Pernice as the wall finish from wainscot

height to above the elevator door; Breche Nouvelle for the door surround; Asiago Red for the narrow bands at eye level; and Creama Valencia as punctuation points and wainscot. The four colors used together as a single composition imply more complexity than the design actually possesses—a *trompe l'oeil* effect that is intensified as the pattern repeats around all four elevators in the 3,500-square-foot lobby.

The laminated panels are joined with grout that is tinted to match the marble. In grout lines that run through several different colors of marble, the grout changes color correspondingly. The panels rest on the concrete subfloor and stack against the structural wall. The panels are held to the wall by wire ties and splined to the adjacent panels (*jamb detail; head detail*). Each panel is grooved on one side, fitting into a tab on the adjacent panel.

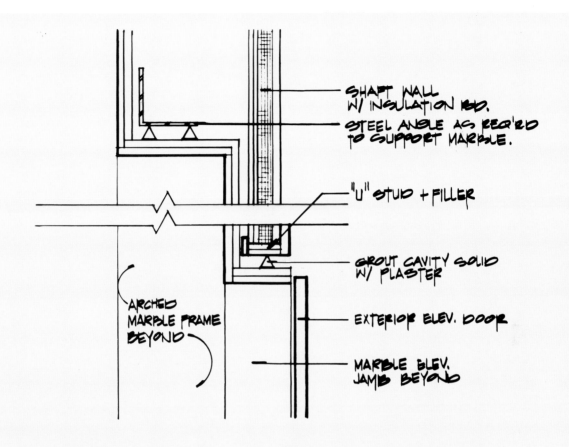

SHAFT WALL
W/ INSULATION BD.

STEEL ANGLE AS REQ'D
TO SUPPORT MARBLE.

"U" STUD + FILLER

GROUT CAVITY SOLID
W/ PLASTER

EXTERIOR ELEV. DOOR

MARBLE ELEV.
JAMB BEYOND

ARCHED
MARBLE FRAME
BEYOND

HEAD DETAIL @ ELEV. OPENING

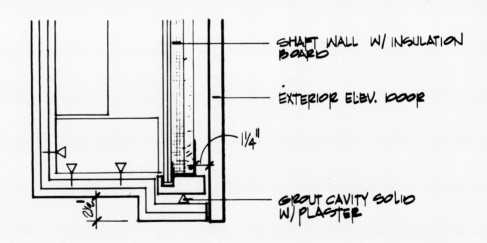

SHAFT WALL W/ INSULATION
BOARD

EXTERIOR ELEV. DOOR

1¼"

GROUT CAVITY SOLID
W/ PLASTER

JAMB DETAIL @ ELEV. OPENING

FILING WALL

MERRILL LYNCH & CO. OPERATIONS CENTER
Princeton, New Jersey

Interior Design
Daroff Design Inc.
Design Team
Karen Daroff, James Rappoport, Chuck Driesen
Fabrication
Specifications Built Corp.
Photography
© Tom Crane

IN A COPYRIGHTED design Daroff Design Inc. of Philadelphia developed for Merrill Lynch's operations center in Princeton, New Jersey, voluminous paper filing—which otherwise would have overwhelmed even this one-million-square-foot project—is accommodated not in cabinets braced against or built into the walls but in the walls themselves.

The cubic volume of records that Merrill Lynch must have on readily accessible file required that the storage system be correspondingly scaled. Because shifting business needs within an industry infamous for constant change may result in replanning the entire space within thirty-month increments, the client required that elements of the wall/storage system be demountable and easily reconfigured without disrupting the work environment.

The design team estimates that the custom filing system saved about 18,000 square feet of floor space, while still providing adequate storage for current needs and immediate growth. Completely modular construction along with the elimination of most interior partitions fulfilled the flexibility requirement—if the units are moved, the rooms' dimensions may be concurrently changed.

In addition to providing a solution for bulk storage and footprint flexibility, the Daroff storage system offers Merrill Lynch an opportunity for facilities management. The Daroff team designed the system to be *completely* free standing and movable. The units rest on the carpet, and the transom glass fits into (but is not affixed to) a fine-line ceiling groove cut out of the acoustical ceiling at modular 2-foot intervals (*section; detail*). By utilizing amphenol connectors, even the electrical system is made portable.

Certain designated wall components, such as box cabinets and file drawers, may be interchanged without structural modification (*elevation*). The file drawers contain complete suspension file carriage units. When offices are moved, each carriage unit with its files intact is removed and transferred to the new location.

Drawers and storage doors are hung on 7-foot-high cabinets constructed of laminate panels, which have been screwed together with blind connectors. Completed units are correspondingly connected to one another, creating office spaces in 12'-0" by 12'-0", 16'-0", or 20'-0" sizes, corresponding to the 4'-0" building module. Door hinges are spring action, self-aligning, fully concealed behind, and socket recessed. The six-pin locking system is keyed on both a corporate and a departmental basis.

Ambient lighting is provided by the same 3100° K octron fluorescent parabolic reflector fixtures that are used throughout the building. The office fixtures are mounted on the cabinet tops to ensure a constant color temperature (*section*).

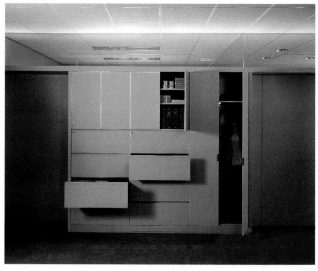

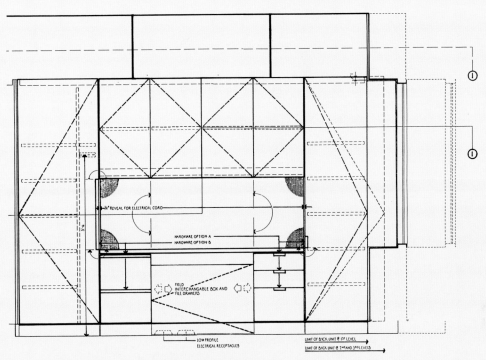

2 STORAGE WALL
ELEVATION

Labels within elevation (image 2):
- ½" REVEAL FOR ELECTRICAL CORD
- HARDWARE OPTION A
- HARDWARE OPTION B
- FIELD INTERCHANGABLE BOX AND FILE DRAWERS
- LOW PROFILE ELECTRICAL RECEPTACLES
- LIMIT OF BACK UNIT @ 1ST LEVEL
- LIMIT OF BACK UNIT @ 2ND AND 3RD LEVELS

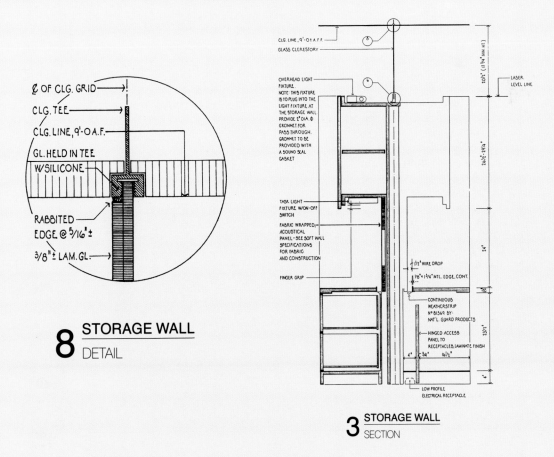

8 STORAGE WALL
DETAIL

Labels within detail:
- ℄ OF CLG. GRID
- CLG. TEE
- CLG. LINE, 9'-0 A.F.
- GL. HELD IN TEE W/ SILICONE
- RABBITED EDGE @ 5/16"±
- 3/8"± LAM. GL.

Labels within section:
- CLG. LINE, 9'-0± A.F.F.
- GLASS CLERESTORY
- OVERHEAD LIGHT FIXTURE. NOTE: THIS FIXTURE IS TO PLUG INTO THE LIGHT FIXTURE AT THE STORAGE WALL. PROVIDE 2" DIA. Ø GROMMET FOR PASS THROUGH. GROMMET TO BE PROVIDED WITH A SOUND SEAL GASKET
- TASK LIGHT FIXTURE W/ON-OFF SWITCH
- FABRIC WRAPPED ACOUSTICAL PANEL - SEE SOFT WALL SPECIFICATIONS FOR FABRIC AND CONSTRUCTION
- FINGER GRIP
- 1½" WIRE DROP
- 1/8" x 1 3/4" MTL. EDGE, CONT.
- CONTINUOUS WEATHERSTRIP N° 81369 BY: NAT'L. GUARD PRODUCTS
- HINGED ACCESS PANEL TO RECEPTACLES, LAMINATE FINISH
- LOW PROFILE ELECTRICAL RECEPTACLE
- LASER LEVEL LINE

3 STORAGE WALL
SECTION

121

FILING WALL

FIRST REPUBLIC BANK
Houston, Texas

Interior Design
Gensler and Associates/Architects,
Houston
Design Team
Antony Harbour, Bill Livingston,
Gregory Burke (drawings)
Fabrication
Brochsteins
Photography
© Peter Mauss, ESTO

BECAUSE THE CENTERPIECE of the First
Republic Bank in Houston, Texas, is a
soaring five-story atrium opening
onto each tangential floor, Gensler
and Associates/Architects of Houston
recommended that complementary
finish detailing be distributed uniformly throughout the building.

Gensler's early participation in the
project paid off in detailing that would
have been impossible to include during a later phase of construction. By
raising the fifth-floor ceilings 3′-0″
above the base building norm, the
design team was able to build in floor-
to-ceiling walls of recessed filing cabinets (*section B*). The cabinets provide
an unusual amount of vertical storage
and also appear to buttress a barrel-
vaulted ceiling and bridge archway.

The deceptive load-bearing appearance of the filing-wall system is
the calculated result of a crucial
abutment between the ceiling's 11⅜-
inch barrel-vault apron and the 11⅜-
inch filing-wall frame (*elevation*). The
effect is successfully substantiated by
two secondary design devices: the
imposition of a flush-fitted concealed
spline ceiling, which is suspended in
front of the filing-wall recess on either
side of the barrel vault, and the filing-
wall paneling, whose oversized dimensions and rich, dark finish lend
visual mass to the wall's "supportive"
function.

The filing-wall module is constructed of plywood overlaid by ma-
hogany-veneered plywood. The
veneers are both straight grained and
figured, and were cut from a single
log so that the grain patterns would
be uniformly distributed across the
facade of each unit (*elevation*).

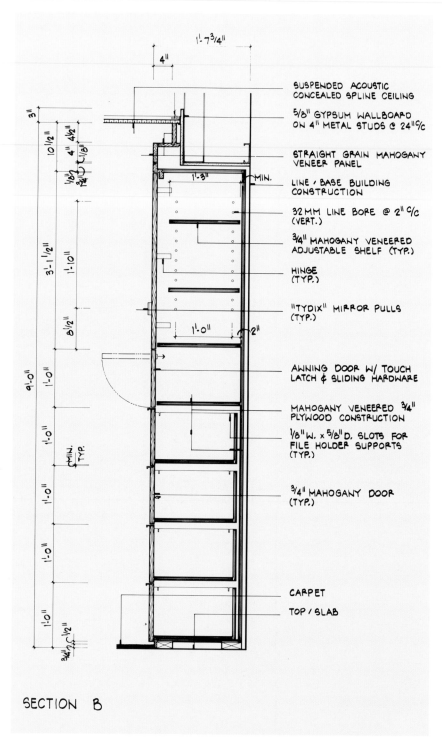

SUSPENDED ACOUSTIC
CONCEALED SPLINE CEILING

5/8" GYPSUM WALLBOARD
ON 4" METAL STUDS @ 24" o/c

STRAIGHT GRAIN MAHOGANY
VENEER PANEL

LINE / BASE BUILDING
CONSTRUCTION

32 MM LINE BORE @ 2" o/c
(VERT.)

3/4" MAHOGANY VENEERED
ADJUSTABLE SHELF (TYP.)

HINGE
(TYP.)

"TYDIX" MIRROR PULLS
(TYP.)

AWNING DOOR W/ TOUCH
LATCH & SLIDING HARDWARE

MAHOGANY VENEERED 3/4"
PLYWOOD CONSTRUCTION

1/8" W. x 5/8" D. SLOTS FOR
FILE HOLDER SUPPORTS
(TYP.)

3/4" MAHOGANY DOOR
(TYP.)

CARPET

TOP / SLAB

SECTION B

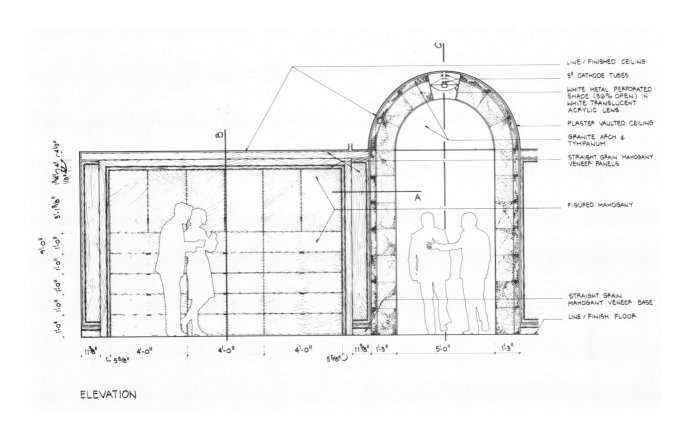

LINE / FINISHED CEILING

3" CATHODE TUBES

WHITE METAL PERFORATED
SHADE (36% OPEN) IN
WHITE TRANSLUCENT
ACRYLIC LENS

PLASTER VAULTED CEILING

GRANITE ARCH &
TYMPANUM

STRAIGHT GRAIN MAHOGANY
VENEER PANELS

FIGURED MAHOGANY

STRAIGHT GRAIN
MAHOGANY VENEER BASE

LINE / FINISH FLOOR

ELEVATION

FILING WALL

NALCO CHEMICAL COMPANY
Naperville, Illinois

Architecture/Interior Design
ISD Incorporated, Chicago
Design Team
Mel Hamilton, Gary Lee,
Angelina Lee, Sharon Singer,
John Bauman, Susan Freeman
Fabrication
Parenti & Raphaelli
Photography
© Nick Merrick, Hedrich-Blessing

THE OUTER-OFFICE WORK areas of secretaries and administrative assistants traditionally have not been planned to incorporate the same level of architectural detailing of adjacent executive offices. The support staff workstations at Nalco Chemical Company are an exception to this rule—thanks to a progressive in-house management philosophy that was interpreted graphically by ISD Incorporated of Chicago.

Despite a sincere executive request for "simplification and subtle elegance" in their support-staff areas, budget stipulations allowed for the expenditure of less than $100 per square foot. The design team's task, therefore, was to imbue 30,000 square feet of outer-office space on the executive floor with a strong architectural identity while staying within the budget.

Before the ISD design team went to work, nothing on the site was built in. Nor was the existing office furniture designed to accommodate the corporation's computers and other miscellaneous technologically advanced componentry. ISD's solution began with a "spring-cleaning" purge of outmoded equipment (which was phased to coincide with the delivery of customized desks) and the on-site construction of file cabinets that are architecturally built into the office-wall structure (*axonometric*).

Although the filing cabinet is, in fact, built out from the private-office party wall, ISD integrated the functional filing system into the surrounding paneling by maintaining the same vertical dimensions for the file cabinets as for adjacent paneling sections. Integration was also achieved by carrying a standardized soffit panel across the tops of the cabinets and paneling sections. The perception of the cabinets as part of the architectural whole is intensified by finishing them in the pomele mahogany veneers that were used, in both flat and burl grains, to panel all of the vertical surfaces in the space.

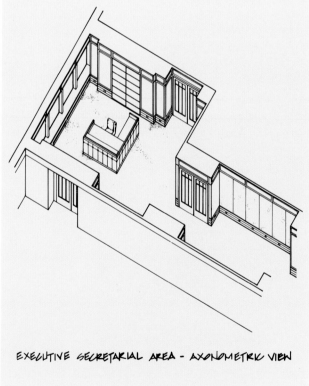

EXECUTIVE SECRETARIAL AREA - AXONOMETRIC VIEW

FLOOR PATTERN

MUSEUM OF ART AND ARCHAEOLOGY, MICHAEL C. CARLOS HALL

Emory University, Atlanta, Georgia

Architecture/Interior Design
Michael Graves, Architect

Design Team
Michael Graves, Theodore Brown, Patrick Burke, Karen Wheeler Nichols, Anita Rosskam, Thomas Rowe, Susan Butcher, Leslie Mason, Michael Kuhling, David Rockwood, Rico Cedro, Randall King

Fabrication
Michael Graves, Architect

Specialty Painters
Debra O'Brien, Patrick Burke, Susan Butcher, David Dymecki, James Prico, Suzanne Strum, Peter Twombley

Photography
© Steven Brooke

OF THE MANY POSITIVE qualities attributed to the work of Michael Graves, one that is often overlooked is humor. But humor—or whimsy—is certainly part of this celebrated architect's vocabulary, as is specific historical referencing.

Nowhere is this unique combination of intentions exhibited more clearly than within Emory University's Museum of Art and Archaeology in Atlanta, Georgia. There the Graves design team developed and implemented a series of stenciled floor treatments that pay witty homage to the floors that are inlaid with architectural plans at Carnegie Mellon University's Henry Hornbostel building.

Graves and his staff worked through a charrette weekend to chalk, tape, and sponge-paint appropriate footprints onto the oak floors of a several-room exhibition space, in which pre-Colombian, Mayan, ancient Greek and Roman, and ancient Near Eastern antiquities are displayed. The laborious two-coat sponging process was selected so that the floor's natural wood grain would show through the pochéed borders of the plans when dry. The composition was finished with several coats of polyurethane.

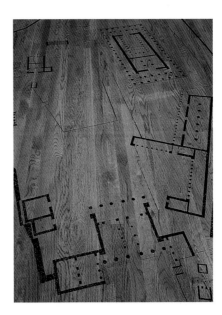

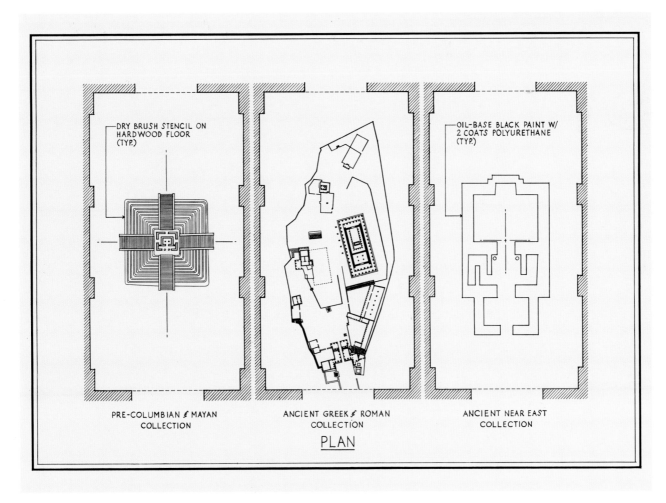

—DRY BRUSH STENCIL ON HARDWOOD FLOOR (TYP.)

—OIL-BASE BLACK PAINT W/ 2 COATS POLYURETHANE (TYP.)

PRE-COLUMBIAN & MAYAN COLLECTION

ANCIENT GREEK & ROMAN COLLECTION

ANCIENT NEAR EAST COLLECTION

PLAN

FLOOR PATTERN

SUSHI ZEN
New York City

Architecture/Interior Design
Haverson-Rockwell Architects
Design Team
David S. Rockwell, Jay M. Haverson
Fabrication
Tiger Construction Corporation
Photography
© Mark Ross Photography, Inc.

THAT THE SAFETY-CONSCIOUS restaurateur/proprietor of Sushi Zen in Manhattan would have his customers walking on glass is, at first glance, a curious anomaly. A second glance at the narrow 2,000-square-foot space reveals that a concern for safety—as

well as the wish to evoke an abstracted Japanese sensibility—was precisely the reason Haverson-Rockwell Architects of New York City designed the Sushi Zen lighted brick floor, whose circular translucent glass blocks define a ceremonial traffic pattern from entry to sushi bar.

The glimmering "rock-garden" effect that customers see (*plan*) is only one layer of the restaurant's flooring. Underneath the finish floor, cool white fluorescent tubes are attached to flooring joists. Beneath them a suspended acoustical tile ceiling, accessed from the kitchen basement below, was installed to form the base of a giant reflective light box. The acoustical panels can be easily

removed to change or replace fluorescent tubes (*section*).

The pattern of the glass blocks was determined by drilling into the existing wood floor joists to establish the pattern around and between them. Small holes were drilled into the existing floor while larger ones were drilled into the overlaid plywood floor so that the glass blocks could be wedged snugly between them. The glass blocks were anchored to the carpeted finish floor by ¾-inch brass mounting rings, which prevent the carpet from fraying.

The Sushi Zen restaurant won a 1985 Illumination Society Award for Haverson-Rockwell Architects.

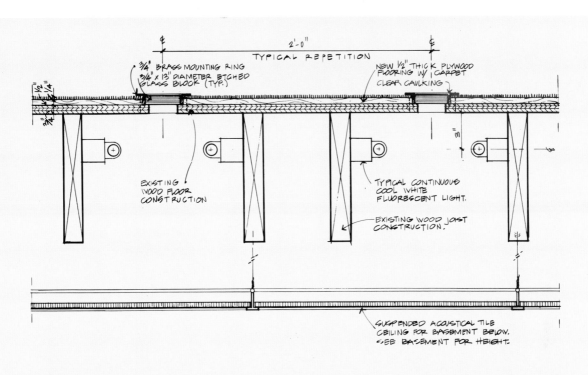

2'-0"
TYPICAL REPETITION

3/4" BRASS MOUNTING RING
3/4" X 13" DIAMETER ETCHED
GLASS BLOCK (TYP.)

NEW 1/2" THICK PLYWOOD
FLOORING W/ CARPET
CLEAR CAULKING

EXISTING
WOOD FLOOR
CONSTRUCTION

TYPICAL CONTINUOUS
COOL WHITE
FLUORESCENT LIGHT.

EXISTING WOOD JOIST
CONSTRUCTION.

SUSPENDED ACOUSTICAL TILE
CEILING FOR BASEMENT BELOW.
SEE BASEMENT FOR HEIGHT.

SECTION THRU FLOOR LIGHTING CONSTRUCTION
0   4   8   1²

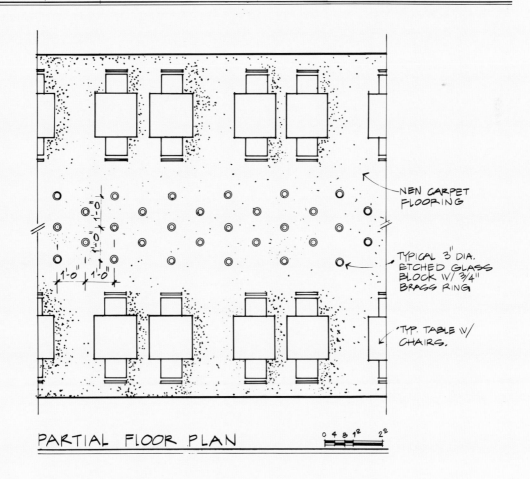

NEW CARPET
FLOORING

TYPICAL 3" DIA.
ETCHED GLASS
BLOCK W/ 3/4"
BRASS RING

TYP. TABLE W/
CHAIRS.

1'-0" 1'-0"

PARTIAL FLOOR PLAN
0 4 8 1²   2²

127

FOUNTAIN

THE BIG SPLASH
Miami, Florida

Architecture/Interior Design
Haverson-Rockwell Architects
Design Team
David S. Rockwell, Jay M. Haverson,
Hans Baehler
Fabrication
Hall Fountains
Photography
© Mark Ross Photography, Inc.

AT THE BIG SPLASH restaurant in Miami, Florida, "buoyant" refers not only to the establishment's predominant water motif but also to the mood such evocative detailing engenders in its patrons. Haverson-Rockwell Architects of New York City developed the festive Neoconstructionist environment to suggest the "open-seafood-market" atmosphere the owner requested.

Central to the success of the plan are six coral-block fountains that surround and define, in staggered formation, a buffet island overflowing with an exuberant display of fresh fish, vegetables, and salads. Behind and above the fountains Haverson-Rockwell installed draped canvas sails, which not only enhance the suggestion of market stalls, but also work in conjunction with the fountains to buffer sound within the 14,000-square-foot open space.

In dimensioning the fountains, the design team's primary concern was to angle the water jets high enough to be clearly seen without causing spillage outside the perimeter of the basin. The problem was resolved by mounting extra-fine nozzles 3 inches on center on the outer face of the trough. The water trajectory was then calibrated so that the water hits the backsplash in an arc and cascades down the face of the coral-block wall (*elevation/section*). Spillage is contained by a tiled concrete curb, which matches the floor around the island.

The design team added visual warmth to the fountain construction by bathing the coral-block walls with evenly distributed 300-watt underwater quartz uplights.

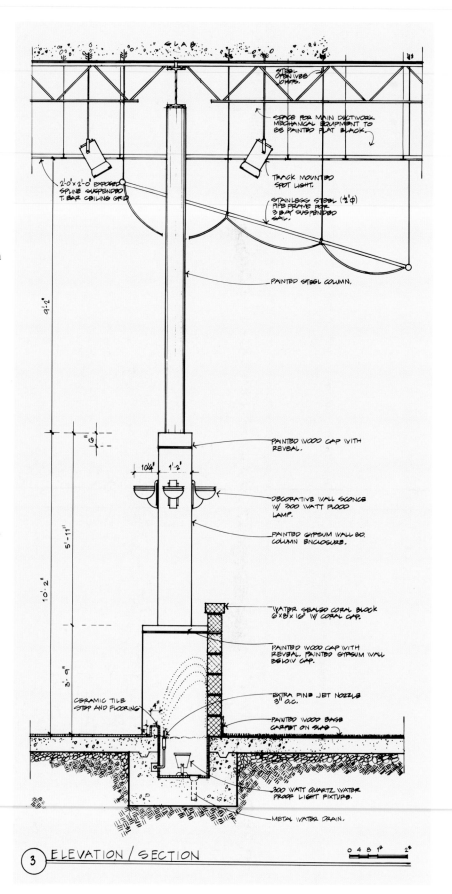

③ ELEVATION / SECTION

FOUNTAIN

HOLONIC STADIUM HEALTH CLUB

Shiseido, Inc., Tokyo, Japan

Architecture/Interior Design
Michael Graves, Architect;
Hamano Institute, Associate Architects
Design Team
Michael Graves, Eric Regh,
Michael Crackel, Suzanne Strum,
Stuart Parks, Ron Berlin (drawings)
Fabrication
Hakusuisha, Inc.
Photography
© Hamano Institute

INDOOR POOLS, especially those without access to natural light, may be dark, uninviting spaces. As a result, they are little used. Shiseido, Inc., owners of the franchised Holonic Stadium Health Clubs, commissioned Michael Graves to transform just such a cavernous space into "an airy facility with the contemporary feeling so important to the modern Japanese, but which respectfully observes the traditions of an ancient Japanese bath house."

The 14,000-square-foot health club occupies a portion of the ground floor and lower level of a new, 25-story, mixed-use tower in downtown Tokyo. The lower level already housed an Olympic-size lap pool covered by a shallow vaulted ceiling. Graves used the "generous but not lavish" budget to develop details that, by manipulating running water, carved-out space, and indirect lighting, achieve a light, airy ambience.

The thoughtful consideration and balancing of scale, form, and color within the space are the cornerstones of Michael Graves's successful design solution. Of particular note are four small fountains, which work subtly with details of grander proportion to effect changes in the perception of the space. The fountains are recessed into wall niches that echo, on a small scale, the positive/negative punching in and out of the long colonnade and light-washed back wall (*section/elevation*).

Graves specified a terra-cotta and ceramic-tile palette of finish materials in response to a client directive that the project exhibit "only Japanese materials" (*detail elevation; detail section*). The expanded checkerboard patterning of variously hued tiles in slate gray, basic white, blue-green, and gold reinforces a "kinetic-quality-of-water" abstraction that is both aesthetically appealing and appropriate to a Japanese sensibility.

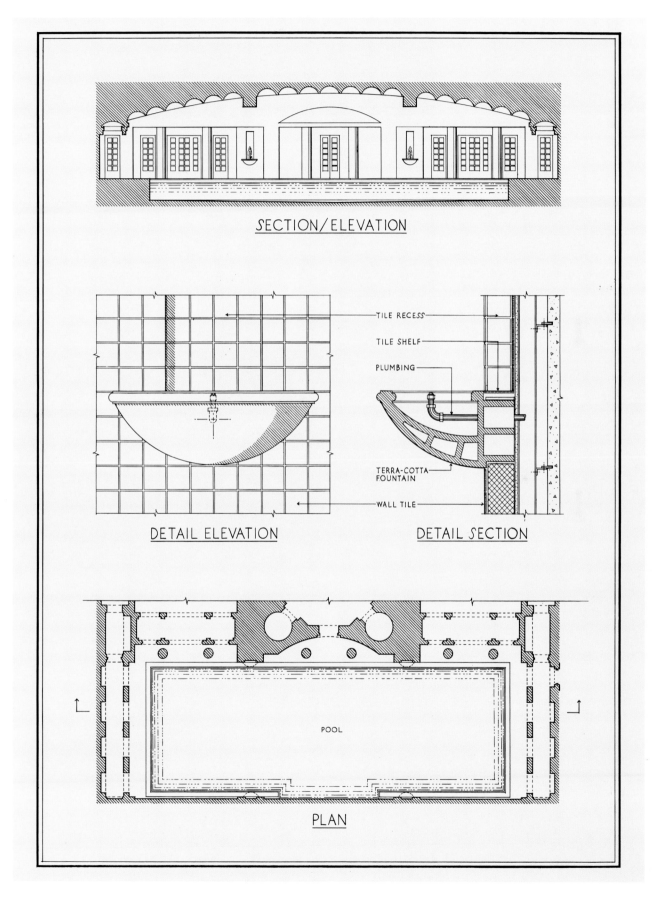

SECTION / ELEVATION

DETAIL ELEVATION

DETAIL SECTION

TILE RECESS

TILE SHELF

PLUMBING

TERRA-COTTA
FOUNTAIN

WALL TILE

POOL

PLAN

FOUNTAIN

PROCTER & GAMBLE COMPANY
Cincinnati, Ohio

Architecture
Kohn Pedersen Fox Associates PC
Metalwork
Tarpenning-Lafollette
Marble Fabrication
Blakleys Corporation
Photography
© Peter Aaron, ESTO

DOWNTOWN CINCINNATI'S central plaza, Fountain Square, is built around an ornate bronze, nineteenth-century exterior fountain that has become a nationally recognized architectural symbol of the city itself. Procter & Gamble Company, headquartered in Cincinnati, Ohio, serves as an internationally recognized symbol of the city's successful business community. When Procter & Gamble decided to construct its new world headquarters complex a few blocks east of Fountain Square, at the end of one of the city's main business thoroughfares, it seemed a natural "symbolic fusion" for architects Kohn Pedersen Fox Associates PC of New York City to design and install a focal-point fountain in the center of the building's main public lobby.

Kohn Pedersen Fox designed the Procter & Gamble fountain as a structural complement to its Fountain Square counterpart. The fountain is sited indoors rather than outdoors. The construction is marble rather than bronze, and the overall design exhibits stylistic restraint rather than the rococo flamboyance of its precursor. The design team conceptualized the fountain as a multifunctional detail: It generates warmth in the cool lobby; provides a sense of scale in the 6,400-square-foot high-ceilinged space; and produces soothing background noise.

The 13-foot-high fountain is built in three tiers (*elevation*). At the top is a metal basin from which water spills consecutively into two marble basins. The water cascades 6'-7" into the upper trough (which is 10 feet on the diagonal) and then 3'-0" into the lower trough (which is 17'-8" on the diagonal) (*plan*).

The internal structure of the fountain consists of a galvanized, welded steel frame—of 2-inch by 3-inch tubes and 3-inch channels—which is bolted to the floor (*section*). The visible exterior is constructed of 1-inch-thick white Vermont marble cladding panels and coping strips. The panels were cut to fit, hung from clips welded to the frame, and then caulked together (*section*). The cascade of water is actually contained by interior steel basins (*section*) made of 16-gauge stainless steel sheets welded to one another and to the frame.

The water pumping room is located on the floor below. The only part of the circulation system located inside the fountain is the feed pipe itself, which propels water up through the structure's core and out through eight spouts at the top of the column crowning the fountain (*section*). The body of the column was constructed of welded, solid bar stock. The column's capital—the upper basin—was configured of bent-and-welded 11-gauge stainless steel sheet.

The lobby—as well as the building's entire interior—was intended to exist in juxtaposition to the structure's massive exterior elements. The more lineal interior detailing was intended to give each design element a "strong sense of figural reading." The design team also took a cue from the Viennese Secessionist architect Otto Wagner in the choice of interior color palette and the emphasis on "ephemeral surface qualities."

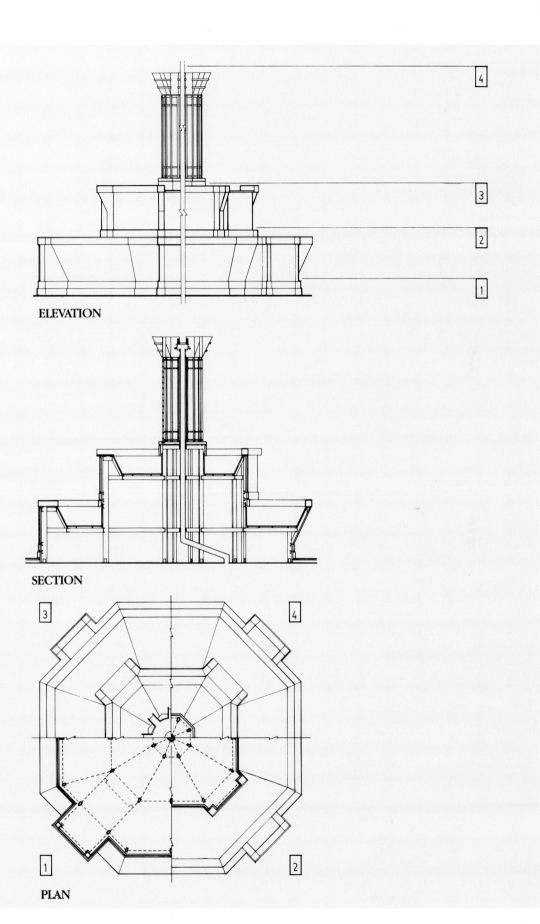

ELEVATION

SECTION

PLAN

KIOSK

**FIDELITY INVESTMENTS
SALES CENTER**
New York City

Interior Design
ISD Incorporated, New York City
Design Team
Daniel Gundrum, Paul Muench,
James Gueguierre, Henry Dreyfuss
(graphic design consultant)
Display/Graphic Fabrication
Rathe Productions
Lighting Consultant
Focus on Lighting (Steve Hefferan)
Photography
© Wolfgang Hoyt, ESTO

PROHIBITED BY THEIR laws of incorporation from offering investment advice
directly to the consumer, Boston-
based Fidelity Investments has done
the next best thing. Utilizing the
design resources of ISD Incorporated
of New York City, in November 1986
Fidelity opened a self-service information center for potential investors at
the corner of Park Avenue and 51st
Street in Manhattan.

The center's most outstanding design feature is a series of modular
electronic kiosks, handsomely clad in
horizontal cross-fire fiddleback Sapele
mahogany and inlaid with strips of
brushed stainless steel. ISD developed
the modular kiosk in response to the
client's request for "display flexibility"
in a format that would "combine high-
tech componentry within traditional
cabinetry."

Each of the five 7'-0"-high by 2'-0"-
wide by 6'-4"-long kiosks can house a
video monitor, a backlit transparency
screen, silk-screened laminate faces
for signage panels, and pigeonholes
for forms. The kiosks are divided
vertically into four equally dimensioned modular compartments. These
are connected and strengthened by
dowels, so that componentry can be
switched from one location to another—vertically and from side to
side (*elevation*). Any six panels can be
popped out and replaced.

Because the base construction con-

crete slab floor was installed 6 inches
below grade, the ISD design team
installed an independent finish floor.
Built-up from wood sleepers and
three plywood subfloors running in
opposite directions, the raised terrazzo floor platform allowed the imposition of an underfloor duct system
and installation of extensive concealed
wiring. The independent floor also
protects the space from the rumbling
vibrations emanating from the sub-

urban train tracks running underneath
the site.

Not content with the impressive
flexibility built into the kiosk units
themselves, ISD provided six configurations for their placement within
the information lobby. Circular
stainless steel bands embedded in the
terrazzo floor conceal electrical connections that provide power sources
for each of the six layout patterns
(*plan*).

7'-0"

VIDEO MONITOR

ACRYLIC FACE

ACRYLIC CARD HOLDER
ON VELCRO PAD

LACQUER FINISH TO MATCH
PLASTIC LAMINATE

3'-4"

FIXED PANEL WITH SHELF
PLASTIC LAMINATE FACE

CABLE DROPS

BRUSHED STAINLESS STEEL
BASE

0'-0"

1/2" DOWEL CONNECTIONS
(TYPICAL)

FIXED LAMINATE PANEL
WITH SILKSCREEN GRAPHICS

1/4" OPAL PERSPEX

FLUORESCENT LAMP
MOUNTED ON PERFORATED
MASONITE

1/4" CLEAR PERSPEX

SPRAY LACQUER ALL
INTERIOR SURFACES
TO MACH LAMINATE

HINGED PLASTIC LAMINATE
FACE PANEL

V C R RACKS

LOCK

LOCKING CASTORS

ELEVATION

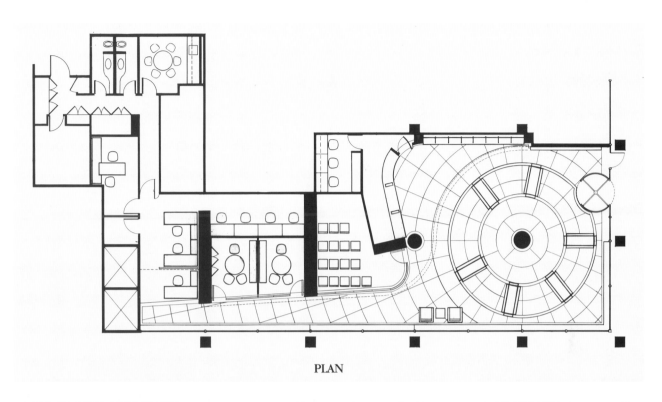

PLAN

KIOSK

CROCKER NATIONAL BANK
San Francisco, California

Architecture/Interior Design
Gensler and Associates/Architects,
San Francisco
Design Team
John Bricker, Barbara Leistico
Fabrication
Thomas-Swan Sign Co.
Photography
© David Wakely

FREE-STANDING KIOSKS ARE one of the better ways to convey information in public spaces. Because kiosks are constructed to human scale, people find them eminently approachable. For architects and designers charged with the task of looking out for the public's "health, safety, and welfare," these are important signage considerations.

When Crocker National Bank asked Gensler and Associates/Architects of San Francisco to plan and execute the renovation of its banking hall, Gensler immediately took the signage portion of the project to its in-house graphic-design department. The graphic design team promptly produced a highly effective series of kiosks that not only provide clear-cut departmental directions but also enliven the spaces they occupy.

The bank's kiosk module is unusual in that it is designed as a vertical tablet rather than as a cylindrical or multifaceted construction. The kiosk consists of only two pieces: a 4'-6" by 1'-6" slab of ½-inch tempered green glass, supported by a 1'-4½" by 1'-6" satin-finish bronze base of US3 bar stock. The glass slab fits into a raised slot in the bronze base and is secured by concealed brass-set screws to en-

sure a tight fit (*detail, side view*). The base is massive enough to permit the kiosk to be free standing. As requested by the client, the kiosk is movable.

The edges of the glass slab have been eased with an abrasive compound. The back of the slab, or its second surface, is sandblasted to create a translucent contrast for the lettering; decorative rules are applied to the front surface (*front elevation*).

The lettering on the kiosks was silk-screened onto the glass. Horizontal rules above and below the typography were appliquéd in gold leaf. The patterned rules were adapted from the ornamental pattern of an existing wall-mounted air grille (see page 207).

The bank is now a Wells Fargo Bank.

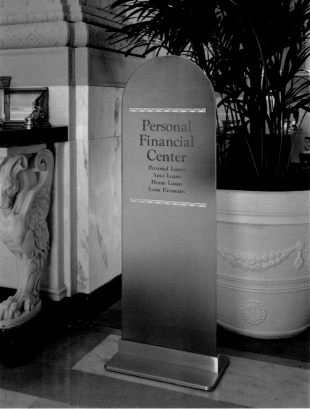

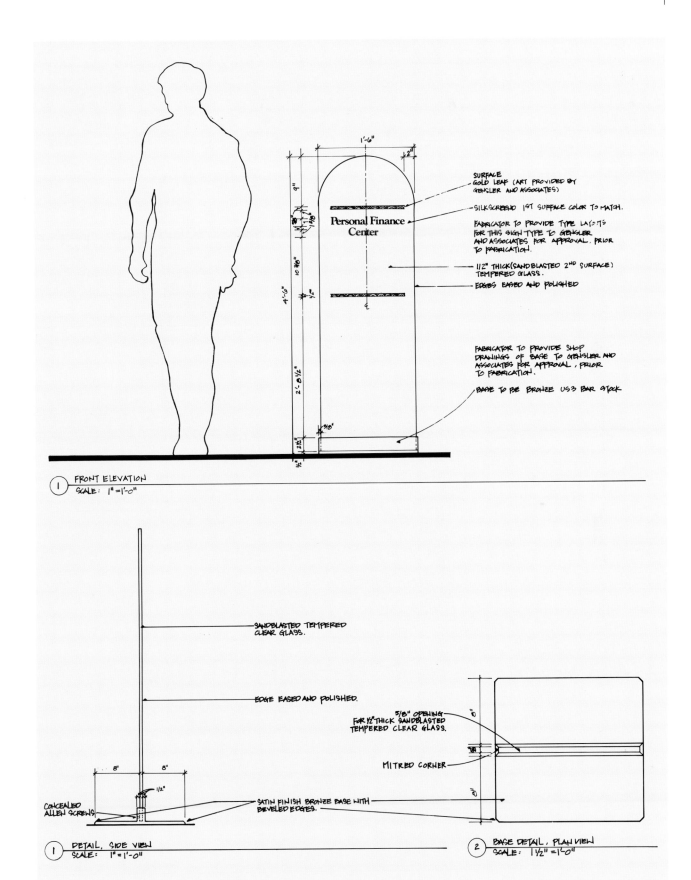

Personal Finance Center

SURFACE
GOLD LEAF (ART PROVIDED BY GENSLER AND ASSOCIATES)

SILKSCREEN 1ST SURFACE COLOR TO MATCH.

FABRICATOR TO PROVIDE TYPE LAYOUTS FOR THIS SIGN TYPE TO GENSLER AND ASSOCIATES FOR APPROVAL PRIOR TO FABRICATION.

1 1/2" THICK (SANDBLASTED 2ND SURFACE) TEMPERED GLASS.

EDGES EASED AND POLISHED

FABRICATOR TO PROVIDE SHOP DRAWINGS OF BASE TO GENSLER AND ASSOCIATES FOR APPROVAL , PRIOR TO FABRICATION.

BASE TO BE BRONZE US3 BAR STOCK

① FRONT ELEVATION
SCALE: 1"=1'-0"

SANDBLASTED TEMPERED CLEAR GLASS.

EDGE EASED AND POLISHED.

5/8" OPENING FOR 1/2" THICK SANDBLASTED TEMPERED CLEAR GLASS.

MITRED CORNER

CONCEALED ALLEN SCREWS

SATIN FINISH BRONZE BASE WITH BEVELED EDGES.

① DETAIL, SIDE VIEW
SCALE: 1"=1'-0"

② BASE DETAIL, PLAN VIEW
SCALE: 1 1/2"=1'-0"

137

KIOSK

BPC INDUSTRIES SHOWROOM
Chicago, Illinois

Architecture/Interior Design
GN Associates
Design Team
Thomas Mahoney, Kurt Monigle
Fabrication
General Exhibits and Displays
Photography
© Abby Sadin

THE VARIOUSLY SIZED and constructed display cabinets designed by GN Associates of New York City for the Chicago Merchandise Mart showroom of BPC Industries, a manufacturer of office accessories and architectural graphic signage products, were so useful that BPC asked the design team for "more." Specifically, GN Associates was asked to adapt a free-standing kiosk for use as a portable unit not only at the Merchandise Mart but also in dealers' showrooms throughout the United States.

The criteria for the creation of a portable kiosk was straightforward. Because showrooms vary in spatial character, the units were to be entirely self-contained, both structurally and aesthetically. The kiosks were to incorporate as much product display in as little space as possible. Finally, the units were to be relatively inexpensive to produce.

GN Associates responded with a kiosk of rigid triangular shape, constructed of plastic laminate for its durability (showroom maintenance is not necessarily tender), as well as for its color depth and resistance to fading. The cabinet, which is fabricated of three 3-foot-wide panels, rises 7'-4" above a plastic-laminated 2-inch base of contrasting color. An interior bracing system of wooden struts and steel clamps is screwed to the laminate at the top and bottom of the kiosk. Side panel joints are mitered and glued. A fitted laminate top caps the unit (*axonometric*).

The office accessories and signage products are displayed on projecting or recessed laminated lucite shelves (*axonometric*). A shelf's position may be changed by moving the stainless steel pin supports to other receptacle holes (*sections*).

The interior of the kiosk contains four vertical fluorescent tubes housed in standard fixtures screwed to the frame. The fixtures provide the unit with self-contained lighting without regard to the fixed display lighting of any particular space. The illumination is emitted through a milk-white lucite panel window at the back of the recessed shelving on one elevation of the kiosk (*sections*) and is refracted through the lucite shelving on a second side.

The company's logos are silk-screened onto the laminated surface by GN Associates.

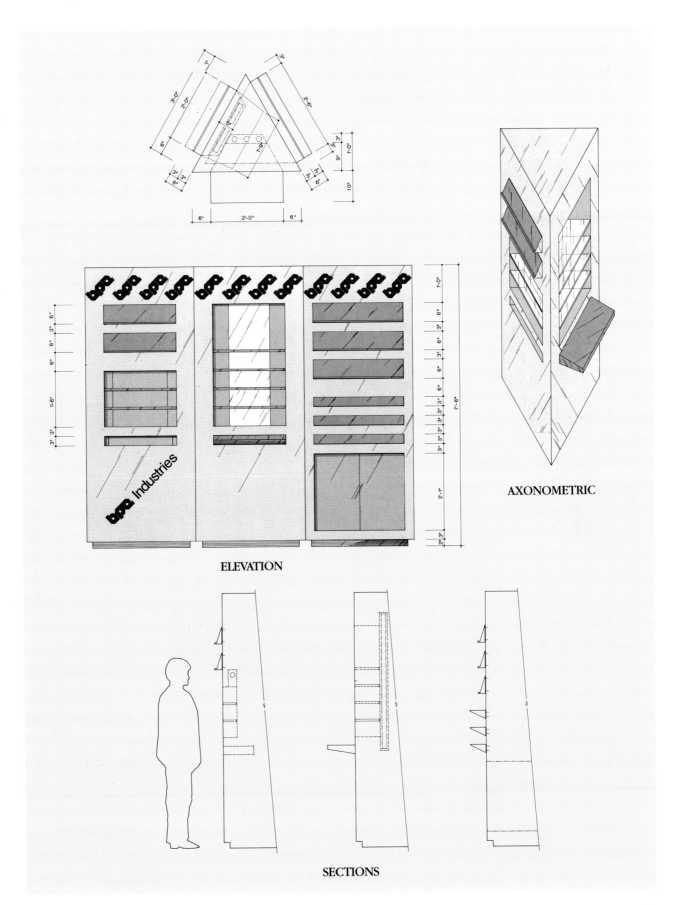

AXONOMETRIC

ELEVATION

SECTIONS

LIBRARY CIRCULATION DESK

DRINKER BIDDLE AND REATH
Philadelphia, Pennsylvania

Interior Design
H2L2 Architects/Planners

Design Team
Barry N. Eiswerth, Vibeke Lichten, Margaret Michel

Millwork
Knipp & Company

Photography
© Tom Bernard

LIBRARIES, WHETHER PUBLIC or private, must appear both accessible and authoritative if their books and periodicals are to be enthusiastically used but also responsibly returned. H2L2 Architects/Planners of Philadelphia achieved that delicate balance in the circulation desk they designed as a "control center" for the library at Drinker Biddle and Reath, a century-old Philadelphia law firm.

H2L2 was asked to design a desk that would accommodate book-card slots and a book-return drop, as well as provide storage and work-surface space for the librarian. Because the desk's construction was part of an overall expansion and renovation project, Drinker Biddle and Reath asked H2L2 to render the desk—as well as other custom pieces—in a "transitional but time-honored" style appropriate to the firm's extensive collection of early Philadelphia, floral, and sporting prints.

H2L2 was given a "quality-oriented" budget to develop the library detailing. The generous budget allowed them to choose solid cherry and fiddleback anigre panels as finish materials for the moldings and window mullions, as well as for the custom casework in the 4,800-square-foot library space. In order to blend the anigre (which is naturally white) with the cherry, a light stain was applied to each panel.

The circulation desk was shop-built in components to accommodate delivery by freight elevator, and the parts were assembled on site. As installed in the space, the elbow-shaped desk is anchored at one end by the librarian's office window wall and door; it is anchored at the other extremity by a substantial boxed-in structural column (*plan at top*).

The behind-the-scenes componentry of the circulation desk belies its smooth exterior facade. In addition to a full expanse of tackboard running the length of the work surface, two file cabinets and nine storage drawers are concealed behind the long section of the desk (*section at drawer unit*); a book-return chute and a rolling book cart are concealed behind the shorter dogleg component (*section thru end*). A cathode light strip, mounted in task-light position behind a cherry end cap, follows the configuration of the entire desk.

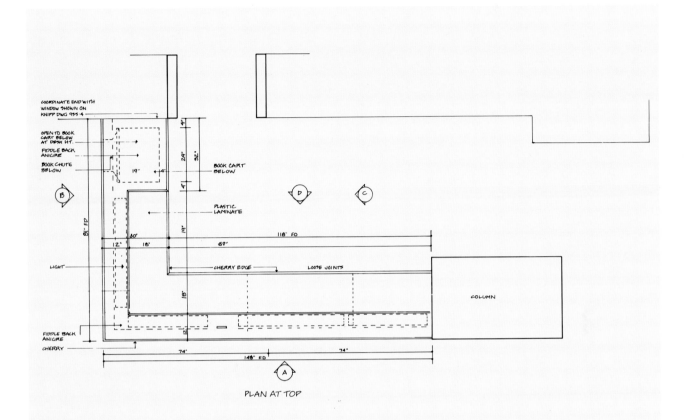

COORDINATE END WITH
WINDOW SHOWN ON
KNIPP DWG 995.4

OPEN TO BOOK
CART BELOW
AT DESK HT.

FIDDLE BACK
ANIGRE

BOOK CHUTE
BELOW

19"

BOOK CART
BELOW

B

PLASTIC
LAMINATE

D

C

81" FD

30"
12" 18"
59"
118" FD

LIGHT

CHERRY EDGE   LOOSE JOINTS

18"

COLUMN

FIDDLE BACK
ANIGRE

CHERRY

74"
146" FD
74"

A

PLAN AT TOP

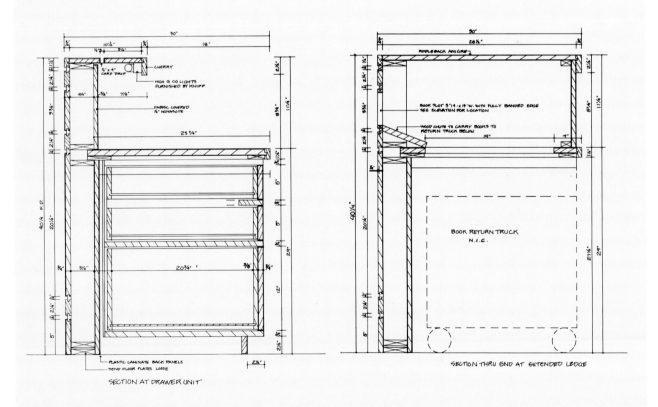

30"
10½"
18"
½" 3⅝"

CHERRY
¾" x 4"
CARD DROP

HIGH O CO LIGHTS
FURNISHED BY KNIPP

4¼" 3⅝" 7⅞"

FABRIC COVERED
½" HOMASOTE

25¾"

2½"

8¾"

11¼"

6"

40¼" FD
20¼"

5

23"

20¾"

3⅜" ¾"

12"

5"

2½"

PLASTIC LAMINATE BACK PANELS
SEND FLOOR PLATES LOOSE

2½"

SECTION AT DRAWER UNIT

30"
26½"

FIDDLEBACK ANIGRE

BOOK SLOT 3"H x 14"W. WITH FULLY BANDED EDGE
SEE ELEVATION FOR LOCATION

WOOD CHUTE TO CARRY BOOKS TO
RETURN TRUCK BELOW

19"

2½"

8¾"

11¼"

1"

40¾"
20¼"

BOOK RETURN TRUCK
N.I.C.

27⅛"

24"

5

SECTION THRU END AT EXTENDED LEDGE

LIBRARY REFERENCE DESK

THE NEW YORK PUBLIC LIBRARY
New York City

Architecture/Interior Design
Davis, Brody & Associates
Design Team
Norman Dorf, John Torborg,
Elin Avery, Madeline Lynch,
John McCoy, Ellen Albert,
Michael Lavoie
Millwork
Jaff Bros. Woodworks, Inc.
Photography
© Peter Aaron, ESTO

WHEN THE MAGNATES of New York City awarded Carrère & Hastings the original architectural commission in 1897 for The New York Public Library, the result of their common vision became one of the grand architectural monuments of the Western World—as well as one of its greatest public research resources.

So it remained for nearly a century, despite the fact that by the early 1980s decay of the landmark Beaux-Arts masterpiece was far advanced. In many parts of the building, maintenance had been put off for years. In other parts, clumsy and uninformed attempts at maintenance, renovation, or restoration had resulted in actual destruction. Worst of all, the floor plan had been repeatedly altered in violation of the architects' original intent. The result was a floor-level maze of "temporary" partitioned office space in nearly every major room.

In 1983 the library's board of trustees commissioned Davis, Brody & Associates of New York City to masterplan a massive restoration and modernization project—with the emphasis on strictly interpreted restoration. The overriding factor during every phase of the project was the smooth integration of the new with the old. There-fore, the trustees requested that all structural and decorative alterations to the building look, in as far as possible, like part of the original.

Although structural damage was not as evident in the 6,400-square-foot public catalog room as in some other areas of the building, renovation was clearly needed. The library's use of three separate computer networks required that, post renovation, each desk in the reference-deck enclosure function as a computer workstation for at least one of the systems. To centralize and incorporate state-of-the-art library-operations computer technology, the obvious solution was to reconfigure and expand the central reference-desk island. However, reconciling the expansion with the requirement that the new features be consistent with the original design created logistical and ethical problems. Because the reference desk was originally a small center island, there was not enough original millwork available to be reorganized into a larger enclosure. Moreover, the computer desks were to be constructed as standing height stations and, as such, were a new and potentially disruptive design element.

The designers kept faith with their mandate and accomplished a subtle integration of the systems and stations by enlarging the reference-desk island with millwork that duplicated the original segments. To accommodate computer wiring systems, the design team buried conduit pathways in the floor and concealed the access panels in the millwork (*north/south section thru reference counter*). They then built an "unfolded" version of the original desk (*floor plan*) and incorporated into it the hand-carved ornamental paneling and pilasters of the original structure. The size of the reference-desk service area now accounts for approximately forty percent of the floor area. The original paneling segments, which comprise about fifteen percent of the total millwork in the new enclosure, were placed in the 33'-4" new south elevation, which faces the public (*south elevation*). The design vocabulary of the new millwork, which includes columns, entablatures, gate enclosures, and computer desks, is based on other details of the reference room and the adjacent reading room (*reference counter elevation*).

Although the 2.6-million-dollar project was reasonable, it was not generous enough to preclude judiciously selected economies. In consequence, certain interior sections of the reference-desk island use fabric panels and plastic laminate instead of millwork; and new paneling and shelving was constructed of plywood veneer. In contrast, the exposed, public-facing woodwork is constructed of quarter-sawn solid white oak.

Solid columns strengthened with steel rods and sturdy, self-joined millwork in the bases bear much of the structure's weight. In elevation, the counter interior is braced with steel angles that were steel bolted to the cabinet frame (*section thru column & valence*). The entire unit is bolted to the quarry tile-over-concrete floor with 5-inch expansion bolts.

Lighting is built into the periphery of the entablature. Over the columned areas, incandescent uplight spots are mounted on swivels screwed to the inner frame. Over the computer desks, fluorescent tubes are mounted over grilles at the outer edge of the entablature to provide downlighting for the work surfaces below (*north/south section thru reference counter*).

LIBRARY REFERENCE DESK

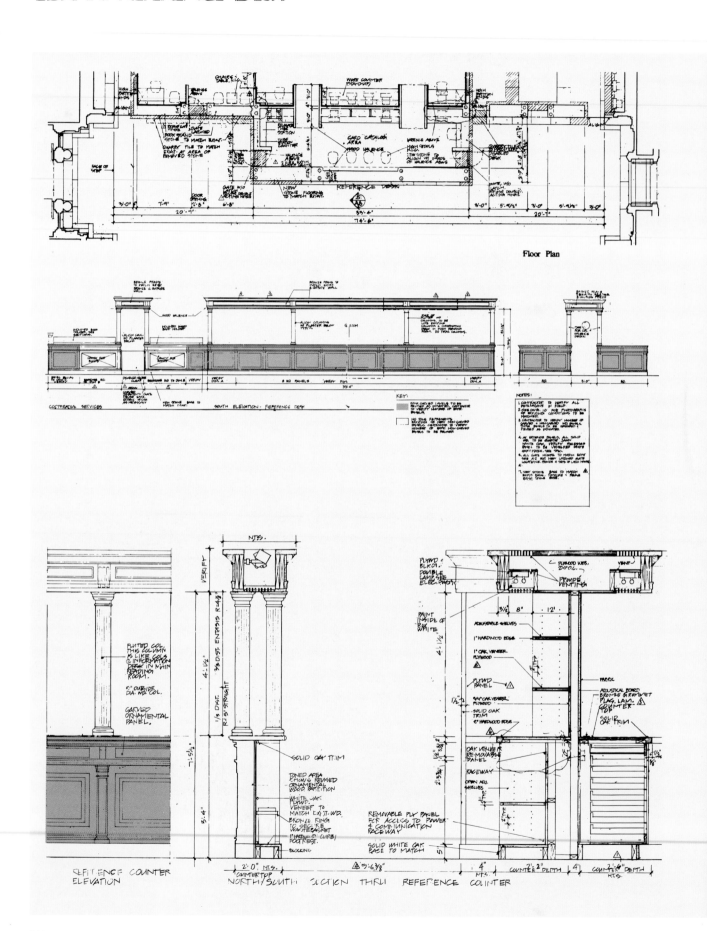

Floor Plan

SOUTH ELEVATION - REFERENCE DESK

KEY:

NOTES:

REFERENCE COUNTER ELEVATION

NORTH/SOUTH SECTION THRU REFERENCE COUNTER

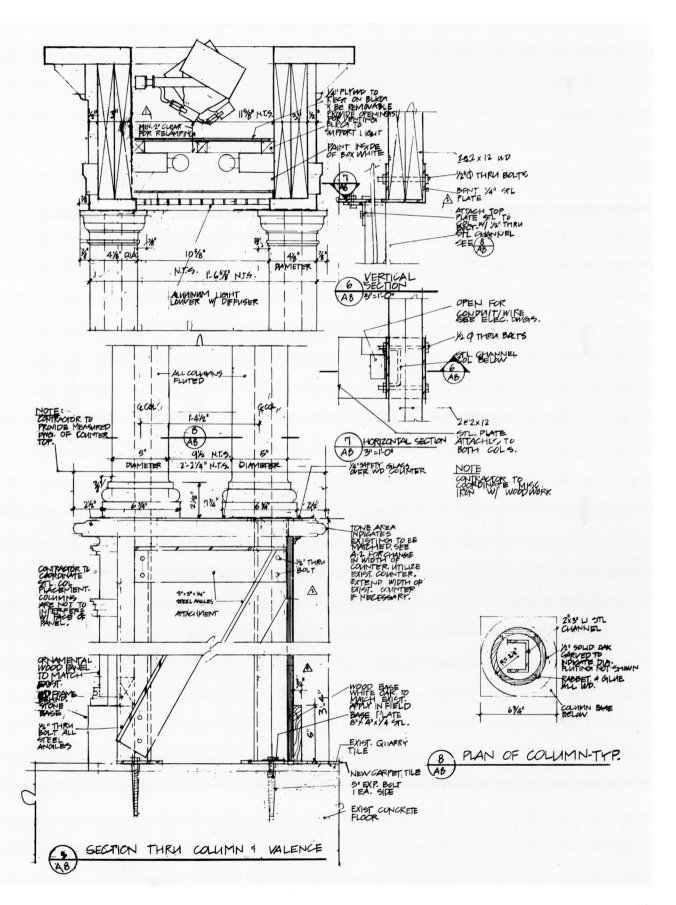

MIN. 2" CLEAR FOR RELAMPING

11 5/8" N.T.S.

4 1/2" 3" 3 1/2" 1/2"

1/4" PLYWD TO REST ON BLKG & BE REMOVABLE PROVIDE OPENINGS FOR ELEC. TO SUPPORT LIGHT

PAINT INSIDE OF BOX WHITE

2@2x12 WD

1/2" Ø THRU BOLTS

BENT 1/4" STL PLATE

ATTACH TOP PLATE STL TO BOLT W/ 1/2" THRU STL CHANNEL SEE 8/A8

3/8" 1/8"

3/8" 4 1/8" DIA 10 5/8" 4 1/8" DIAMETER 3/8"

N.T.S. 1'-6 5/8" N.T.S.

ALUMINUM LIGHT LOUVER W/ DIFFUSER

VERTICAL SECTION 6/A8 3"=1'-0"

OPEN FOR CONDUIT/WIRE SEE ELEC. DWGS.

1/2" Ø THRU BOLTS

STL CHANNEL COL BELOW 6/A8

ALL COLUMNS FLUTED

NOTE: CONTRACTOR TO PROVIDE MEASURED DWG. OF COUNTER TOP.

Ø COL 1'-4 1/2" Ø COL 8/A8

5" 9 1/2" N.T.S. 5"

DIAMETER 2'-2 1/4" N.T.S. DIAMETER

2@2x12

STL PLATE ATTACHES TO BOTH COLS.

HORIZONTAL SECTION 7/A8 3"=1'-0"

1/4" SAFETY GLASS OVER WD COUNTER

NOTE CONTRACTOR TO COORDINATE MISC IRON W/ WOODWORK

3/4" 2 1/4" 2 1/2" 7 3/4" 6 1/4" 2 1/2"

2 1/4" 6 3/4"

CONTRACTOR TO COORDINATE STL. COL PLACEMENT. COLUMNS ARE NOT TO INTERFERE W/ FACE OF PANEL.

3"x3"x1/4" STEEL ANGLES ATTACHMENT

1/2" THRU BOLT

TONE AREA INDICATES EXISTING TO BE MATCHED. SEE A-2 FOR CHANGE IN WIDTH OF COUNTER. UTILIZE EXIST. COUNTER. EXTEND WIDTH OF EXIST. COUNTER IF NECESSARY.

ORNAMENTAL WOOD PANEL TO MATCH EXIST. WD FRAME BEHIND STONE BASE 1/2" THRU BOLT ALL STEEL ANGLES

3/4" 3'-4" 5"

WOOD BASE WHITE OAK TO MATCH EXIST. APPLY IN FIELD BASE PLATE 8"X 4"X 1/4" STL.

EXIST. QUARRY TILE

NEW CARPET TILE

5" EXP. BOLT 1 EA. SIDE

EXIST CONCRETE FLOOR

SECTION THRU COLUMN & VALENCE 5/A8

2"x3" U STL CHANNEL

1/2" SOLID OAK CARVED TO INDICATE DIA. FLUTING NOT SHOWN RABBET & GLUE ALL WD.

R=3 1/4"

6 3/4"

COLUMN BASE BELOW

PLAN OF COLUMN-TYP. 8/A8

LIGHT FIXTURE

GREENWOOD GRILLE
Jenkintown, Pennsylvania

Architecture/Interior Design
The Hillier Group
(Barbara Hillier)
Glass Chandelier Fabrication
Ray King
Millwork
Woodlore
Photography
© Mark Ross Photography, Inc.

TRAIN STATIONS ARE NOT merely sites for the arrival and departure of trains and their passengers. Historically, they have also been gathering places— where people meet for a few minutes or even for a few hours of conversation. When SEPTA (the Southeastern Pennsylvania Transportation Authority) offered the Jenkintown, Pennsylvania, train-station building for business development, Benchmark Corporation, a New Jersey developer, seized the opportunity. Benchmark chose The Hillier Group of Princeton, New Jersey, to renovate the 9,000-square-foot space as a restaurant, named the Greenwood Grille.

Because the client wanted "a cost efficient means of renovating and adding on to the building," Hillier's design team opted to retain the slate floors, the terra-cotta tile walls, and the lofty barrel-vaulted ceilings extant from the original 1931 construction. The Hillier Group added a 3,000-square-foot addition under the existing platform canopy to accommodate a new bar and a gourmet take-out food service called The Market at Greenwood Grille. The design team then turned its attention to defining and detailing the 160-seat dining room.

The designers positioned the main dining room against the long wall of windows overlooking the platform. They separated the dining area from exterior noise and traffic congestion by imposing the bar area, as a buffer, in between. The design team defined the two interior "walls" of the space by constructing a painted drywall privacy partition, topped by a two-tiered, square-edge mahogany railing.

Hillier used the often-disregarded right-angle corners of the partition and railing wall as locations in which to integrate functional and decorative light fixtures. The fixtures are 1'-0"-square by 5'-1"-tall pedestals fabricated of solid mahogany panels. The corners of the polished panels are protected by mahogany molding. The

pedestals are similarly protected by additional segments of railing, which wrap the cut-out corners of the drywall partition (*plan/section @ corner post; axonometric*). The fixtures are topped by translucent cone shades, which echo, by inversion, Ray King's sculptural glass chandeliers.

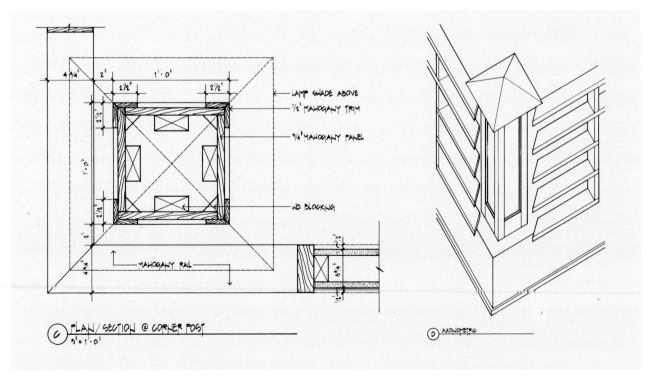

C PLAN/SECTION @ CORNER POST
3"=1'-0"

LAMP SHADE ABOVE
1/2" MAHOGANY TRIM
3/4" MAHOGANY PANEL
NO BLOCKING
MAHOGANY RAIL

D AXONOMETRIC

LIGHT FIXTURE

PROCTER & GAMBLE COMPANY
Cincinnati, Ohio

Architecture
Kohn Pedersen Fox Associates PC
Fabrication
Bergen Art Metal Works
Photography
© Jock Pottle

THE DETAILING OF Procter & Gamble Company's new headquarters in Cincinnati, Ohio, designed by Kohn Pedersen Fox Associates PC of New York City, was inspired, according to William Pedersen, by Frank Lloyd Wright's 1904 Unity Temple in Oak Park, Illinois. Wright's influence is evident throughout the project (see also pages 132 and 244). Nowhere is this influence more evident than in the suspended and cantilevered light fixtures Kohn Pedersen Fox designed for the headquarter's main public spaces.

The light fixtures serve as "glowing objects" that illuminate and further define tangential reflective surfaces, while functioning as ornamental geometric forms.

The design team constructed the fixture's open framework in stainless steel to emphasize the subtlety of the essentially "monochromatic" detailing palette that is reiterated throughout the interior. A frame-mounted 1'-7½"-high by 11½"-diameter sandblasted glass cylinder within the steel fixture provides color contrast (*plan*).

The fixture is suspended from the ceiling by four ⅝-inch-diameter, #4 stainless steel sleeves, which articulate to the framework's horizontal members that are constructed of 1-inch by 1-inch #4 stainless steel tubing (*rod and fixture section/elevation*). The joints of the sleeve and tubing segments are welded or internally screwed. The actual glass mounting is constructed of two vertical shafts of 1-inch by 1-inch tubing, which are connected to the frame by three ¾-inch segments of ½-inch tubing. The shafts are screwed to five 1-inch-wide #4 stainless steel sheet bands that encircle the glass cylinder. Each band is edged with bronze strips. The fixtures are suspended by brackets constructed of stainless steel bolted to the sheetrock wall.

The fixtures' electric feed lines run through one of the suspension tubes to a junction box suspended within the cylinder from a top horizontal 1-inch by 1-inch tube (*fixture section*).

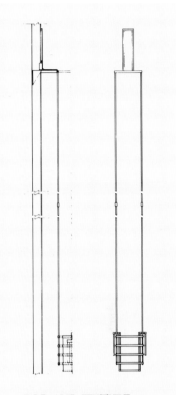

ROD AND FIXTURE SECTION/ELEVATION

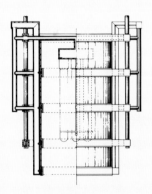

FIXTURE SECTION

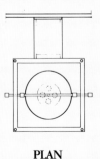

PLAN

LIGHT FIXTURE

**AMERICAN EXPRESS
HEALTH & FITNESS CENTER**
New York City

Interior Design
Swanke Hayden Connell Architects
Design Team
Don Kiel, Steve Cramer
Sculpture
Alexander Danel
Mannequin Fabrication
Goldsmith, Inc.
Neon
Say It In Neon, Inc.
Photography
© Wolfgang Hoyt, ESTO

THE DESIGN FIRM OF Swanke Hayden Connell Architects of New York City has designed a series of whimsical, humanoid light fixtures for the American Express employee health club in Manhattan which prove the point that good detailing can also supply good, light-hearted fun.

American Express asked the design team to visually enhance a series of exercise rooms that had been purposely pared to standard building finishes: carpeted floors, white-painted sheetrock walls, and a utilitarian lay-in ceiling. Because it was necessary for floor space to remain free of impedimenta, SHCA's team exercised their creativity by developing two details that addressed the client's mandate of visual enhancement—first, a straightforward built-out wall partition covered with mirror panels surmounted by cove lighting, and second, the supernatural human-form light fixtures, which occupy a nonintrusive series of alcoves created by the irregular perimeter of the building.

SHCA's design concept centered on the conversion of neon tubes to symbolic exercise objects. Each human-form fixture was modified to demonstrate to the end-user the type of exercise activity planned for each room. The fixtures display ergonomically correct postures for the exercises in question. The androgenous character of the fixtures was intentionally planned as a nonsexist statement.

Although the design concept of the fixtures was relatively simple, their fabrication and installation on site was a complicated matter of crucial sequencing. The unfinished fiberglass figures, sculpted by Alexander Danel, were brought to the construction site for "fittings" of steel support and electrical feed locations, internal mannequin armature, and partition-wall modifications (*figure section*). Representatives from the neon and mannequin fabricator firms, as well as a talented team of electricians, were on hand to make final adjustments to the installed product.

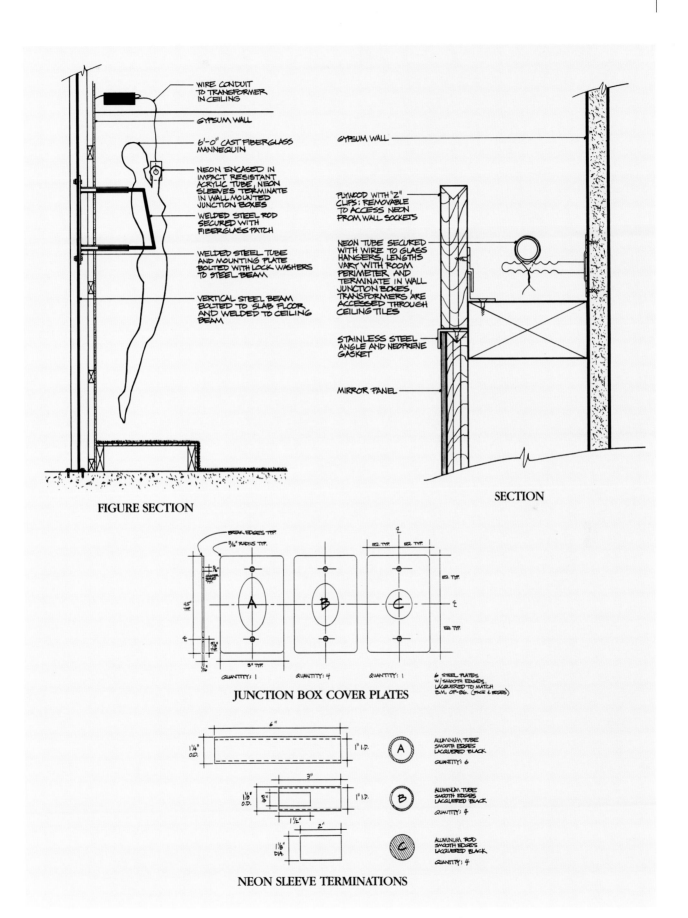

WIRE CONDUIT TO TRANSFORMER IN CEILING

GYPSUM WALL

6'-0" CAST FIBERGLASS MANNEQUIN

NEON ENCASED IN IMPACT RESISTANT ACRYLIC TUBE, NEON SLEEVES TERMINATE IN WALL MOUNTED JUNCTION BOXES

WELDED STEEL ROD SECURED WITH FIBERGLASS PATCH

WELDED STEEL TUBE AND MOUNTING PLATE BOLTED WITH LOCK WASHERS TO STEEL BEAM

VERTICAL STEEL BEAM BOLTED TO SLAB FLOOR AND WELDED TO CEILING BEAM

FIGURE SECTION

GYPSUM WALL

PLYWOOD WITH "Z" CLIPS; REMOVABLE TO ACCESS NEON FROM WALL SOCKETS

NEON TUBE SECURED WITH WIRE TO GLASS HANGERS, LENGTHS VARY WITH ROOM PERIMETER AND TERMINATE IN WALL JUNCTION BOXES, TRANSFORMERS ARE ACCESSED THROUGH CEILING TILES

STAINLESS STEEL ANGLE AND NEOPRENE GASKET

MIRROR PANEL

SECTION

BREAK EDGES TYP

3/16" RADIUS TYP.

A   B   C

QUANTITY: 1   QUANTITY: 4   QUANTITY: 1

6 STEEL PLATES W/ SMOOTH EDGES LACQUERED TO MATCH B.M. OP-86. (FACE & EDGES)

JUNCTION BOX COVER PLATES

6"
1 1/4" O.D.   1" I.D.

A   ALUMINUM TUBE SMOOTH EDGES LACQUERED BLACK
QUANTITY: 6

3"
1 1/8" 5/8" O.D.   1" I.D.
1 1/2"

B   ALUMINUM TUBE SMOOTH EDGES LACQUERED BLACK
QUANTITY: 4

2"
1 1/8" DIA.

C   ALUMINUM ROD SMOOTH EDGES LACQUERED BLACK
QUANTITY: 4

NEON SLEEVE TERMINATIONS

LIGHT FIXTURE

GOLDEN TULIP BARBIZON HOTEL
New York City

Interior Design
Judith Stockman & Associates
Design Team
Judith Stockman, Michael Zuckerman
Fabrication
Urban Archaeology
Lighting Consultant
Howard Brandston
Photography
© Langdon Clay

FINDING CREATIVE detailing solutions in a quasi-historic renovation project sometimes means evoking an era without copying its stylistic symbols. Judith Stockman & Associates, however, succeeded in designing a wholly original Art Nouveau wall sconce for The Barbizon (now called Golden Tulip Barbizon Hotel) in New York City.

Floral allusion, one of the most prominent symbols of the Art Nouveau era, is one of the principal motifs of the redesign of the venerable hotel, which was famous in its past as the archetypal women's residence. Floral allusion was also the inspiration for Stockman's sconce. The sandblasted glass "shade" consists of three stylized petals, and the sconce's bronze base is a representation of a flower's calyx.

The sconce's form and color restate the hotel's stylistic themes. The tea-rose hue of the petal glass reiterates the midrange tonal value of a carefully selected palette of interior surface finishes. Similarly, the transmission of light through the translucent glass of the sconce reiterates in miniature the honey onyx glow emitted by mezzanine-level light boxes that line the railing.

The construction of the sconce was

facilitated by casting the base—a process that reduces the number of visible assembly pieces to three (*elevation*). Concealed within the fixture's base are three angled steel brackets, which were slotted to permit set screws to pass through into the base itself (*plan*). Each glass petal is held in place by a bracket, tightened by its set screw. The petals themselves are not attached to one another. The base is affixed to the wall in two ways: by the casting itself, which is screwed to a steel backplate; and by the backplate, which, in turn, is expansion anchor bolted through a carborundum backing to the gypsum-board wall. The diffused quality of the light emitted from the sconce is caused by the use of a perforated, three-sided aluminum diffuser screwed to the backplate (*section*).

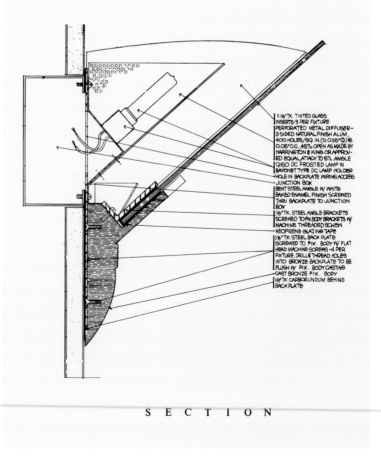

1⅛"TK. TINTED GLASS
INSERTS-3 PER FIXTURE
PERFORATED METAL DIFFUSER—
3 SIDED NATURAL FINISH ALUM,
400 HOLES/SQ. IN. (0.038"⌀) @
0.05"O.C., 46% OPEN AS MADE BY
HARRINGTON & KING OR APPROV-
ED EQUAL.ATTACH TO STL. ANGLE
Q150 DC FROSTED LAMP IN
BAYONET TYPE DC LAMP HOLDER
HOLE IN BACKPLATE WIRING ACCESS
JUNCTION BOX
BENT STEEL ANGLE W/ WHITE
BAKED ENAMEL FINISH SCREWED
THRU BACKPLATE TO JUNCTION
BOX
⅛"TK. STEEL ANGLE BRACKETS
SCREWED TO FIX.BODY BRACKETS W/
MACHINE THREADED SCREW
NEOPRENE GLAZING TAPE
⅛"TK.STEEL BACK PLATE
SCREWED TO FIX. BODY W/ FLAT
HEAD MACHINE SCREWS -4 PER
FIXTURE. DRILL& THREAD HOLES
INTO BRONZE.BACKPLATE TO BE
FLUSH W/ FIX. BODY CASTING
CAST BRONZE FIX. BODY
⅛"TK CARBORUNDUM BEHIND
BACK PLATE

S E C T I O N

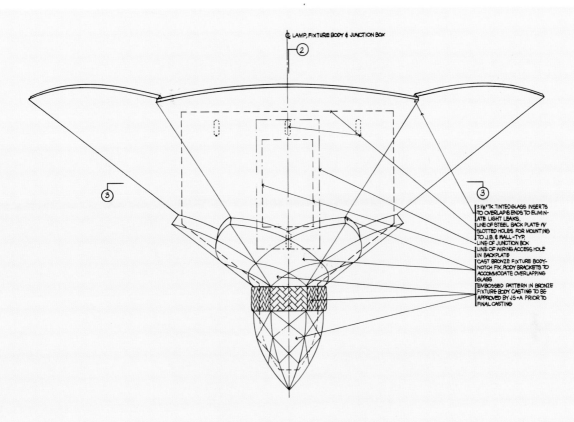

CL LAMP, FIXTURE BODY & JUNCTION BOX
②

③   ③

±1/8"TK TINTED GLASS INSERTS
TO OVERLAP 6 ENDS TO ELIMIN-
ATE LIGHT LEAKS.
LINE OF STEEL BACK PLATE W/
SLOTTED HOLES FOR MOUNTING
TO J.B. & WALL -TYP.
LINE OF JUNCTION BOX
LINE OF WIRING ACCESS HOLE
IN BACKPLATE
CAST BRONZE FIXTURE BODY-
NOTCH FIX. BODY BRACKETS TO
ACCOMMODATE OVERLAPPING
GLASS
EMBOSSED PATTERN IN BRONZE
FIXTURE BODY CASTING TO BE
APPROVED BY JS + A PRIOR TO
FINAL CASTING

E L E V A T I O N

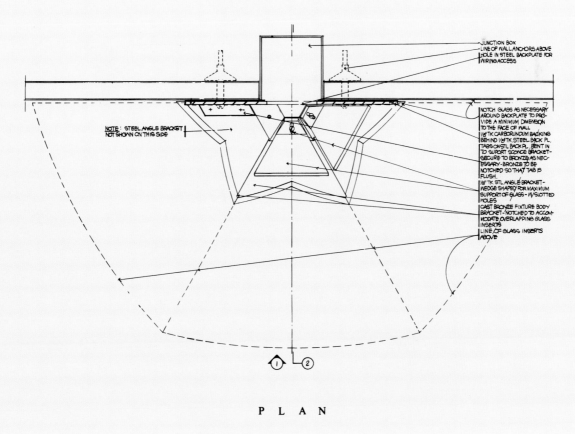

JUNCTION BOX
LINE OF WALL ANCHORS ABOVE
HOLE IN STEEL BACKPLATE FOR
WIRING ACCESS

NOTE : STEEL ANGLE BRACKET
NOT SHOWN ON THIS SIDE

NOTCH GLASS AS NECESSARY
AROUND BACKPLATE TO PRO-
VIDE A MINIMUM DIMENSION
TO THE FACE OF WALL
1/8"TK. CARBORUNDUM BACKING
BEHIND 1/8"TK STEEL BACK PL.
TABS ON STL BACK PL. BENT IN
TO SUPORT SCONCE BRACKET-
SECURE TO BRONZE AS NEC-
ESSARY-BRONZE TO BE
NOTCHED SO THAT TAB IS
FLUSH.
1/8" TK STL ANGLE BRACKET-
WEDGE SHAPED FOR MAXIMUM
SUPPORT OF GLASS - W/SLOTTED
HOLES
CAST BRONZE FIXTURE BODY
BRACKET-NOTCHED TO ACCOM-
MODATE OVERLAPPING GLASS
INSERTS
LINE OF GLASS INSERTS
ABOVE

◇① ②

P L A N

LIGHT FIXTURE

THIRD NATIONAL BANK
Nashville, Tennessee

Architecture/Interior Design
Kohn Pedersen Fox Associates PC
Fabrication
National Lighting Company
Photography
© Jock Pottle

ALTHOUGH ARCHITECTURE and interior design wend a cautious, sometimes awkward, and occasionally inspired path toward a Modernist/Traditionalist fusion, light-fixture design still suffers from polarized extremes. As a result, many design firms now devise their own transitional fixtures in order to finish a project in coordinated detail.

For the Third National Bank in Nashville, Tennessee, Kohn Pedersen Fox Associates PC of New York City graced the bank's massively scaled lobby with suitably scaled, custom-designed chandeliers. The fixtures are suspended from the center ceiling points of eight column bays. The 30'-0" height of the ceilings determined the 16'-0" proportionate length of the fixtures, which are suspended from painted escutcheon plates by single verdegris finished iron rods. On each chandelier, the suspension rod "pierces" a satin-finished bronze cap. The rod "fragments," at its lower extremity, into nine narrow rod sections that articulate with hooks to a tripartite barred cradle around four frosted hemisphere, or bowl, shades (*elevation*). Four smaller ornamental bronze spheres, placed at diagonal corners of the cradle's central section, define and "finish" the chandelier frame (*reflected plan*).

The opalescent bowl shades are constructed of double layers of plastic, a process that prevents visual perception of the lamps and wiring that may produce hot spots in ordinary light fixtures.

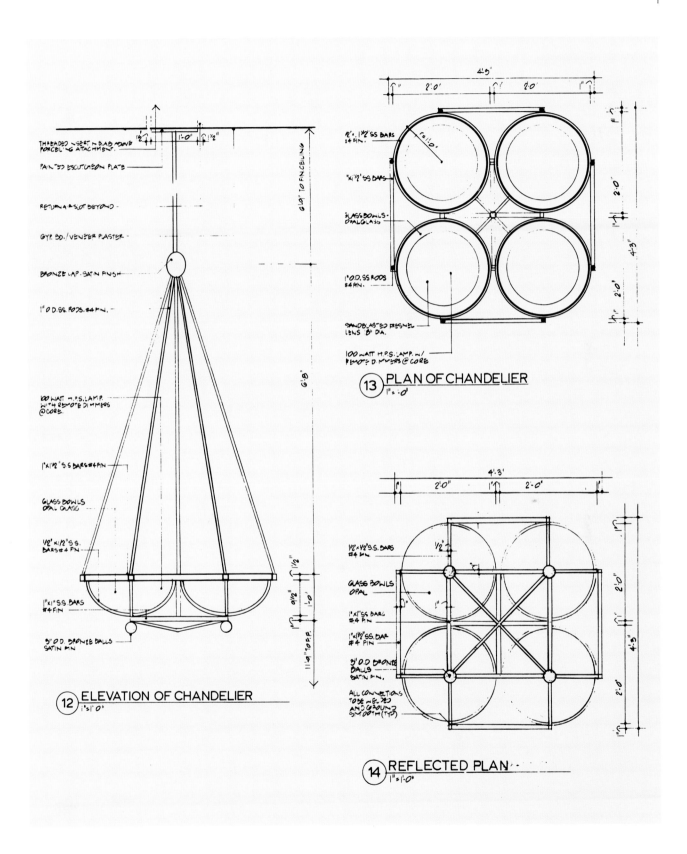

THREADED INSERT IN SLAB ABOVE FOR CEILING ATTACHMENT.

PAINTED ESCUTCHEON PLATE

RETURN AIR SLOT BEYOND

GYP. BD. / VENEER PLASTER

BRONZE CAP. SATIN FINISH

1" O.D. S.S. RODS. #4 FIN.

6'-9" TO FIN. CEILING

6'-8"

100 WATT H.P.S. LAMP. WITH REMOTE DIMMERS @ CORE.

1" x 1/2" S.S. BARS #4 FIN

GLASS BOWLS OPAL. GLASS

1/2" x 1/2" S.S. BARS #4 FIN

1" x 1" S.S. BARS #4 FIN

3" O.D. BRONZE BALLS SATIN FIN

1/2" 1/2"

1'-0"

9 1/2"

1'-0"

1'-9" TO FIN.

11'-9" TO F.F.

⑫ ELEVATION OF CHANDELIER
1" = 1'-0"

4'-5"

2'-0"   2'-0"

1"   1"   1"

1/2" x 1/2" S.S. BARS #4 FIN

"x 1/2" SS BARS

GLASS BOWLS OPAL GLASS

1" O.D. S.S. RODS #4 FIN.

SANDBLASTED FRESNEL LENS 8" DIA.

100 WATT H.P.S. LAMP. W/ REMOTE DIMMERS @ CORE.

2'-0"

2'-0"

4'-3"

1"   1"

⑬ PLAN OF CHANDELIER
1" = 1'-0"

4'-3"

1"   2'-0"   2'-0"   1"

1/2" x 1/2" S.S. BARS #4 FIN

1/2"

GLASS BOWLS OPAL

1" x 1" S.S. BARS #4 FIN

1" x 1/2" S.S. BAR #4 FIN

3" O.D. BRONZE BALLS SATIN FIN.

ALL CONNECTIONS TO BE WELDED AND GROUND SMOOTH (TYP.)

2'-0"

2'-0"

4'-5"

⑭ REFLECTED PLAN
1" = 1'-0"

153

MAGAZINE RACK

PENNSYLVANIA HOSPITAL
Bala Cynwyd, Pennsylvania

Interior Design
Wischmann Design Associates, Inc.
Design Team
Caroline Wischmann, Kim Siebert
Fabrication
Rohner Construction Co.
Photography
© Jack Neith

RIGHT-ANGLE GEOMETRY promotes efficient space planning. Paradoxically, in terms of square footage, right-angle planning often makes useless corners.

For a corner in the waiting area of Pennsylvania Hospital's OB-GYN satellite office in suburban Bala Cynwyd, Pennsylvania, Wischmann Design Associates, Inc., of Philadelphia has designed an innovative and inexpensive magazine rack/storage cabinet that makes every square inch count.

The design team divided the 4'-0"-high cabinet vertically into three concentrically stepped 10-inch racks over four 12- by 17-inch storage drawers (*elevation*). Each 4-inch-deep rack accommodates at least six magazine issues. The publications are held in place by solid mahogany bullnose guardrails, which, like the cabinet shell, have been mitered and scribed to the right-angle walls (*plan*). Drawers on roll-out glides (*section*) currently store informational pamphlets but were designed to accommodate a cache of children's toys as well.

The corner unit is constructed of inexpensive fiberboard, finished in Colorcore laminate for ease of maintenance. The soft teal green laminate was chosen to coordinate with the Zolatoned walls, mint green upholstery fabric, and pastel-flecked purple carpeting. The choice of color was in response to Pennsylvania Hospital's request, voiced by project coordinator Judy Faust, for "an office environment that is feminine without being stereotypically fussy."

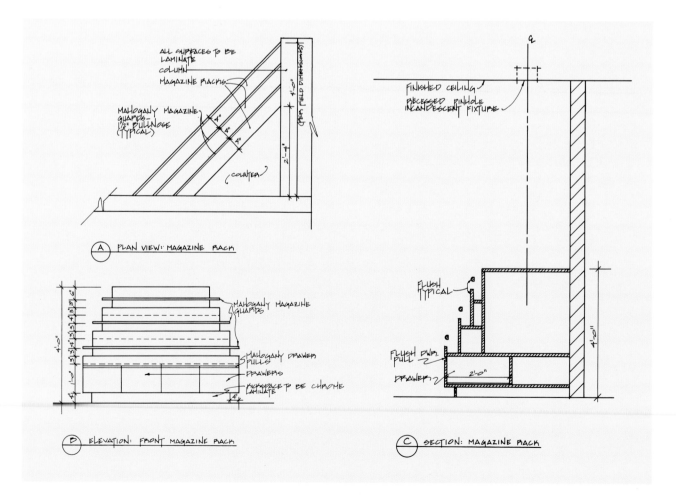

154

Maître D'Hôtel Stand

CAROLINE'S
New York City

Architecture/Interior Design
Dorf Associates

Design Team
Martin Dorf, Ivonne Dorf, Hugh Boyd, Andrea McBride (rendering)

Sculptural Mosaic
Lauren B. Miller

Graphic Design
de la Houssaye Design

Tile
Nemo Tile; American Olean; Hastings

Cabinetry and Ornamental Foot
Hamilton Woodworking

Patina
Metal Forms, Inc.

Photography
© Durston Saylor

THE IMAGINATIVE RE-USE of obsolete industrial space adds a certain hard dynamism to Manhattan's nightlife that flows from the commercial power of the metropolis by day. Dorf Associates of New York City undertook such a conversion project when they designed Caroline's, a trendy comedy club-cum-restaurant located near the Fulton Fish Market.

The design team chose to capitalize on—rather than downplay—the "trashy" elements of the neighborhood by bringing subtly integrated rusty metal, broken glass, and rubble into the project in order to project an environment of "excitement rather than of squalor." Where the actual elements would not work, Dorf conveyed its texture and appearance through stylized shapes and application methods.

Intended to create an immediate, strong visual focus, the massive maître d'hôtel stand is the most important of several sculptural details that give definition to the club's interior space. The stand is designed as an inverted section of a square-base pyramid; thus it seems to tower—as a skyscraper would—viewed from above. The stand is built of birch plywood mounted on two sections of pipe. The visual surface is created by ¼-inch-thick, glazed ceramic tiles that were hand-selected and glued to the plywood (*elevation*). Four drawers of analine-stained, oak veneer plywood, opening to the rear of the cabinet, are mounted on heavy-duty glides (*section*).

The design team was so determined to make this free-standing quasi-sculpture a successful foil to the neutral space of the warehouse that they constructed a full-scale cardboard mock-up to enable them to judge proportion and design. The designers also experimented with various tile patterns and colors. The result expresses the crazy-quilt character of the tumble-down fish market surroundings of the club—but also the polished, chic atmosphere of the club itself.

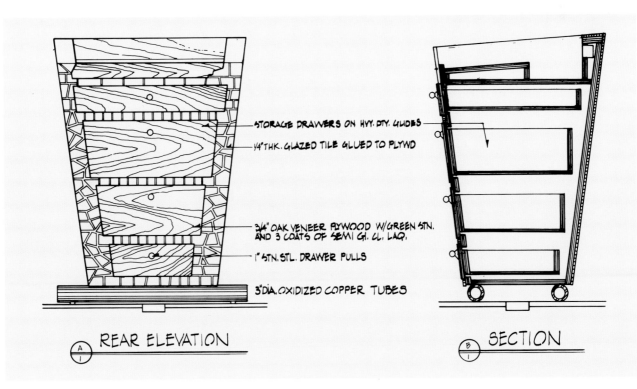

STORAGE DRAWERS ON HVY. DTY. GLIDES

¼"THK. GLAZED TILE GLUED TO PLYWD

¾" OAK VENEER PLYWOOD W/GREEN STN. AND 3 COATS OF SEMI GL. CL. LAQ.

1" STN. STL. DRAWER PULLS

3"DIA. OXIDIZED COPPER TUBES

Ⓐ/1 REAR ELEVATION

Ⓑ/1 SECTION

MEMO/AV CABINET

ALABAMA POWER COMPANY
Birmingham, Alabama

Architecture/Interior Design
Geddes Brecher Qualls Cunningham;
Gresham, Smith and Partners
Design Team
James P. Snyder, Adrienne Bussey
Fabrication
Akira Wood
Photography
© Durston Saylor

A DETAIL THAT visually enhances a space may be said to be "good." A detail that also performs a specific function within that space is thought to be "better." The "best" details offer some nuance of technical innovation as well. At the Alabama Power Company in Birmingham, Alabama, one of the best details, designed by Geddes Brecher Qualls Cunningham of Philadelphia in joint venture with Gresham, Smith and Partners of Birmingham, is a memo/audio-visual/graphic display cabinet, which appears in every executive-floor conference room.

Although company executives had definite usage requirements in mind for the cabinet, accommodating the technical paraphernalia those requirements necessitated within the pre-existing structural restrictions of the conference rooms presented the more difficult design challenge.

For example, to retain free circulation around the conference table the depth dimension of mandated audio-visual equipment suggested recessing the cabinet into the wall. However, wiring in the wall prevented the design team from recessing the cabinet completely (*section A*). Lateral restrictions created even more difficulties. A previously installed cove light, a curtain, and audio-visual switch controls not only limited the outside dimensions of the cabinet when closed but, more importantly,

made it necessary for the cabinet doors to swing open in sections (*elevation*).

The design team divided the cabinet horizontally. An upper cabinet, closed by mirror-image doors, houses a television monitor and pinup tackboard surfaces. The lower cabinet, concealed by a conventional space-saving flipper door, provides storage for a projector, a coffee set, and a telephone and conference-call equipment (*axonometric*).

The creation of a completely innovative, laterally opening, two-section L-shaped door with flush pulls on the upper cabinet neatly circumvents the switch panel. The concealed hinge is positioned midway between the front

corner and the wall within the bull-nosed secondary side door panel, rather than on the facade corner of the cabinet. As the cabinet door swings open, the hinge pivots a full 180 degrees, allowing the two right-angle sections of the door to lie flush with the cabinet and the wall—a position exactly opposite to the way it rests when closed (*jamb detail; door detail*).

The aesthetic quality of the cabinet is as impressive as is its functionalism. The doors and trim were constructed of ¾-inch-thick plywood over which a plain-sliced mahogany was applied. The interior of the unit was veneered in mahogany and plastic laminate (*sill at horizontal door*).

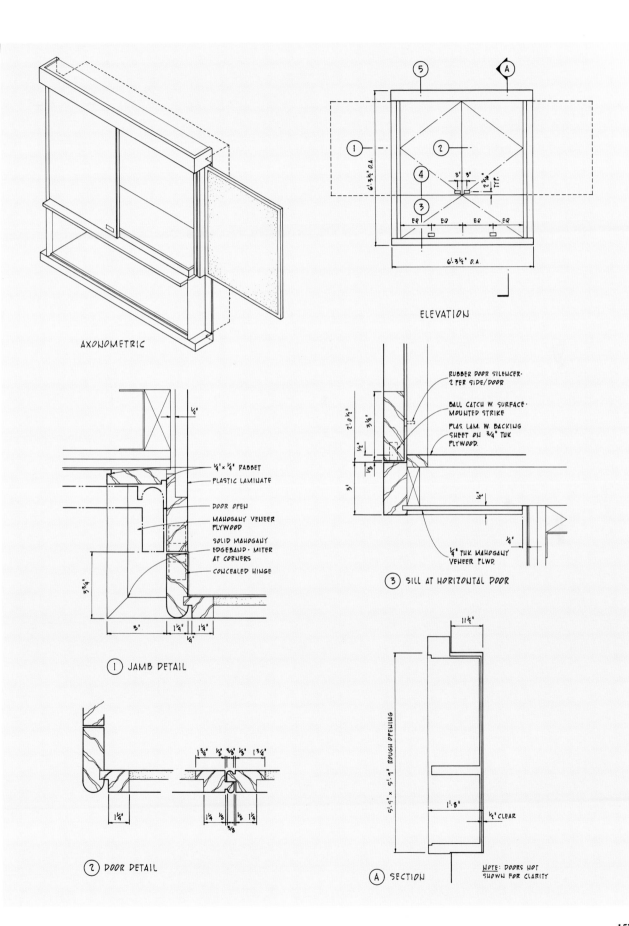

AXONOMETRIC

ELEVATION

① JAMB DETAIL

- ¼" × ¼" RABBET
- PLASTIC LAMINATE
- DOOR OPEN
- MAHOGANY VENEER PLYWOOD
- SOLID MAHOGANY EDGEBAND · MITER AT CORNERS
- CONCEALED HINGE

② DOOR DETAIL

③ SILL AT HORIZONTAL DOOR

- RUBBER DOOR SILENCER · 2 PER SIDE/DOOR
- BALL CATCH W. SURFACE · MOUNTED STRIKE
- PLAS. LAM. W. BACKING SHEET ON ¾" TUK PLYWOOD.
- ¼" THK MAHOGANY VENEER PLWD.

Ⓐ SECTION

NOTE: DOORS NOT SHOWN FOR CLARITY

OPERATIONS CENTER

**AMERICAN TELEPHONE &
TELEGRAPH OPERATIONS CENTER**
Atlanta, Georgia

Architecture/Interior Design
Thompson, Ventulett, Stainback &
Associates, Inc.
Design Team
Sheri Raiford, Becky Ward
Millwork
Murphy and Orr
Photography
© Jonathan Hillyer

AT&T ADVERTISES that "long distance is the next best thing to being there." Based on company statistics that tabulate the number of telephone calls generated each day to domestic and foreign destinations, the American consumer agrees. To maintain efficient management of an ever-increasing network load demands not only the continuous installation and maintenance of state-of-the-art technology but also the development of a number of regional operations centers from which that technology can be monitored.

Thompson, Ventulett, Stainback & Associates, Inc., of Atlanta, Georgia, designed the AT&T Atlanta Regional Network Operations Center with the obvious understanding that the ultimate purpose of high technology—no matter how complex its componentry—is to simplify. Bearing that technological truth in mind, the firm's goal was to create an interior in which the simplicity of the construction and appearance would match that of the operations themselves.

The function of the operations center is, in a sense, a super-sophisticated version of the old-fashioned telephone switchboard. Here, instead of switching one call at a time, traffic managers monitor immense computers that continuously switch and route long-distance calls through regional long-distance circuits. The traffic manager's role is essentially one of passive nonintervention. However, if the computer makes a directional error or if overload occurs, the manager can override the computer manually with console-mounted controls at his or her workstation. AT&T's mandate was to assure each traffic manager full visual access to the computerized display panels located on the control room's front wall.

The design team divided the control-room floor into three levels by building a two-tiered and bilaterally angled stair-stepped platform above the base floor level. The differing elevations are connected by a ramp (*plan @ network operations area*). Free-standing workstations, which conform to the shape of the platform, were installed on both levels. The upper tier of four workstations was raised 1'-9" above the lower level (*profile @ bookcase w/CRT*) to afford the traffic managers seated at these stations an equal view of the display panels. Recesses within the fascia of the rear platform also provide open storage space for those seated on the lower level.

The desks were constructed of ¾-inch plywood for ease of assembly. The structural integrity of the three-sided shape permits each desk unit to be entirely free standing; there are no knee-grazing interior supports or braces (*profile @ CRT*). The plywood surfaces are faced with plastic laminate for durability and ease of maintenance. The joints are mitered and glued. Installed within each workstation is a custom-designed screen-tilt mechanism that enables each manager to set the CRT screen at his or her own preferred angle with the twist of a thumb screw.

The color scheme of beige, warm brown, and blue was chosen to avoid distraction from the visual focus of activity on the main display panels. A strip of stainless steel, which suggests molding, was set into the fascia reveal of each desk as the only concession to ornament in the design scheme.

The design team included a small observation amphitheater on the second story of the center, from which visitors and trainees may watch the activity below through a plate glass window wall.

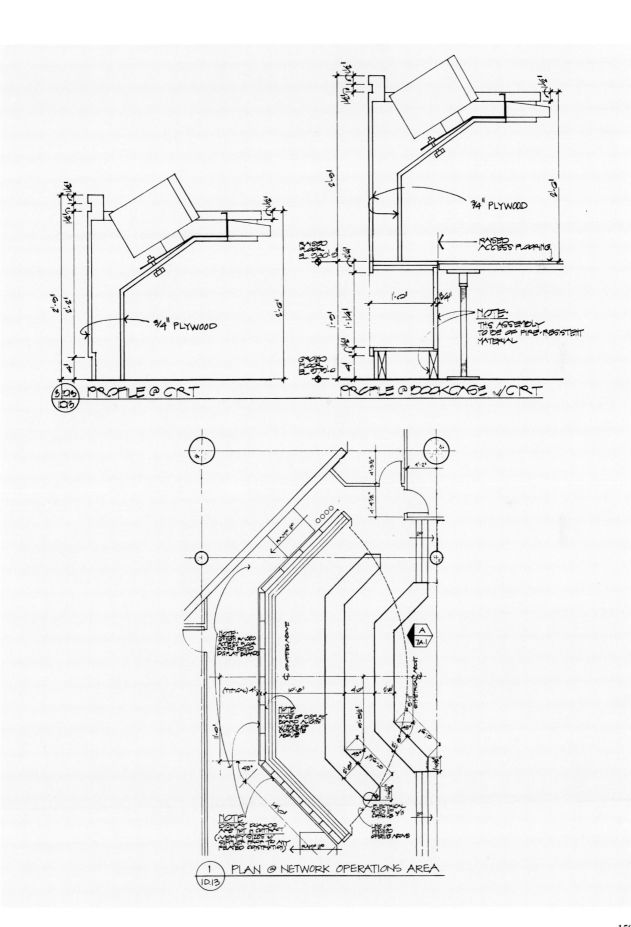

¾" PLYWOOD

PROFILE @ CRT

¾" PLYWOOD

RAISED
ACCESS FLOORING

NOTE:
THIS ASSEMBLY
TO BE OF FIRE-RESISTENT
MATERIAL

PROFILE @ BOOKCASE w/CRT

NOTE:
THIS RAISED
ACCESS FLOOR
EXTENDS BEHIND
DISPLAY BOARDS

NOTE:
FACE OF DISPLAY
BOARD ALIGNS
w/POCKET
ABOVE

NOTE:
DISPLAY BOARDS
ARE NOT IN CONTRACT
(VERIFY SIZES w/
SUPPLIER PRIOR TO ANY
RELATED CONSTRUCTION)

ELECTRICAL
CONTRACTOR
CAULK

THIS IS
FINISHED
OPENING ABOVE

A
7A.1

1   PLAN @ NETWORK OPERATIONS AREA
10.13

ORGAN ENCLOSURE

**ST. PATRICK'S
EPISCOPAL CHURCH**
Washington, D.C.

Architecture/Interior Design
Hartman-Cox Architects
Design Team
George Hartman, Peter Grina,
Lee Becker
Organ-Enclosure Fabrication
Holtkamp Organ
Photography
© Harlan Hambright

IT IS MORE DIFFICULT NOW than it was a few centuries—or even a few decades—ago for church congregations to raise money for facility renovation. More difficult still is the financing of completely new construction. Therefore, it is rare for an architect or designer today to land as substantial an ecclesiastical commission as that given to Hartman-Cox Architects by St. Patrick's Episcopal Church in Washington, D.C.

Hartman-Cox responded handsomely to the opportunity by designing a beautifully detailed church and day school that expresses the "updated American Gothic look" the congregation requested.

The focal point of the new 2,500-square-foot church is a 31'-3"-high organ entablature scribed to the rear wall of the chancel. One of the advantages of locating the organ console and pipe entablature on the ceremonial chancel dais was the provision of a natural cover for the instrument's tracking rods (*side elevation/section*). The organ, which was moved in pieces from the old facility, was originally designed to fit into a low-ceilinged nave. Refitting the instrument into the more prominent chancel location accomplished two goals outlined by the parish steering committee: a credible end axis and a backdrop. Enclosed in its new tripar-

tite cabinetry (*front elevation*), the organ establishes a termination to the church's main axis and provides a visually interesting "ecumenical" backdrop to increasingly varied chancel activities.

The increased height of the organ-enclosure casework allowed not only a reconfiguration of the instrument's existing voice pipes but also the possibility of future additions. In re-

turn for the organ's architectural reinforcement of the new space, the chancel backdrop location provided a more suitable acoustical environment for the organ.

The Hartman-Cox team specified sturdy midwestern poplar for the enclosure's construction. Enameled beadboard paneling, varied in scale and frontal projection, elaborates the reference to Arts and Crafts styling.

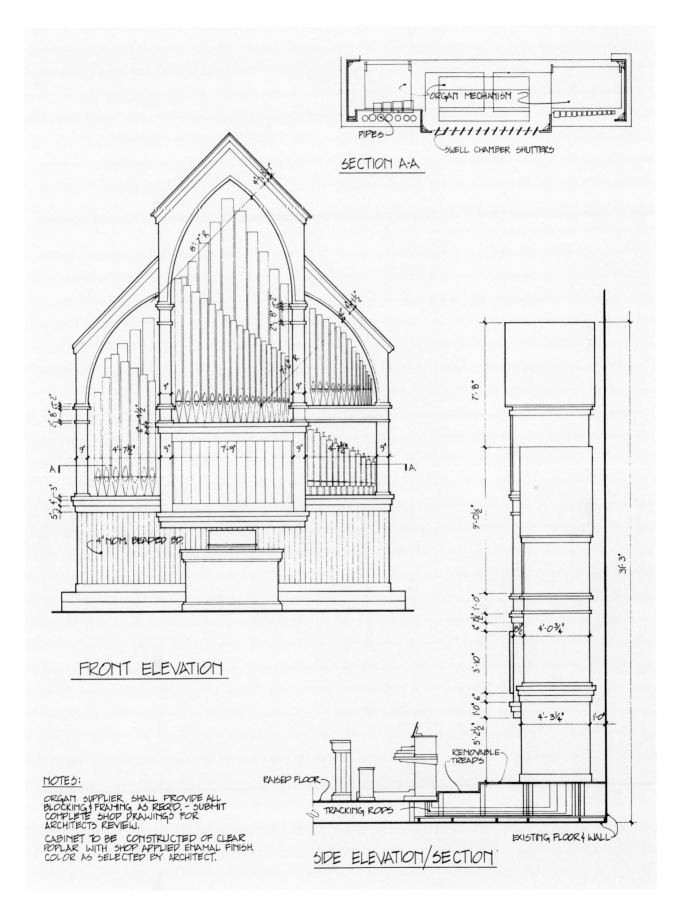

SECTION A-A

ORGAN MECHANISM

PIPES

SWELL CHAMBER SHUTTERS

FRONT ELEVATION

4" NOM. BEADED BD.

SIDE ELEVATION/SECTION

RAISED FLOOR

TRACKING RODS

REMOVABLE
TREADS

EXISTING FLOOR & WALL

NOTES:

ORGAN SUPPLIER SHALL PROVIDE ALL
BLOCKING & FRAMING AS REQ'D. - SUBMIT
COMPLETE SHOP DRAWINGS FOR
ARCHITECTS REVIEW.

CABINET TO BE CONSTRUCTED OF CLEAR
POPLAR WITH SHOP APPLIED ENAMEL FINISH,
COLOR AS SELECTED BY ARCHITECT.

PARTITION

THE CENTER CLUB
Baltimore, Maryland

Architecture/Interior Design
RTKL Associates Inc.
Design Team
Les Bates, Michael Gotwald,
Dennis Gaffney, Susan Basile
Fabrication
Valley City
Photography
© Victoria Lefcourt

IT WOULD BE DIFFICULT to estimate the number of franchised restaurants, bars, and private dining rooms in America that have adopted a privacy partitioning system constructed of paneling and etched glass in combination. The partitioning RTKL Associates Inc. of Baltimore/Washington, D.C., designed for The Center Club in Baltimore, Maryland, however, is in no way diminished by statistics. Rather, it serves as a striking example of the way in which good detailing transcends what may have become design cliché elsewhere.

The Center Club, which has become known as "Baltimore's premier private dining and business club," occupies the fifteenth and sixteenth floors of a modern high-rise tower overlooking Baltimore's celebrated waterfront. RTKL Associates developed the low partitioning system in response to a client request for "dining room privacy which does not conflict with harbor views." Because a granite guardrail outside the windows blocked direct downward views, the design team installed 1'-0" raised platforms to accommodate the sightline of diners seated near the window. The partitioning not only makes the platform transition less visible, it also serves as a safety railing around the raised platform (*"A" elevation*).

RTKL Associates conceived the 210-seat dining area as an open space, subdivided at seating level with partitions to give diners a sense of privacy. For versatility in form and enclosure function, the 3'-0"-high base unit partitions were designed in both rectangular and curvilinear modules. The

transom glass in the curved sections is not curved but simply placed straight, section by section, through each arc of the curve (*"C" plan section*).

In a symbolic nod to Baltimore's status as a world port, RTKL Associates used an international palette of rich woods as partition finishing materials. The design team specified a West African Bubinga veneer for the paneling. (All 30,000 square feet of Bubinga veneer in the project came from a single tree, guaranteeing uniformity of color and grain.) The trim was applied in solid Honduras mahogany.

In order to promote a sense of openness, the partitions were de-

signed with glass transom panels in the 1'-0" upper segment (*"B" section*). Etched beveled glass (with a 1-inch clear margin) was used to maintain privacy.

The partitions are constructed of ¾-inch veneered plywood panels bolted to steel angles, which are bolted to the concrete floor. The partitions are hollow but are braced internally with hardwood blocking and with 2⅞-inch studs (*"B" section; "C" plan section*). The trim is glued to the blocking and paneling (*"B" section*). The brass supports for the solid brass handrails are screwed through the paneling into the studs at the ends of panels.

STRAIGHT PANELS CURVED PANELS

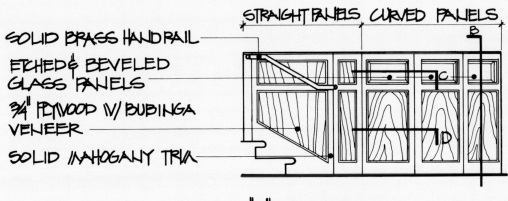

SOLID BRASS HANDRAIL

ETCHED & BEVELED
GLASS PANELS

3/4" PLYWOOD W/ BUBINGA
VENEER

SOLID MAHOGANY TRIM

A. "A" ELEVATION

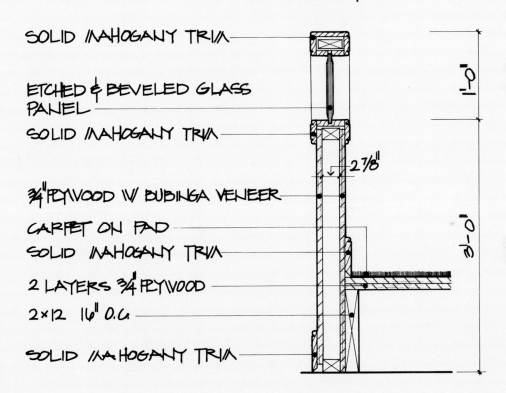

SOLID MAHOGANY TRIM

ETCHED & BEVELED GLASS
PANEL

SOLID MAHOGANY TRIM

2 7/8"

3/4" PLYWOOD W/ BUBINGA VENEER

CARPET ON PAD

SOLID MAHOGANY TRIM

2 LAYERS 3/4" PLYWOOD

2×12 16" O.C.

SOLID MAHOGANY TRIM

1'-0"

3'-0"

B. "B" SECTION

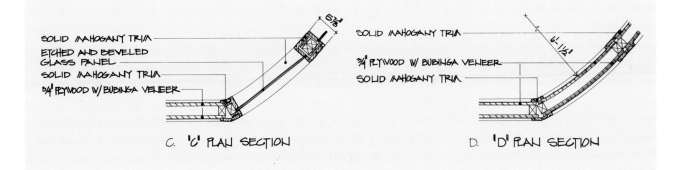

SOLID MAHOGANY TRIM
ETCHED AND BEVELED
GLASS PANEL
SOLID MAHOGANY TRIM
3/4" PLYWOOD W/ BUBINGA VENEER

5 7/8"

SOLID MAHOGANY TRIM

3/4" PLYWOOD W/ BUBINGA VENEER
SOLID MAHOGANY TRIM

6'-1 1/2"

C. "C" PLAN SECTION

D. "D" PLAN SECTION

PARTITION

SITE PROJECTS, INC.
New York City

Architecture/Interior Design
SITE Projects, Inc.
Design Team
Alison Sky, Joshua Weinstein,
Wendy Tippetts
Fabrication
Gordon Construction
Photography
© Peter Aaron, ESTO

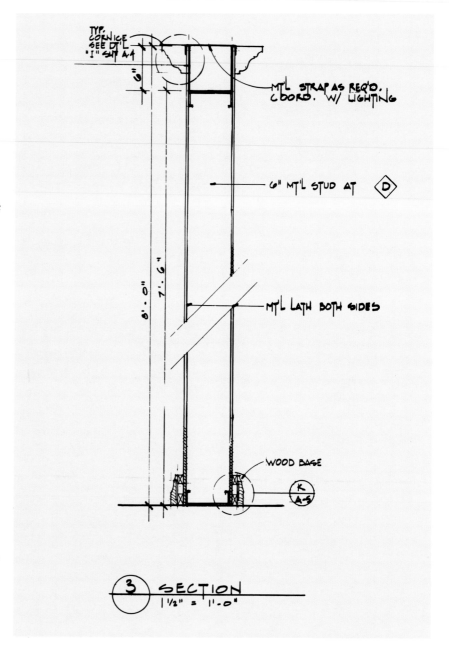

IT PAYS TO CHECK IN periodically with the innovators at SITE Projects, Inc. in New York City to see what's happening on the whimsical, witty fringe of architecture, interior design, and detailing. What can be found in-house at SITE's own offices is a Neoconstructionist, yet Neoclassical, partition wall.

SITE's studio and offices occupy a loft in the Bayard Building, Louis Sullivan's only New York City project. The 1898 structure was originally designed for light industrial use. The building later became a factory and was partly destroyed. SITE took over the building's loft in 1984 and immediately restored the original plaster walls and ceiling, as well as the Sullivan-designed structural column capitals.

The SITE loft functions both as an "open" office and as a gallery for models and drawings. SITE's belief in the open-office concept springs from its commitment to "an ongoing collaborative design process." Recognizing the need for intrastaff accessibility, however, did not preclude the inverse necessity for the firm to provide minimal personal privacy, as well as an adequate number of hanging display surfaces.

SITE built several 8'-0"-high see-through partitions (*elevations*) within the 6,800-square-foot space. By virtue of their stamped sheet-metal egg-and-dart cornices, the partitions evoke the industrial elements of the Sullivan era. The partitions' cleverly contrived wire-lath framework elicits the reaction of delighted surprise we anticipate from this firm's work.

Each partition is built up from a steel runner screwed into the hardwood floor, onto which light-gauge, 6-inch cold-form studs have been mounted (*section*). A sheet-metal light trough (the only custom-built piece of the wall) was positioned above the studs. The covering lath was screwed to the studs and to the trough. Uplighting provided by the troughs is produced by standard 8'-0" double-tube fluorescent fixtures (*section*). The edges and corners were joined with standard corner and J-beads. All of the junctions were screwed. Three-and-one-half-inch stock pine base-boards were screwed to the studs, and cornices were top mounted with screws on either side of the trough.

To remove residual oils left over from the manufacturing process, SITE had each metal piece cleaned in a vinegar solution before applying paint primer. The metal was then spray painted white, producing a "ghost-of-the-past" interior—the surreal "scrimlike" effect of which is enhanced by the daily flurry of staff and client movement.

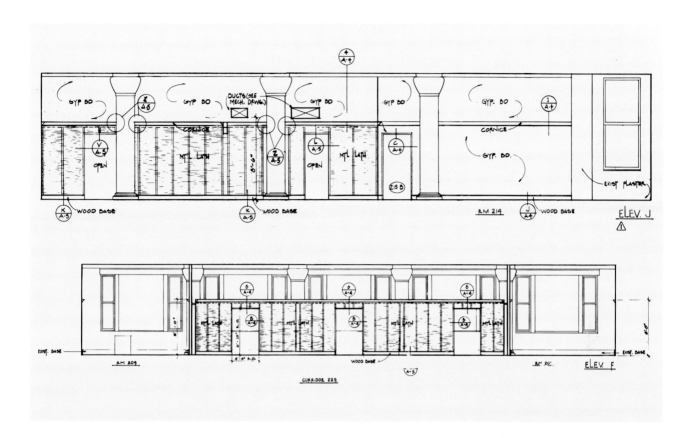

PARTITION

HEARST & COMPANY ARCHITECTURE, INC. OFFICES
San Francisco, California

Architecture/Interior Design
Hearst & Company Architecture, Inc.
Design Team
Nan Hearst, Patrick Carney,
T.C. Chen, Michael Garavaglia
Fabrication
Dirk Espinosa-Setchko Construction
Photography
© Tim Street-Porter

PUTTING GROUP SPACE into perspective is one of the things Hearst & Company Architecture, Inc., of San Francisco does best. Nowhere is this more evident than in the design firm's own offices, which radiate an Eastern-inspired tranquility and elegance of line that is usually seen only in the Orient.

Preexisting conditions, such as the lack of windows in the reception area, stimulated a design concept responding to natural lighting conditions. Fortunately, of the two offices on either side of the reception area, one is blessed with a skylight, while the other office boasts three windows. This natural light played a significant role in the final design. To prevent the loss of this valuable natural illumination, the design team used transparent doors. The remaining structure is made of a corresponding translucent material that provides privacy for the firm's workers without interfering with the transmission of light.

This goal was accomplished by using Japanese-like partitions of transparent and translucent glass panels in a grid of black-lacquered wood. The grid pattern, which is actually a mod-

ern interpretation of a Japanese shoji screen, is repeated strikingly in the floor's black granite border and light gray carpet. The partition not only maximizes light but also encourages interoffice communication, while, at the same time, reducing the overall noise level.

The grid was made of vertical-grain, black-lacquered, Douglas fir and was simply nailed together. The glass was sandblasted to create translucent panels and was then easily installed in place. The next step added wood stops and muntins to the frame. Finally, the window-wall frame was bolted to both the floor and the ceiling to hold it in place (*head detail*). Surprisingly, the design was relatively inexpensive because, as the designer says, "It is just carpentry."

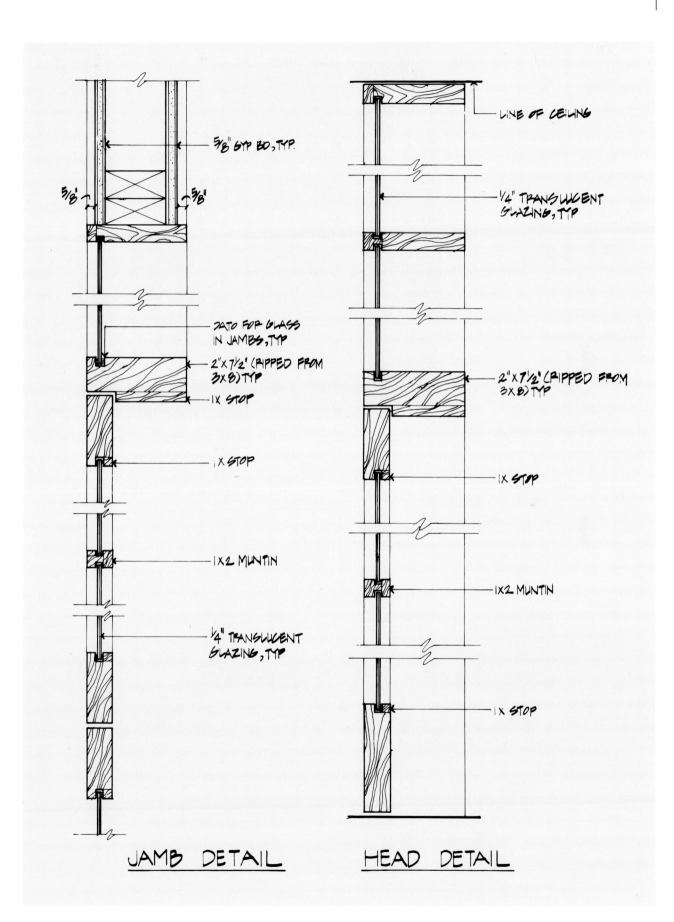

⁵⁄₈" GYP BD, TYP.

⁵⁄₈"   ⁵⁄₈"

DATO FOR GLASS
IN JAMBS, TYP

2"x 7½" (RIPPED FROM
3x8) TYP

1X STOP

1X STOP

1X2 MUNTIN

¼" TRANSLUCENT
GLAZING, TYP

LINE OF CEILING

¼" TRANSLUCENT
GLAZING, TYP

2"x 7½" (RIPPED FROM
3x8) TYP

1X STOP

1X2 MUNTIN

1X STOP

JAMB DETAIL   HEAD DETAIL

PARTITION

**FINANCIAL GUARANTY
INSURANCE COMPANY**
New York City

Architecture/Interior Design
Emilio Ambasz & Associates, Inc.
Design Team
Emilio Ambasz, Evan Douglis,
Gary Chan, Mark Robbins,
Ken Laser, Terry Kleinberg,
Dominique Leferin
Glass Fabrication
Active Glass Corporation
Sandblasting
Shefts Carved Glass Company
Photography
© Paul Warchol

INSURING MUNICIPAL BONDS against default is the business of the Financial Guaranty Insurance Company (or FGIC). Because FGIC's "product" may be regarded as risk evaluation, acceptance, and management, company executives searched for an architect "of like mind" to design their headquarters in the Wall Street area.

FGIC commissioned Emilio Ambasz & Associates, Inc., of New York City to design the 60,000-square-foot space. At FGIC, Ambasz upheld his reputation as a risk-taking visionary and trend-setting pioneer by developing a plan and detail package that visually redefines the conservative, "rich" atmosphere traditionally associated with Wall Street financial offices. Ambasz declares: "The suggestion of richness comes from that which cannot be measured. Intimations of expanding limits, of multilayered meanings, are far more effective than the obvious grand gesture."

"Multilayered" takes on literal significance in the FGIC offices by virtue of two related details—beaded silk-thread partitioning curtains that define spatial divisions in open areas and complementary vertically striped sandblasted glass partitions that enclose the offices and circular conference rooms. The beaded-curtain

partition is an Ambasz signature detail originally designed for the Belgian Banque Bruxelles Lambert. The sandblasted glass partition was developed specifically for FGIC.

To maximize the proportion of usable space within the relatively small 254-square-foot conference rooms, the design team imposed the glass partition in a circular form. The circular motif was then amplified by a free-standing circular credenza, which hugs the room's circumference, and a circular conference table centered in the space.

The glass partition detail is constructed of twenty-four abutted 2'-2¼"-width by 8'-0"-height glass panels, plus two similarly sized glass doors (*reflected ceiling plan*). Each panel is anchored in place at the top and at the bottom by a 1¾-inch by 4-inch anodized aluminum rail. The bottom

rail rests on a metal sidelight track that is bolted to the concrete slab (*glass wall detail at threshold*). The top rail is supported by a 1¾-inch steel I-beam, which is buttressed by welded steel struts and attached to the upper slab (*glass wall detail at ceiling*).

The partition panes are fabricated of ½-inch-thick tempered glass, sandblasted with ¼-inch stripes that alternate between the front and back surfaces (*glass pattern detail*). The alternate-side sandblasting technique achieves semitransparency in oblique views and translucency when viewed directly.

Recessed ambient lighting is generated by a peripheral circle of garbo fluorescent light fixtures, which are supplemented by four radially mounted modolinear diffusers (*reflected ceiling plan*).

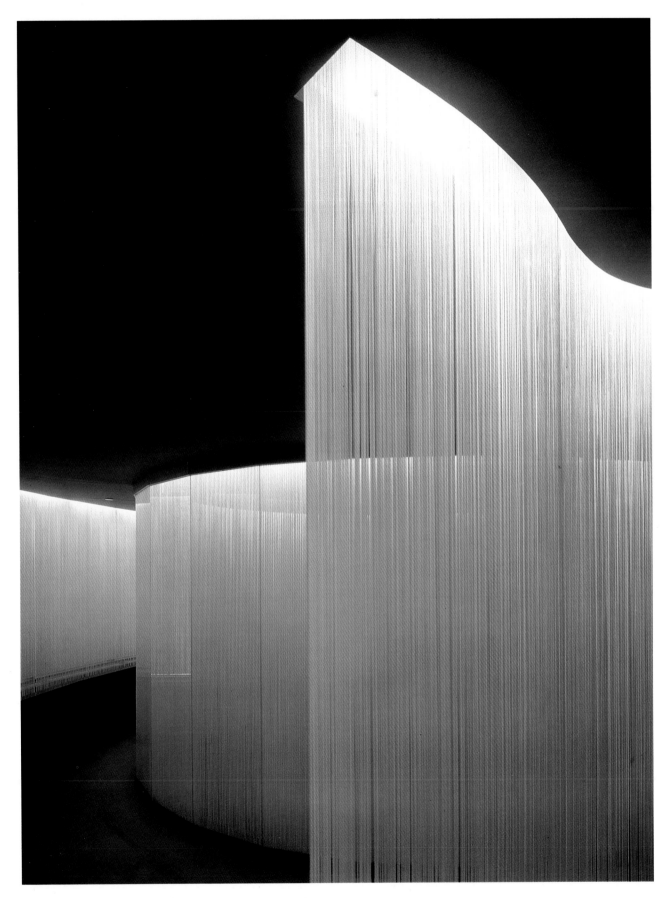

PARTITION

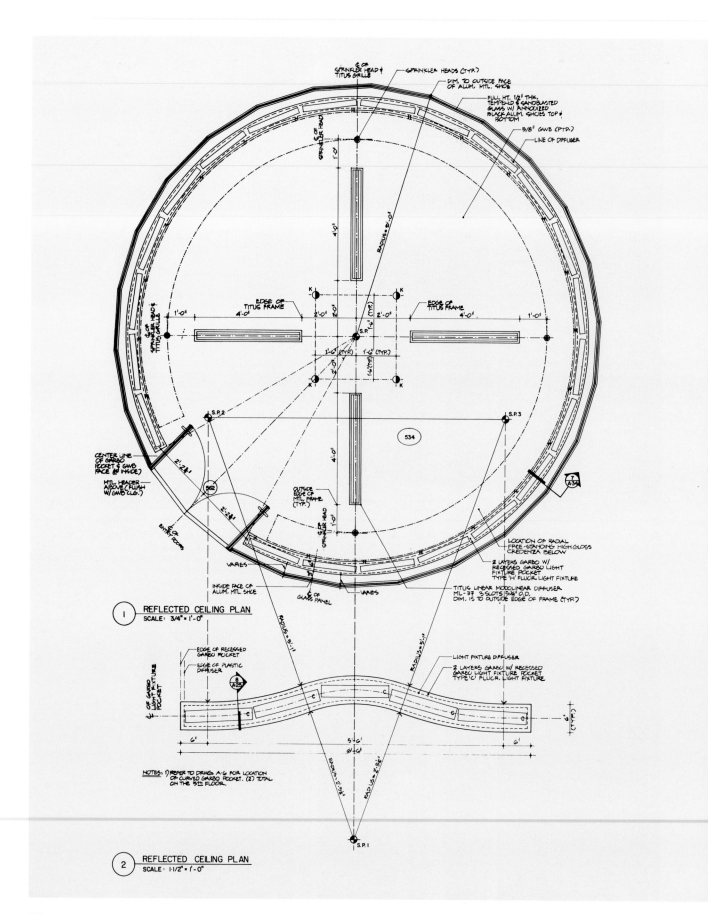

170

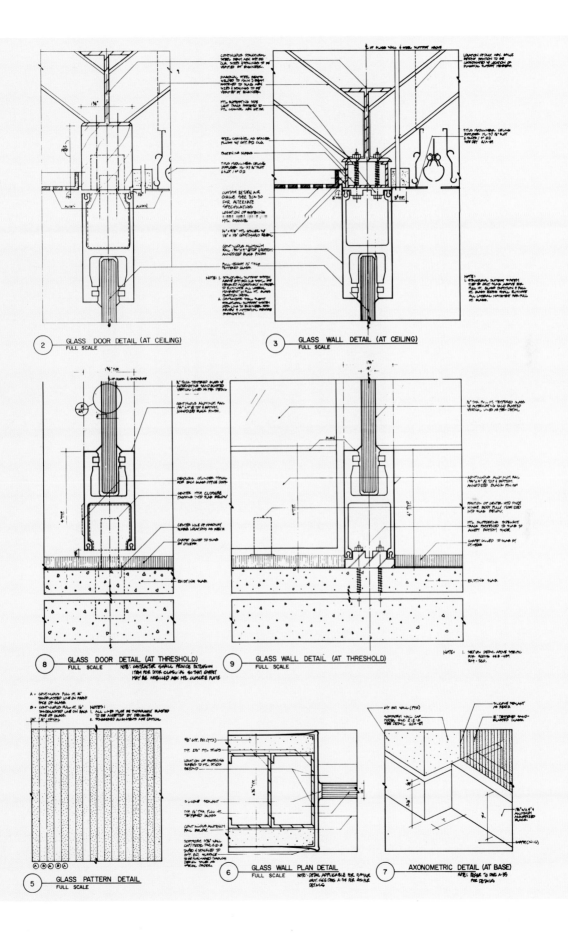

2 GLASS DOOR DETAIL (AT CEILING)
FULL SCALE

3 GLASS WALL DETAIL (AT CEILING)
FULL SCALE

8 GLASS DOOR DETAIL (AT THRESHOLD)
FULL SCALE

9 GLASS WALL DETAIL (AT THRESHOLD)
FULL SCALE

5 GLASS PATTERN DETAIL
FULL SCALE

6 GLASS WALL PLAN DETAIL
FULL SCALE

7 AXONOMETRIC DETAIL (AT BASE)

PILASTERS

180 EAST 70TH STREET
New York City

Architecture/Interior Design
Kohn Pedersen Fox Associates PC
Millwork
Midhattan
Photography
© Chun Lai

ARCHITECTS AND DESIGNERS who have already proven their ability to innovate are quite often the industry leaders who confidently choose to re-create. At 180 East 70th Street, a small but prestigious cooperative apartment building in New York City, William Pedersen of Kohn Pederson Fox Associates PC has painstakingly evoked the Beaux-Arts detailing signature of turn-of-the-century architects McKim, Mead and White. The focal point of Pedersen's lobby design is a Beaux-Arts paneling system of protruding columns and pilasters, surmounted by a barrel-vaulted *trompe l'oeil* ceiling painted as an infinite sky.

Kohn Pedersen Fox developed the detailing for Trafalgar House Real Estate, Inc., a distinguished British firm in one of its first American ventures. Trafalgar favored the Classicist approach, finding it "appropriate to both our public image and to the building's tangential neighborhood character." Trafalgar's generous budget permitted Kohn Pederson Fox to realize its conceptual design without cutting any corners.

The 429-square-foot lobby, which serves fewer than 100 apartments, provides an elegant but relatively intimate setting for guest reception. Paired columns and pilasters, grouped symmetrically around the room, convey a sense of classical order (*floor plan; elevation*). Each 9'-6" columnar group is separated from adjacent pairs by framed panels of linen moire. The fabric's aquamarine tint blends with the sky blue of the 14'-0" *trompe l'oeil* ceiling. To add dramatic impact to the space as well as to unify disparate elements, the design team specified Belgian black marble as the border for the diagonal checkerboard marble floor and for the millwork baseboard.

The custom millwork is constructed of African Bubinga mahogany. Veneer

was specified for the paneling, and solid hardwood for the columns, cornices, and trim. Each of the twenty 5'-6" Tuscan columns was shop constructed in twelve doweled-and-glued vertical sections. The columns were then turned to a 10-inch diameter and shaped (*column section*). The trim and cornices were shop-milled and carved. The pilaster/column units were shipped to the site for dowel-and-glue, nail-and-wood-blocking screw assembly (*section elevation*).

To expose and maximize the natural wood grain, the columns and pilasters were treated with a clear, hand-rubbed finish—an effect most evident in the veneers on each pedestal where the grains were book matched.

The vaulted ceiling is constructed in two layers of molded gypsum board.

The ceiling is finished with a skim coat of plaster and hung from the structural ceiling with a standard wire-and-clip system (*elevation*). Three crystal-and-brass chandeliers hang directly from the structural ceiling, through a gypsum-board panel within the mahogany frame at the top of the vault. The light-box frame is bolted to the structural ceiling and contains twelve downspouts with diffusion lenses.

A cove lighting system is concealed by the cornice. Fluorescent tubes illuminate the "sky" from the edges, heightening the sky illusion by creating an apparently more distant horizon (*section elevation*). Pinhole incandescent downlights were installed between each column and its pilaster in order to avoid somber, shadowy recesses.

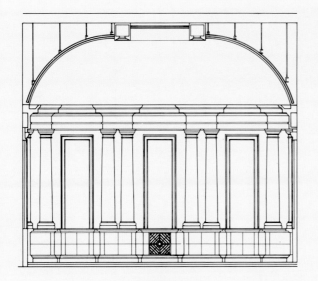

ELEVATION

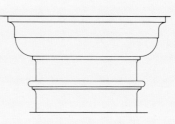

CAPITAL ELEVATION

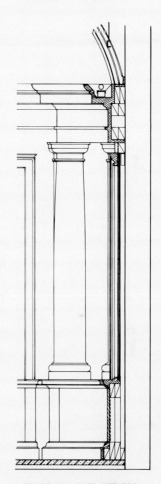

SECTION ELEVATION

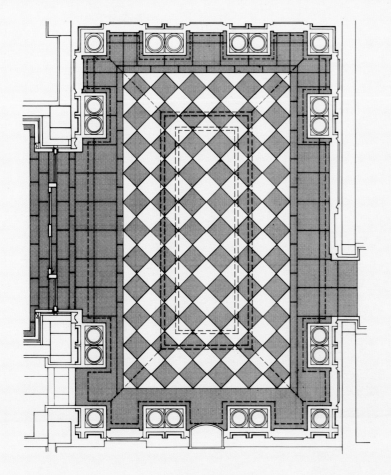

FLOOR PLAN

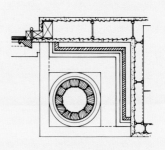

COLUMN SECTION

PODIUM

ALABAMA POWER COMPANY
Birmingham, Alabama

Architecture/Interior Design
Geddes Brecher Qualls Cunningham;
Gresham, Smith and Partners
Design Team
James P. Snyder, Lisa Hansel
Fabrication
Akira Woodworking
Photography
© Durston Saylor

ACCORDING TO Dr. Diana Robertson, professor at the Wharton School of Economics, "corporate culture" is a catchall phrase used to characterize and quantify the system of essential values that drive company activities. Although the Alabama Power Company's corporate culture would receive a commendation on the basis of any one of these issues, its headquarters environment, designed as a joint-venture project between Geddes Brecher Qualls Cunningham of Phila-

delphia and Gresham, Smith and Partners of Birmingham, is exemplary.

No detail at the Alabama Power Company was considered to be too small or too insignificant to receive the thoughtful planning that typifies the entire project. Therefore, in developing details for the executive-floor staff conference and boardrooms, the design team went beyond the requisite development of tables and audio-visual cabinetry and developed a visually complementary, ergonomically scaled speaker podium as well.

Like other adjustable-height podiums, the Alabama Power Company's model may be electrically raised and lowered to accommodate the height of the speaker. Unlike more prosaic versions, which raise at the base and look correspondingly "tipsy" in their fully extended position, only the top section of the podium is movable. The solid base remains stationary (*isometric*). When the podium

is fully lowered, it appears to be a one-piece construction. As the podium telescopes 8 inches upward, a handsome reveal panel is exposed.

The motor for the podium lift is concealed in the base section behind a removable access panel. The momentary-contact operating switch is located in a recessed cutout on the slanting desk surface (*section A*). Audio-visual controls are also located on the slanted surface within a brass concealed box that links the podium, through the floor, to similar control panels in the table and screen partition wall (*section*).

The podium was veneered in mahogany over a ¾-inch particleboard substructure. Veneer grains were selected to match those of each room's table and partition paneling, resulting in quarter-sliced veneer for the conference room and plain-sliced veneer for the boardroom.

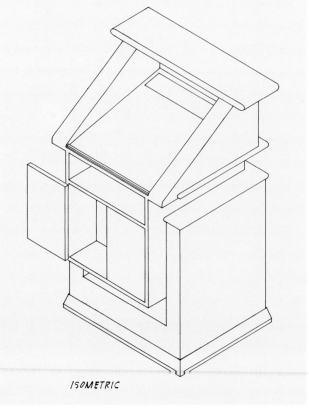

ISOMETRIC

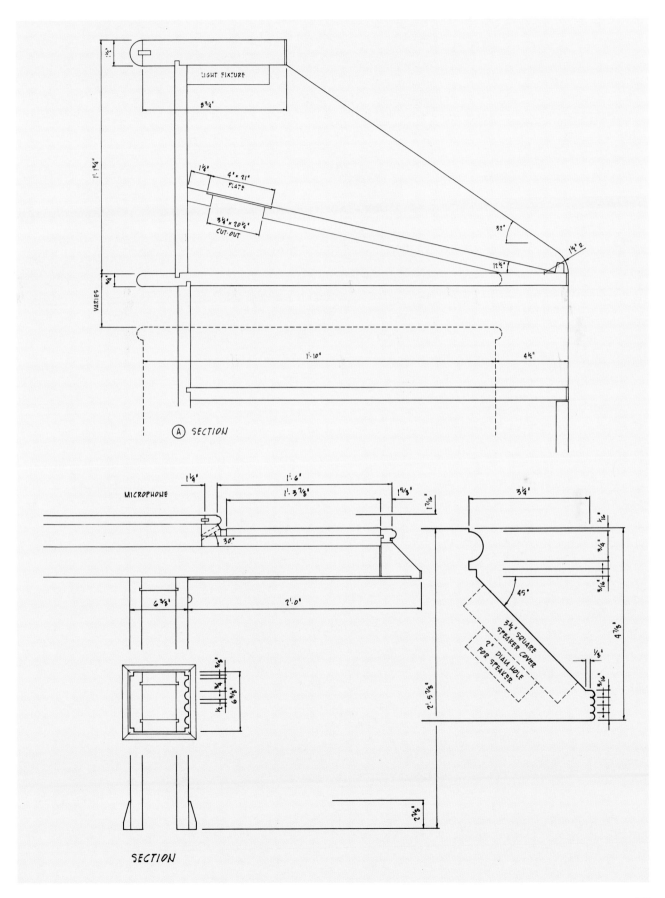

LIGHT FIXTURE

8¾"

1½"

1'-1¾"

VARIES

¾"

1¼"

4" x 21"
PLATE

3¼" x 20¼"
CUT·OUT

32°

12½"

1½" R

1'-10"

4½"

Ⓐ SECTION

MICROPHONE

1¼"

1'-6"

1'-3⅞"

1⁵⁄₈"

1⁷⁄₁₆"

30°

6⅜"

2'-0"

3¼"

¼"

45°

3¾" SQUARE
SPEAKER COVER

2" DIAM HOLE
FOR SPEAKER

4⅞"

⅛"

¾"

¾"

6⅜"

¾"

¾"

2'-5⅞"

2⅛"

SECTION

RAILING

UNIVERSITY OF PENNSYLVANIA
Philadelphia, Pennsylvania

Architecture/Interior Design
Davis, Brody & Associates
Design Team
Albert Grossman, Nathan Hoyt,
Fred Chomowicz, Pamela Veit,
John Locke, John Romana,
John McCoy, Leon Joseph,
Kate Warner, Julie Holmes
Fabrication
Central Metals, Inc.
Photography
© Nick Wheeler

IN 1984 Davis, Brody & Associates of
New York City was commissioned by
the University of Pennsylvania to con-
vert two dormitory floors of the
Jacobean Revival quadrangle's turreted
Provost Tower into an in-house study
room/library. University trustees
wanted the new library to "respect
Cope & Stewardson's original architecture" but also required that Davis,
Brody create the "intimate, but open,
atmosphere found in the libraries of
small colleges." To achieve both aims,
the design team first gutted the two-
story, 900-square-foot space. They then
girded the soaring new room with a
mezzanine-level gallery, which recalls
Stewardson ironwork.

Because existing windows were relatively small, the design team mini-
mized the gallery's structural density.
Except for the concrete deck and the
oak handrail, the gallery and stairs are
constructed entirely of narrow-profile,
welded steel components (*elevation;
section at bracket*). The cutout
brackets, cutout railing trim, and 6-
inch-spaced safety rods enhance the
wall surfaces with delicately traced
shadows but do not interfere with
even light distribution (*elevation*).

The ironwork railing was constructed of 6-gauge steel plates
pierced by circular cutouts. The plates
were welded to ½-inch-square rails at
6-inch intervals (*elevation*). The rails
were welded, in turn, to channels that
serve also as edge moldings. To support the balcony and restate the
cutout circle motif in reverse, eight
steel brackets were welded to channels within the structural wall.

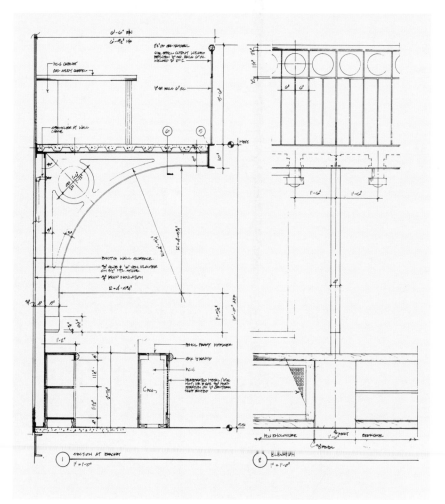

176

RAILING

1001 PENNSYLVANIA AVENUE
Washington, D.C.

Architecture/Interior Design
Hartman-Cox Architects
Design Team
George Hartman, Graham Davidson
Fabrication
Custom Art and Metals
Photography
© Durston Saylor

A CERTAIN AMOUNT of detailing one-upmanship prevails in the highly competitive real-estate development game played in earnest in Washington, D.C., and in other major cities across the United States. Because developers need a visual hook to attract tenants for their buildings, architects and designers who detail well are in demand.

1001 Pennsylvania Avenue in Washington, D.C., is the spectacular by-product of a collaboration between Cadillac-Fairview Urban Development Corporation of Dallas, Texas, and Hartman-Cox Architects of Washington, D.C. At 1001, the project team took the path least trodden in spec-

building development—the generous application of sumptuous materials throughout both public and private spaces of the building.

To connect the second-floor office suites, which are bisected by the two-story vaulted lobby, Hartman-Cox suggested the installation of a 15-foot bridge, surmounted by a brass-tube-and-bar "union jack" railing (*detail elevation A*). The developer understood the detail's potential for adding "sparkle" to the public area and readily agreed to the proposal.

The bridge railing consists of a series of six 2'-4¾" square panels, built of 1-inch by ¾-inch brass bars. The vertical and horizontal components are ½-inch by ½-inch single bars. The diagonal segments are double bars, each one of which is ¼-inch by ½-inch. The intersection cross-over point of the components is covered by a 2½-inch-diameter circular brass boss.

Each square is peripherally framed-in by vertical posts of 1½-inch by 1½-inch square tubes—strengthened inside by concealed 1-inch by ⅜-inch steel bars and on top by horizontal

segments of the same reinforced tube (*detail elevation A*). The handrail itself is a solid brass bloom screwed to a 1½-inch by 1-inch by ⅛-inch channel (*typical section*).

At the base of each post, a steel bar concealed by a bronze fascia plate is screwed through the brass tube to the ½-inch steel plate backing (*section C*). The backing is then welded to a steel angle in the concrete floor. A Muntz metal panel base, with rectangular recesses between posts, reinforces the horizontality of the railing (*detail elevation A; section C*).

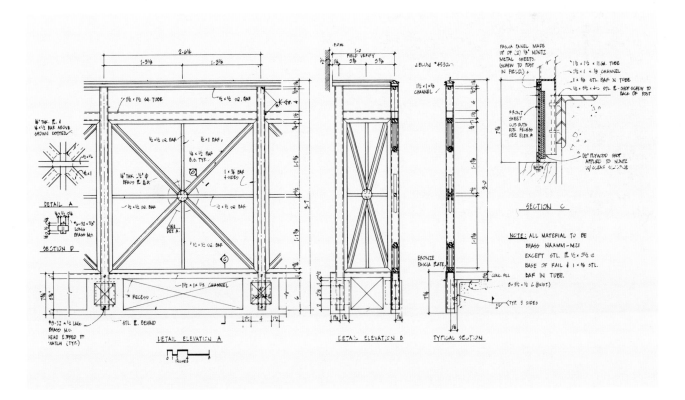

RAILING

FIRST REPUBLIC BANK
Houston, Texas

Architectural Design
John Burgee Architects
(John Burgee, Partner;
Philip Johnson, Design Consultant)
Design Team
John Burgee, Philip Johnson,
Scott Johnson, Ronette Riley,
David Fiore
Metal Fabrication
Midwest Ironwork
Photography
© Richard Payne

THE RAILINGS THAT architects design for
staircases, bridges, and low-height partitioning often give clues about which
stylistic mode is currently in favor.
During the sixties and early seventies,
brass, steel, and wood bannisters
topped flush-fitted sheets of clear
glass. Those railing talismans of the
Modernist school were superseded in
the late seventies and early eighties by
diagonally crossed braces of bronze
or steel, which were often centered
by decorative medallions—a
Postmodern motif that signaled the
resurgence of a Neoclassical genre.

Now, at the First Republic Bank
center in Houston, Texas, the John
Burgee and Philip Johnson team has
designed a softly twisting wrought-
iron railing which advertises their
interest in a new, and as yet unnamed,
genre that incorporates the sculptural
sensibilities of Italian ironworker/
sculptor Alberto Giacometti.

One-and-one-eighth-inch-diameter
ballister railing panels appear in the
First Republic Bank's low-rise banking
pavilion, as well as in the arcade that
separates it from the adjacent office
tower. The railing panels answer practical as well as aesthetic concerns: as a
safety barrier on bridges and walk-
ways and as psychological dividers
between the personal and public
banking areas of the main floor.

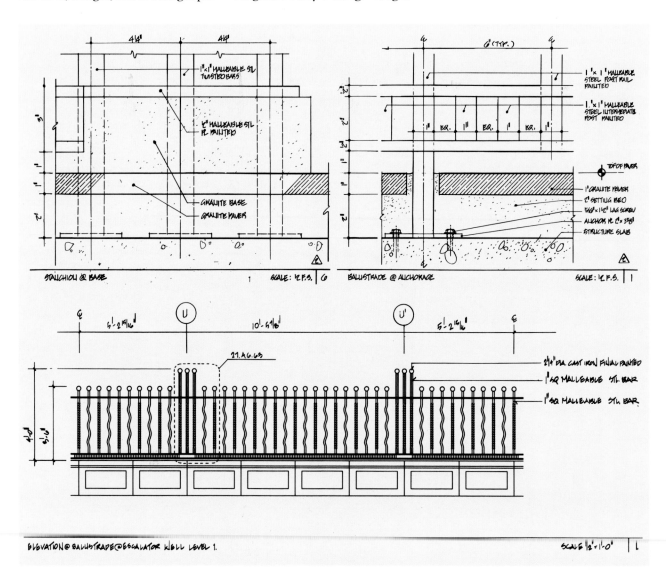

RAMP

YVES SAINT LAURENT SHOWROOM
New York City

Interior Architectural Design
The Switzer Group, Inc.
Design Team
Lou Switzer, Joan Petersen,
Robert Kellogg, Christopher Leary,
Stewart Fishbein, Steven Smith
Fabrication
Hakon, Inc.
Photography
© Durston Saylor

ANYONE WHO FOLLOWS the world of high fashion knows to expect the unexpected from Yves Saint Laurent. According to company executives, "stimulating a sense of pleasurable anticipation" is the cornerstone of the YSL marketing approach.

In designing the company's Manhattan showroom, The Switzer Group, Inc., of New York City exhibited a similar flair for sophisticated showmanship. Bidermann Industries U.S.A. Inc., YSL's American distributors, wanted a space that would be "different, have impact, and convey an international sensibility." Switzer designer Christopher Leary's response was to develop a "deconstructionist" entrance, which draws customers into a spacious 18- by 18-foot reception area via an intriguing and unusual granite ramp enclosure.

The enclosure detail accomplishes much more than merely exciting curiosity, however. In addition to establishing a sense of immediate drama, the ramp's 1-in-12 ascending pitch elevates the awkward and lengthy walk from the elevator bank to a process of ceremonial progression.

The enclosure's finish materials, granite slabs and heavy-gauge stainless steel, convey an elemental strength that was intentionally planned to balance—yet not compete with—the boldness and strength of the displayed clothing. According to Leary, that initial focus on appropriate juxtapositioning led to refinement of the detail's form. In the final version, the ramp enclosure plays a subtle game of "implied geological violence."

The ramp is perceived as a solid block of granite that has exploded; its end cap is imploded, or "buried," in the wall behind the reception desk,

leaving a "hole" through which to enter the space. Leary embellished this effect by removing a forward section of ceiling and cantilevering it instead from the entry soffit. This sleight-of-hand device implies that the ceiling has slipped backward, opening the enclosure to natural daylight.

The granite slabs that face the walls and floor of the ramp enclosure appear to be 2 feet thick; in fact, they are ⅝-inch veneer panels. The *trompe l'oeil* effect was achieved by setting the stone into expanded metal-mesh mortar beds built up and out from the plywood subfloor and cementitious board walls (*section*).

The ¾-inch granite ceiling panels are held tightly together by dowels suspended by threaded steel pins from a ⁵⁄₁₆-inch steel angle. The metal angle is suspended from the cement

slab ceiling by ⅜-inch-diameter threaded steel rods. Crude leveling, or angling, adjustment of the ceiling panels is accommodated by the rod system, and fine tuning is accomplished by adjustments to the steel pins (*sketch detail*). The complicated system (updated to utilize modern technology) was designed by Leary after a comprehensive study of nineteenth-century stone ceiling detailing.

Although based on historical norms, the ramp enclosure is embellished by secondary detailing that firmly establishes it as a contemporary structure. A series of recessed outdoor step lights (*elevation*) leads the eye to a futuristic light fixture framed by the enclosure. Stainless steel handrails, as well as the flame (or thermal) finish of the granite panels, gracefully respond to current code requirements.

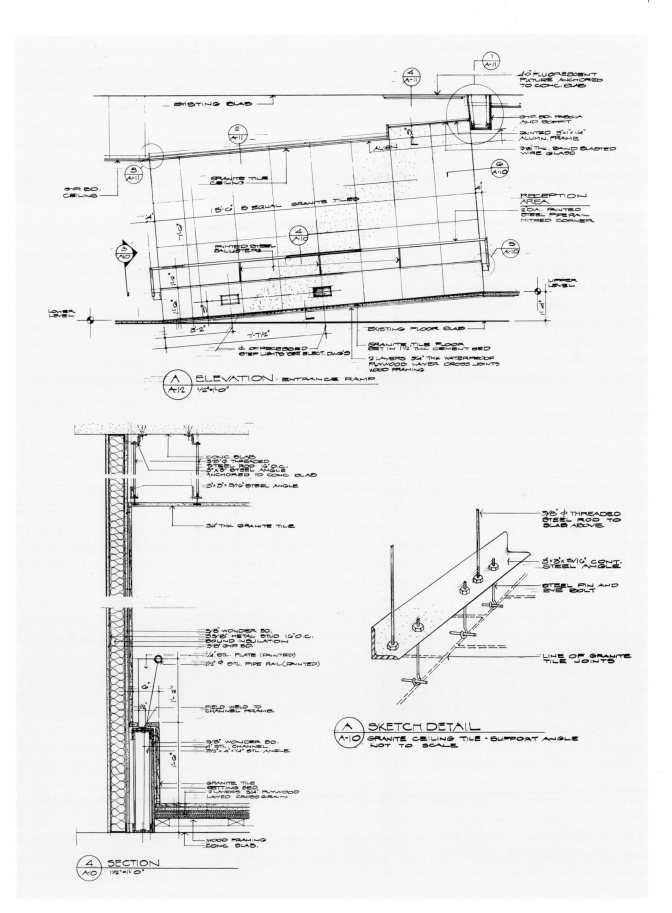

ⓐ ELEVATION · ENTRANCE RAMP
A·12   1/2"=1'-0"

④ SECTION
A·10   1 1/2"=1'-0"

ⓐ SKETCH DETAIL
A·10   GRANITE CEILING TILE · SUPPORT ANGLE
        NOT TO SCALE

RECEPTION DESK

LARSON ASSOCIATES, INC.
Chicago, Illinois

Architecture/Interior Design
Larson Associates, Inc.
Design Team
George Larson, Susan B. Larson,
B. Timothy Desmond, Mark Roeser,
Charlotte Maassen, Jong Lee,
Jorge A. Reyes, Sandi Gold
Fabrication
Interior Woodworking Corp.
Photography
© François Robert

LARSON ASSOCIATES, INC., of Chicago liked the Printers Row location and the general feeling of Holabird and Roche's 1891 steel-frame Pontiac Building so much that they took a full floor for their own offices, despite the fact that the move entailed a complete architectural and interior renovation.

The design team encountered several logistical headaches, however. A sheer wall running horizontally through the building obstructed the flow of traffic from one end of the office to the other. Although it meant relocating the building exit stairs—a major structural undertaking—the Larson design team capitalized on the opportunity to utilize the two large open-office spaces resulting from the sheer wall by designating two functional areas: an architectural studio space and an administrative conference area. A round reception desk was created to channel traffic from one wing to the other in a circular, roundabout pattern.

The desk, which has an 7'-6" diameter, follows a 60-degree angled curve around its circumference. The subframe is constructed of hardwood blocking sandwiched between and screwed to two layers of ¾-inch particleboard. The circular polyurethane countertop overlays the frame and is held in place by concealed screws underneath (*elevation*). The entire exterior was lacquered "Larson red."

The interior of the desk is finished in black laminate. The desk's work surface is bilevel—one section is lowered as a keyboard base (*section*). Storage shelves and cantilevered storage pedestals are attached by continuous blocking around the interior elevation of the desk unit. A sosshinged gate provides access to the work space. The three hinges pivot 270 degrees when the entry door is open. When the door is closed, the hinges recess into themselves for an invisible closure seal (*reception desk plan*).

Lighting for the desk is provided by continuous incandescent strips that are recessed under the countertop lip (*section*). The wiring for the workstation emanates from a small transformer located beneath the pedestal.

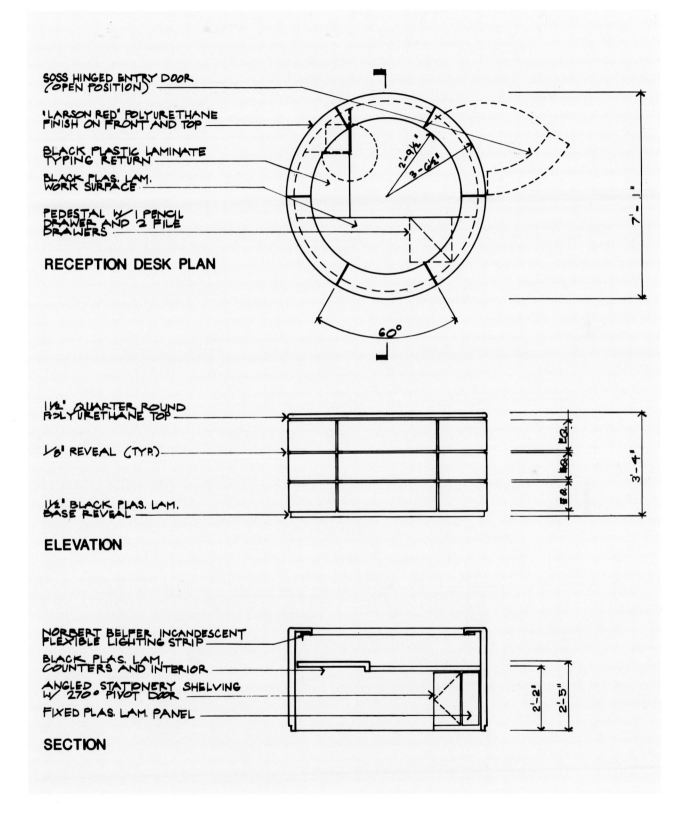

SOSS HINGED ENTRY DOOR
(OPEN POSITION)

'LARSON RED' POLYURETHANE
FINISH ON FRONT AND TOP

BLACK PLASTIC LAMINATE
TYPING RETURN

BLACK PLAS. LAM.
WORK SURFACE

PEDESTAL W/ 1 PENCIL
DRAWER AND 2 FILE
DRAWERS

RECEPTION DESK PLAN

2'-9½"

3'-6½"

7'-1"

60°

1½" QUARTER ROUND
POLYURETHANE TOP

⅛" REVEAL (TYP.)

1½" BLACK PLAS. LAM.
BASE REVEAL

ELEVATION

3'-4"

E.Q. E.Q. E.Q.

NORBERT BELFER INCANDESCENT
FLEXIBLE LIGHTING STRIP

BLACK PLAS. LAM.
COUNTERS AND INTERIOR

ANGLED STATIONERY SHELVING
W/ 270° PIVOT DOOR

FIXED PLAS. LAM. PANEL

SECTION

2'-2"

2'-5"

RECEPTION DESK

USG INTERIORS, INC., SHOWROOM
*The International Design Center, New York
Long Island City, New York*

Architecture/Interior Design
Daroff Design Inc.
Design Team
Karen Daroff, James Rappoport,
Charles Driesen
Fabrication
Azzarone Contracting Company
Photography
© Norman McGrath

BECAUSE GYPSUM BOARD—a humble but heroic building material—is the product manufactured by USG Interiors, Inc., Philadelphia-based Daroff Design Inc. developed an ambience for the company's showroom in The International Design Center, New York, that emphasizes the diverse usages of bare-bones construction materials. The result is an embellished Neoconstructionist industrial shell.

The Daroff design team boldly declared its Neoconstructionist intentions by installing a piano-curved, fresco-washed, poured-concrete reception desk just inside the showroom's front door. The design team built the desk in concrete to complement an undulating concrete ramp that is the showroom's other primary detail. The fine-arts painted finish on the desk refers subtly to another species of shell—an inside/out oyster, rough on the inside, sculptured, pearlized, and smooth on the exterior.

The desk was constructed in stages, which began with pouring epoxy onto the concrete slab floor. Concrete was poured into a shaped plywood frame form, supported internally by steel reinforcing rods and two 2'-0" sections of embedded wiremold (*detail*). When the form was removed, a plywood subframe was placed on top of the concrete wall and bolted to the rebar that extends above it. The plywood serves as a cushion for the lustrous Italian Cremo marble countertop that is further protected by ¼-inch-thick plastic laminate (*plan of countertop*), which also maintains the marble's immobility.

Marble was cut to fit over and around the plywood and was secured with mastic. The marble sections were butted with grout. Brass dowels, set into the plywood and concrete, laterally stabilize the marble sections.

Bridge plates are installed with counter connectors beneath the actual workspace counter. To eliminate the tendency of aluminum stretchers to bow with weight, the design team bolted the stretchers to the concrete wall. A continuous 1¼-inch cord drop was installed between the countertop and the concrete wall. The counter was edged with a raised steel strip just in front of the cord drop to keep pencils and other narrow objects from falling through. Wiremold is placed under the counter near the anterior edge to hide the cords.

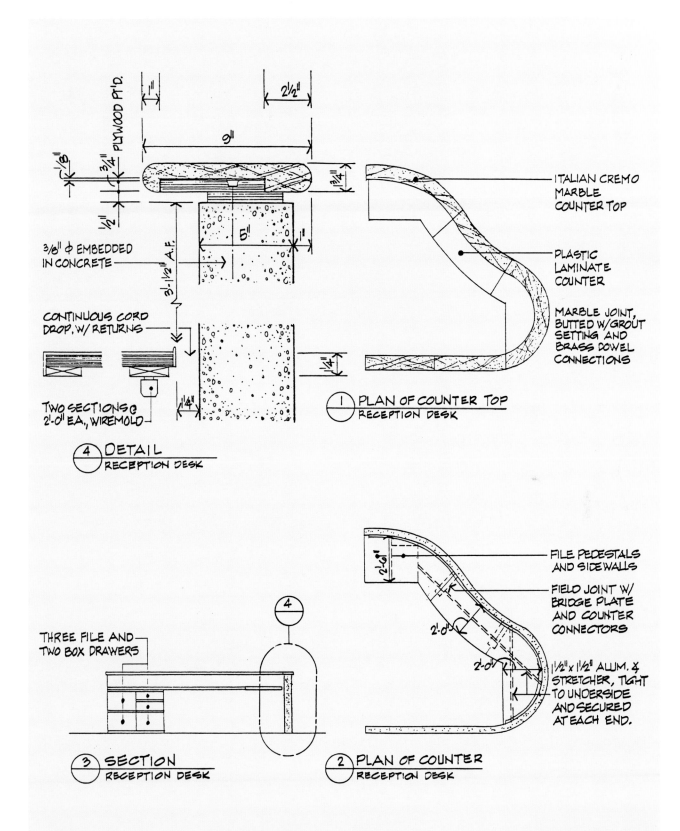

PLYWOOD PT'D.

3/8"⌀ EMBEDDED IN CONCRETE

CONTINUOUS CORD DROP, W/ RETURNS

TWO SECTIONS @ 2'-0" EA., WIREMOLD

4 DETAIL
RECEPTION DESK

2½"

9"

3'-1½" A.F.

5"

1"

3¾"

1"

¼"

¼"

⅛"

¾"

½"

ITALIAN CREMO MARBLE COUNTER TOP

PLASTIC LAMINATE COUNTER

MARBLE JOINT, BUTTED W/GROUT SETTING AND BRASS DOWEL CONNECTIONS

1 PLAN OF COUNTER TOP
RECEPTION DESK

THREE FILE AND TWO BOX DRAWERS

4

3 SECTION
RECEPTION DESK

2'-0"

2'-0"

2'-0"

FILE PEDESTALS AND SIDEWALLS

FIELD JOINT W/ BRIDGE PLATE AND COUNTER CONNECTORS

1½" x 1½" ALUM. ∯ STRETCHER, TIGHT TO UNDERSIDE AND SECURED AT EACH END.

2 PLAN OF COUNTER
RECEPTION DESK

185

Reception Desk

ELLERBE ASSOCIATES, INC.
Minneapolis, Minnesota

Architecture/Interior Design
Ellerbe Associates, Inc.
(Kenneth A. LeDoux)
Fabrication
Vern Holberg; Thompson Woodcraft
Photography
© Steve Greenway

ELLERBE ASSOCIATES, INC., of Minneapolis, Minnesota, added a three-dimensional exclamation point to the logo of its interior-design division, then called Inside!, whose name appeared on a glass block wall in the reception area.

Even in the most imaginatively designed offices, a desk is usually just a desk. However, according to the designers at Ellerbe: "In designing the reception desk for our own offices, we had more conceptual latitude than we might have had for another client. We wanted to inject an element of surprise into the overall impression of the reception area. The sphere as table base grew from that priority." The element of surprise, however, did not preclude an elegant statement based on simple, classic forms.

The whimsical desk, designed by Kenneth A. LeDoux, consists of three elements: the upper surface, which is 2'-6" high; the return surface, which is 2'-3½" high; and a six-file-drawer credenza, located under the return (*EE section*). The main work surface is a rakish parallelogram, measuring 11'-6" by 4'-0" with 45°/135° interior angles. The credenza/return surface is a combination triangle and rectangle whose 8'-0"-long side parallels the back wall of the reception area. The triangular end of the credenza/return passes under the upper surface, with which it shares a single 6'-0" vertical support panel (*reception desk plan*). From the front, the side support panel is not conspicuous. The result is that the main desktop appears to be cantilevered from the sphere on which it rests.

The 2'-3½"-diameter sphere is constructed of custom-cast fiberglass of thicknesses varying from ¼ inch to 2 inches. The two hemispheres were cast separately, each with a section of 2-inch steel pipe passing through its focal point. When the halves were mated and glued, the pipe sections were threaded into a joining sleeve. The sphere is like a threaded pearl—with the pipe as the thread.

Each end of the pipe is threaded:

The bottom is screwed to a pipe cap; the top is screwed to a steel flange, which, in turn, is bolted to the underside of the desktop (*EE section; elevations*). The weight of the desk rests on the pipe.

The sphere is enameled dark burgundy; the work surfaces are pale mauve laminate on particleboard. The most visible edges, or those most likely to be brushed by clients, are bullnosed (*EE section; detail*).

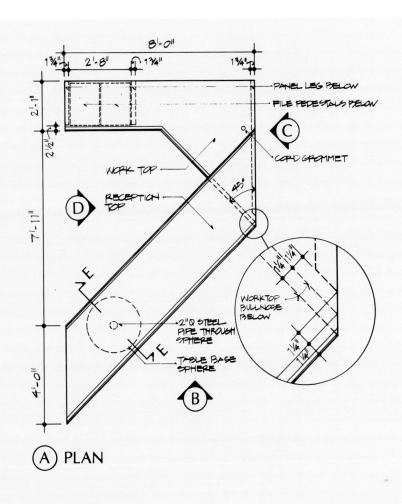

8'-0"
1 3/4"
2'-8"
1 3/4"
1 3/4"
2'-1"
2 1/2"
7'-11"
4'-0"
45°

PANEL LEG BELOW
FILE PEDESTALS BELOW
CORD GROMMET
WORK TOP
RECEPTION TOP
2"Ø STEEL PIPE THROUGH SPHERE
TABLE BASE SPHERE

WORKTOP BULLNOSE BELOW
1/4" 1 1/4"
1/4"
1/4"

(C)
(D)
(B)
E
E

(A) PLAN

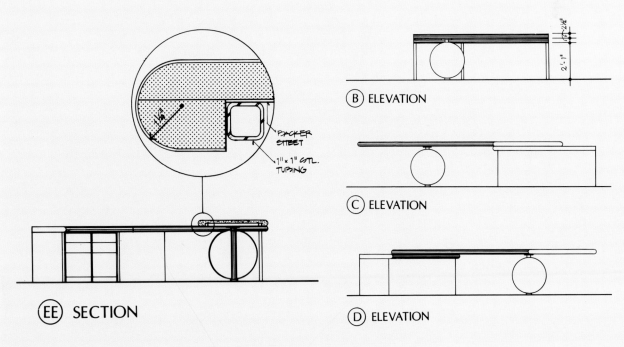

PACKER STEEL
1" x 1" STL. TUBING
1/4"

(EE) SECTION

(B) ELEVATION
1'-2 1/2"
2'-1"

(C) ELEVATION

(D) ELEVATION

ROTUNDA

PONDEROSA, INC.
Dayton, Ohio

Interior Design
ISD Incorporated, Chicago
Design Team
Mel Hamilton, Nick Luzietti,
Angelina Lee, Joseph Martino,
Donna Becco, Lauria Dunne,
Jennifer Holt-Tucker
Woodwork
Imperial Woodworking
Photography
© Nick Merrick, Hedrich-Blessing

IN A DETAILING tour de force that debunks the claim that smashing design appears only in America's major cities, ISD Incorporated of Chicago integrated a historically referenced rotunda into Ponderosa, Inc.'s modern, 5,000-square-foot corporate headquarters in Dayton, Ohio.

The ISD team developed the rotunda as part of a comprehensive detailing program for a client who requested "an enriching but not heavy-handed office atmosphere," which would recall "the luxury of the Orient Express train cars." According to ISD's principal-in-charge Mel Hamilton, "we recognized, as did our clients, that a literal interpretation of Orient Express detailing within the confines of an I. M. Pei office tower would seem contrived." The ISD team resolved what might have been a jarring juxtaposition by focusing on the streamlined spirit of the train, rather than on its literal form. Gerald S. Office, president of Ponderosa, concurs. "What we now have is the best of both worlds—sumptuous European materials applied in a straightforward American way."

To accommodate the curve of the rotunda, which is both round and concave in diminishing dimension as it rises toward the ceiling, ¹⁄₁₆-inch to ⅛-inch veneers of heavily figured pomele and straight-grain sapele mahogany were flat cut in triangles. The triangles were then glued back together on site, in a process described by Hamilton as being similar to "laying out and opening a child's pop-up book."

ISD lit the rotunda with a custom cathode fixture concealed in the ogee cove (*elevation*). Intense light bounces off the apex of the ogee, spilling an even wash of more temperate light across the fascia of the cornice, which is inlaid with figured cherry, satinwood, and ebony (*cornice detail*).

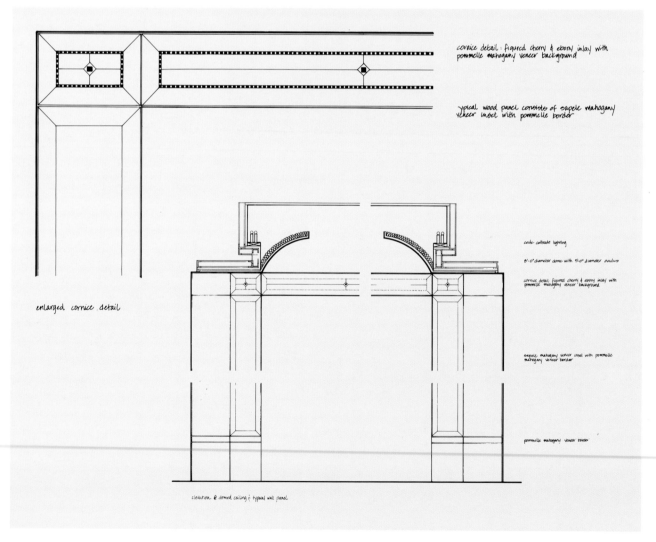

cornice detail: figured cherry & ebony inlay with pommelle mahogany veneer background

typical wood panel consists of sapele mahogany veneer inset with pommelle border

enlarged cornice detail

code cathode lighting

8'-0" diameter dome with 5'-0" diameter oculus

cornice detail: figured cherry & ebony inlay with pommelle mahogany veneer background

sapele mahogany veneer inset with pommelle mahogany veneer border

pommelle mahogany veneer border

elevation @ domed ceiling & typical wall panel

ROTUNDA

WORLD FINANCIAL CENTER
New York City

Architecture/Interior Design
Cesar Pelli & Associates;
Adamson Associates Architects Planners
Design Team
Thomas Morton, Mark Shoemaker,
Jeffrey Paine
Lighting Consultants
Jules Fisher, Paul Marantz
Stenciling
Rambusch
Photography
© Timothy Hursley

THE GRACEFUL EXTERIOR configuration of the World Financial Center, designed by Cesar Pelli & Associates of New Haven, Connecticut, in association with Adamson Associates Architects Planners of Toronto, Canada, and Haines Lundberg Waehler of New York City, has done much to restore faith in the architectural integrity of New York City's skyline. The center's clustered, octagonal towers and plaza revive the human-scale orientation of fine urban spaces. From a late-afternoon, Hudson River perspective, the sun-drenched, gold-leafed domes inspire poetic reflection.

A pair of octagonal high-rise towers house the two formal gateways to the 7-million-square-foot complex. The developer, Olympia & York Companies (U.S.A.), wanted the gateways to be "impressive and monumental

overtures" to the overall composition of the project. That directive suggested that a large open space should be created. Because the octagonal form of the buildings had already established their exterior identity, the Pelli design team decided that an interior octagonal domed rotunda in Tower A would establish both the impressive gateway the client required and a symmetrical "inside-outside dialogue."

In detailing the lobby as a domed rotunda, the design team struck an aesthetic chord of universal and timeless appeal. Rotundas continue to be popular even though their original function—as a device for eliminating interior supports—has long since been obviated by modern construction methods and materials. Steel, in particular, has allowed modern architects to play with forms, allowing the creation of spatial effects denied their predecessors. The center's dome appears to "float," an illusion that would have been impossible in the days of masonry construction. The subtle floating effect was achieved by straightforward design that permitted simple construction.

The design team chose a segmented ceiling to control the relative complexity of the curved form (*axonometric; partial reflected ceiling plan*). The "ribs" between the segments are reveals, which emphasize the separate construction of the seg-

ments. Each segment is constructed of gypsum board on metal studs, hung from the structural ceiling by standard techniques. Where articulation was desired, as in the molding at the segments' edges and in the octagonal base (*section/elevation thru base of dome*), sections of fiberglass-reinforced plaster were factory molded then assembled, screwed, and taped to the gypsum board on site. The octagonal soffit beneath the dome was also premolded and assembled in the same manner.

The intervening window is the element that does most to create the floating dome effect. The window severs the dome from the soffit that would otherwise be perceived as its base, as well as from the structural columns below. The window is fabricated in clear plate glass that is butt-jointed to avoid any trace of verticality (*section/elevation thru base of dome*).

The dome ceiling, which spans 60 feet and rises 16 feet from the window to an apex 60 feet above the lobby floor, is finished in stenciling over a base of sanded off-white paint, in a pattern that suggests coffering (*partial reflected ceiling plan—extended*). Incandescent lamps in stainless steel fixtures mounted on the soffit illuminate the ceiling. Mirrors within the fixtures focus the light up and across the ceiling.

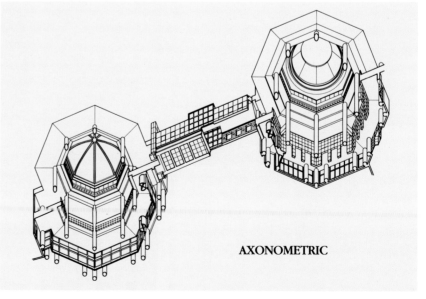

AXONOMETRIC

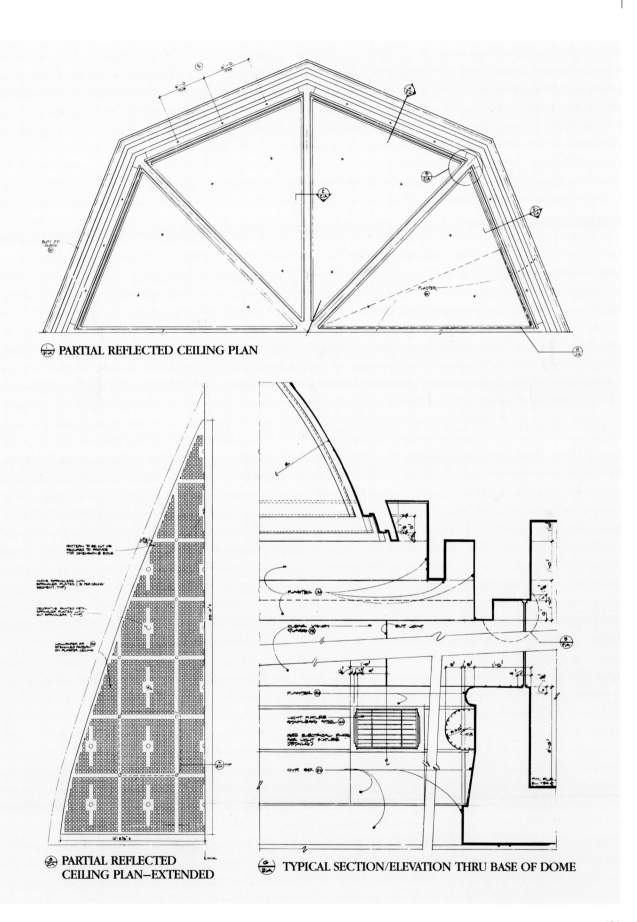

PARTIAL REFLECTED CEILING PLAN

PARTIAL REFLECTED CEILING PLAN—EXTENDED

TYPICAL SECTION/ELEVATION THRU BASE OF DOME

ROTUNDA

THE GRAND HOTEL
Washington, D.C.

Architecture
Skidmore, Owings & Merrill,
Washington, D.C.
Interior Architecture/Interior Design
Charles Pfister Associates
Design Team
Charles Pfister, Richard Brayton,
Gerry Jue, Miguel Solé,
James Leal, Michael Collins
Fabrication
George Hyman Construction
Lighting Consultant
Claude R. Engel
Photography
© Jaime Ardiles-Arce

IN THE FIERCELY competitive Washington, D.C., hotel market, the only designers whose work will satisfy the discerning owner are those who are known for accomplished and sophisticated design. It is no surprise, therefore, that The Kaempfer Companies selected Skidmore, Owings & Merrill of Washington, D.C., as project architects and Charles Pfister Associates of San Francisco as interior architects and designers for the new 242-room Regent Hotel, now The Grand Hotel.

The owners initially envisioned the hotel's interior as a revival of the traditional design that is prominent throughout the capital city. Pfister convinced them otherwise, pointing out that the economic advantages of utilizing a transitional design would not preclude achieving a similar, but more timely, elegance and grace. "In every project, it comes down to a question of where to spend the money that is available. We decided to allocate money on The Grand Hotel to finely wrought detailing and finish materials."

The rotunda of the main lounge, a double-column–supported dome constructed of coves in graduated sizes that step down from an oculus, creates an obvious classical allusion. So do the rotunda's finish materials, which include figured mahogany columns, Rosso Levanto column capitals and bases, genuine plaster coves, and applied gold leaf on the oculus and moldings.

What is definitely not historical in the design and construction of the rotunda is the deft incorporation of HVAC equipment, sprinklers, and sophisticated recessed lighting. Because good heating and ventilating systems must be partially exposed for efficiency, Pfister's team worked with manufacturers to develop a curved air-slot diffuser that could be subtly integrated into the curve of the plaster coves without arbitrary imposition (*detail*). Standard sprinklers were adapted for lateral diffusion, reducing their vertical protrusion to a nearly invisible ¾ inch (*detail*). Lighting consultant Claude Engel added his expertise in developing color ranges for recessed incandescent and halogen fixtures, settling on a scheme with a red underbase to enhance the glow of the gold leaf trim.

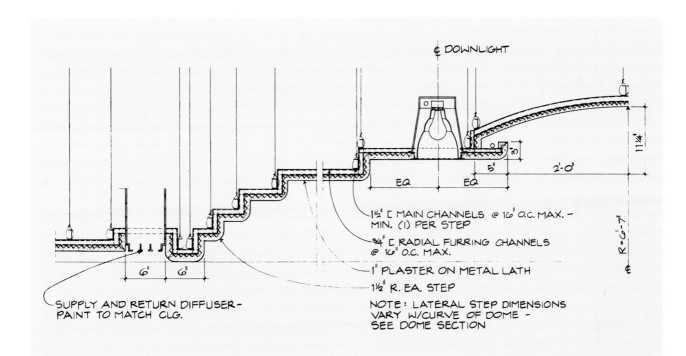

¢ DOWNLIGHT

1½" [MAIN CHANNELS @ 16" O.C. MAX. —
MIN. (1) PER STEP

¾" [RADIAL FURRING CHANNELS
@ 16" O.C. MAX.

1" PLASTER ON METAL LATH

1½" R. EA. STEP

NOTE: LATERAL STEP DIMENSIONS
VARY W/CURVE OF DOME —
SEE DOME SECTION

SUPPLY AND RETURN DIFFUSER—
PAINT TO MATCH CLG.

EQ   EQ

5"   2'-0"

11¼"

R=6'-7"

PLASTER CLG. & DIFFUSER DETAIL @ DOME

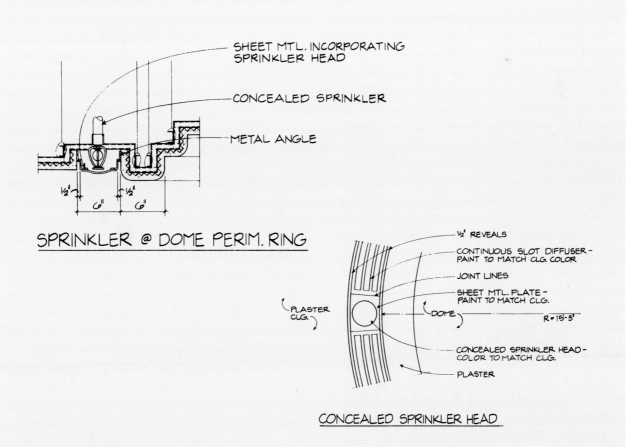

SHEET MTL. INCORPORATING
SPRINKLER HEAD

CONCEALED SPRINKLER

METAL ANGLE

½" 6" ½" 6"

SPRINKLER @ DOME PERIM. RING

PLASTER
CLG.

½" REVEALS

CONTINUOUS SLOT DIFFUSER—
PAINT TO MATCH CLG. COLOR

JOINT LINES

SHEET MTL. PLATE—
PAINT TO MATCH CLG.

DOME

R=15'-3"

CONCEALED SPRINKLER HEAD—
COLOR TO MATCH CLG.

PLASTER

CONCEALED SPRINKLER HEAD

ROTUNDA

LARSON ASSOCIATES, INC.
Chicago, Illinois

Architecture/Interior Design
Larson Associates, Inc.
Design Team
George Larson, Susan B. Larson,
B. Timothy Desmond, Mark Roeser,
Charlotte Maassen, Jong Lee,
Jorge A. Reyes, Sandi Gold
Photography
© François Robert

ALTHOUGH BY PRIMARY definition a rotunda is a dome supported by a colonnade, the reception area at Larson Associates, Inc., in Chicago qualifies as a rotunda without a dome or column in sight. Allusory verisimilitude is the case in point at the design firm's office, where a flat ceiling and four awkward, asymmetrically placed columns were concealed by a rotundalike room.

Larson's aim was to create a centrally located reception area just off the floor's elevator lobby that would promote the flow of traffic from one end of the office to the other (*floor plan*). Because the span of the space was a relatively modest 18′-0″, the designers first contrived a round reception desk (see page 182) and then the rotunda itself—in order to recess guest seating within curved corner niches, which thereby eliminates the need for cumbersome sofas and chairs.

According to George Larson, the spatial enclosure "maintains the virtues of durability, practicality, and economy of construction." The enclosure conveys the impression of a rotunda even though it has no dome—the 9-foot ceiling is entirely flat (*rotunda section*). The ceiling's convincing illusion of concavity is accomplished by the suspension of a

2′-0″-wide circular ring, built of fire-resistant particleboard over plywood, that contains and separates two concentric tiers of cove lights (*rotunda section; exploded axonometric of rotunda*). The light from the inner circle diminishes in intensity toward the center of the ceiling and "builds" a dome rising from the ring. The rotunda illusion is exaggerated by the four seating niches, which give the schematic impression of vaults and pendentives.

The construction of the rotunda support walls was straightforward and practical, consisting of gypsum board screwed to metal studs. Muted elevation colors that do not compete with the firm's own design products were chosen. The walls were finished with easy-to-maintain satin sheen white paint, and the niche benches were cushioned in black leather.

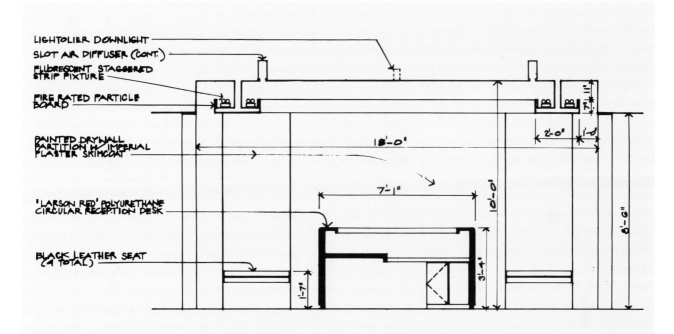

LIGHTOLIER DOWNLIGHT

SLOT AIR DIFFUSER (CONT.)

FLUORESCENT STAGGERED
STRIP FIXTURE

FIRE RATED PARTICLE
BOARD

PAINTED DRYWALL
PARTITION W/ IMPERIAL
PLASTER SKIMCOAT

'LARSON RED' POLYURETHANE
CIRCULAR RECEPTION DESK

BLACK LEATHER SEAT
(4 TOTAL)

18'-0"

7'-1"

10'-0"

2'-0"

1'-0"

7'-11"

8'-6"

3'-4"

1'-7"

ROTUNDA SECTION

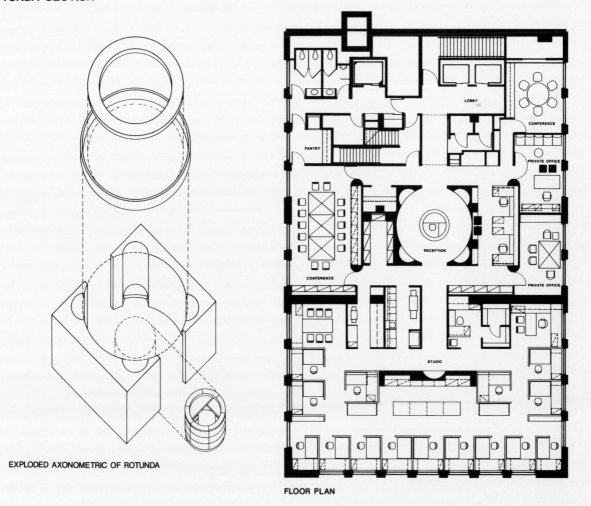

EXPLODED AXONOMETRIC OF ROTUNDA

LOBBY

CONFERENCE

PRIVATE OFFICE

PANTRY

CONFERENCE

RECEPTION

PRIVATE OFFICE

STUDIO

FLOOR PLAN

Salad Bar

TEXACO INC. REGIONAL OFFICE
Universal City, California

Interior Design
Cole Martinez Curtis and Associates
Design Team
Jill Cole, Maggie Mandel,
Howard Cherry, Tim Brandt (drawing)
Fabrication
Roger B. Phillips, Inc.
Photography
© Toshi Yoshimi

TEXACO'S SELF-SERVICE cafeteria serves otherwise locationally isolated Texaco employees, other building occupants, and nearby business people once (and sometimes twice) a day. Because the facility is also used in conjunction with an adjacent 98-person conference center, as well as for regularly scheduled special events, Texaco executives asked Marina del Rey design firm Cole Martinez Curtis and Associates to come up with a planning solution that would meet corporate requirements for "attractive but sensibly priced and durable cafeteria design" in their regional office.

Durability was the least of the design team's problems when it became clear that in order to meet stringent California code requirements for ingress, egress, and exhaust

ventilation, the only economically viable location for the new cafeteria was an annexed concrete parking garage. There, instead of facing mundane restrictions like limited square footage and oppressively low ceilings, CMC faced open air and 8,700 square feet of massive, raw concrete structural columns set 10'-0" from the peripheral wall and attached by tie beams.

As part of their design solution, the CMC team decided to "make a feature of" both the columns and the tie beams. The column spacing was utilized to modulate drywall ceiling beams that create a framework for indirect-light coves. Texaco red horizontal reveals break up the long perspective in high ceiling areas. At the window wall, a red linear light tube provides lighting at night.

Detailing in the cafeteria servery evolved naturally from two sources: the strong architectural elements of the original structure and the spatial/storage requirements requested by both food-service operator Sergio Gluschankoff and kitchen consultants Laschober & Sovich Inc. A racetrack-oval salad-bar island became the focal point of the servery area. The island was integrated with the overall space by echoing column forms and beam colors.

The base cabinet of the salad bar is constructed of heavy-duty, ¾-inch clear birch veneer for visual warmth. To accommodate built-in refrigeration units, ventilation slots were carved into two of the equal-sized birch panels that face the island in elevation. The vertical column shafts at the polar ends of the island are actually enameled and varnished 12-inch hollow Pittcon softforms, which disguise plumbing and electrical lines. The column shafts are anchored to the island cabinetry by stainless steel collars that match the counter surface. The brass and wire-glass sneeze guard, required by health code, is freely suspended on aircraft cable by a stub end turnbuckle hidden by a sheetrock cove recessed into an acoustical lay-in ceiling (*elevation; section*).

Of particular interest in the overall planning of the servery is CMC's attention to details within details. The design team developed a lively signage program for the cafeteria, which incorporates the Texaco logo into its typography (*elevation*). Signage panels are rendered in enameled metal and are suspended by the same aircraft cable used to suspend the sneeze guard.

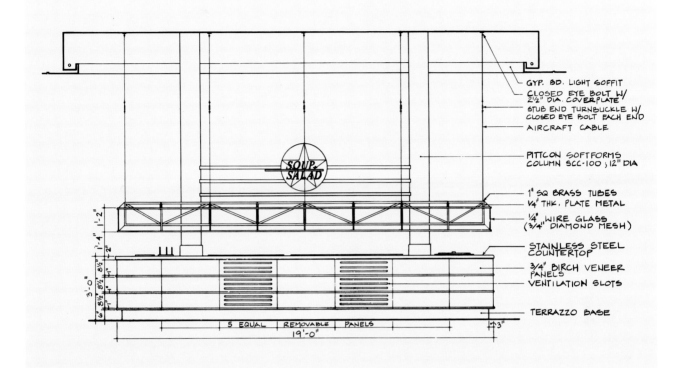

GYP. BD. LIGHT SOFFIT
CLOSED EYE BOLT W/ 2½" DIA. COVERPLATE
STUB END TURNBUCKLE W/ CLOSED EYE BOLT EACH END
AIRCRAFT CABLE

PITTCON SOFTFORMS COLUMN SCC-100 ; 12" DIA

1" SQ BRASS TUBES
¼" THK. PLATE METAL
¼" WIRE GLASS (¾" DIAMOND MESH)

STAINLESS STEEL COUNTERTOP
¾" BIRCH VENEER PANELS
VENTILATION SLOTS

TERRAZZO BASE

5 EQUAL REMOVABLE PANELS
19'-0"

ELEVATION

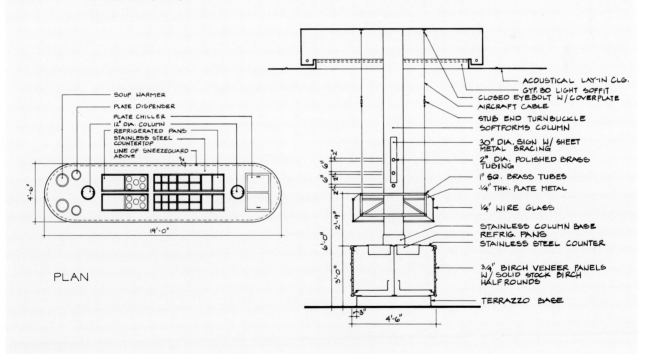

SOUP WARMER
PLATE DISPENSER
PLATE CHILLER
12" DIA. COLUMN
REFRIGERATED PANS
STAINLESS STEEL COUNTERTOP
LINE OF SNEEZEGUARD ABOVE

4'-6"
19'-0"

PLAN

ACOUSTICAL LAY-IN CLG.
GYP. BD. LIGHT SOFFIT
CLOSED EYEBOLT W/ COVERPLATE
AIRCRAFT CABLE
STUB END TURNBUCKLE
SOFTFORMS COLUMN

30" DIA. SIGN W/ SHEET METAL BRACING
2" DIA. POLISHED BRASS TUBING
1" SQ. BRASS TUBES
¼" THK. PLATE METAL
¼" WIRE GLASS

STAINLESS COLUMN BASE
REFRIG. PANS
STAINLESS STEEL COUNTER

¾" BIRCH VENEER PANELS W/ SOLID STOCK BIRCH HALF ROUNDS

TERRAZZO BASE

4'-6"

SECTION

SALAD BAR

ALABAMA POWER COMPANY
Birmingham, Alabama

Architecture/Interior Design
Geddes Brecher Qualls Cunningham;
Gresham, Smith and Partners
Design Team
James Snyder, Mark Williams,
Charles Alexander
Fabrication
Masonry Arts
Kitchen Consultant
Romano Gatland
Photography
© Durston Saylor

As a public-relations gesture, the cafeteria at the Alabama Power Company's corporate headquarters in Birmingham, Alabama, is available to the general public as well as to the corporation's 1,800 in-house employees. To comfortably accommodate the daily crowds who use the ground-floor facility for breakfast and snacks as well as for lunch, the servery and the 450-seat cafeteria were given over half of the 56,000 square feet allocated to the building's sun-drenched, four-story entrance atrium.

To project-associated architects Geddes Brecher Qualls Cunningham of Philadelphia and Gresham, Smith and Partners of Birmingham, Alabama, moving people efficiently through the servery to the cafeteria seating area meant using the "scatter system." (The scatter system allows customers to proceed directly to individual service counters where they are served a designated food category, rather than being detained by a single traffic line.) In order to permit the imposition of more servery stations, the design team created staggered offset counter areas. The resulting servery windows add intimacy to the space as a whole by breaking up what would otherwise have been long expanses of flat walls.

Free-standing salad-bar islands provide similar advantages. The design team chose to locate the salad bars on the diagonal, parallel to the offset servery windows. To establish visual unity, both with the servery-station walls and with the existing cashier counters and hot-beverage island, the

design team specified that the salad bars be finished in three shades of granite. Similarly, the stainless steel shelves and tray glides reiterate the stainless steel used for the signage panels and trim.

The salad bar's subframe is constructed of concrete masonry units resting on a mortar setting bed on the concrete slab floor. The granite fascia panels rest on continuous steel angles anchored to the masonry. All panels are also attached to the masonry with steel ties. Granite joints are caulked; corners are quirk jointed. To create a kickspace, the panels were hung 4 inches above the floor. At each end of the cabinet, a stainless steel panel is recessed 4 inches and is hinged for easy access to the concealed drainage system.

The two 1'-0"-wide dark granite tray-glide shelves on each island rest on the masonry substructure at a height of 36 inches, leaving a 1-inch reveal beneath them. The stainless steel tray glides are routed into the granite and glued with silicone sealant. Thus, the tray glide is both mechanically and chemically attached to the granite.

Two cold pans and three cylindrical salad-dressing containers are recessed into the top surface of the island (*axonometric*). The insulated cold pans, which are self-rimming units fabricated in 16-gauge stainless steel, are mounted on rigid plastic foam. A channel stiffener lies under the cold pan to hold the plastic foam.

In deference to health-code stipulations, salad ingredients are lit by standard fluorescent fixtures screwed into the underside of a stainless steel cap. Each fluorescent fixture is equipped with an explosion plate to provide a safe, sanitary means for the display of fresh vegetables. The cap, which doubles as a display shelf, is supported by four 1'-6"-high square stainless steel bracing posts. On either horizontal side of the cap, a quarter-circular Plexiglas sneeze guard projects down 1'-0". Each Plexiglas canopy is held to shape by a curved metal glazing channel sealed to the Plexiglas and screwed to the steel cap.

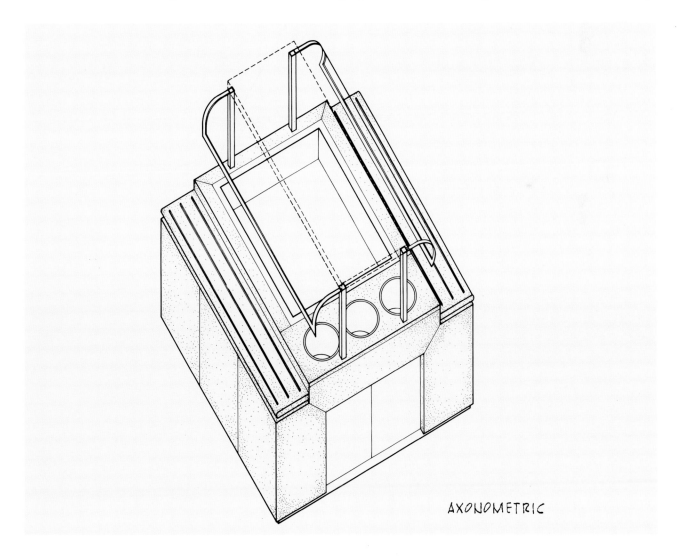

AXONOMETRIC

SALAD BAR

GENERAL CINEMA CORPORATION
Newton, Massachusetts

Architecture/Interior Design
The Stubbins Associates, Inc./Interior
Design Group
Design Team
Philip T. Seibert, Jr., Sebastian L. LaBella,
Sandra Mika, David D. Stone
Fabrication
Chain Construction Corporation
Light Fixture Manufacturer
Guardco
Photography
© Edward Jacoby, Jacoby Photography

GENERAL CINEMA CORPORATION commissioned The Stubbins Associates, Inc./ Interior Design Group, of Cambridge, Massachusetts, to install a new employee dining facility in its Newton, Massachusetts, executive office building. The 3,600-square-foot facility includes a kitchen, a servery, and three dining areas, which accommodate three daily breakfast and lunch seatings of seventy people each.

General Cinema Corporation wanted its dining facility to provide a pleasant environment that would act as an inducement to employees to remain in the office building during lunch. In the servery, the Stubbins team responded with a design that lends a "theatrical touch of excitement" to the area by utilizing bright tiles, bold shapes and colors, and signage executed in lively, multicolored neon script.

The servery's central feature is the red tiled stainless steel salad bar, with its bright yellow and clear acrylic sneeze guard-cum-light fixture. The 45-degree twist of each end of the bar in combination with the boldly suspended sneeze guard transforms an otherwise heavy form into a free-floating shape that sets the tone for the entire area.

The sneeze guard, which is positioned asymmetrically over the 5-foot cold pan (*plan of tube fixture*), is required by health code. It is constructed of two basic elements: an 8'-0" commercial fluorescent lighting fixture in the form of a 4-inch-radius tube of enameled, rolled aluminum and the guard itself, a 5'-0"-long molded sheet of 3/16-inch clear acrylic

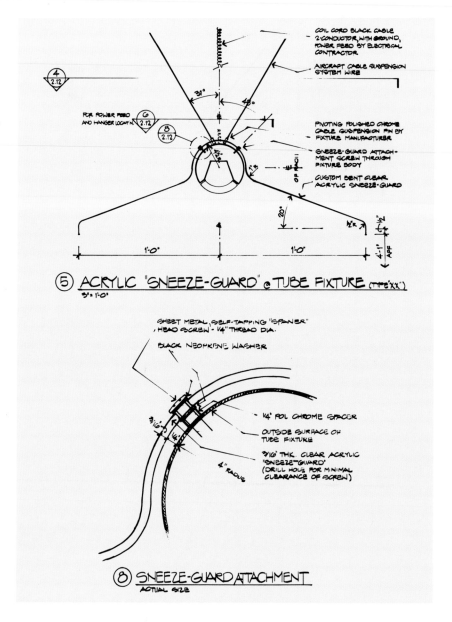

⑤ ACRYLIC "SNEEZE-GUARD" @ TUBE FIXTURE (TYPE 'XX')

⑧ SNEEZE-GUARD ATTACHMENT
ACTUAL SIZE

plastic. A plastic explosion protector is fitted into the bottom of the fixture. The middle of the acrylic sheet is bent to fit the curvature of the tube light fixture, which extends the length of the bar's 8-foot main axis. The sheet is affixed to the fixture's aluminum skin with ¼-inch, self-tapping sheet-metal screws set 45 degrees off the vertical on both sides and held ¼ inch away from the aluminum with chrome spacers (*acrylic "sneeze-guard" @ tube fixture; sneeze-guard attachment*). Each side of the guard slopes 9¾ inches away from the light fixture at a 20-degree angle, ending with a

vertical 1½-inch flange. The resultant height above the floor of each flange's bottom edge is 4'-1".

The entire unit is suspended from the ceiling with aircraft cable attached to chrome suspension pins that were fitted to the aluminum skin of the fixture by the contractor. The design team used two sets of two cables, with each cable angled 31 degrees away from the vertical to eliminate sway (*acrylic "sneeze-guard" @ tube fixture*). The fixture's electrical feed comes from the ceiling through a discreet, black, vertically suspended coiled wire.

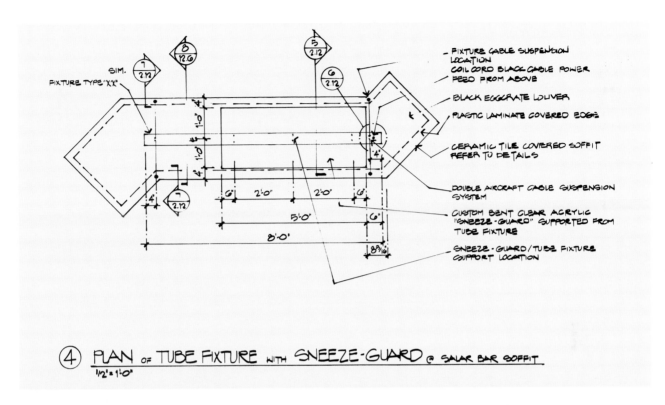

FIXTURE CABLE SUSPENSION LOCATION
COIL CORD BLACK CABLE POWER FEED FROM ABOVE

BLACK EGGCRATE LOUVER

PLASTIC LAMINATE COVERED EDGE

CERAMIC TILE COVERED SOFFIT
REFER TO DETAILS

DOUBLE AIRCRAFT CABLE SUSPENSION SYSTEM

CUSTOM BENT CLEAR ACRYLIC "SNEEZE-GUARD" SUPPORTED FROM TUBE FIXTURE

SNEEZE-GUARD/TUBE FIXTURE SUPPORT LOCATION

SIM.

FIXTURE TYPE "XX"

④ PLAN OF TUBE FIXTURE WITH SNEEZE-GUARD @ SALAR BAR SOFFIT
1/2" = 1'-0"

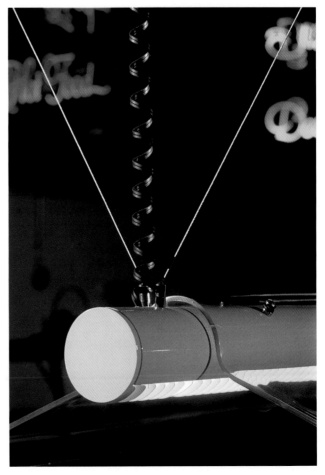

SECURITY DESK

1001 PENNSYLVANIA AVENUE
Washington, D.C.

Architecture/Interior Design
Hartman-Cox Architects
Design Team
George Hartman, Graham Davidson
Fabrication
MX Marble & Granite, Inc.
Photography
© Durston Saylor

THE PRODUCERS OF *Broadcast News*, a 1987 movie about television journalism, needed to find an impressive Washington, D.C., office building for location shooting background. 1001 Pennsylvania Avenue, developed by Cadillac-Fairview Urban Development Corporation of Dallas and designed by Hartman-Cox Architects of Washington, D.C., provided just the right "traditional but larger-than-life" atmosphere.

Of the many beautifully rendered details (pages 85, 112, and 177) that drew the production crew to the building, the most striking was the ground-floor security desk, grandly

situated underneath a six-story barrel-vaulted lobby ceiling at the convergence point of four entrance concourses, or two central axes. To accommodate working space for lobby attendants, a twenty-four-hour security guard, and the building's concierge, the desk was designed as an octagon with a 12'-6" diagonal and two entry gates on the primary axis. Although correspondingly imposing in scale, the desk is entirely in keeping with the scale of the expansive 75-foot by 75-foot area of the lobby. In fact, the desk and its 20-foot-high, four-faced Victorian clock bring the scale of the lobby into human focus and anchor the area as the building's center of vitality.

The style and materials specified for the desk and clock echo the finish materials of the concourses and lobby. Recessed panels in the desk fascia reiterate pilaster detailing (*elevations*). The carved edge of the desktop is suggestive of the concourse cornices. The desk's fascia of Verde St. Nicholas marble repeats the marble of the pilasters and cornices—a color theme

that recurs in the elaborately patterned green floor stone. The clock, although fabricated of cast aluminum, is painted to resemble the brass used for the lobby doors and the concourse bridge railing.

The desk substructure is a frame of steel channels and angles, which are bolted to the concrete slab. Gypsum board is screwed to the frame, and ¾-inch- to 2-inch-thick marble fascia panels, which were precut in Italy, are glued to the gypsum board with epoxy. The joints of the panels are treated with a dark grout to disguise the seams. Desk attendants use a work surface beneath and protruding 6 inches out from the countertop. The desk's steel frame serves as a bracket to support the white Carrara marble work surface. Dark gray plastic laminate panels run vertically from the top side of the shelf to the bottom side of the countertop; the top is screwed to the support and bolted to the steel frame. In-floor wiring boxes provide the electricity needed for security monitors and other technical reception-area equipment.

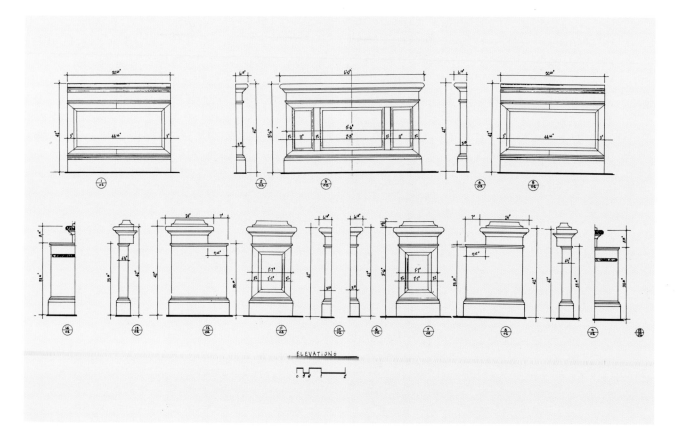

ELEVATIONS

Servery

ENRON CORP OFFICES
Houston, Texas

Interior Design
Gensler and Associates/Architects,
Houston
Design Team
Antony Harbour, Mark Shinn,
Gary Grether, Evelyn Fujimoto,
Gregory Burke (drawings)
Fabrication
Kitchen Equipment Fabricators
Photography
© Nick Merrick, Hedrich-Blessing

ENRON CORP IS A newly established natural-gas pipeline company formed by the merger of the Houston Natural Gas Company and Internorth of Omaha, Nebraska. Enron's managing directors asked their designers, Gensler and Associates/Architects of Houston, Texas, to plan new facilities in an upscale office building that would reflect "an aesthetic as modern, upbeat, and progressive as the corporation's current position within its industry."

Twenty-four thousand square feet of the 1,250,000-square-foot Enron facility are devoted to the company's cafeteria, which comfortably serves fifteen hundred employees two meals and two snacks per day. Code restrictions made it necessary to locate the cafeteria on the second floor. Because the building's elevators do not stop at that level, the cafeteria is accessed from the ground floor by escalator or staircase.

The design team divided the space into a servery corridor, two private dining rooms, and a 320-seat open-seating dining room. The sophisticated styling of the Enron cafeteria belies its $140-per-square-foot construction cost. Gensler accomplished such pedestrian panache by keeping the plan simple, eliminating extraneous detailing, and rendering the remaining basics with considerably more flair than financial investment.

The focal point of the servery "street" are the storefront canopies, which demarcate scatter-plan serving bays spaced 15 feet on center. The serving bays are separated by 3'-10" steel frames enclosed in laminate-covered peninsular partitions, which allow discreet storage of rolling carts

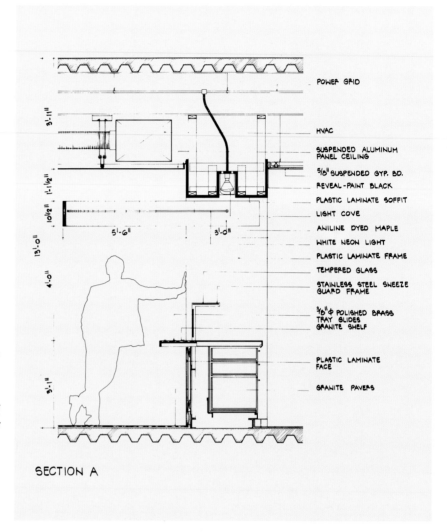

POWER GRID

HVAC

SUSPENDED ALUMINUM
PANEL CEILING

5/8" SUSPENDED GYP. BD.

REVEAL - PAINT BLACK

PLASTIC LAMINATE SOFFIT

LIGHT COVE

ANILINE DYED MAPLE

WHITE NEON LIGHT

PLASTIC LAMINATE FRAME

TEMPERED GLASS

STAINLESS STEEL SNEEZE
GUARD FRAME

3/8"∅ POLISHED BRASS
TRAY GLIDES
GRANITE SHELF

PLASTIC LAMINATE
FACE

GRANITE PAVERS

SECTION A

and other kitchen-related paraphernalia (*plan*). The serving bays themselves are framed-in with steel and metal studs to support and prevent torque from heavy granite countertop shelves. Z-clips position plastic laminate fascia covers (*elevation*).

The serving bays' custom-designed sneeze guards, tray glides, and window cover panels add elegance to the overall composition. The sneeze guards are constructed of right-angle stainless steel brackets that hold clear panels of tempered glass—not the usual Plexiglas—in place. The solid brass tray glides are ⅜-inch plugs driven into pre-drilled granite shelves. Window cover panels appear to float between painted steel rods, reiterating in square geometry the positive/negative relationship established by the round tray glides.

The servery's eye-catching canopies are constructed of aniline-dyed maple veneer over a simple particleboard subframe (*section A*). The design team's intention to "keep the detailing tight and clean" is boldly demonstrated by the neon lighting strip that sweeps the interior curve of each canopy. The neon tubes are held in place by fifteen equally spaced anchors imbedded in the wood and plugged with analine maple circles. Clear Plexiglas shields (a health code requirement) protect the serving area from glass shards should the tubes ever shatter.

The design team finished the horizontal planes of ceilings and floors with high-quality materials. The suspended metal-panel ceiling and granite floor pavers add a glossy finish to an already slick design package.

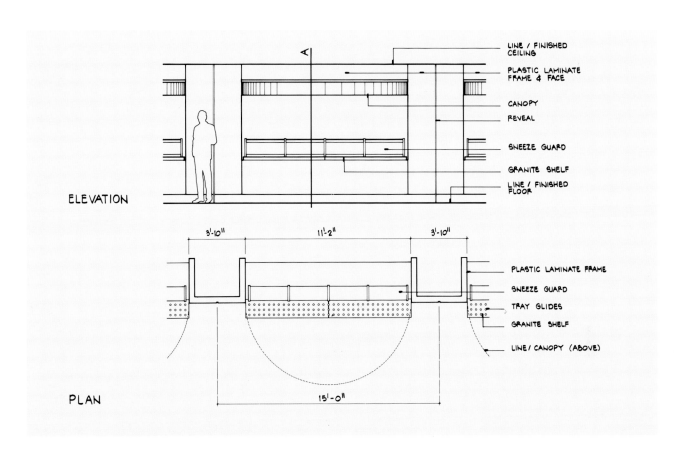

ELEVATION

LINE / FINISHED CEILING

PLASTIC LAMINATE FRAME & FACE

CANOPY

REVEAL

SNEEZE GUARD

GRANITE SHELF

LINE / FINISHED FLOOR

3'-10"   11'-2"   3'-10"

PLAN

15'-0"

PLASTIC LAMINATE FRAME

SNEEZE GUARD

TRAY GLIDES

GRANITE SHELF

LINE / CANOPY (ABOVE)

SIGNAGE

ALABAMA POWER COMPANY
Birmingham, Alabama

Architecture/Interior Design
Geddes Brecher Qualls Cunningham;
Gresham, Smith and Partners
Design Team
Steven Yarnall, Alice Word
Fabrication
Cooper Architectural Signs
Photography
© Durston Saylor

THE NEW BIRMINGHAM headquarters of the Alabama Power Company is replete with detailing subtleties designed by Geddes Brecher Qualls Cunningham of Philadelphia and Gresham, Smith and Partners of Birmingham. Proving that no detail was too small to receive special handling, signage throughout the building was also treated to the project team's standard of excellence.

The company's executives agreed with the graphic-design team that signage should "fully integrate the building's graphics with the interiors." In consequence, signage details were designed to complement the surroundings—rather than compete with them.

Signage is three-dimensional and is either carved in stone or applied in relief on stainless steel. The elevator-bank entrance on the ground floor exemplifies the designers' graphic approach. Typography on the gray slate walls is deeply incised, broadly enough that letters do not appear shadowed. The curved surfaces of the carvings are finished more smoothly than is the wall surface surrounding them, which causes the letters to appear lighter than the stone in which they are cut. On the other hand, the appliqué lettering on the transom valance appears to be darker than the brushed stainless steel from which it stands out.

Because Alabama Power Company's corporate headquarters has a consistently modest public traffic flow, it was not necessary to proclaim information in a dominant manner that would be appropriate for more public spaces. The choice of five-inch letters produces an effect that is visual but not

focal. The applied stainless steel letters were precision cut from ¼-inch No. 4 brushed-finish stainless steel, with the grain of the letters matching that of the valance as an effective way to reduce glare. The letters were mounted on the valance with industrial epoxy adhesive, which was then held in place by jigs and gaffer's tape until secure. Because the design team chose this chemical-adhesion method rather than the use of penetrating bolts or studs, the valance was not prone to oil-can buckling.

The executives of the Alabama Power Company had originally decided to impose the use of the corporate-logo typeface (a style similar to Optima) within the new headquarters building, but GBQC graphic designer Steven Yarnall convinced management that Times New Roman was more in keeping with the dignified image of the new building. Standard logo typography was appropriately relegated to older company buildings, to satellite facilities, and to other less image-conscious corporate buildings.

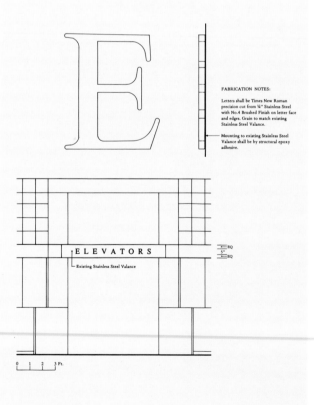

FABRICATION NOTES:

Letters shall be Times New Roman precision cut from ¼" Stainless Steel with No.4 Brushed Finish on letter face and edges. Grain to match existing Stainless Steel Valance.

Mounting to existing Stainless Steel Valance shall be by structural epoxy adhesive.

ELEVATORS
Existing Stainless Steel Valance

0 1 2 3 Ft.

SIGNAGE

CROCKER NATIONAL BANK
San Francisco, California

Architecture/Interior Design
Gensler and Associates/Architects,
San Francisco

Design Team
John Bricker, Barbara Leistico

Fabrication
Zebra Awnings

Bracket Fabrication
Manuel Palos

Photography
© David Wakely

ALTHOUGH MODEST SIGNS are appropriate in most public locations, there are times when the ordinary must become extraordinary. Such is the case with the signage that the Crocker National Bank (now a Wells Fargo Bank) hired Gensler and Associates/Architects of San Francisco to develop. The client mandate required functional, information-providing signs that would not detract from the elegant turn-of-the-century landmark building in San Francisco's financial district that houses the bank's headquarters.

The bank's offices occupy 20,000 square feet of polished, Beaux-Arts grandeur. In keeping with the dignity

of the marble interior, the design team installed elegantly designed signs on the ground level (see pages 84 and 136) and draped nine dramatic banners through the enormous space above the main banking floor.

The banners are made of a luxurious silk fabric, custom-dyed blue-gray to match the bank's corporate color. A geometric pattern has been silk-screened onto the fabric as a subtle textural contrast to the base color of the silk. The "grille" motif that is silk-screened in gold over the metallic blue background was adapted by the design team from an existing wall-mounted air grille. On the five purely ornamental banners, the pattern continues top to bottom. On the other four, the "grille" pattern ends halfway down the banner's 12'-0" length. The 4-inch-high opaque white typography is silk-screened approximately four feet up from the bottom of the banner.

Each banner is actually a double length draped over an inverted bracket. The ornamental curved upper part of each bracket is antiqued plaster, cast from a mold based on an assemblage of various detail parts adapted from the existing building.

The horizontal bar is steel. Slippage of the draped banner is prevented by a metal plate over the banner, which is screwed through the banner into the bar. In addition, metal bars sewn into the banners' hems prevent flapping. Wall brackets are screwed to steel plates that are either bolted to a wall or, in the case of each of two 8'-5" banners announcing new accounts, the brackets are welded to a 13'-10¼" brass pole, which is bolted to the marble floor (*elevation*).

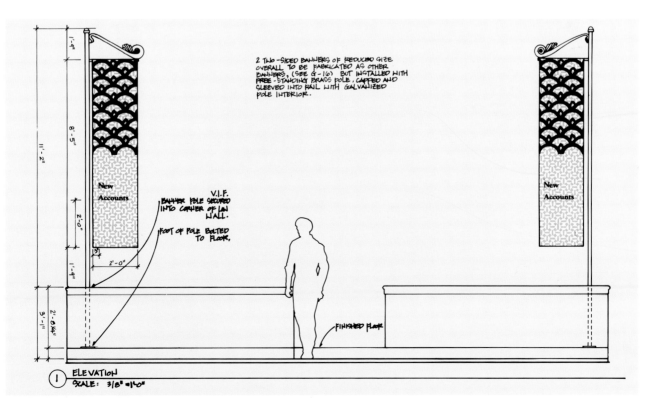

2 two-sided banners of reduced size overall to be fabricated as other banners, (see G-16) but installed with free-standing brass pole, capped and sleeved into rail with galvanized pole interior.

New Accounts

BANNER POLE SECURED INTO CORNER OF LOW WALL. V.I.F.

FOOT OF POLE BOLTED TO FLOOR.

New Accounts

FINISHED FLOOR

1 ELEVATION
SCALE: 3/8" = 1'-0"

SODA FOUNTAIN

BROADWAY SOUTHWEST
Denver, Colorado

Interior Design
Cole Martinez Curtis and Associates
Design Team
Leo Martinez, Dennis Takeda,
Jayne Peterson, Cynthia Rubin,
Paul Lechleiter, Joseph Magnetti,
Matthew Marten (drawing)
Fabrication
Hochberg Bros. Schan of California, Inc.
Photography
© Toshi Yoshimi

THE BROADWAY SOUTHWEST stores believe that children—as well as adults—deserve entertainment and opportunities for refreshment while shopping. Cole Martinez Curtis and Associates of Marina del Rey, California, was hired to design a prototype soda fountain for the Broadway Southwest store in Denver, Colorado.

Project executive Dennis Takeda and project designer Paul Lechleiter were given a 446-square-foot area in the children's department for the installation of a modern-day soda fountain. Because their end-users would necessarily fall short of adult ergonomic standards, their first priority was to develop an appropriate planning scale. Every detail in the soda fountain is scaled down 6 inches from the norm—from the counters and revolving stools to the standard restaurant equipment. Seat heights are 25 inches from the floor. The counter and equipment heights are 3'-0". Adjustments were also made in the positioning and angling of the sneeze guards (required by health code), which are placed directly over the counter rather than suspended above it.

The soda fountain accommodates seven seated customers, as well as four standing customers at the central ordering station. Larger crowds are dispersed to pint-sized standing counters, which are cantilevered from the side walls as well as from the interior side of the entrance partition walls (*axonometric*). The counter and the bar at the rear are constructed of laminate-covered particleboard for durability and ease of maintenance. The utilitarian construction of the soda fountain and backbar is enlivened by the visual rhythm of alternating angles and curves and by mirrors that are applied with adhesives to the rear partition wall. The cheerful ice-cream colors of the fiberglass column covers, laminates, and vinyl upholstery finishes give this shoppers' stopover a playful and lively ambience.

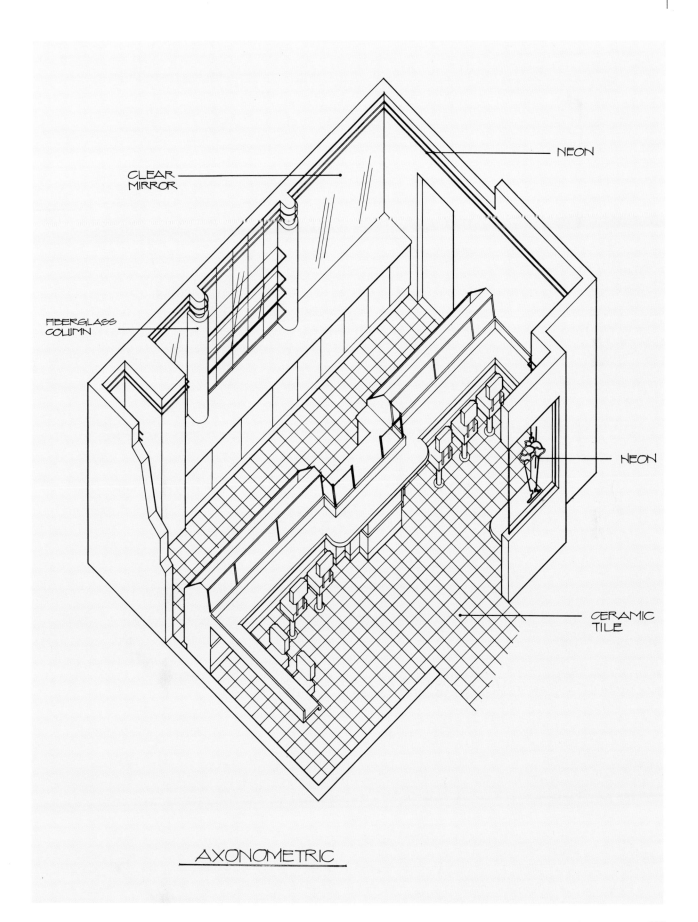

NEON

CLEAR
MIRROR

FIBERGLASS
COLUMN

NEON

CERAMIC
TILE

AXONOMETRIC

SOFFIT

VENTANA CANYON GOLF AND RACQUET CLUB
Tucson, Arizona

Architecture/Interior Design
Anderson DeBartolo Pan, Inc.
Design Team
Jack DeBartolo, Jr., Michael Osburn
Fabrication
Sundt Construction
Photography
© Timothy Hursley

THE BAR IN THE Ventana Canyon Golf and Racquet Club in Tucson, Arizona, is intended to be an interior oasis. The bar's cool angularity was planned to contrast with the undulating foothills and fiery heat of the Santa Catalina desert landscape outside.

Anderson DeBartolo Pan, Inc., of Tucson designed the club's main bar to advance the plan with an original,

four-tiered soffit. The angularity of the design was emphasized by the right-angled 1'-0" setbacks, which step down from the 12'-0" ceiling (*section A*). Angularity was reemphasized by scooping out the exposed corner of each tier into eight 1'-0" square faces, each at a right angle to the next. Since the 1'-0" setbacks were continued in the corner, the effect is the apparent erosion of the corner into an inverted pile of 1-foot cubes (*elevation*). The design team carried the setback motif from the soffit to the corbeled door and to the front of the bar itself, where the pattern is repeated in inlaid brass (*axonometric; elevation*).

Vertical faces of the tiers and "cubes" were painted alternately teal blue or mauve, creating a color design in addition to the geometric play of forms. The design team chose these particular colors in an effort to

create a relaxed, intimate atmosphere that would harmonize with the desert sunsets that are visible from the bar.

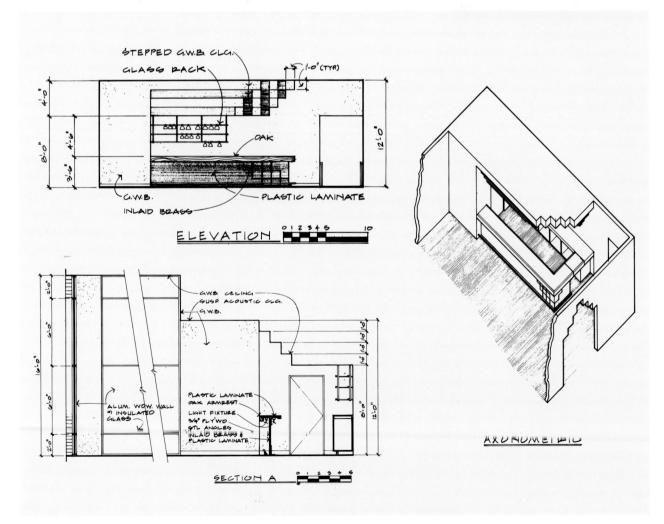

ELEVATION

SECTION A

AXONOMETRIC

SOFFIT

POMPANO SQUARE MALL
Pompano Beach, Florida

Architecture/Interior Design
Walker Group/CNI
Design Team
Edwin Sierra, Sandra Hagashi,
Michael Guilroy, Steven Kitezh
Fabrication
M-P Contractors
Photography
© Kate Zari

FROM THE 1950S until the early 1980s, "shopping-mall design" might have been construed as a contradiction in terms. That was before retailing specialists like Walker Group/CNI of New York City began to show developers that the design ambience of the shopping facility as a whole was as important a traffic draw as the quality of individual retail stores.

LaSalle Partners, Inc., commissioned Walker Group/CNI to reconfigure and facelift the 1950s-era Pompano Square Mall in Pompano Beach, Florida. The design team was asked to integrate a second-floor space, which had been occupied formerly by a series of closed manage-ment offices, into the retail floor below. The purpose of the revised plan was to replace a franchised fast-food restaurant on the second floor with a 10,000- to 12,000-square-foot food court. A secondary concern was to visually soften and make more inviting the uncompromising angularity of the mall's interior.

Walker Group/CNI utilized both its former specialty in graphic design and its skill in retail planning to develop a series of boldly painted break-out balconies, which are incorporated into the gutted and simply refurbished second floor. As viewed from the lower courtyard, colorful stair-stepped soffit fascias on the balconies recur at regular intervals along the two-story walkway, adding an important element of architectural and graphic unity to the vast interior.

The soffit balconies are cantilevered out 6'-0" to 8'-0" from existing structural beams and are constructed of steel-reinforced concrete, which is faced with standard gypsum board over aluminum studs. The pastel colors of the fascia were chosen to reflect the semitropical locale and to emphasize the broad curves (56-foot radius)

and the steps of the balconies against the angular surfaces of the existing building.

Originally, the second floor had no access from the public areas below. Walker Group/CNI added an escalator that required the inclusion of new columns for support. The design team enclosed the columns in plaster cones—a shape that adds interest and reduces bulk.

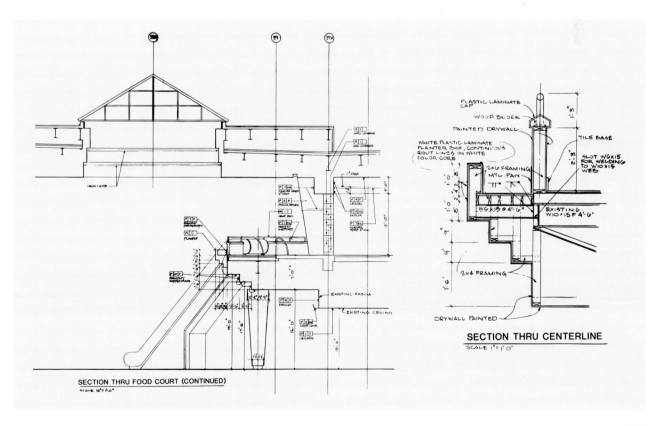

SECTION THRU CENTERLINE
SCALE 1"=1'-0"

SECTION THRU FOOD COURT (CONTINUED)
SCALE ⅛"=1'-0"

SOFFIT

FIDELITY INVESTMENTS SALES CENTER
New York City

Interior Design
ISD Incorporated, New York City
Design Team
Daniel Gundrum, Paul Muench,
James Gueguierre
Mural Fabrication
SLAG
Photography
© Wolfgang Hoyt, ESTO

FOR YEARS, Fidelity Investments, head-quartered in Boston, conducted its business in New York City with print ads placed in magazines and newspapers, supplemented by an 800-number telephone line. However, changing times and stiffer competition convinced the officers of Fidelity to take a more aggressive marketing approach.

As step one in the implementation of a new marketing program, the firm leased ground-floor office space on the corner of Park Avenue and 51st Street in Manhattan. Because the intended purpose of the 5,000-square-foot space was to disseminate mutual fund information to the public in an educational, self-service, sales-center format, step two was to hire ISD Incorporated of New York City to design an interior "with enough graphic style to draw in pedestrian traffic, which at the same time conveys a sense of permanence and solidity."

Working with base building construction in a postwar building that project director Daniel Gundrum described as "bogus Mies," the ISD design team developed a floor plan that in one fell swoop connects the differing ceiling heights of closed offices to public spaces by means of a prominent curved soffit (*axonometric*).

A horizontal display of digital market information runs across the lower edge of the soffit construction; above, a Rockefeller Center–like mural de-picts a series of financially oriented New York City landmarks.

The soffit is constructed of bent gypsum board overlaid with pre-painted canvas panels, which are affixed to the soffit surface with wall-paper glue. The composition of the mural was carefully planned to conceal seams; for example, strategically placed rays of light and built-up tones eliminate the viewer's awareness of seam junctures. The digital display is held in place by a recessed stainless steel apron that is bolted and seam-welded to the subframe (*elevation*).

The Rockefeller Center allusion is reiterated in other finish materials: paneling is finished in Sapele fiddle-back mahogany; both the paneling and the terrazzo flooring are banded in stainless steel.

The Fidelity Investments Sales Center was a fast-track project. The ISD design team completed the entire job from inception to installation in just three months.

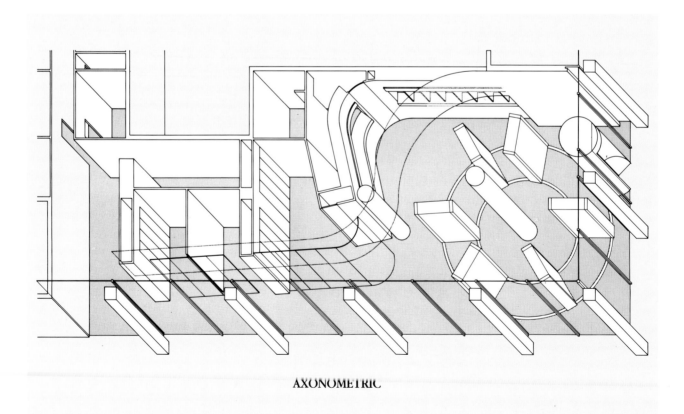

AXONOMETRIC

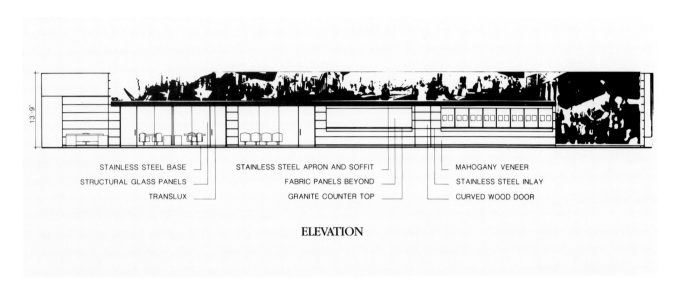

STAINLESS STEEL BASE   STAINLESS STEEL APRON AND SOFFIT   MAHOGANY VENEER

STRUCTURAL GLASS PANELS   FABRIC PANELS BEYOND   STAINLESS STEEL INLAY

TRANSLUX   GRANITE COUNTER TOP   CURVED WOOD DOOR

ELEVATION

STAIRCASE

THE PRUDENTIAL INSURANCE COMPANY OF AMERICA EASTERN HOME OFFICE
Dresher, Pennsylvania

Architecture/Interior Design
Daroff Design Inc.
Design Team
Karen Daroff, James Rappoport,
Norman Holloway, Martin Komitzky,
John Borne, David Layton
Fabrication
Marcantonio, Inc.
Photography
© Matt Wargo

IN THE EARLY 1970s, The Prudential Insurance Company of America built its eastern home office in Dresher, Pennsylvania. The manner in which the five separate sections of the building converged created a unique space planning and design challenge; the overriding impression retained by visitors was one of directional confusion. The company concluded that the original design would have to be modified and commissioned Daroff Design Inc. of Philadelphia to plan and implement the renovation.

The Daroff design team analyzed the traffic patterns of the complex and decided that the creation of an orientation point at the core of the central building would bring psychological and visual order to the maze of corridors. The most obvious location for an orientation area was the two-story "white-box" lobby. However, the lobby's uncompromisingly sheer walls gave rise to a practical as well as an aesthetic problem: Without a mezzanine or balcony, the second floor was accessible only through arterial interior staircases. As a result, the lobby performed no apparent function other than to usher people into the building.

The design team's solution was to open up the lobby to the second floor, install a balcony, and connect the two floors with a "monumental" staircase that would improve circulation as well as provide visual focus. To relieve the lobby's angularity, the Daroff team designed a curved staircase that reiterates the column-and-round-shape motif found elsewhere in the building. As a bonus, the curved stair saves space (a true helix around a narrow core is the most efficient stair design) and provides sculptural grace. Suspended, it becomes still more graceful.

The design team refined the staircase by winding the 6'-0"-wide steps within a relatively narrow radius of 9'-0". A secondary refinement limited the relatively narrow working-point angle of the stair treads to 33¾ degrees (*architectural plan lower level*). The result is a tautly controlled sinuous curve that is ideally proportioned to both the center column and the lobby's dimensions (*elevation*).

The staircase is constructed of reinforced concrete that was poured in place. To construct the staircase's 2'-4"-high walls, lengths of 1¼-inch steel pipe were attached to the concrete 4'-0" on center. Steel channels were welded between the pipes. Steel studs were screwed to the channel 16 inches on center, and two layers of gypsum board were applied over each side of the studs. A painted hardwood cap was then screwed to the wood blocking between the studs, leaving a narrow reveal between the cap and the wall. The gypsum board was finished with Zolatone, and the steps were covered in seafoam green carpeting.

The aluminum railing is screwed into the staircase wall. Railing supports on the balcony are welded to a steel channel, which is, in turn, welded to the steel pipes (*section*).

214

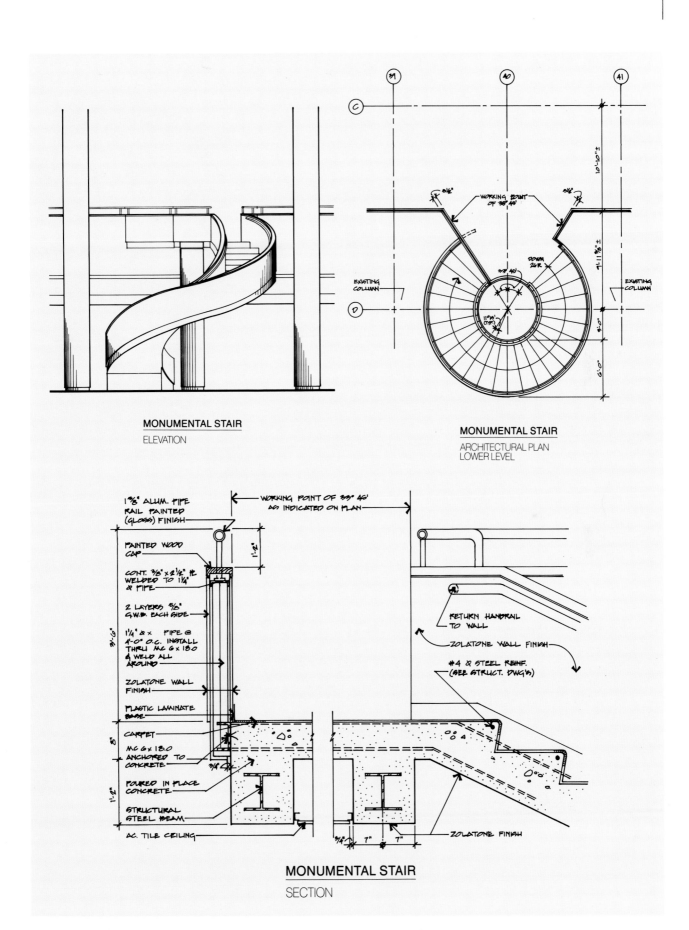

MONUMENTAL STAIR
ELEVATION

MONUMENTAL STAIR
ARCHITECTURAL PLAN
LOWER LEVEL

1⅜" ALUM. PIPE
RAIL PAINTED
(GLOSS) FINISH

WORKING POINT OF 33° 45'
AS INDICATED ON PLAN

PAINTED WOOD
CAP

CONT. ⅜" X 2½" PL.
WELDED TO 1¼"
Ø PIPE

2 LAYERS ⅝"
G.W.B. EACH SIDE

1¼" Ø X PIPE @
4'-0" O.C. INSTALL
THRU MC 6 X 18.0
& WELD ALL
AROUND

ZOLATONE WALL
FINISH

PLASTIC LAMINATE
BASE

CARPET

MC 6 X 18.0
ANCHORED TO
CONCRETE

POURED IN PLACE
CONCRETE

STRUCTURAL
STEEL BEAM

AC. TILE CEILING

RETURN HANDRAIL
TO WALL

ZOLATONE WALL FINISH

#4 Ø STEEL REINF.
(SEE STRUCT. DWG'S)

ZOLATONE FINISH

MONUMENTAL STAIR
SECTION

215

STAIRCASE

STATUE OF LIBERTY
New York Harbor

Architecture/Interior Design
Swanke Hayden Connell Architects
Associate Architect
The Office of Thierry W. Despont
Design Team
Richard S. Hayden, Robert Landsman
Engineers
Ammann and Whitney
Photography
© Dan Cornish, ESTO

THE REHABILITATION OF the Statue of Liberty, America's premier public monument, required more than technical skill on the part of the design team. It also required a commitment that prior to construction their solution be sanctioned, by consensus of all of the project's participants, as one that would be visually and psychologically *right*. Swanke Hayden Connell Architects of New York City won the commission for the renovation because of their long-established reputation in restoration work.

The design team worked under the demanding aegis of the Preservation and Historical divisions of the National Park Service and through The Statue of Liberty/Ellis Island Foundation and were also "subject to advice" from various city, state, and federal historical preservation societies. However, according to William Koelling, spokesperson for Swanke Hayden Connell Architects, parrying preservationist zeal against logistical reality was the least of the design team's problems. More difficult by far were the tasks of sorting out and identifying those structural elements in the statue that were original and those that had been altered or added during its lifespan, as well as identifying and implementing those alterations and additions that were deemed necessary to the statue's structural integrity.

In studying the available archival records of the statue, the design team and the National Park Service agreed that there had been no original plan for a staircase. Instead, the staircase had been installed shortly after the statue opened. Despite the timing of the staircase's installation, both the design firm and the National Park Service believe that because of its striking similarity to the staircase in the Eiffel Tower, the statue's staircase was designed by Alexandre Gustave Eiffel as well.

During the research phase of the project, the design team and the Park Service identified other elements, both original and nonoriginal, as targets for elimination, replacement, alteration, or repair. After review, a consensus of the project committee established that the screens in the secondary structure were to be eliminated and glass balustrades installed to open up the interior to visitor view; the torch flame was to be replaced with a replica of the original; "rest" platforms were to be installed intermittently along the ascending curve of the staircase balustrade; the staircase risers and treads were to be replaced; and a new emergency elevator was to be installed. The more politically delicate issue of repair or replacement of the statue's shoulder fell out on the side of repair rather than replacement in deference to the wish of the Park Service rather than that of the design team.

New concerns demanding resolution included a reassessment of the actual annual volume of sightseeing traffic and a corresponding revision of the statue's traffic pattern. The SHCA team also decided to install a stainless steel observation platform and 25 bronze window frames at the top of the statue.

Despite all these complex issues, the renovation of the staircase itself presented the most difficult challenge. The double-helix staircase begins at the top of the masonry pedestal and rises 112 feet 0 inches to Liberty's eyebrow level. The existing staircase was fabricated entirely of cast iron, much of which had worn or corroded to the point of danger. Since the preservation of as much "original" structure as possible had been agreed on as a paramount goal, the design team's first tasks were to determine

how much of the staircase could be used as it was, how much could be used with reinforcement, and how much would need to be replaced.

The design team used without change the staircase's main structural element, the 18-inch diameter central pipe around which the stairs wind (*elevation of helical stairs E-2 & E-3*). The designers did impress the pipe into double service as a ready-made air-conditioning duct, replacing its former solid cap at the upper-platform level with a grille (*plan of helical stair grille*). The designers retained all except the worst-worn stair treads, but they covered all existing treads with new stainless steel castings (*typical new tread*). The entire balustrade needed replacement, which the design team effected with stainless steel sheeting onto which is welded a stainless pipe railing (*section through crown platform*).

The design team changed only two other significant elements in the staircase design: the rest platforms and a new platform in the crown.

Replacing the old balustrade enabled the designers to replace an antiquated and unsafe system of seats mounted on the balustrade with a

series of intermediate balconylike rest platforms (*elevation of helical stairs E-2 & E-3*). The addition of the last of these platforms, at a height of 45 feet on the down staircase, appeared to produce vertigo in some visitors when they saw it in conjunction with the floor below. The designers countered the psychological effect by installing a second handrail welded to the interior pipe for the last 45 feet of the descent.

In the crown, the design team made a fundamental design decision based on an external aesthetic consideration—that visitors arriving at the goal of their pilgrimage should face the Manhattan skyline. To allow the view, the designers reversed the traffic flow on the staircases and redesigned the viewing platform accordingly, in stainless steel (*plan of crown platform; interior elevation of crown windows; plan of helical stair from crown down*). They also replaced the viewing window frames with new bronze frames.

The use of stainless steel was occasioned by the metal's durability and ease of maintenance. However, its use also caused two unusual problems. The juxtaposition of iron and stainless steel, which have differing electrochemical properties, can induce a slight electrical current—potentially enough to corrode junction points. In order to avoid that possibility, the design team inserted Teflon isolators between the stainless steel and the iron and used Teflon-coated screws to attach the new treads to the old. In order to make the steps as slip-proof as possible, the designers wanted to meld carborundum directly into the new tread castings. This required close collaboration with the foundry to devise a new casting technique.

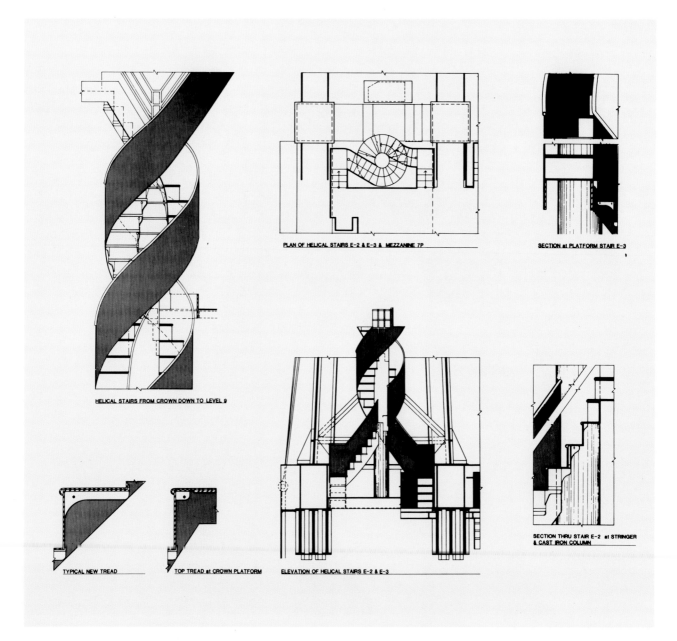

HELICAL STAIRS FROM CROWN DOWN TO LEVEL 9

PLAN OF HELICAL STAIRS E-2 & E-3 & MEZZANINE 7P

SECTION at PLATFORM STAIR E-3

TYPICAL NEW TREAD

TOP TREAD at CROWN PLATFORM

ELEVATION OF HELICAL STAIRS E-2 & E-3

SECTION THRU STAIR E-2 at STRINGER & CAST IRON COLUMN

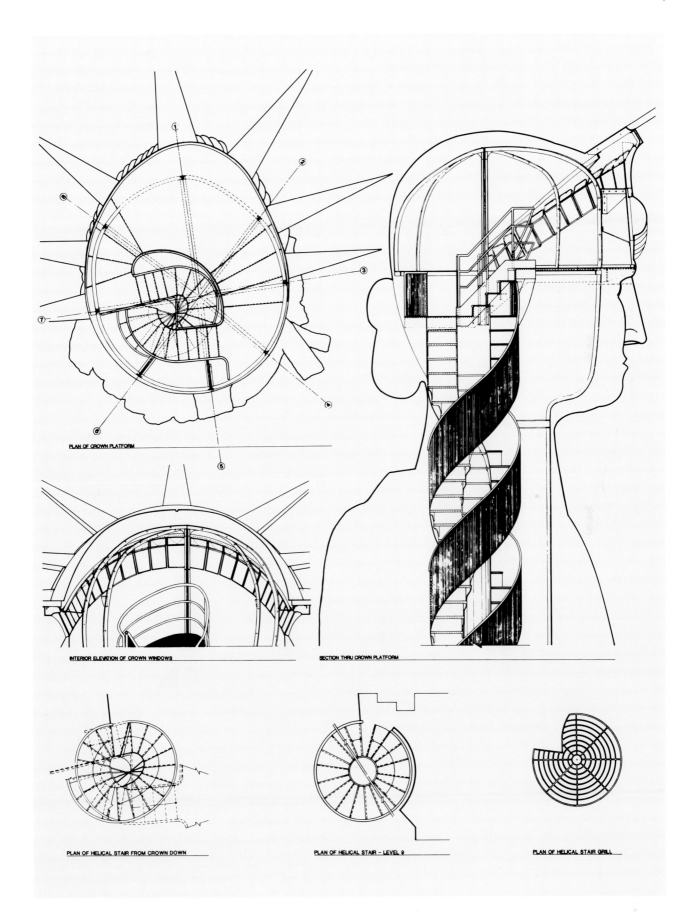

PLAN OF CROWN PLATFORM

INTERIOR ELEVATION OF CROWN WINDOWS

SECTION THRU CROWN PLATFORM

PLAN OF HELICAL STAIR FROM CROWN DOWN

PLAN OF HELICAL STAIR - LEVEL 9

PLAN OF HELICAL STAIR GRILL

STAIRCASE

**DEUTSCHE BANK
TAUNUSANLAGE**
Frankfurt, West Germany

Architecture/Interior Design
Charles Pfister Associates;
Robinson Mills + Williams;
ABB Architekten
Design Team
Charles Pfister, Joseph Matzo,
Sara Galbraith, James Leal
(Charles Pfister Associates);
Andrew Belschner, James Budzinsky
(Robinson Mills + Williams)
Photography
© Jaime Ardiles-Arce

DEUTSCHE BANK'S NEW Frankfurt, West Germany, headquarters consists principally of twin 44-story skyscrapers. Local regulations required that the bank include a space dedicated to the public. ABB Architekten, the building architects, responded by designing an exhibition gallery in a separate building adjacent to the two skyscrapers.

The gallery lobby needed a staircase to connect its two floors. The lobby also presented two notable difficulties: Two expansion joints ran through it, and a ramp led down from the ground floor to an underground parking garage. The collaborating designers, Charles Pfister Associates and Robinson Mills + Williams, both of San Francisco, addressed these conditions by producing a staircase of massive, theatrical proportions that serves as a cover for both the expansion joint and the down ramp. The team's solution "floats" giant slabs of polished granite over the expansion joint and encloses the ramp entrance in granite-block walls.

The first visual impression of the staircase is one of confusion. Were these steps left over from a Wagnerian stage set, down which giants strode? On closer inspection, it becomes evident that the giants' steps are not really the staircase at all but are only an ornamental element that tends to hide the actual, relatively modest granite steps. On still closer analysis, one gradually discovers that the apparent profusion of different shapes and angles is also illusory. The staircase is structurally simpler than it seems.

The staircase moves around three sides of a rectangular firestair enclosure (*plan*). Twelve triangular slabs of polished granite radiate from the "enclosed" corner of the stairwell, offering a suggestion of a broken circular staircase. Four more slabs radiate from near the opposite end of the firestair, completing the downward sweep of the whole mass.

The structural framework for the staircase is reinforced concrete poured in place (*section/elevation*). The steps themselves consist of precut pieces of solid thermal granite laid on a mortar bed over the concrete and are held in place with steel angles bolted into the concrete (*detail section at stairs*).

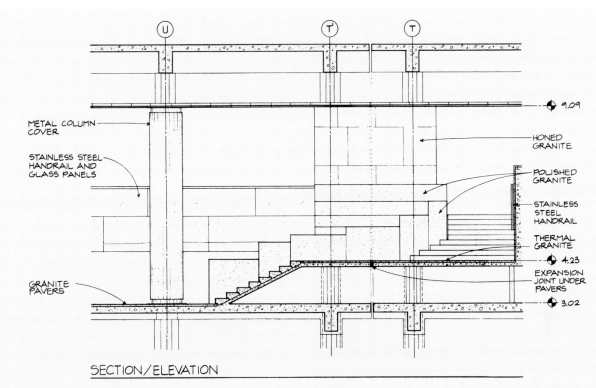

METAL COLUMN COVER

STAINLESS STEEL HANDRAIL AND GLASS PANELS

GRANITE PAVERS

HONED GRANITE

POLISHED GRANITE

STAINLESS STEEL HANDRAIL

THERMAL GRANITE

◈ 9.09

◈ 4.23

EXPANSION JOINT UNDER PAVERS

◈ 3.02

SECTION/ELEVATION

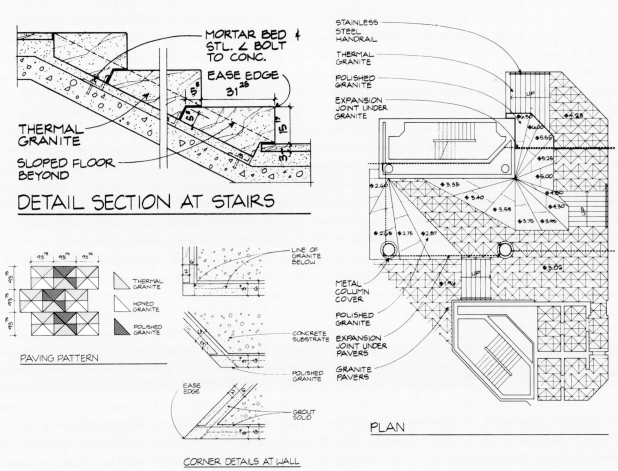

MORTAR BED & STL. ∠ BOLT TO CONC.

EASE EDGE 31²⁵

THERMAL GRANITE

SLOPED FLOOR BEYOND

DETAIL SECTION AT STAIRS

STAINLESS STEEL HANDRAIL

THERMAL GRANITE

POLISHED GRANITE

EXPANSION JOINT UNDER GRANITE

METAL COLUMN COVER

POLISHED GRANITE

EXPANSION JOINT UNDER PAVERS

GRANITE PAVERS

PLAN

THERMAL GRANITE

HONED GRANITE

POLISHED GRANITE

PAVING PATTERN

LINE OF GRANITE BELOW

CONCRETE SUBSTRATE

POLISHED GRANITE

EASE EDGE

GROUT SOLID

CORNER DETAILS AT WALL

STORAGE WALL

ALABAMA POWER COMPANY
Birmingham, Alabama

Architecture/Interior Design
Geddes Brecher Qualls Cunningham;
Gresham, Smith and Partners
Design Team
James Snyder, Kim Haskell,
Lisa Hansel
Fabrication
Walter P. Sauer & Sons Inc.
Photography
© Durston Saylor

ACCORDING TO JAMES SNYDER, director of interiors for Geddes Brecher Qualls Cunningham of Philadelphia, the problem with the design of most executive wall-storage casework is that "they look too heavy and the various components rarely are visually integrated." Geddes Brecher Qualls Cunningham and Gresham, Smith and Partners of Birmingham avoided these errors in the storage wall they designed for the executives of the Alabama Power Company by concentrating on the power of positive and negative composition.

The designers were obliged to build the storage unit within an existing wall alcove, measuring 12'-5⅛" long, 7'-0" high, and 2'-0" deep. The unit was shop built in order to fit it into trucks and elevators, and it was constructed in parts that were assembled at the project site. Each closet (one is for clothes and the other contains shelving) was constructed as a unit, as was the credenza. The back wall panel and bookcase was also constructed as a separate unit.

The designers made it an important objective to hide all traces of the joining of the parts. Assembly proceeded with the credenza (which contains a cabinet, two file drawers, and six box drawers) being screwed to the back wall. The back panel was fitted into a slot at the back of the credenza, and the bookshelf's end-supports were screwed into the head

frame of the existing alcove and also into the closet units at the sides. Finally, the two closets were slid into place and screwed to the ends of the bookcase. Each closet door was designed to close flush with the front edge of the bookcase "unit," so that no joinery is visible between the closet and the shelving (*door strike at bookcase; perspective*). The "built-in" look is preserved at the top of the bookcase by leaving a ⅜-inch reveal between the bookcase molding and the existing casing, with continuous mahogany blocking barely visible at the back of the reveal (*head at bookcase*).

The use of positive/negative composition is best exemplified by the bookshelves' placement 10 inches in front of the back panel (*plan*). The

back panel is lit by a fluorescent strip fixture screwed to the ledge on the back of the lowest shelf. Thus, there is an effective contrast between the relatively illuminated background and the shelving itself—where the natural darkness of the mahogany prevails. The shelves seem to float in the spacious recess above the credenza.

A reverse light/dark contrast is effected by having kept 1'-0" of open space above the closets. Here the recesses are dark, above doors whose planes are illuminated with ambient light.

All woodwork is mahogany and was finished to match other office furniture. Joints are mortised and glued, with interior joints being screwed. The hardware is brass, including the cabinet hinges on the closet doors.

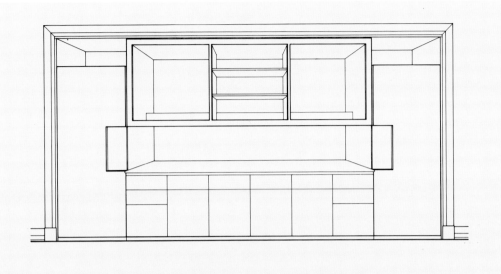

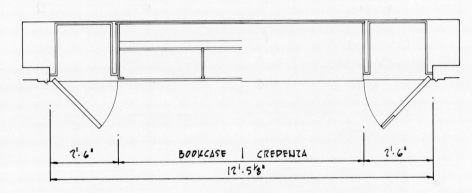

BOOKCASE | CREDENZA
2'-6"   12'-5⅛"   2'-6"

PLAN
PERSPECTIVE

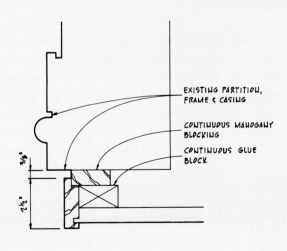

EXISTING PARTITION, FRAME & CASING

CONTINUOUS MAHOGANY BLOCKING

CONTINUOUS GLUE BLOCK

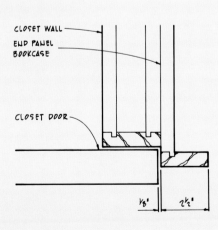

CLOSET WALL

END PANEL BOOKCASE

CLOSET DOOR

⅛"   2½"

(1) HEAD AT BOOKCASE

(2) DOOR STRIKE AT BOOKCASE

TRADING DESK

FIRST EASTERN CORPORATION
Wilkes Barre, Pennsylvania

Interior Design
H2L2 Architects/Planners
Design Team
Barry N. Eiswerth, Howard Maresch,
Robert Bray, Carolyn Simons
Millwork
Dorranceton Millwork
Photography
© Tom Bernard

WALL STREET IS NOT the only place where bonds, stocks, and options are traded. Feverish hives of trading activity are found everywhere—including one in Wilkes Barre, Pennsylvania, where H2L2 Architects/Planners of Philadelphia has designed a cluster trading desk for the First Eastern Corporation.

First Eastern asked the design team to sandwich ten traders and eighteen sellers into a 240-square-foot department, located within an overall seven-story, 70,000-square-foot headquarters building. H2L2 rose to the challenge by developing a clean line face-off between traders and sellers. To allow for unobstructed visibility and plenty of maneuverability between the two groups, the trading platform was raised 8 inches above grade.

In order to maintain the generous traffic alley between and around the two lines, H2L2 limited the width of each trading station to 6'-0". In order to facilitate visual communication, stations were limited to 3'-2½" in height. The design team compensated for such dimensional constraints by allocating 8'-0" in length for the well of each station and, because stations are

paired so that monitor screens may be shared, allocated 12'-0" of workspace overall (*plan*).

The trading desk is constructed of straightforward materials in response to a client request for "contemporary styling on a moderate budget." Oak bullnosed molding and oak veneer plywood accent gray-toned plastic laminate panels, which have been glued to ¾-inch particleboard subframes (*section; elevation C*).

Each trading station houses two display monitors, two drawer files, a work surface, a tackboard, a document tray, a keyboard control, and a shelf for optional equipment (*elevation B*). The monitors are recessed at a 15-degree angle and vented through a louvered panel on the countertop (*section*).

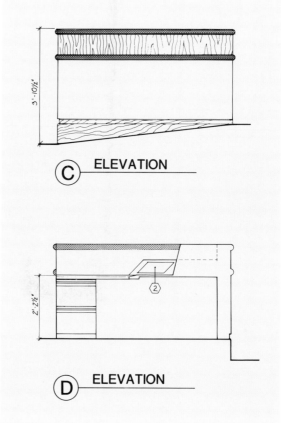

C **ELEVATION**

D **ELEVATION**

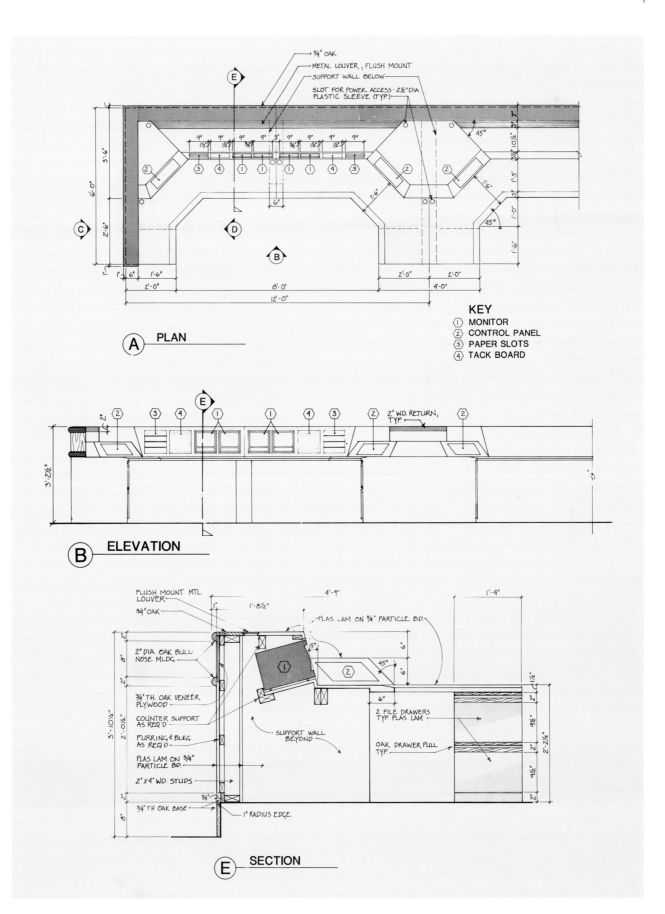

¾" OAK
METAL LOUVER, FLUSH MOUNT
SUPPORT WALL BELOW
SLOT FOR POWER ACCESS · 2½"DIA
PLASTIC SLEEVE (TYP.)

KEY
① MONITOR
② CONTROL PANEL
③ PAPER SLOTS
④ TACK BOARD

Ⓐ PLAN

Ⓑ ELEVATION

2" WD. RETURN, TYP.

FLUSH MOUNT MTL. LOUVER
¾" OAK
PLAS LAM. ON ¾" PARTICLE BD.
2" DIA. OAK BULL-NOSE MLDG.
¾" TH. OAK VENEER PLYWOOD
COUNTER SUPPORT AS REQ'D
FURRING & BLKG. AS REQ'D.
PLAS. LAM. ON ¾" PARTICLE BD.
2" X 4" WD. STUDS
¾" TH OAK BASE
1" RADIUS EDGE
SUPPORT WALL BEYOND
2 FILE DRAWERS TYP. PLAS. LAM.
OAK DRAWER PULL TYP.

Ⓔ SECTION

TRADING DESK

BANKERS TRUST COMPANY
New York City

Architecture/Interior Design
Interior Facilities Associates, Inc.
Design Team
Robert J. Orlando, Valerie Hoffmann
Fabrication
Specifications Built Corp.
Lighting Consultant
Jules Fisher & Paul Marantz, Inc.,
Architectural Lighting Design
Photography
© Norman McGrath

IN THE WALL STREET financial district of New York City, the trading of securities, bonds, and commodities is an intensely competitive business in a state of perpetual flux. Therefore, facilities must be planned that will be responsive to projected changes in business volume and personnel not only tomorrow and next month, but also a year to five years hence. To further complicate the challenge for the architect or interior designer commissioned to effect trading-room planning or renovation, the time frame allocated to the project is invariably short. The Bankers Trust Company gave industry experts Interior Facilities Associates, Inc., of New York City, just twelve months to plan and install a trading-room renovation for 240 traders and affiliated sales staff.

Central to the success of the renovation was the development of a flexible trading-desk workstation that could be ganged in runs side by side and front to front according to departmental focus. The runs are tiered on a steel-pedestal-supported raised floor system in three levels, each 6 inches high, to enhance the visual communication among traders and sales staff.

Simple mathematical calculations established that to fit 240 stations into the 15,000 square feet available, allowing for twenty-percent growth and plenty of clearance for traffic circulation around the desk runs and file-cabinet banks, would result in a 4'-0"-wide by 3'-0"-deep trading-desk module. Once the raw dimensions of the unit had been established, IFA designed logically sequenced componentry for the trading desk from the inside out. Roughly one-third of the desk's undercounter anterior space

was allocated to wire management. A hollow 1'-0" by 1'-8" box, concealed by a finished kneehole access panel, feeds wiring from the desktop to linear channels cut in the floor. The channels, in turn, feed the cabling to core equipment rooms located elsewhere on the floor (*detail*). Two shelves for personal storage are fitted in an undercounter cabinet covered by double doors on one side of each station.

Because the goal of trading-desk design is to improve work efficiency, close attention was given to the logical arrangement of the industry's requisite high-tech componentry. Desktops are not seen primarily as writing surfaces but, rather, as horizontal keyboard surfaces from which to achieve interfacing by computer, telephone, and intercom. At the Bankers Trust Company, trading desks accommodate an average of four computer monitors, a telephone turret that contains push-button direct-access lines, "hoot-and-holler" speaker boxes, and an intercom line (*type "A" : 54" dedicated desk*). The components, which may also include a paper-

storage bin, run across an angled backsplash panel in 10-inch by 10-inch lift-out increments that may be replaced by the same size monitor module or rearranged to suit the individual needs of each trader.

The trading desk is finished in pale gray laminate, which was selected to reduce eye strain. End panels and back framing panels that surround each run are veneered in mahogany and trimmed with a narrow brass reveal and bullnosed solid cherry edges.

Of particular note is the barrel-vaulted ceiling. IFA designed the ceiling to diffuse and reflect fluorescent light that emanates upward, as well as down from, long suspended tubular fixtures designed by Jules Fisher & Paul Marantz, Inc., Architectural Lighting Design. The reflection off the vaulted ceiling provides even ambient light for the room and prevents glare on the monitor screens. The generous ceiling height, ranging from 8'-0" on the highest platform tier to 10'-8" on the lowest platform, diffuses physical and temperamental heat during the frantic working day.

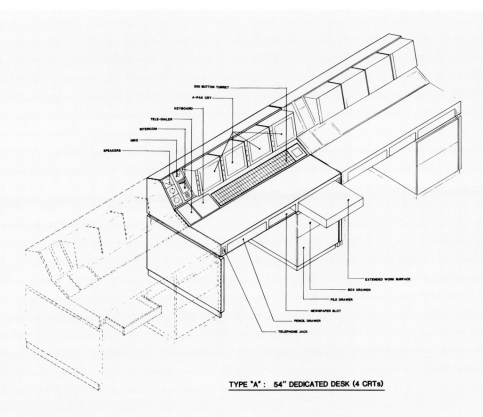

TYPE "A" : 54" DEDICATED DESK (4 CRTs)

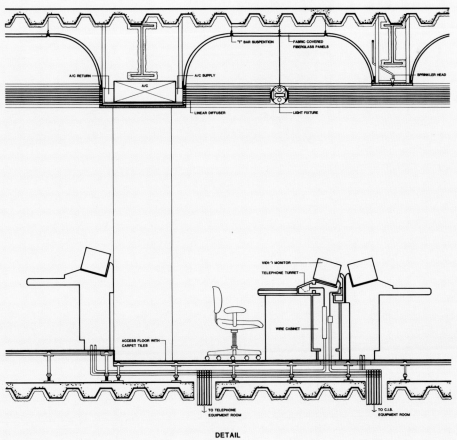

DETAIL

TRELLIS

STEELCASE INC. SHOWROOM

The International Design Center/New York
Long Island City, New York

Architecture/Interior Design
The Hillier Group (Barbara Hillier)
Fabrication
Premier Mill Corporation
Photography
© Peter Paige

WHAT A PRODUCT SHOWROOM client requires from an architect or interior designer is a subtly lighted and eye-catching, but not stage-grabbing, framework in which to display merchandise to wholesale customers. Steelcase Inc., the world's largest office-furniture manufacturer, commissioned The Hillier Group of Princeton, New Jersey, to design its 20,000-square-foot showroom in The International Design Center, New York, mandating a showroom with a strong "regional identity" that would still respond to the requirements of the company's "diverse customer base."

The Hillier Group interpreted the regional-identity aspect of the firm's mandate liberally rather than literally, utilizing a trellis, or pergola walkway, that gives literal form to a product-display framework concept. Although trellises and pergolas are not much in evidence on New York City streets, style and the indoor/outdoor concept for the exhibition of merchandise definitely are. Barbara Hillier's trellis substantiates her overall design theme of "a stroll along a New York avenue."

According to Barbara Hillier, the pergola's elemental shapes are architecturally related to the cornices and grids the design team had already decided to use in other areas of the showroom. The shapes relate psychologically to the company's fabric samples by suggesting that the samples be seen against the trellis as colorful climbing flowers.

The result is a 56-foot pergola framework that contains approximately 220 feet of lineal fabric display shelving. Customers stroll through the pergola walkway, picking samples from the shelving on one side and examining them on maple counter-

tops on the other side (*exploded axonometric*).

The free-standing pergola must bear a considerable amount of unevenly distributed weight and is subject to customer buffeting. These were factors that demanded strong construction. The design team used steel generously. The countertops are screwed to ¼-inch steel plates welded to a ½-inch by 1¼-inch steel bar. The steel bar is, in turn, welded to a 1¾-inch by ¾-inch 10-gauge bent steel plate, which is bolted to the hardwood posts. Shelves are supported by similar steel assemblies screwed to the posts. Posts are anchored to ½-inch steel plates bolted to the con-

crete subfloor with 10-gauge steel shoes welded to the plates (*plan—shelf at post; counter support at post*). The upper assembly is made of hollow beams and crossbeams (*section*).

The design team specified hardwood construction for the trellis/pergola. All surfaces are spray painted white except for the countertops, which were fabricated in quarter-sawn maple with a transparent finish and solid maple nosing.

Three types of lighting fixtures are suspended from the crossbeams: warm white fluorescent tubes, dimmable quartz, and dimmable incandescent. All are arranged to spread light evenly on the textile displays.

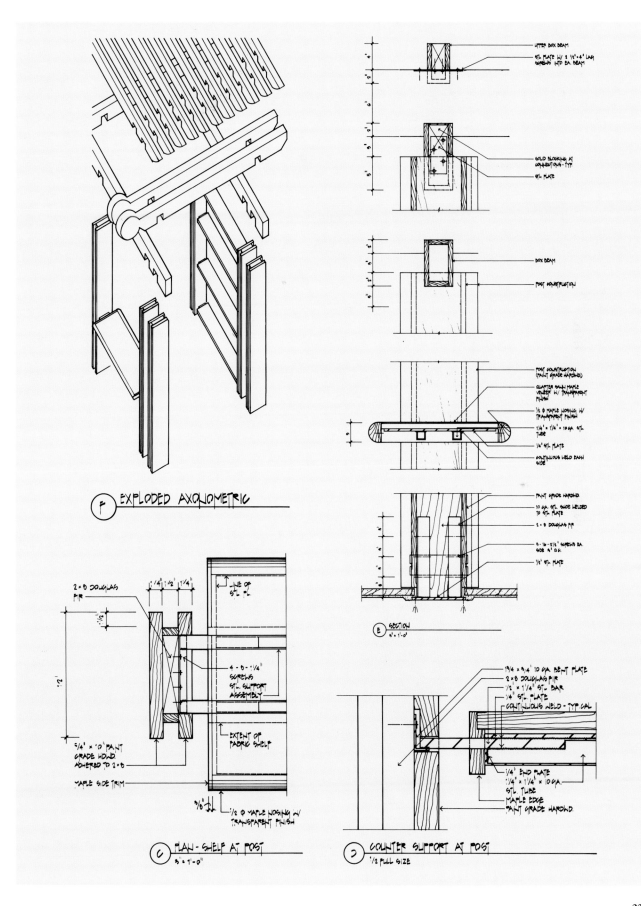

EXPLODED AXONOMETRIC

UTTER BOX BEAM
STL PLATE W/ 2 1/2"×4" LAG SCREWS INTO EA. BEAM

SOLID BLOCKING AT CONNECTIONS - TYP
STL PLATE

BOX BEAM
POST CONSTRUCTION

POST CONSTRUCTION (PAINT GRADE HARDWD)
QUARTER SAWN MAPLE VENEER W/ TRANSPARENT FINISH
1/2 ∅ MAPLE NOSING W/ TRANSPARENT FINISH
1/4" × 1 1/4" × 10 GA. STL TUBE
1/4" STL PLATE
CONTINUOUS WELD EACH SIDE

PAINT GRADE HARDWD
10 GA. STL SHOE WELDED TO STL PLATE
1 × ∅ DOUGLAS FIR
5 - 16 - 3 1/2" SCREWS EA. SIDE 3" O.C.
1/2" STL PLATE

E SECTION
    3" = 1'-0"

2 × ∅ DOUGLAS FIR

LINE OF STL. PL.

1/4" | 1/2" | 1 1/4"

4 - ∅ - 1 1/4" SCREWS STL SUPPORT ASSEMBLY

EXTENT OF FABRIC SHELF

5/4" × ∅" PAINT GRADE HDWD. ADHERED TO 2×∅

MAPLE SIDE TRIM

1/2 ∅ MAPLE NOSING W/ TRANSPARENT FINISH

C PLAN - SHELF AT POST
    3" = 1'-0"

1 3/4 × 3/4" 10 GA. BENT PLATE
2 × ∅ DOUGLAS FIR
1/2" × 1 1/4" STL. BAR
1/4" STL PLATE
CONTINUOUS WELD - TYPICAL

1/4" END PLATE
1/4" × 1 1/4" × 10 GA. STL TUBE
MAPLE EDGE
PAINT GRADE HARDWD.

D COUNTER SUPPORT AT POST
    1/2 FULL SIZE

229

TRELLIS

THE POYNTER INSTITUTE
St. Petersburg, Florida

Architecture/Interior Design
Jung/Brannen Associates, Inc.
Design Team
Robert Brannen, Robert Hsiung,
Tom Walsh, Jerry Seelen
Fabrication
Anderson Lumber Co.;
Federal Construction Company
Photography
© Steven Brooke

THE PRESTIGIOUS Poynter Institute in St. Petersburg, Florida, is a nonprofit foundation that provides continuing education seminars for journalists. In 1983 when the board of directors made the decision to build new facilities, the Institute's president resolved that the architects' aim should be to design "a world-class building that will attract world-class talent." Jung/Brannen Associates, Inc., of Boston, Massachusetts, was given the architectural and interior-design commission.

Although the design team was given a detailed program, no direction as to aesthetic form was given. The design team opted for a generalized expression of "good" Florida architecture, without specific precedent. The building Jung/Brannen designed is a low-pitched, tiled roof complex surrounding a reflecting pool planted with palm trees. The spaces within are drenched in sunlight that passes through floor-to-ceiling windows. The windows are detailed by a 75-foot trellis that, like the sunlight it filters, passes through the window wall into the great hall of the main space to form an interior/exterior detail of significant elemental strength.

The trellis detail was envisioned as a particularly vivid expression of the regional idiom. The design echoes the construction of the exposed wooden truss system that supports the 4,000-square-foot hall's 50-foot ceiling (*trellis elevation*). The upper level of the two-layer trellis begins at the line of 2-foot-square concrete columns and extends 2′-10″ to the steel-supported window wall, where it penetrates the facade to project 10′-3″ over the reflecting-pool terrace outside. The lower layer extends only 6 feet from the window wall.

The trellis frame is constructed of welded steel tubing. The upper-level horizontal joists (or "outriggers") are made of 10-inch by 2-inch by ⅜-inch tubes and the lower level joists of 6-inch by 2-inch by ⅜-inch tubes. The tubes are welded to 6-inch by 6-inch by ⅜-inch steel-tube window-wall supports and are bolted to the concrete columns. On the upper level, the designers enhanced the trellis effect by running 2-inch by 10-inch mahogany ribs, spaced at 6-inch intervals, across the 11′-6″ distance from outrigger to outrigger. The pattern is continued for 7 feet on the outside projection of the outriggers.

All steel and concrete elements are clad in solid wood rather than veneers. Interior woodwork is Honduras mahogany. Woodwork on the exterior is western red cedar. The design team created a custom lacquer-and-wax finish for the mahogany.

The mahogany cladding over the vertical tubes in the window wall is attached with bolted connections, which are either concealed within other wood segments or countersunk and plugged. The concrete columns have stud walls built up from the floor and bolted to them. Panels are then screwed to the studs. Outrigger tubes are sandwiched between 14-inch by 2-inch planks.

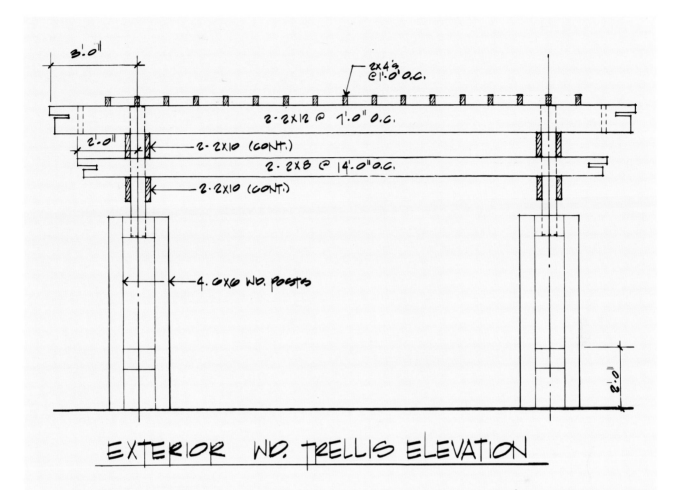

3'.0"

2x4's
@ 1'.0" O.C.

2 - 2x12 @ 7'.0" O.C.

2'.0"

2 - 2x10 (CONT.)

2 - 2x8 @ 14'.0" O.C.

2 - 2x10 (CONT.)

4 - 6x6 WD. POSTS

2'.0"

EXTERIOR WD. TRELLIS ELEVATION

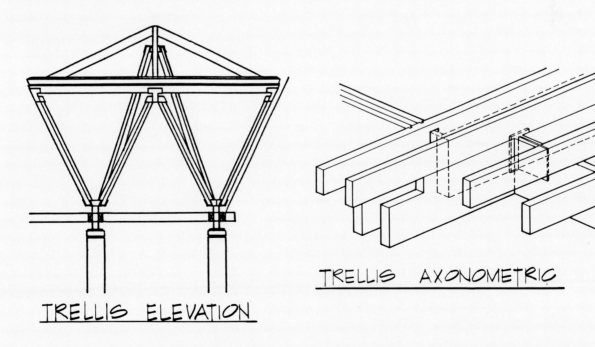

TRELLIS ELEVATION

TRELLIS AXONOMETRIC

TRELLIS

MONADNOCK BUILDING
San Francisco, California

Architecture/Interior Design
Whisler-Patri
Design Team
Rod Glasgow, Kevin Dill,
Dean Randle
Fabrication
C. E. Toland & Son
Photography
© Mark Citret

SAN FRANCISCO'S landmark Monadnock Building is a survivor. Under construction at the time, it survived the 1906 earthquake, and it also survived the urban decay of the postwar decades. Finally, in the mid-1980s, it was rewarded by its new owner, Eastdil Realty, Inc., with a comprehensive restoration and renovation. Eastdil chose Whisler-Patri of San Francisco to spearhead the project.

Like most office buildings of its vintage, the Monadnock Building is built around a large light well. As renovation proceeded, Eastdil became concerned about the growing disparity between the elegance being created inside and the starkness of the light well. Eastdil asked Whisler-Patri to "do something with that airshaft"— but without spending a lot of money. In response, and bearing in mind American architect Louis Kahn's admonition that two things are free in architecture—light and people— Whisler-Patri designed a delicately traced, trellised arcade that now provides an inexpensive but elegant framework for a courtyard sculpture gallery. Here light plays, and people mingle freely.

Eastdil's objectives were to harmonize the four walls of the light well, to embellish the courtyard space, to link two doors on opposing sides of the space, and to make commercial use of the area. The masterful *trompe l'oeil* unifies the light well. The sculpture gallery operates commercially.

The 15'-8"-high trellised arcade gracefully connects the doors with a delicate canopy and establishes a strikingly proportioned three-dimensional lattice motif that also helps tie together the entire court. Its 39'-4" length includes two end segments, each 14'-2" square. Each segment is constructed of four 11'-4" columns, 1'-6" square, on which four arch trusses and a ceiling unit rest (*axonometric*). Each ceiling unit is reinforced with warren-trussed joists spaced at 2'-8½" intervals (*section*). Between the two end segments, two 10'-5" lintel trusses (which support a third ceiling unit) are suspended by ledger angles (*elevation*).

The trellis is constructed of aluminum tubes joined primarily with aluminum rivets. All vertical supporting pieces are 1-inch by 1-inch by ⅛-inch. The crosspieces measure 1-inch by ½-inch by ⅛-inch. The supports and crosspieces form a modular grid of 6-inch squares.

To complete the elegant passageway, Whisler-Patri paved the canopied area with granite in two colors and designed two rusticated wall arches to frame the fountains.

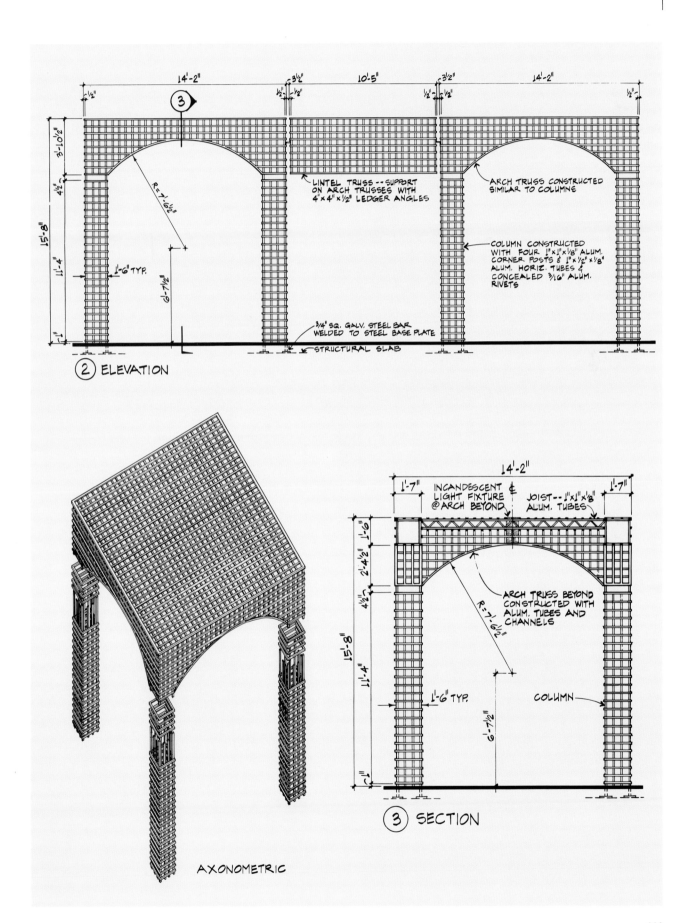

14'-2"   3½"   10'-5"   3½"   14'-2"

③

LINTEL TRUSS -- SUPPORT
ON ARCH TRUSSES WITH
4" x 4" x ½" LEDGER ANGLES

ARCH TRUSS CONSTRUCTED
SIMILAR TO COLUMNE

COLUMN CONSTRUCTED
WITH FOUR 1"x1"x⅛" ALUM.
CORNER POSTS & 1"x½"x⅛"
ALUM. HORIZ. TUBES &
CONCEALED 3/16" ALUM.
RIVETS

R=7'-6½"

1'-6" TYP.

9'-7½"

3'-10½"   4½"   15'-8"   1'-4"   1"

¾" SQ. GALV. STEEL BAR
WELDED TO STEEL BASE PLATE

STRUCTURAL SLAB

② ELEVATION

AXONOMETRIC

14'-2"

1'-7"   INCANDESCENT ℄
LIGHT FIXTURE
@ ARCH BEYOND

JOIST -- 1"x1"x⅛"
ALUM. TUBES   1'-7"

ARCH TRUSS BEYOND
CONSTRUCTED WITH
ALUM. TUBES AND
CHANNELS

R=7'-6½"

1'-6" TYP.

COLUMN

9'-7½"

1'-6"   2'-4½"   4½"   15'-8"   1'-4"   1"

③ SECTION

VESTIBULE

KWASHA LIPTON
Fort Lee, New Jersey

Architecture/Interior Design
Hambrecht Terrell International
Design Team
Michael J. McGowan, Daniel J. Barteluce,
James E. Terrell, James B. Nicoloff,
Bret Kelln
General Contracting
Herbert Construction Co.
Glass-Block Fabrication
George Panetta
Photography
© Peter Paige

KWASHA LIPTON IS A leading actuarial firm whose work depends on mainframe computer use. Hambrecht Terrell International is an architectural interior design firm, whose work is known for its stylish flair. What brought the "punch-card" identity of Kwasha Lipton together with the pizzazz of Hambrecht Terrell was a similarity in work methodology—a problem-solving approach that resulted in a twenty-four-hour computer facility for Kwasha Lipton's Fort Lee, New Jersey, offices that is both efficient and attractive.

The executives of Kwasha Lipton asked the design team to create a functional, comfortable interior that would produce a "a mood conducive to concentrated work." Because eye fatigue from glare is an occupational hazard for computer operators, special attention was to be given to lighting, particularly to the perception of light through transparent, translucent, and reflective surfaces.

Large computer installations are usually carefully controlled atmospheric environments that are isolated from other departments. The designers were determined to avoid that isolation. Specifically, the design team wanted to retain a visual connection between the computer area and the corridors and offices around it. For that purpose, the team chose glass block as the primary material for the room's entry vestibule and corridor walls, exploiting the medium in a

unique interplay of subtly lighted glass and mirrors.

The 8'-0" walls of glass block rest on 4-inch by 4-inch steel angles, which are bolted to backup angles that are in turn bolted to the concrete slab. The top of the glass wall is held by another continuous 4-inch by 4-inch steel angle. The bottom angles are open to the corridor, leaving a 4-inch kickspace, faced with ceramic tile, between the wall base and the floor (*section*). The wall's vertical integrity is maintained by bolting the horizontal support angles to 3-inch by 3-inch vertical steel tubes that are bolted to the slab and secured to the structural ceiling with cross angles.

The glass blocks are installed in two sizes, 6-inch squares and 12-inch squares. At the entry corners of the vestibule and on the corridor wall directly outside the vestibule, the smaller blocks rise the full elevation of the wall to the lighting cove. The blocks are then stepped down at 2-foot intervals to become a 2-foot bot-

tom border along the 58-foot length of the glass-block wall (*elevation*). The step motif reiterates certain exterior details of the building. The contrast between the 12-inch and the 6-inch blocks, as well as the general play of light in the corridor area, is enhanced by the treatment of the smaller blocks as mirrors. Silvering was applied to the back side (the side facing the computer room) of each block.

The glass motif continues inside the vestibule, where the side walls are constructed of butt-glazed, ½-inch smoke gray tempered panes. The vestibule doors and 3'-5" sidelight glass on the adjacent wall are built of similar gray panes. The remaining 2'-4" of the back wall is gypsum board (*plan*).

Three steps lead up from the corridor floor to the 2-foot height of the raised computer-room floor. Each riser is faced with black anodized aluminum, which is illuminated by lucifer lights tucked under the nosing of each stair in a routed edge.

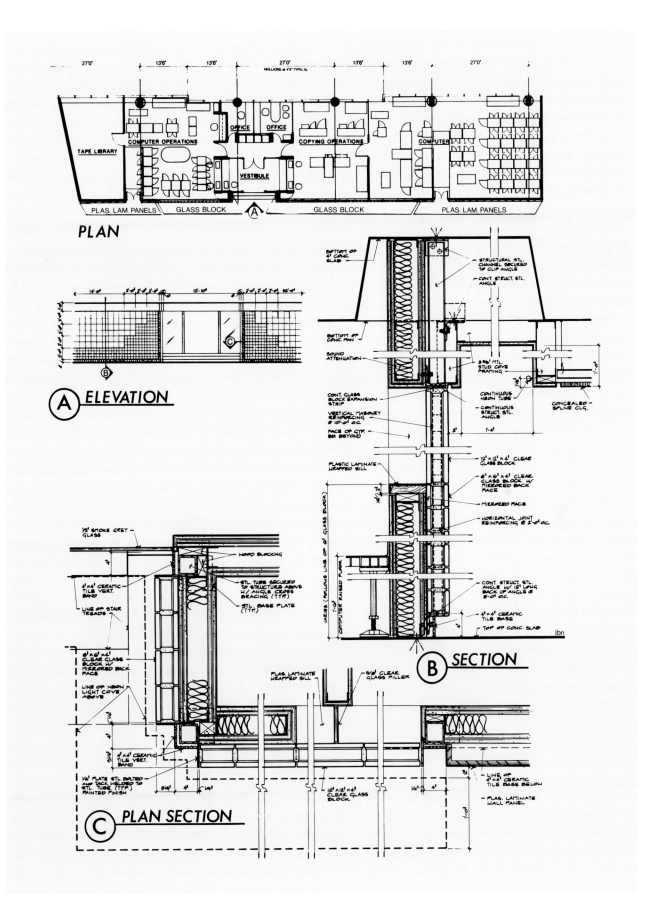

PLAN

27'0"   13'6"   13'6"   27'0"   MULLIONS at 4'6" TYPICAL   13'6"   13'6"   27'0"

TAPE LIBRARY

COMPUTER OPERATIONS   OFFICE   OFFICE   COPYING OPERATIONS   COMPUTER

VESTIBULE

PLAS. LAM. PANELS   GLASS BLOCK   (A)   GLASS BLOCK   PLAS. LAM. PANELS

14'-0"   12'-0"   12'-10"

(A) ELEVATION

(B)

(C)

(B) SECTION

- BOTTOM OF 4" CONC. SLAB
- STRUCTURAL STL. CHANNEL SECURED TO CLIP ANGLE
- CONT. STRUCT. STL. ANGLE
- BOTTOM OF CONC. PAN
- SOUND ATTENUATION
- 3 5/8" MTL. STUD COVE FRAMING
- CONTINUOUS NEON TUBE
- CONTINUOUS STRUCT. STL. ANGLE
- CONCEALED SPLINE CLG.
- CONT. GLASS BLOCK EXPANSION STRIP
- VERTICAL MASONRY REINFORCING @ 10'-0" O.C.
- FACE OF GYP. BD. BEYOND
- 12" X 12" X 4" CLEAR GLASS BLOCK
- PLASTIC LAMINATE WRAPPED SILL
- 6" X 6" X 4" CLEAR GLASS BLOCK W/ MIRRORED BACK FACE
- MIRRORED FACE
- HORIZONTAL JOINT REINFORCING @ 2'-0" O.C.
- VARIES (FOLLOWS LINE OF G' OF GLASS BLOCK)
- CONT. STRUCT. STL. ANGLE W/ 12" LONG BACK UP ANGLE @ 3'-0" O.C.
- COMPUTER RAISED FLOOR
- 4" X 4" CERAMIC TILE BASE
- TOP OF CONC. SLAB

jbn

(C) PLAN SECTION

- 1/2" SMOKE GREY GLASS
- HOOD BLOCKING
- STL. TUBE SECURED TO STRUCTURE ABOVE W/ ANGLE CROSS BRACING (TYP.)
- STL. BASE PLATE (TYP.)
- 4" X 4" CERAMIC TILE VERT. BAND
- LINE OF STAIR TREADS
- 6" X 6" X 4" CLEAR GLASS BLOCK W/ MIRRORED BACK FACE
- LINE OF NEON LIGHT COVE ABOVE
- PLAS. LAMINATE WRAPPED SILL
- 3/8" CLEAR GLASS FILLER
- 4" X 4" CERAMIC TILE VERT. BAND
- 1/4" PLATE STL. BOLTED AND TACK WELDED TO STL. TUBE (TYP.) PAINTED FINISH
- 12" X 12" X 4" CLEAR GLASS BLOCK
- LINE OF 4" X 4" CERAMIC TILE BASE BELOW
- PLAS. LAMINATE WALL PANEL

235

WALL

McDONALD'S
Berwyn, Illinois

Architecture/Interior Design
SITE Projects, Inc.
Design Team
Joshua Weinstein, James Wines,
Peter Kincl, Robin Hoffman
Photography
© Russell Phillips

To CITE detailing excellence and McDonald's in the same breath might at first seem anomalous, if not incredible. These snap judgments are made, however, before learning that the fast-food industry's most successful corporation commissioned SITE Projects, Inc., of New York City to detail a commemorative franchise near the original restaurant in the founder's hometown of Berwyn, Illinois.

The directors of the McDonald's Corporation believe that the restaurant owes a significant part of its marketing success to thematic continuity. In architectural terms, that translates into ubiquitous "golden arches" over a one-design, easy-to-construct, easy-to-use, and easy-to-recognize 4,500-square-foot restaurant building. Therefore, although the

mandate to SITE was to "do anything," the design team was also instructed that "nothing in the standard design should be changed."

SITE prefers to treat buildings as "Duchampian found objects" and to emphasize the Cubist influence in modern architecture. In its work for the McDonald's Corporation, SITE alluded specifically to the Cubist juxtaposition of flat elements crisscrossing at different levels that is exemplified architecturally in Frank Lloyd Wright's Unity Temple in nearby Oak Park, Illinois. In making that reference, SITE executed McDonald's directive almost literally, retaining the elements of the standard design but altering their spatial relationships. The result is a design that redeems the original building module by reordering the restaurant's brick walls, soffits, and "Colonial" windows and vestibules. At certain angles, the revised building has the appearance of an exploded axonometric.

The most striking change in the building is the apparent suspension of the brick exterior and interior walls above the perceived foundation line. Mounted on and surmounted by glass window panels, the walls now seem

to float freely—as does the roof, which appears to be unconnected to the walls (*west and north elevations*). To further the illusion, some walls were thrust out from the structural elevation line. Thus, they appear to be cantilevered; although, in fact, they are not. The conjuring effects were achieved structurally by replacing the typical concrete bearing walls with a 10-inch by 10-inch steel tube framework. The 3'-4¾" steel tube struts were welded to the frame in moment connections. Metal studs were screwed onto the struts, then ½-inch plywood was screwed to the studs, and ½-inch-thick bricks were affixed to the plywood with adhesive and then grouted (*wall section–dining room*).

Because McDonald's policy requires that all windows be cleaned twice a day, easy window access was an important maintenance consideration. The "cantilevered" wall panels were connected, top and bottom, to the structural elevation line by custom windows that were hinged to open inward for cleaning (*wall section–dining room*).

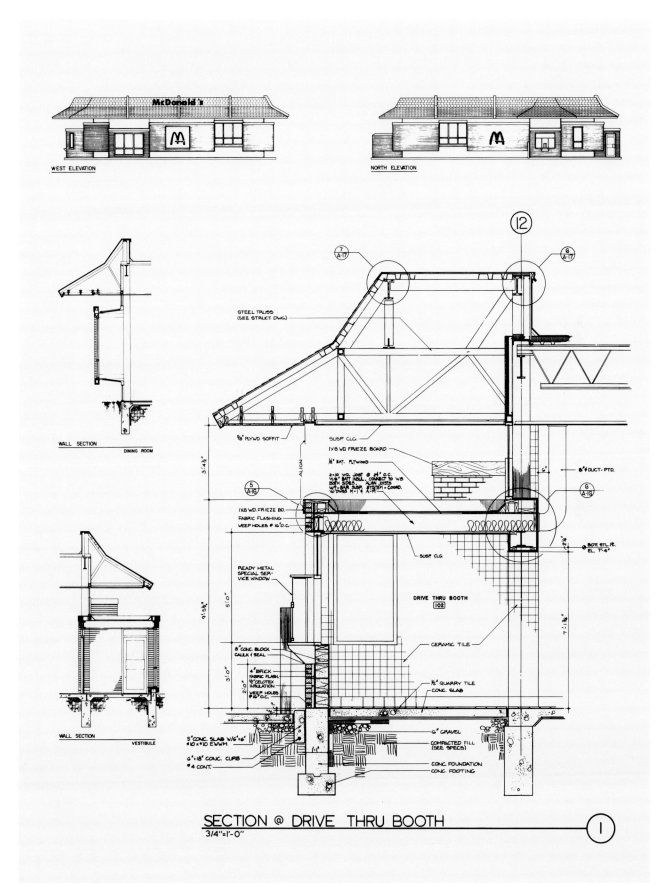

WEST ELEVATION

NORTH ELEVATION

WALL SECTION

DINING ROOM

WALL SECTION

VESTIBULE

7
A-17

12

6
A-17

STEEL TRUSS
(SEE STRUCT. DWG)

5/8" PLYWD. SOFFIT

SUSP. CLG.

1X8 WD. FRIEZE BOARD

1/2" EXT. PLYWOOD

2×10 WD. JOIST @ 24" O.C.
W/6" BATT INSUL., CONNECT TO WB
BOTH SIDES. ALIGN JOISTS
W/ BAR SUSP. SYSTEM - COORD.
W/ DWGS M-14 A-14

6"

8"ø DUCT- PTD.

5
A-16

1X8 WD. FRIEZE BD.
FABRIC FLASHING
WEEP HOLES @ 16"O.C.

SUSP. CLG.

6
A-16

2'-4"

BOTT. STL. PL.
EL. 7'-4"

READY METAL
SPECIAL SER-
VICE WINDOW

DRIVE THRU BOOTH
102

CERAMIC TILE

7'-1 3/4"

8" CONC. BLOCK
CAULK & SEAL

4" BRICK
FABRIC FLASH.
1/2" CELOTEX
INSULATION
WEEP HOLES
@ 16"O.C.

1/2" QUARRY TILE
CONC. SLAB

3'-0"

2'-0"

6" GRAVEL

5'-0"

9'-5 1/2"

3'-4 1/2"

COMPACTED FILL
(SEE SPECS)

5" CONC. SLAB W/ 6"×6"
#10 ×#10 EWWM

6"×18" CONC. CURB
#4 CONT.

CONC. FOUNDATION
CONC. FOOTING

SECTION @ DRIVE THRU BOOTH
3/4"=1'-0"

1

WALL

THE MADDEN CORPORATION
New York City

Architecture/Interior Design
Sidney Philip Gilbert & Associates
Design Team
Sidney Gilbert, Williams Whistler,
Richard Nininger
Fabrication
Nordic Interior Inc.
Photography
© Paul Warchol

AN OFFICE BUILDING is the last place one expects to be reminded of a dense Finnish forest. But that abstract suggestion is exactly what Sidney Philip Gilbert & Associates of New York City has achieved in the curved and carved wood-paneled wall designed for the executive reception area of The Madden Corporation, America's largest importer of Finnish newsprint paper. The design team executed the detail in response to the client's request for "an environment related in some way to our product."

Madden executives had made it clear to SPGA from the outset of the project that they subscribed to a Scandinavian corporate philosophy that dictates allocating the bulk of budget to public, rather than private, spaces within an office complex. SPGA reserved judgment on such an egalitarian approach until their own analysis of on-site conditions had been completed. The tunnellike aspect of the office suite, caused by an unusually obtrusive mechanical core, provided the key to a less hierarchical solution. According to principal Sidney Gilbert, "we were relieved and excited when we realized that we could offer a detailing solution that would enrich *both* public spaces and private offices."

What the design team had divined was that by developing an asymmetrical floor-to-ceiling wall treatment to screen the mechanical awkwardness of the core wall, it would be a matter of relative ease and modest expense to wrap the detail around adjacent walls—until the entrances to all of the private offices had been incorporated as well. The executives at Madden endorsed the concept enthusiastically.

The design team initially envisioned the wall treatment as an elaborate paper construction. That concept was rejected for two reasons: ideologically, because the solution was regarded as being "too literal," and pragmatically, because a paper construction might ultimately prove to be a fire hazard. Going back to square one, the design team found their solution by reexamining, in literal terms, the "nature" of the company's product. Paper comes from trees, and trees are made of wood. The Madden Corporation's product came from Finnish trees, and Finnish trees are primarily white ash.

Because Alvar Aalto was the acknowledged master of the use of Finnish ash in furniture design, SPGA developed a sinuous, curvilinear wall of tongue-and-groove ash reminiscent of Aalto's classic furniture forms. The pattern was drawn on paper then drawn, refined, and chalked on the floor on site. Adjustments were necessary, according to Gilbert, because "the simple act of walking up and down a corridor causes objects in elevation to advance and recede in a way that is impossible to forecast accurately in a plan. We moved things around until they both felt and looked 'right'."

Once the plan was approved, Nordic Interior Inc. built a single-stud, fireproof wood frame 16 inches on center. Plywood sheeting was water-soaked and then bent to conform to curve. Simple 1½-inch tongue-and-groove ash paneling was applied vertically after being pattern cut to accommodate the dimensions of the office's windows and doors. The cuts and baseboard were finished in simple birch molding trim (*elevation; detail*).

As a finishing touch, a concentric light cove was built when the paneled wall was completed. The paneling was protected with ½-inch homosote panels during construction of the cove, which houses incandescent wall washers approximately 11 inches on center (*section*).

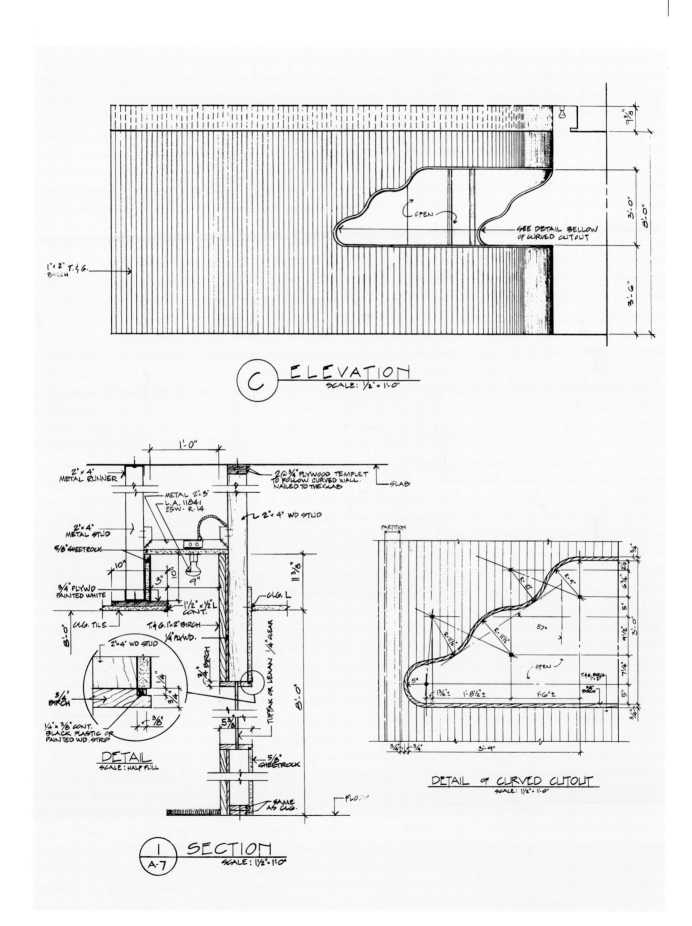

$1'' \times 2''$ T.$\frac{1}{4}$ G.
BIRCH

OPEN

SEE DETAIL BELLOW
OF CURVED CUTOUT

$9\frac{1}{8}''$

$3'-0''$

$6'-0''$

$3'-6''$

$\overline{C}$ ELEVATION
SCALE: $\frac{1}{2}'' = 1'-0''$

$1'-0''$

$2'' \times 4''$
METAL RUNNER

$2'' \times 4''$
METAL STUD

$5/8''$ SHEETROCK

$3/4''$ PLYWD.
PAINTED WHITE

$8'-0''$

CLG. TILE

$2'' \times 4''$ WD STUD

$3/4''$
BIRCH

$1/4'' \times 3/8''$ CONT.
BLACK PLASTIC OR
PAINTED WD. STRIP

METAL 2"x 3"
L.A. 11841
25W. R-14

$10''$

$3''$

$9''$

$1\frac{1}{2}'' \times \frac{1}{2}''$ L
CONT.

T.$\frac{1}{4}$ G. $1\frac{1}{2}''$ BIRCH

$\frac{1}{4}''$ BIRCH

$2 @ 3/4''$ PLYWOOD TEMPLET
TO FOLLOW CURVED WALL.
NAILED TO THE SLAB

SLAB

$2 \cdot 2'' \times 4''$ WD STUD

$11\frac{3}{8}''$

CLG. L

$1/4''$ PLYWD.

TUFFAK OR LEXAN $1/4''$ CLEAR

$8'-0''$

$5/8''$

$3/8''$

$3/4''$

DETAIL
SCALE: HALF FULL

$\frac{1}{A-7}$ SECTION
SCALE: $1\frac{1}{2}'' = 1'-0''$

$5/8''$
SHEETROCK

SAME
AS CLG.

FLOOR

PARTITION

R-10''

R-9''

R-11½''

R-11½''

57°

OPEN

T.$\frac{1}{4}$ G. $1\frac{1}{2}''$
BIRCH

$3/4''$

$2\frac{1}{4}''$

$6\frac{1}{4}''$

$5''$

$9\frac{1}{2}''$

$3'-0''$

$7\frac{1}{4}''$

$5''$

$3/4''$

$5''$

$1\frac{3}{4}'' \pm$

$1'-8\frac{1}{2}'' \pm$

$1'-6'' \pm$

$2\frac{1}{4}''$
BIRCH

$3/4'' \pm$ $3/4''$

$3'-9''$

DETAIL OF CURVED CUTOUT
SCALE: $1\frac{1}{2}'' = 1'-0''$

WALL

20/20 RESTAURANT
New York City

Architecture/Interior Design
Haverson-Rockwell Architects
Design Team
David S. Rockwell, Jay M. Haverson
Fabrication
G.P. Winter Assoc.
Neon
Alan Bank Neon
Photography
© Timothy Hursley

NEOCONSTRUCTIONIST detailing requires a thorough understanding of building material qualities and the capacity for innovative application of those materials. Haverson-Rockwell Architects of New York City exhibited that balance of knowledge and talent in the detailing they designed for 20/20, an upscale restaurant owned by singers Ashford & Simpson in Manhattan's Flatiron District.

Haverson-Rockwell utilized walls of Zolatoned gypsum board, faux-painted fire escapes, and lighted window boxes to create a series of street-scene vignettes, which according to Jay Haverson "allude to the steamy evening underside of life in any crowded urban center." The window-wall vignettes offer more than an insouciant sociological commentary, however. By emphasizing the plan's strong asymmetrical geometry, the vignettes, seen along the back wall, both introduce a skewed perception of the space's depth and control the flow of traffic (*axonometric*).

As in most of Haverson-Rockwell's work, the tightly controlled lighting at 20/20 is a design element in and of itself. Each full-height window-wall vignette is furred out six inches from a brick base construction wall to accommodate sheet metal–backed light boxes, which are framed-in by metal studs and ⅝-inch gypsum wallboard. A neon striplight, concealed by a painted wood fascia suspended from a gypsum-board soffit, washes the window wall from within in color ranging in intensity from full saturation at the ceiling to dark shadow

near the floor. As an added effect, 300-watt uplights are imbedded in poured-concrete troughs recessed below a finish slate over the wood subfloor. The uplights, diffused by ½-inch-thick tempered glass lenses, are abruptly angled to accentuate the contrast between light and shadow emanating from the neon-fixture wash near the ceiling (*section*).

The design team built several "window" light-box mock-ups off site in their search for the perfect blend of low-voltage light fixtures and covering construction material. In their final configuration, the light boxes house

low-voltage belfer lighting strips, which are concealed horizontally and vertically directly behind the main muntins. Two panes of fluted translucent glass, installed with their ribs running perpendicularly to each other, diffuse the light to the desired soft glow.

The window-box frames and fire escapes are constructed of faux-finish wood to simulate granite. The *trompe l'oeil* effect, according to David Rockwell, "specifically emphasizes a world, or dimension beyond reality, which seems to be entirely appropriate to the Manhattan scene."

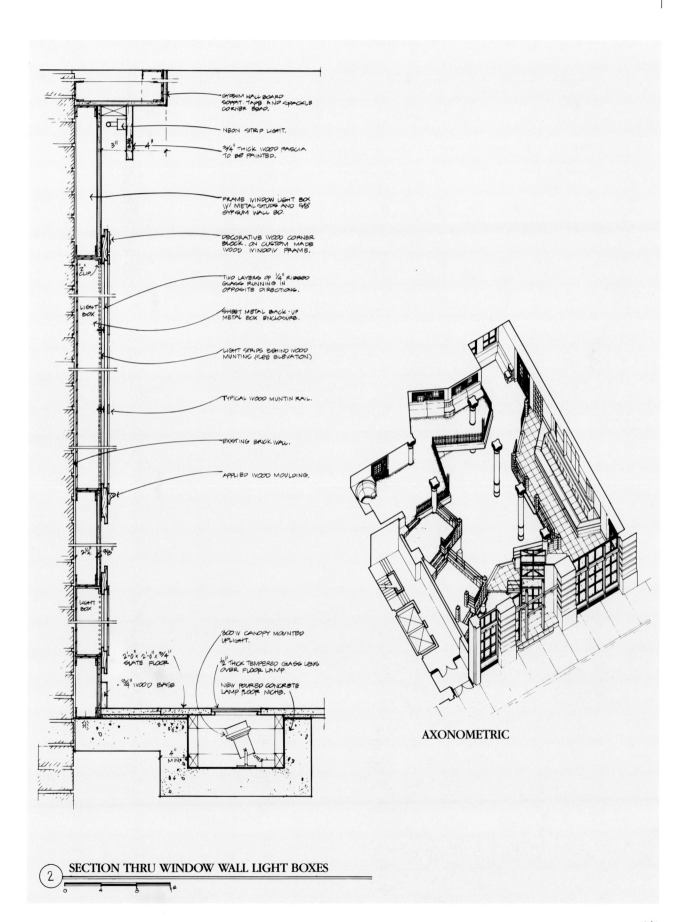

GYPSUM WALL BOARD
SOFFIT. TAPE AND SPACKLE
CORNER BEAD.

NEON STRIP LIGHT.

3/4" THICK WOOD FASCIA
TO BE PAINTED.

FRAME WINDOW LIGHT BOX
W/ METAL STUDS AND 5/8"
GYPSUM WALL BO.

DECORATIVE WOOD CORNER
BLOCK. ON CUSTOM MADE
WOOD WINDOW FRAME.

TWO LAYERS OF 1/4" RIBBED
GLASS RUNNING IN
OPPOSITE DIRECTIONS.

SHEET METAL BACK-UP
METAL BOX ENCLOSURE.

LIGHT STRIPS BEHIND WOOD
MUNTINS (SEE ELEVATION)

TYPICAL WOOD MUNTIN RAIL.

EXISTING BRICK WALL.

APPLIED WOOD MOULDING.

300 W CANOPY MOUNTED
UPLIGHT.

1/2" THICK TEMPERED GLASS LENS
OVER FLOOR LAMP.

NEW POURED CONCRETE
LAMP FLOOR NICHE.

2'-0" x 2'-0" x 3/4"
SLATE FLOOR

3/4" WOOD BASE

3"   4"

2"
CLIP

LIGHT
BOX

2 1/2"   3/8"

LIGHT
BOX

4"
MIN.

2 SECTION THRU WINDOW WALL LIGHT BOXES

0   2   4   8   12

AXONOMETRIC

WALL

DANIEL HECHTER SHOWROOM
New York City

Interior Architectural Design
The Switzer Group, Inc.

Design Team
Lou Switzer, Steven Smith,
Robert Kellogg, Marilyn Richter,
Joan Petersen, Stewart Fishbein,
Susan Steinler

Fabrication
Pilot Woodworking

Photography
© Durston Saylor

DANIEL HECHTER, a principal player in the *haut monde* French fashion industry, places a premium on design consistency—whether it be in men's clothing or in a worldwide showroom image. Bidermann Industries U.S.A. Inc., the distributor of Daniel Hechter clothing in the United States, commissioned The Switzer Group, Inc. of New York City to design the Hechter showroom in Manhattan on the basis of the work the firm had done for another fashion magnate, Diane Von Furstenberg. Bidermann communicated to Switzer's design team Hechter's request for a "light, airy, and open showroom finished in beige and white," which would provide "privacy in both office and showroom space."

Switzer's solution took its cue from the Hechter endorsement of high-quality natural materials, which Switzer identifies as "soft-tech countryish," conveying a "Japanese sensibility." Transforming that sensibility from clothing design to architectural detailing resulted in an interior graced by a series of set-back office/showroom walls that preserve transaction privacy, while admitting light through gridded window muntins crafted in solid cherry (*office elevation*). The grids' cherry construction, which recurs along the main office corridor, conveys the desired Japanese reverence for natural materials—an element that is reinforced by the juxtaposition of a short serpentine wall inset with naturally cut stone (*office elevation*). The serpentine stone wall offsets the passageway's linear character and screens secretarial workstations that lead to management offices.

The showroom walls are standard gypsum board and metal stud construction. The grid-over-gypsum surfaces are made of 1-inch clear-finished solid cherry strips mitered and glued to form 1'-2" squares. Over windows the squares' sides are doubled (*office elevation*). The grids are not affixed to the surfaces over which they fit. Instead, they are beveled and screwed to solid cherry baseboards and wall corners, which are glued to the gypsum and hold the grid in place. Thus,

the grids can easily be removed for window repairs.

Fiberglass sound attenuation blankets between the gypsum sheets and the ¼-inch plate glass in the windows assure sound privacy.

The cove ceilings on the corridor side of each grid wall conceal both return-air registers and fluorescent light fixtures that provide ambient lighting (*section*). The fixtures are overlapped to avoid dark spots on the walls they wash.

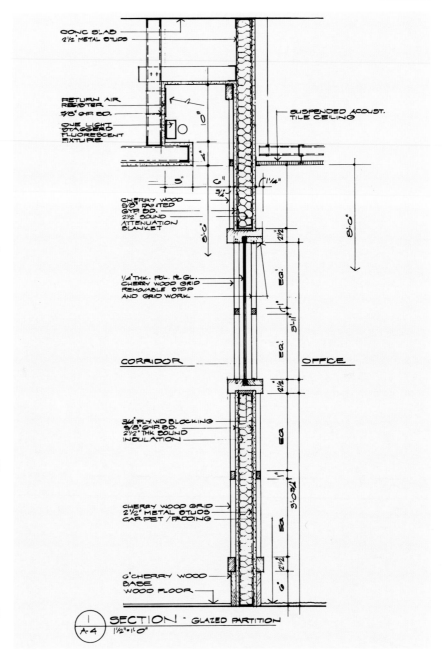

1 / A-4   SECTION · GLAZED PARTITION
1½"=1'-0"

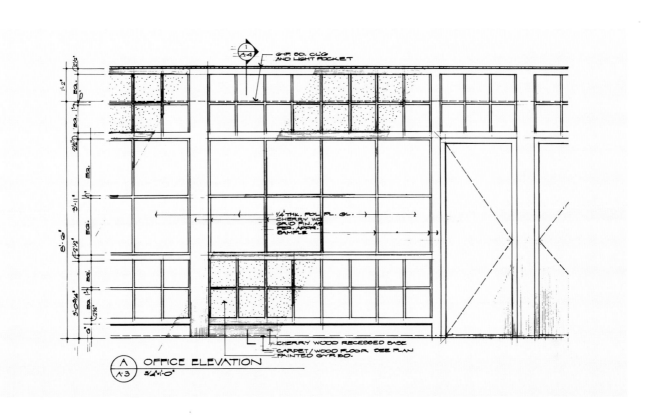

WATERWALL

PROCTER & GAMBLE COMPANY
Cincinnati, Ohio

Interior Design
Kohn Pedersen Fox Conway
Design Team
Patricia Conway, Randolph Gerner,
Judy Swenson, Keith Rosen
Fabrication
Huber, Hunt and Nichols
Photography
© Peter Aaron, ESTO

THE EXECUTIVES OF the Procter & Gamble Company wanted the firm's world headquarters, located in Cincinnati, Ohio, to reflect their "conservative-but-strong" corporate self-image. New York City–based Kohn Pedersen Fox Associates PC interpreted that wish architecturally by conceiving a building of restrained but powerfully massed exterior shapes—side-by-side broad octagonal towers, flanked by lower rectangular wings.

The wings' interiors might have seemed squat and dull in comparison with the forceful presence of the towers, but Kohn Pedersen Fox Conway, the interior-design subsidiary of Kohn Pedersen Fox Associates PC, introduced "forceful verticality" into the space by splitting each of the ancillary buildings with a tall and relatively narrow (130-foot-long by 20-foot-wide by 51-foot-high) atrium that originates on the fourth-floor level and stretches four further stories to the roof.

KPFC was required to locate a 3½-story firestair at the far end of each atrium. The design team also wanted to introduce a subtle play of light and sound into the elegant, but static, calm of the spaces. An inexpensive solution that would combine the two needs was a 3½-story ornamental glass waterwall tower, to be placed directly in front of the firestair as the focal point of the longer atrium.

The primary construction material of the waterwall is standard window wall: ¼-inch clear tempered glass in a frame of anodized aluminum mullions. Visual consistency with the stainless steel and bronze motifs that appear throughout the atrium was accomplished by the application of removable brushed stainless steel covers held to the mullions with tapped fastenings and through the use of bronze plaques on welded studs at setback levels of the framework. Mullions are pressure sealed to the glass with elastomeric gaskets and silicone sealant (*waterfall details*).

The fountain's water is pumped from a subfloor recirculating station located immediately beneath the water tower to regulating weirs located at three heights: for the central channel, at the center of the circular ornament at the top of the tower; for the two intermediate flanking channels and for the two outside channels, at the third- and first-story heights. The water is released at each point through a flush floor grate of welded stainless steel bar stock. The stream of water then cascades down the glass into a shallow stainless steel trough, from which the water is pumped to begin the cycle again.

KPFC designed the tower so that it appears to be free standing. In fact, the tower is braced with stainless steel tubing against the sheetrock exterior of the firestair behind it. Steel-tube cross bracing with stainless cladding was also installed as additional support at each setback.

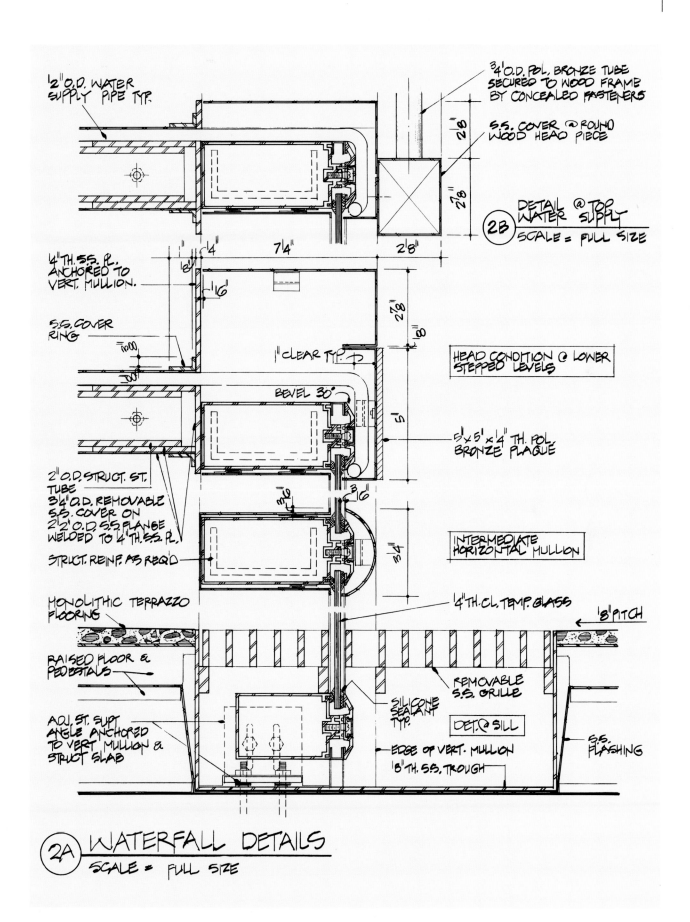

¾" O.D. POL. BRONZE TUBE
SECURED TO WOOD FRAME
BY CONCEALED FASTENERS

S.S. COVER @ ROUND
WOOD HEAD PIECE

½" O.D. WATER
SUPPLY PIPE TYP.

2B DETAIL @ TOP
WATER SUPPLY
SCALE = FULL SIZE

¼" TH. S.S. PL.
ANCHORED TO
VERT. MULLION.

S.S. COVER
RING

HEAD CONDITION @ LOWER
STEPPED LEVELS

1" CLEAR TYP.

BEVEL 30°

5" x 5" x ¼" TH. POL.
BRONZE PLAQUE

2" O.D. STRUCT. ST.
TUBE
¾" O.D. REMOVABLE
S.S. COVER ON
2½" O.D. S.S. FLANGE
WELDED TO ¼" TH. S.S. PL.

STRUCT. REINF. AS REQ'D

INTERMEDIATE
HORIZONTAL MULLION

MONOLITHIC TERRAZZO
FLOORING

¼" TH. CL. TEMP. GLASS

⅛" PITCH

RAISED FLOOR &
PEDESTALS

REMOVABLE
S.S. GRILLE

ADJ. ST. SUPT.
ANGLE ANCHORED
TO VERT. MULLION &
STRUCT. SLAB

SILICONE
SEALANT
TYP.

DET. @ SILL

EDGE OF VERT. MULLION

⅛" TH. S.S. TROUGH

S.S.
FLASHING

2A WATERFALL DETAILS
SCALE = FULL SIZE

245

WATERWALL

TRUMP TOWER
New York City

Architecture/Interior Design
Swanke Hayden Connell Architects
Design Team
John Peter Barie, Fannie Gong,
Domenic Scali
Fabrication
Peter Bratti Associates Inc.
Landscaping
Balsley Kuhl
(now Thomas Balsley Associates)
Water-Systems Engineer
Gerald Palevsky
Photography
© Durston Saylor

IF A BUILDING IS taller, splashier, and more crowd pleasing than its competition, the building is likely to be the inspiration of New York City real-estate developer Donald Trump. Trump practices the design gospel he preaches, living and working within a Fifth Avenue tower that bears his name and epitomizes his personal style.

If one were to select the single architectural detail that sums up the Trump design philosophy, it would certainly be the six-story waterwall cascade that serves as the spectacular focal point of Trump Tower's shopping atrium. The 85-foot vertically sloped waterwall was designed by Swanke Hayden Connell Architects of New York City with landscape architects Balsley Kuhl and water-systems engineer Gerald Palevsky and fabricated by Peter Bratti Associates Inc.

So that visitors to the building may enjoy the waterwall at close range without being soaked in spray, Thomas Balsley designed a series of fiberglass troughs, or basins, that contain the cascade in random steps of incrementally increasing forward projection from the top to the bottom of the structure (*section C*). The stepped troughs serve as stanchions for theatrical underwater spotlights that en-

hance both the refraction of water and the suggestion of natural outcroppings of rock (*detail E*).

The basins are supported by stainless steel angles bolted to a unistrut frame, which is, in turn, anchored by waterproofed concrete beams (*detail F*).

A pumping station located on the floor below the atrium sends an unregulated surge of water to the

waterwalls' fifth-story level for initial dispersion (*detail D*). At the point of entry, a weir plate with a finely adjustable lip regulates the horizontal dispersion of the water to maximize waterwall coverage.

The entire wall, as well as the trough fascias, are covered in Rose Breccia Pernice marble panels to integrate the detail into the wall and floor finishes of the atrium's interior.

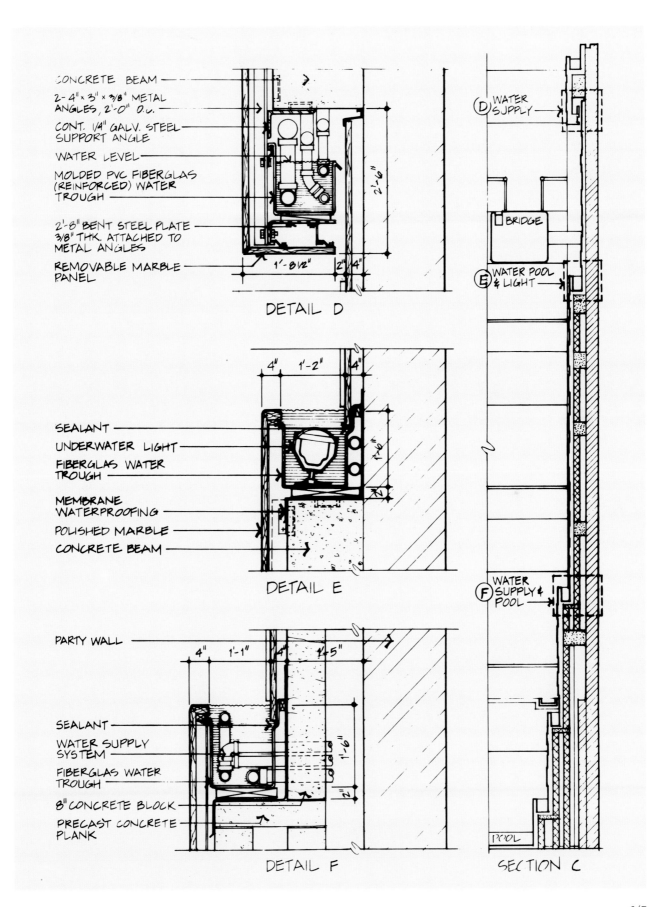

DETAIL D

CONCRETE BEAM

2- 4" x 3" x 3/8" METAL ANGLES, 2'-0" O.C.

CONT. 1/4" GALV. STEEL SUPPORT ANGLE

WATER LEVEL

MOLDED PVC FIBERGLAS (REINFORCED) WATER TROUGH

2'-8" BENT STEEL PLATE 3/8" THK. ATTACHED TO METAL ANGLES

REMOVABLE MARBLE PANEL

2'-6"

1'-8½" 2" 4"

DETAIL E

SEALANT

UNDERWATER LIGHT

FIBERGLAS WATER TROUGH

MEMBRANE WATERPROOFING

POLISHED MARBLE

CONCRETE BEAM

4" 1'-2" 4"

1'-6"

DETAIL F

PARTY WALL

SEALANT

WATER SUPPLY SYSTEM

FIBERGLAS WATER TROUGH

8" CONCRETE BLOCK

PRECAST CONCRETE PLANK

4" 1'-1" 4" 1'-5"

1'-6"

2"

SECTION C

D WATER SUPPLY

BRIDGE

E WATER POOL & LIGHT

F WATER SUPPLY & POOL

POOL

WATERWALL

OLD PUEBLO MUSEUM

Tucson, Arizona

Project Designer
Rory McCarthy
Consulting Architect
Design and Building Consultants
(Paul T. Edwards)
Artists
Charley Brown, Mark Evans
Consulting Engineer
RGA Engineering Corporation
Lighting Consultant
Grenald Associates, Ltd.
Photography
© Mark Citret

ARCHAEOLOGISTS OF THE future will be puzzled if they excavate the Foothills Center in Tucson, Arizona. This suburban shopping mall bears little resemblance to its more prosaic late-twentieth-century counterparts. Although Foothills Center houses the usual number of stores, several restaurants, and a movie theater, the unique and primary traffic draw to the complex is Old Pueblo Museum, a showplace that visually recounts a regional archaeological narrative.

Consultant Don Baker from Eastdil Realty, Inc. of San Francisco created the innovative museum-in-a-mall concept as an antidote to Foothill Center's steadily falling consumer patronage. The project was then designed and implemented as a collaborative effort among interior designer Rory McCarthy and architect Paul T. Edwards, both of Tucson, and San Francisco artists Charley Brown and Mark Evans.

An important task for the design team was to create a transitional visual relationship between the 6,000 square feet of internal vacant storefront, which had been allocated to the museum, and a tangential atrium food court. Although a series of existing stone archways located between the two areas provided enough architectural interest to lead the eye as far as the periphery of the court, what was needed to actually draw patrons into the museum space was a strong focal point detail that would outweigh the framing archway element.

The design team agreed that the focal-point detail should reinforce the archaeological narrative concept with both literal and abstract allusion. Because the floors of the museum exhibit space were to be tiled to provide transitional unity (the atrium food court was already tiled), a secondary priority was to create a detail that would provide "white noise," or sound masking, for the space.

The design team achieved both objectives by designing a spectacular waterwall, which, although constructed of "abstract" futuristic industrial materials, accurately evokes the rough-and-tumble cascade of water through mountain boulders. The waterwall detail evolved after months of careful planning, consulting, and trial-and-error on-site adaptations—a painstaking process that contributed immeasurably to the structure's success.

There are four main structural components to the waterwall. The first is a copper wall that serves as a "weather-battered mountain crag" backdrop while alluding, in its finish material, to the mining industry that once supported the region's economy (*section*). The second is a Corten steel, two-tier waterstair, or sluice, which simulates the irregular contours of boulders, while paying homage, in color, to the residual derelict mining equipment seen in the local landscape. The third element is a 30-foot, steel-covered monolith, which suggests a sheered mountainside in shadow (*pedestal plan*). The fourth and final component is a granite-rimmed basin or pool, which appears to have been formed as the natural result of a rock slide (*waterfall plan*). The rock slide allusion and the fractured floor around its base reinforce the design team's effort to portray the museum space as part of an organic and ever-changing process, rather than as a static *fait accompli*.

The tremendous weight of the monolith, which is constructed of a solid concrete slab armatured and plated in bolted and welded steel, as well as the corresponding weight of the granite boulder slabs, made it necessary to engineer an anchoring footing of poured concrete pedestals below grade (*pedestal plan*). To prevent real-life rather than merely illusory geological disasters (an earthquake code consideration), the granite slabs surrounding the poured concrete pool were floated 6 inches above grade on threaded stainless steel pins specially milled for the project (*section*). The water cascade is generated in a pump room located 3 feet below grade, which propels water to a reservoir at the top of the structure through pipes enclosed by the copper wall. Adjustable weirs in the reservoir and in each stepped trough were individually fine tuned, both to vary the amount of spill as well as to control the rack and twist that caused the troughs to side-slosh water prior to adjustment. Atomizers ranging from bubblers to fine mist heads enhance the cascade's natural effect—bubblers create mounding jets of water to simulate the rush of water through narrow crevices and fine heads create clouds of realistic mist over the granite pool.

Not content to provide just audio and visual stimulation, the design team emphasized the "over, under, around, and through" sensory experience of the space by locating a traffic staircase under the cascade. The traffic stair allows museum visitors tactile contact with the copper wall and enhances the impression of descending into an actual archaeological excavation site. Final filips to the project include a *trompe l'oeil* desert sky painted on the ceiling and neon-fabricated lightning bolts, which simulate a timed-sequence desert storm.

The members of the collaborative design team are not strangers to success. Rory McCarthy, project designer, won the *Progressive Architecture* International Furniture Competition in 1985, as well as the *Industrial Design* Product Competition in 1984. Charley Brown and Mark Evans painted the murals in the award-winning Monadnock Building in San Francisco.

WATERWALL

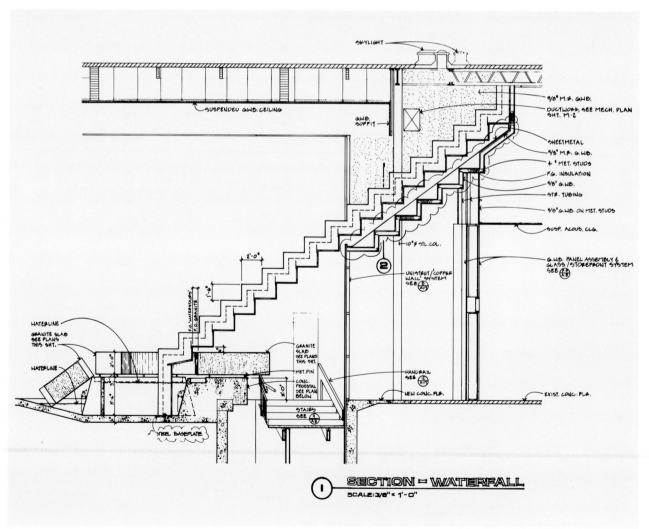

SKYLIGHT

SUSPENDED G.W.B. CEILING

G.W.B. SOFFIT

3/8" M.R. G.W.B.

DUCTWORK, SEE MECH. PLAN SHT. M-2

SHEETMETAL

5/8" M.R. G.W.B.

4 ° MET. STUDS

F.G. INSULATION

5/8" G.W.B.

STR. TUBING

5/8" G.W.B. ON MET. STUDS

SUSP. ACOUS. CLG.

G.W.B. PANEL ASSEMBLY & GLASS/STOREFRONT SYSTEM SEE

2'-0"

10"∅ STL. COL.

UNISTRUT/COPPER WALL' SYSTEM SEE

WATERLINE

GRANITE SLAB SEE PLANS THIS SHT.

WATERLINE

F.O. 'WATERSTAIRS'
F.O. GRANITE

GRANITE SLAB SEE PLANS THIS SHT.

MET. PIN

CONC. PEDESTAL SEE PLAN BELOW

STAIRS SEE

HANDRAIL SEE

NEW CONC. FLR.

EXIST. CONC. FLR.

STEEL BASEPLATE

① SECTION ≈ WATERFALL

SCALE: 3/8" = 1'-0"

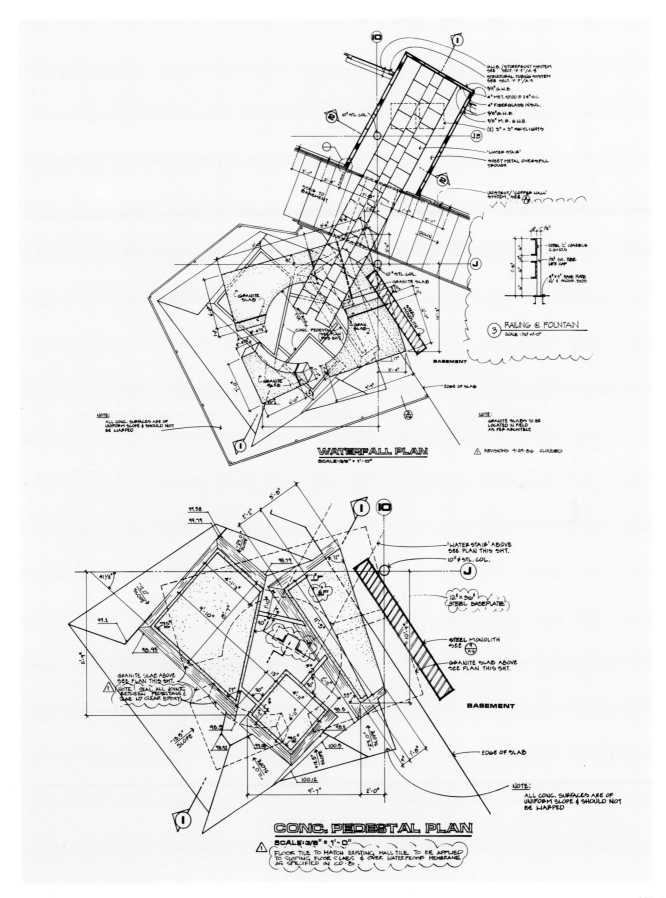

WATERFALL PLAN
SCALE: 3/8" = 1'-0"

CONC. PEDESTAL PLAN
SCALE: 3/8" = 1'-0"

RAILING @ FOUNTAIN
SCALE: 1½" = 1'-0"

NOTE:
ALL CONC. SURFACES ARE OF UNIFORM SLOPE & SHOULD NOT BE WARPED

NOTE:
GRANITE SLABS TO BE LOCATED IN FIELD AS PER ARCHITECT

REVISIONS 9-29-86 CLOUDED

NOTE:
ALL CONC. SURFACES ARE OF UNIFORM SLOPE & SHOULD NOT BE WARPED

FLOOR TILE TO MATCH EXISTING MALL TILE TO BE APPLIED TO SLOPING FLOOR SLABS & OVER WATERPROOF MEMBRANE AS SPECIFIED IN C.D. 'B'

CREDITS

ARCHITECTS/DESIGNERS

ABB ARCHITEKTEN, Frankfurt, West Germany: *pp. 52–53, 220–21*

EMILIO AMBASZ & ASSOCIATES, INC., New York, New York: *pp. 168–71*

ANDERSON DeBARTOLO PAN, INC., Tucson, Arizona: *p. 210*

ANDERSON/SCHWARTZ, New York, New York: *pp. 36–37*

BEYER BLINDER BELLE, New York, New York: *pp. 44–45*

JOHN BURGEE ARCHITECTS (John Burgee, Partner; Philip Johnson, Design Consultant), New York, New York: *pp. 46–49, 178–79*

COLE MARTINEZ CURTIS AND ASSOCIATES, Marina del Rey, California: *pp. 97, 196–97, 208–9*

DAROFF DESIGN INC., Philadelphia, Pennsylvania: *pp. 120–21, 184–85, 214–15*

DAVIS, BRODY & ASSOCIATES, New York, New York: *pp. 142–45, 176*

DORF ASSOCIATES, New York, New York: *pp. 32–33, 68–69, 155*

DESIGN AND BUILDING CONSULTANTS, Tucson, Arizona: *pp. 248–51*

ELLERBE ASSOCIATES, INC., Minneapolis, Minnesota: *pp. 186–87*

GEDDES BRECHER QUALLS CUNNINGHAM, Philadelphia, Pennsylvania: *pp. 42–43, 54–55, 110–11, 114–15, 156–57, 174–75, 198–99, 206, 222–23*

GENSLER AND ASSOCIATES/ ARCHITECTS, Houston, Texas: *pp. 20–21, 24–25, 122–23, 204–5*

GENSLER AND ASSOCIATES/ ARCHITECTS, San Francisco, California: *pp. 84, 136–37, 207*

GN ASSOCIATES, New York, New York: *pp. 138–39*

MICHAEL GRAVES, ARCHITECT, Princeton, New Jersey: *pp. 56–57, 88–89, 116–17, 125, 130–31*

GRESHAM, SMITH AND PARTNERS, Birmingham, Alabama: *pp. 42–43, 54–55, 110–11, 114–15, 156–57, 174–75, 198–99, 206, 222–23*

HAMBRECHT TERRELL INTERNATIONAL, New York, New York: *pp. 234–35*

HARTMAN-COX ARCHITECTS, Washington, D.C.: *pp. 85, 112–13, 160–61, 177, 202–3*

HAVERSON-ROCKWELL ARCHITECTS, New York, New York: *pp. 28–29, 70–71, 126–27, 128–29, 240–41*

HEARST & COMPANY ARCHITECTURE, INC., San Francisco, California: *pp. 16–17, 166–67*

THE HILLIER GROUP, Princeton, New Jersey: *pp. 146, 228–29*

H2L2 ARCHITECTS/PLANNERS, Philadelphia, Pennsylvania: *pp. 140–41, 224–25*

INTERIOR FACILITIES ASSOCIATES, INC., New York, New York: *pp. 226–27*

ISD INCORPORATED, Chicago, Illinois: *pp. 124, 188–89*

ISD INCORPORATED, Houston, Texas: *pp. 60, 94*

ISD INCORPORATED, New York, New York: *pp. 134–35, 212–13*

JUNG/BRANNEN ASSOCIATES, INC., Boston, Massachusetts: *pp. 118–19, 230–31*

KELLY AND LEHN, Kansas City, Missouri: *pp. 18–19, 34–35, 74–75*

KOHN PEDERSEN FOX ASSOCIATES PC, New York, New York: *pp. 72–73, 132–33, 147, 152–53, 172–73*

KOHN PEDERSEN FOX CONWAY, New York, New York: *pp. 50–51, 76–79, 244–45*

LARSON ASSOCIATES, INC., Chicago, Illinois: *pp. 182–83, 194–95*

LOEBL SCHLOSSMAN & HACKL, Chicago, Illinois: *pp. 66–67*

LOHAN ASSOCIATES, Chicago, Illinois: *pp. 82–83, 96*

RORY McCARTHY, Tucson, Arizona: *pp. 248–51*

EVA MADDOX ASSOCIATES, INC., Chicago, Illinois: *pp. 90–91, 92–93, 98–99*

PAPPAGEORGE HAYMES LTD., Chicago, Illinois: *pp. 86–87*

CESAR PELLI & ASSOCIATES, New Haven, Connecticut: *pp. 190–91*

PERKINS & WILL, New York, New York: *p. 95*

CHARLES PFISTER ASSOCIATES, San Francisco, California: *pp. 10, 38–39, 52–53, 62–63, 104–5, 192–93, 220–21*

ROBINSON MILLS + WILLIAMS, San Francisco, California: *pp. 52–53, 61, 220–21*

RTKL ASSOCIATES INC., Baltimore/ Washington, D.C.: *pp. 22–23, 26–27, 162–63*

SIDNEY PHILIP GILBERT & ASSOCIATES, New York, New York: *pp. 40–41, 238–39*

SITE PROJECTS, INC., New York, New York: *pp. 164–65, 236–37*

SKIDMORE, OWINGS & MERRILL, Washington, D.C.: *pp. 192–193*

ARCHITECTS SNYDER • SNYDER, Philadelphia, Pennsylvania: *pp. 58–59*

SPACE DESIGN INTERNATIONAL INC., Cincinnati, Ohio: *pp. 108–9*

JUDITH STOCKMAN & ASSOCIATES, New York, New York: *pp. 30–31, 100–101, 150–51*

THE STUBBINS ASSOCIATES, INC./ INTERIOR DESIGN GROUP, Cambridge, Massachusetts: *pp. 200–201*

SWANKE HAYDEN CONNELL ARCHITECTS, New York, New York: *pp. 148–49, 216–19, 246–47*

THE SWITZER GROUP, INC., New York, New York: *pp. 180–81, 242–43*

THOMPSON, VENTULETT, STAINBACK & ASSOCIATES, INC., Atlanta, Georgia: *pp. 158–59*

3D/INTERNATIONAL, INC., Dallas, Texas: *pp. 14–15, 106–7*

3D/INTERNATIONAL, INC., Houston, Texas: *pp. 64–65*

WALKER GROUP/CNI, New York, New York: *pp. 102–3, 211*

WHISLER-PATRI, San Francisco, California: *pp. 80–81, 232–33*

WISCHMANN DESIGN ASSOCIATES, INC., Philadelphia, Pennsylvania: *p. 154*

PHOTOGRAPHERS

PETER AARON, ESTO, Mamaroneck, New York: *pp. 56, 104, 132, 143, 165, 244*

JAIME ARDILES-ARCE, New York, New York: *pp. 10, 39, 53, 62, 192, 220*

TOM BERNARD, Berwyn, Pennsylvania: *pp. 140, 224*

STEVEN BROOKE, Miami, Florida: *pp. 88, 125, 230*

PATRICK BROWN, Hamilton, Ohio: *p. 108*

ORLANDO CABANBAN, Chicago, Illinois: *p. 98*

MARK CITRET, Daly City, California: *pp. 232, 249, 250*

LANGDON CLAY, New York, New York: *pp. 30, 150*

DAN CORNISH, ESTO, Mamaroneck, New York: *pp. 216, 217*

TOM CRANE, New York, New York: *p. 120*

STEVE GREENWAY, Minneapolis, Minnesota: *p. 186*

HARLAN HAMBRIGHT, Washington, D.C.: *p. 160*

BILL HEDRICH, HEDRICH-BLESSING, Chicago, Illinois: *p. 81*

JONATHAN HILLYER, Atlanta, Georgia: *p. 158*

WOLFGANG HOYT, ESTO, Mamaroneck, New York: *pp. 135, 148, 213*

TIMOTHY HURSLEY, Little Rock, Arkansas: *pp. 190, 210, 240*

EDWARD JACOBY, Boston, Massachusetts: *p. 201*

BARBARA KARANT, Chicago, Illinois: *p. 92*

ELLIOT KAUFMAN, New York, New York: *p. 36*

CHUN LAI, New York, New York: *p. 172*

VICTORIA LEFCOURT, Baltimore, Maryland: *pp. 22, 26, 162*

CHAS MCGRATH, San Francisco, California: *pp. 14, 21, 24, 60, 94, 106*

NORMAN MCGRATH, New York, New York: *pp. 40, 184, 226*

PETER MAUSS, ESTO, Mamaroneck, New York: *p. 123*

NICK MERRICK, HEDRICH-BLESSING, Chicago, Illinois: *pp. 83, 90, 96, 124, 189, 205*

JON MILLER, HEDRICH-BLESSING, Chicago, Illinois: *p. 47*

JAMES R. MORSE, New York, New York: *p. 95*

JACK NEITH, Mount Laurel, New Jersey: *p. 154*

PETER PAIGE, Harrington Park, New Jersey: *p. 228, 234*

PASCHALL/TAYLOR, Princeton, New Jersey: *p. 117*

RICHARD PAYNE, Midwest, Texas: *p. 179*

PAUL PECK (Robinson Mills + Williams), San Francisco, California: *p. 61*

RUSSELL PHILLIPS, Chicago, Illinois: *p. 236*

JOCK POTTLE, New York, New York: *pp. 72, 147, 152*

FRANÇOIS ROBERT, Chicago, Illinois: *pp. 182, 194*

MARK ROSS PHOTOGRAPHY, INC., New York, New York: *pp. 28, 70, 126, 129, 146*

BARRY RUSTIN, Chicago, Illinois: *p. 66*

ABBY SADIN, Chicago, Illinois: *pp. 86, 138*

DURSTON SAYLOR, New York, New York: *pp. 32, 42, 54 (above), 58, 69, 85, 100, 110, 112, 155, 156, 174, 177, 180, 198, 203, 206, 222, 243, 246*

E.G. SCHEMPF, Kansas City, Missouri: *pp. 18, 34, 75*

BOB SHIMER, HEDRICH-BLESSING, Chicago, Illinois: *p. 11*

ED STEWART, Houston, Texas: *p. 64*

TIM STREET-PORTER, Los Angeles, California: *p. 166*

JOHN WADSWORTH, Norfolk, Virginia: *p. 102*

DAVID WAKELY, San Francisco, California: *pp. 84, 136, 207*

PAUL WARCHOL, New York, New York: *pp. 44 (left), 50, 54 (below), 76, 78, 114, 168, 169, 238*

MATT WARGO, Philadelphia, Pennsylvania: *pp. 16, 214*

NICK WHEELER, Townsend, Massachusetts: *pp. 118, 176*

ROY WRIGHT, New York, New York: *p. 44 (right)*

TOSHI YOSHIMI, Los Angeles, California: *pp. 97, 196, 208*

KATE ZARI, Coral Gables, Florida: *p. 211*

INDEX

Senior Editor: Julia Moore
Editor: Cornelia Guest
Designer: Areta Buk
Production Manager: Ellen Greene
Set in 10-point ITC Garamond Light